Learning Performance and Individual Differences: Essays and Readings

Len Sperry
Marquette University

Gerald S. Lesser
Harvard University

*Academic Advisor in Educational
and Developmental Psychology*

Scott, Foresman and Company
Glenview, Illinois   London

Learning Performance and Individual Differences: Essays and Readings

Library of Congress Catalog Card Number 73-186157

To my parents

Preface

Asked what America should worry about before all else, conservationist David Brower said: "There are no hawks and no doves, no blacks and no whites—on a dead planet." College students responding to *Playboy*'s "Student Survey: 1971" (September 1971) agreed with Brower as they rated ecology their number one concern. Unlike other social problems which affect really only one or another segment of the population, ecology is becoming a growing concern for all Americans. But what does this have to do with education and learning?

Simply put, ecology is the interaction of a person with his environment. Learning, in a classroom setting, involves the interaction of learner and book, learner and programmed unit, learner and discussion group, or more usually, learner and teacher. The learner changes, or is educated, through his responses to this environment. Here, too, an environment can deaden and destroy—or give sustenance.

An increasing number of teachers and researchers are beginning to think that learning effectiveness is related to the quality of the interaction between learner and environment. To foster life and growth, the environment must provide relevant feedback to the learner, feedback which fits the learner's particular way of learning, or learning style.

In *Learning Performance and Individual Differences* the reader will be introduced to a new perspective based on learner-environment interactions in the classroom. From the learner's side, differences in aptitudes (and other attributes) can and do interact with instructional method to affect his learning and performance. And from the teacher's side, different ways of handling information and applying sanctions have different effects on student behavior, including achievement. The focus will be on these two kinds of person-environment interactions, which are central to an understanding of what is happening in the classroom and to teaching to meet individual student needs.

The book is in three main parts, devoted, respectively, to expectations, learning style, and instructional style. For each of these three parts there is first a *context* section, in which an overview is presented to orient the reader to the relevant concepts and issues; next there is a *controversy* section, with an exploration of various viewpoints to enable the reader to develop his own point of view; and finally, there is an *application* section that explores the utility of these ideas for classroom practice and changing of learner performance. The format is an integrative framework of articles and commentary—an "environment" that it is hoped will invoke active response and interaction on the part of the reader.

Learning Performance and Individual Differences intends to convey a message of hope to those who feel disillusioned and discouraged about the future of formal education. It will find a place in undergraduate courses in educational psychology and psychology of human differences, and in advanced courses in psychology of learning, social psychology of education, and educational research. It can also be used as a supplement in educational methods courses.

Gratefully acknowledged are the helpful comments and suggestions offered by Gary M. Ingersoll at Indiana University, Steven V. Owen at the University of Connecticut, Judith V. Torney at the University of Illinois Chicago Circle, James W. Hall at Northwestern University, and by the Academic Advisor in Educational and Developmental Psychology, Gerald S. Lesser, as well as the editorial assistance of John Amacker, John Cox, and Linda Peterson of Scott, Foresman.

Len Sperry

Contents

Correlation Chart, xii

Part One
Learning Performance
and Individual Differences   1

Chapter One
Perspective, 2

Part Two
Expectations   9

Chapter Two
An Introduction, 10

Chapter Three
Context, 13

Robert Rosenthal
Experimenter Expectations, 14

Jacob W. Getzels
Conflict and Role Behavior in the Educational Setting, 23

Gerald Gurin and Patricia Gurin
Expectancy Theory in the Study of Poverty, 37

William J. Gephart and Daniel P. Antonoplos
The Effects of Expectancy and Other Research-Biasing Factors, 55

Chapter Four
Controversy, 64

Robert Rosenthal and Lenore Jacobson
Teachers' Expectancies: Determinants of Pupils' IQ Gains, 65

Richard E. Snow
Unfinished Pygmalion, 68

Robert L. Thorndike
Review of *Pygmalion in the Classroom*, 73

Robert Rosenthal
Empirical vs Decreed Validation of Clocks and Tests, 76

Robert L. Thorndike
But You Have to Know How to Tell Time, 78

Chapter Five
Expectations and Learning Performance, 80

R. Jean Hills
Social Classes and Educational Views, 81

W. Victor Beez
Influence of Biased Psychological Reports on Teacher Behavior and Pupil Performance, 86

Part Three
Learning Style   93

Chapter Six
An Introduction, 94

Chapter Seven
Context, 99

Samuel Messick
The Criterion Problem in the Evaluation of Instruction: Assessing Possible, Not Just Intended, Outcomes, 100

Frank Riessman
The Strategy of Style, 116

Adaia Shumsky
Individual Differences in Learning Styles, 122

Chapter Eight
Controversy, 126

Leonard Cahen
Comments on Professor Messick's Paper, 127

Glenn H. Bracht and Gene V. Glass
Interaction of Personological Variables and Treatment, 132

Chapter Nine
Learning Style and Learning Performance, 140

Herman A. Witkin, Donald R. Goodenough, and Stephen A. Karp
Stability of Cognitive Style from Childhood to Young Adulthood, 141

J. S. Bruner, Jacqueline Goodnow, and G. A. Austin
Selection from *A Study of Thinking*, 157

Jerome Kagan
*Reflection-Impulsivity: The Generality and Dynamics
of Conceptual Tempo*, 165

Philip S. Holzman and Riley W. Gardner
Leveling-Sharpening and Memory Organization, 177

Part Four
Instructional Style   185

Chapter Ten
An Introduction, 186

Chapter Eleven
Context, 193

Ned A. Flanders
Intent, Action, and Feedback: A Preparation for Teaching, 194

James Reed Campbell and Cyrus W. Barnes
Interaction Analysis—A Breakthrough? 207

Samuel E. Wood
*A Multidimensional Model for the Observation, Analysis,
and Assessment of Classroom Behavior*, 213

Chapter Twelve
Controversy, 218

Richard C. Anderson
*Learning in Discussions: A Resume of the Authoritarian-
Democratic Studies*, 219

Lee J. Cronbach
The Logic of Experiments on Discovery, 232

Barak Rosenshine
Interaction Analysis: A Tardy Comment, 246

Chapter Thirteen
Instructional Style and Learning Performance, 251

Robert D. Hess and Virginia C. Shipman
Early Experience and the Socialization of Cognitive Modes in Children, 253

John E. Rhetts
*Attribute-Treatment Interactions and Individualized Instruction:
A Conceptual Framework and an Example from Project PLAN*, 269

Hilda Taba and Freeman F. Elzey
Teaching Strategies and Thought Processes, 286

Gerald S. Lesser
Pedagogical Adaptations to Individual Differences: Some Research Findings, 298

Part Five
Learning Performance
and Individual Differences 311

Chapter Fourteen
Prospective, 312

References, 321

Index, 329

Correlation Chart

Learning Performance and Individual Differences	Biehler Psychology Applied to Teaching Houghton-Mifflin, 1971	Cronbach Educational Psychology Harcourt Brace Jovanovich, 1963	DeCecco The Psychology of Learning and Instruction Prentice-Hall, 1968
1 Perspective	1	1, 2	1
2 Expectations: An Introduction	3	4, 14	5
3 Expectations: Context	3	14	5
4 Expectations: Controversy	3	14	6
5 Expectations and Learning Performance	3	7, 14	5
6 Learning Style: An Introduction	5	3	3
7 Learning Style: Context	5	3, 5	3
8 Learning Style: Controversy	12	6, 7, 16	16
9 Learning Style and Learning Performance	6	5	10, 11
10 Instructional Style: An Introduction	15	11, 15	1
11 Instructional Style: Context	15	11, 15	1
12 Instructional Style: Controversy	11	15, 16	16
13 Instructional Style and Learning Performance	1	12, 15	12
14 Prospective	16		1

Klausmeier and Ripple *Learning and Human Abilities* Harper & Row, 1971	McDonald *Educational Psychology* Wadsworth, 1965	Morse and Wingo *Psychology and Teaching* Scott, Foresman 1969	Perkins *Human Development and Learning* Wadsworth, 1969
1	1, 12	1	1, 5
9	4	1, 10	3
17	4	11	3
17	4	1, 11	3
9	4	1, 3, 10, 11	3
3, 6	5, 6	6, 8	13
3, 6	5, 6	6, 7	15
17, 18	15, 17	14	19
11, 12	5, 6, 7	7, 8, 14	15, 16
8	2, 3, 13	9	17
8	13	9	17, 18
18	13, 16, 17	14	19
6	10, 13	9, 11, 12	21
	3		

Learning Performance and Individual Differences: Essays and Readings

Part One
Learning Performance
and Individual Differences

Chapter One
Learning Performance and
Individual Differences: Perspective

According to estimates by Ralph Tyler (1969), approximately one fifth of the children in the United States do not attain the level of literacy required for available employment, and a similar number may not gain the understanding needed for effective citizenship and satisfying lives. Thirty percent of high school age youth fail to finish high school, and in both rural and urban slum areas, forty to sixty percent of students in the sixth grade perform at second grade level or below on standardized achievement tests. These are only a few of the statistics or indicators of student learning performance that portray the seriousness of America's educational problem.

The reasons for these deplorable conditions are many and varied. However, it is known that for a long time educators and psychologists have tended to ignore the notion of individual differences in learning and instructional style, and expectations. Instead they have focused their attention on motivation, emotion, and personality as causes for learning or failure to learn. In other words, the focus has been on the learner *qua* person. When confronted with an intellectually capable learner whose performance failed to measure up to his supposed potential, psychologists and educators have tended to attribute this failure to an emotional block, a personality conflict, or to social class factors. Little attention was given to how learning could be improved simply by concentrating on the way in which an individual works and learns and whether the expectations and methods of instruction, controlled by the teacher or the machine, sufficiently utilized the strengths in the learner's style of learning.

Today, with emphasis on accountability, performance contracting, and the like, it is imperative that the educator and the psychologist be knowledgeable of the available resources in these areas. Accountability indicates that learning performance is optimal for each learner. This can be accomplished only when individual differences are viewed in a total perspective, that is, by considering the learner *qua* learner, as well as the learner *qua* person. Perhaps the reason there has been so little success in controlling and predicting learning performance is an inadequate understanding and model of learning performance.

Needed: A New Perspective on Learning Performance
Despite the self-evident centrality of classroom learning and cognitive development for the psychological aspects of education, educational psychologists have

2

virtually ignored these areas, both theoretically and empirically, for the past forty years (Ausubel, 1963). Although this withdrawal of educational psychology from the central issues in classroom learning was temporarily expedient, as Ausubel observes, it was highly unfortunate. In recent years many educators and psychologists have been developing, or have been forced to develop, new perspectives of the teaching-learning process, and the learner *qua* learner model is being more seriously studied and discussed than ever before.

Three contemporary concerns which highlight this consideration are individualized instruction, learning disorders, and the disadvantaged learner.

Individualized Instruction: Learning Styles
as an Individual Difference in Learning Performance
On theoretical grounds it seems rather self-evident that individualized learning should be more efficient than traditional group instruction. When instruction is geared to personality and achievement needs, general and specific intellectual capacities, idiosyncratic or personal styles of learning, and within appropriate expectation levels, it would necessarily follow that learning performance should be superior to other methods which are geared to the needs, capacities, styles, and expectation levels of the hypothetical mean student in the classroom group. Milton (1962) has supplied experimental data which appear to confirm this self-evident proposition.

On the other hand, widely publicized claims that individualized instruction has established the educational breakthrough for optimizing learning performance by adapting instruction to individual differences appear to be a gross overstatement. It is true that individualized instruction adapts to the learner's rate of learning, but it is also known that rate is only one dimension of an individual's learning style. In fact, Ausubel (1968) has identified at least twenty different dimensions of learning or cognitive style.

What is learning style? Messick (1969) defines it as information processing habits representing the learner's typical mode of perceiving, thinking, problem-solving, and remembering. For truly effective instruction, the instructor—whether live or automated—must be aware of and respond to these personal differences in the learner. Today, most individualized instruction on the market responds to only one of these differences, rate.

The PLAN (*P*rogram for *L*earning in *A*ccordance with *N*eeds) program is one indication that individualized learning is emerging from its infancy stage. This program attempts to match seven characteristics of the learner with seven characteristics of the programmed material, beyond the learner's rate of learning. The PLAN system has developed a number of Teaching-Learning Units (TLU) which are designed to lead the learner to a mastery of a module of knowledge. A TLU is chosen which matches the learner on the following characteristics: need for teacher supervision; practice; social involvement; single v. multiple media; variety of activity; preference for reading; and reading comprehension rate (Rhetts, 1970).

How effective is PLAN compared to other individualized learning programs? Actually, the question of program effectiveness is becoming a moot issue as researchers are becoming more aware that current research designs and statistical methods are somewhat inappropriate when comparing the effectiveness of different individualized programs, or even the effectiveness of one individualized program for one learner. Typically, the effectiveness of programs was judged statistically by comparing the average gains for learners receiving one treatment or method with average gains for learners receiving the other treatment. Now supposing one method is better for certain types of learners and the other method is better for still other kinds of learners, depending on the mix of learners in the two groups, the two methods might actually exhibit negligible differences on the average, when they actually produce widely different effects upon the learner.

This type of "horse race" evaluation procedure, as Messick (1969) terms it, reflects a problem rooted in the design of experiments themselves. Educational research in general has relied somewhat blindly on classical principles of experimental design borrowed from the animal laboratory and the agricultural field. A human learner is neither a rat nor a plot of land. Breeding and plot-splitting make individuals homogeneous, and random divisions maintain homogeneity; therefore, treatment averages are meaningful and legitimate in the animal laboratory and the agricultural field. But when human learners are involved, it is naïve to assume that all learners are the same and that random assignment will assure homogeneity. Therefore, it seems meaningless to use treatment averages when comparing instructional methods (Snow & Salomon, 1968).

Thus, this questionable methodological assumption is certain to affect theoretical considerations about individual differences in learning style that must be accounted for in the development of really effective individualized learning.

Learning Disorders: Instructional Style
as Individual Differences in Learning Performance

Bateman (1966) described learning disorders as deviations in the learning process that are associated with an educationally significant discrepancy between apparent capacity for language or cognitive behavior and actual level of language or cognitive learning performance. This definition, she feels, could easily describe forty percent of our current school population. Theories of the etiology of learning disorders are myriad, and it is generally agreed that the causes can be multiple and interactive.

Can any one factor be singled out for the blame? Travers (1970) has surveyed four major factors that cause learning disorders: the home, the school, the community, and individual physical and cognitive makeup. Travers singled out the school itself as perhaps the primary cause accounting for the majority of diagnosed learning difficulties. He contends that the school, especially the teacher, has failed to recognize individual differences among learners. Travers feels that "responding to individual differences is the sole proven method of preventing [these] problems" (p. 305). Since brain damage is evident in only a small percentage of those who are diagnosed as learning disorders cases, Travers concludes that instructional style (poor teaching), aided and abetted by poor facilities, poor materials, and a lack of community cooperation, fosters learning difficulties and consequently affects learning performance.

According to Gagné (1967a), two classes of variables influence learning performance: those within the learner, or internal conditions; and those in the learning situation, or external conditions. Instruction, then, is basically the control and arrangement of external conditions in the learning situation. Optimal instruction and learning performance result when instructional style matches the internal conditions of learning, especially the learning style of the learner.

What is instructional style? Instructional style refers to the way in which the external learning situation is controlled: with commanding attention, with presenting stimuli, and with the nature and sequencing of verbal directions given to the learner (Gagné, 1967a). Instructional style is sometimes used synonymously with teaching style. Styles of teaching can be thought of in relation to the following dimensions: authoritarian v. democratic v. permissive; student v. content oriented; and planned v. unplanned. In short, teaching or instructional style appears to be an individual difference of the instructor—either live or automated—that can affect learning performance.

The Disadvantaged Learner: Expectations
as Individual Differences in Learning Performance
Goldberg (1970) has described five theories which have been offered to explain the statistic that sixty percent of urban sixth graders are achieving only at the second grade level: genetic selection; effective power and mastery; cognitive deficiencies; motivation and value clashes; and school and teacher expectation and prejudice. The last one, teacher expectation, has perhaps received the most attention in the popular press. Most often heard among civil rights groups is the belief that the disadvantaged learner is no different from other learners. He comes to school no less ready for learning than others, but the school personnel reject him, fail to teach him, and, obviously, expect very little from him. This *self-fulfilling prophecy* of low expectation found support in the study of Rosenthal and Jacobson (1968), which suggested that there may be a positive relationship between level of teacher expectation and level of learner performance.

But how do expectations affect learning performance? DeCecco (1968) conceives of expectations as learned anticipations of the consequences of one's behavior. And since expectations are products of past experiences, past experiences of success and failure are then the primary basis for predicting one's future successes and failures. DeCecco claims that the *teacher expectancy function* is to maintain or modify the *student's expectations* of success or failure in reaching the stated instructional objectives of the task to be learned. To do this, the teacher must have sufficient knowledge of the learner's previous failures and successes in order to distinguish among realistic, pessimistic, and extravagantly optimistic expectancies. When there has been much failure, the teacher may have to provide such successes.

In the Rosenthal-Jacobson study, it appears that the teachers who were assigned to the "slow" learners groups continually reinforced their students' expectations of failure, thereby resulting in consistently poor learning performance.

The phenomenon of one person's expectations for the performance of another has become a lively consideration in experimental psychology today, just as it was nearly a century ago (Friedman, 1967). *Experimenter bias* is the term used by Rosenthal to describe the experimenter's expectations for performance of his subjects. According to Friedman, the study of experimenter bias has two basic thrusts: studies of the effects of differences between experimenters, called the *personal equation*; and studies of the effects of the experimenter on subjects, called the *interpersonal equation*. The study of the personal equation was actually the birthright of experimental psychology and represented the measurement of individual differences between experimenters. In fact, the study of individual differences began with the study of the personal equation (Anastasi, 1965). So, not only in experimental psychology, but also in the study of the disadvantaged learner, the study of expectations is an important consideration in any discussion of individual differences and learning performance.

Integrative Aspects
Learning style, instructional style, and expectations, then, are three factors that can influence learning performance. Also, the previous discussion suggests that all three of these factors are legitimate areas of study in differential psychology, or the psychology of individual differences. We have looked at each of these factors independently, yet it appears that all three factors are quite intimately related.   Victor Beez (1970) unexpectedly observed this phenomenon in an experiment he conducted with summer Head Start programs. In this study of teacher expectation and learner performance, Beez noted that teachers with the more favorable expectations for their students apparently facilitated the students' expectation of success and then proceeded to teach more material in more different ways than did teachers who had unfavorable expectations. Rosenthal (1968) interpreted Beez' data as an indication that teacher expectations are not only translated into subtle verbal and visual messages to the learner but actually alter instructional style, thus affecting learning style and, ultimately, learning performance.

Trends in the Study of Individual Differences
From the preceding discussion, the reader may have concluded that the study of individual differences has really been operationalized as the study of group differences. Historically this has been the case. Differential psychology has largely been concerned with classifying individuals by intelligence and in relation to such traits as age, sex, race, and social class, and observing the differences within and among these groups.

However, Leona Tyler (1965) has suggested that the study of individual differences has reached a transitional stage. As mentioned previously, the first concern of differential psychology was the study by Wundt and other experimental psychologists in the 1860's and 1870's of the personal equation.

As the field of psychology developed, a split occurred and two disciplines emerged, correlation psychology and experimental psychology (Cronbach, 1957), and interest shifted away from the study of individual differences. According to Cronbach, experimental psychologists tended to see individual differences as an annoyance rather than as a challenge. And since the experimental psychologist's goal was to control behavior, variations within treatments were proof that he had not succeeded in controlling behavior. But with the development of the mental measurement movement at the turn of the century came a transition in thinking about individual differences, so that the focus turned to group differences. Hopes were high in the 1930's and 1940's that such procedures as factor analysis, multivariate experimental designs, and inferential statistics would simplify and integrate the proliferation of behavioral dimensions and variables relating to the new study of group differences. These expectations were frustrated as few multiple correlation coefficients exceeded .60, and there appeared to be little promise of meaningfully interpreting all these data.

Moreover, other factors led to a reconsideration of this theoretical and methodological interpretation of the study of individual differences. Tyler (1965) described this impending second transition as a gradual and subtle change in goal orientation. Whereas the previous theoretical framework of the mental measurement or group differences model was nomothetic, focusing on normative traits and dimensions of behavior, the emerging theoretical framework is now an essentially idiographic or subjective and personal approach, which can more accurately be thought of as a psychology of development rather than a psychology of measurement. Instead of the normal curve, the growth curve will be its graphic symbol. Strategies and types, rather than traits and dimensions, will constitute useful techniques. Furthermore, the search for grand universal principles—such as the principle that males are more variable than females—is being abandoned in place of striving for general conclusions about unique individuals. Ironically, the psychology of individual differences is only now beginning to study the individual *qua* individual.

Practically speaking, this emerging idiographic approach is bound to influence school practice, and hopefully give some sense of legitimacy to the "whole child" rhetoric. Recognition of such individual differences as learning and instructional styles is bound to increase the effectiveness of a teacher. Fredrick and Klausmeier (1970) feel that, in time, a profile of the student's learning style will become as much a part of the student's guidance folder and the school's measurement program as the I.Q. test score. Matching a student's learning style with a teacher's instructional style could be a more rational and effective basis for grouping students than our present criterion. Likewise, considerations about the selection of content and skills, evaluation, discipline, and time factors could be dealt with more in a spirit of informed judgment than is now possible.

Plan of the Book
Much has been written about how individual differences in personality, intelligence, motivation, and social conditions affect learning and school performance. This book is concerned with three other individual differences which may have an even greater influence on learning performance than those previously studied and have heuristic value as a conceptual framework for the study of individual differences in the classroom.

Through a discussion of expectancy, learning style, and instructional style, the reader will be introduced to a new perspective in the study of learning and learning performance based on person-environment interactions. It is becoming increasingly clear that twentieth-century man is not acting and reacting in a vacuum but in a context. Every day he must come to terms with the environment of which he himself is a part. This is particularly true when one considers the dimension of human learning, especially in a classroom setting. Implicitly, it is known that learning is a complex and interactive process. Realistically, students of human learning—whether preservice teachers or educational psychologists—must now come to grips with the learning and teaching process as a person-environment interaction.

This book will focus on two types of these interactions: Aptitude-Treatment Interactions (ATI), in the study of learning style and expectation; and Verbal Interaction Analysis, in the study of instructional style and expectation. The reader will find that by viewing learning performance in terms of these person-environment interactions, it will be possible to study the learner *qua* learner, as well as the learner *qua* person.

Part Two will focus on the theory, research, and controversy surrounding the study of expectations. Part Three will focus on the theory, research, and controversy concerning learning style. Part Four will focus on the theory, research, controversy, and application of instructional styles. Finally, Part Five will summarize and integrate the discussions of Parts One through Four.

Part Two
Expectations

Chapter Two
Expectations: An Introduction

In the literature of psychology and sociology, the terms *expectation* and *expectancy* hold special meaning and a certain prominence in many theories of learning and motivation, as well as in theories of social behavior. This chapter will introduce the reader to these various meanings and models of expectancy, and to the relationship between changes in expectancy level and changes in learning performance. Finally, an introduction to the other chapters of Part Two will follow.

Meanings in the Psychological Literature

In the psychological literature, expectancy, considered a cognitive variable, has gained status in recent years, especially in the learning theory of Tolman and the drive reduction theories of Spence, Mowrer, and Rotter. Tolman used the terms *sign-gestalt, reward expectancy,* and, later, *field expectancy* to refer to an acquired disposition whereby a response to a certain sign object or cue stimuli is expected to bring about a certain other situation. Similarly, Rotter defined expectancy as the probability held by the individual that a particular reinforcement will occur as a function of a specific behavior on his part in a specific situation. Chaplin and Krawiec (1968) have noted that expectancy is one of the three most significant variables in learning theory.

Expectancy has also been central to the theories of motivation developed by Lewin, Atkinson, and Rotter. According to these theorists, motivation of behavior depends on three conditions:

1. a generalized disposition to approach or avoid a given class of objects— motive;
2. the incentive value of the particular goal or objects—the valence; and
3. the estimate of the probability that the behavior will lead to the goal—the expectancy (Gurin & Gurin, 1970).

In the last few years, the term *expectancy* has become part of the current argot and is usually associated with Robert Rosenthal. It was Rosenthal's (1966) early laboratory research with the interaction between experimenter and subject—white rat as well as college sophomore—that set the stage for his controversial study of the interaction between teacher expectation and student learning performance, which is described in *Pygmalion in the Classroom* (1968). The expectancy effect is still little understood and is often confused with four other research biasing effects: halo effect, hawthorne effect, demand characteristics,

10

and placebo effect. Gephart and Antonoplos (1969) have clarified the meaning of these five terms and have given a clear perspective for understanding these types of person-environment interactions.

Meanings in the Sociological Literature

In the sociological literature, expectation is usually designated as role expectation or self-fulfilling prophecy. Suggesting the centrality of this concept in sociology, Robert Merton in his classic treatise, *Social Theory and Social Structure* (1957), states that *role* is considered one of the basic units of social science, while *self-fulfilling prophecy* is one of its basic theorems. Merton explained further that by the theorem of self-fulfilling prophecy, one's expectations for another's behavior could quite unwittingly become a more accurate prediction of that behavior simply for its having been made.

Discussed in its psychological sense, then, expectancy refers to beliefs or anticipations about the outcome or consequences of behavior, usually defined as a personal or idiographic dimension. In its sociological sense, however, role expectancy or expectation is an objective or nomothetic dimension of behavior.

Role may be thought of as the nomothetic elements defining the behavior expected of the occupant of a given status or position and is characterized by certain typical actions and qualities. According to Sarbin (1968), if viewed as actions, these elements of behavior are codified as a job description, such as "The teacher candidate must have a degree, state certification, and five years' experience. . . ."; and if they are viewed as qualities, they are codified as adjectival terms, such as "The teacher candidate must be warm, friendly, outgoing. . . ."

Roles are defined in terms of role expectations. A role has certain normative rights and duties such that, when the role incumbent puts these rights and duties into effect, he is said to be performing his role. The expectations define what the role incumbent should or should not do under various circumstances while occupying the particular role in the social system.

A Model Delineating Various Types of Expectations

Since most behavior is social, it may be helpful to consider a model for studying behavior in a social system and clarify the relationship between the idiographic and the nomothetic dimensions. Adapting from the theory of Getzels and Thelen (1960), one can conceive of a social system as involving three classes of phenomena: first, the institution with certain roles and expectations that will fulfill the goals of the system—the nomothetic dimension; second, the individual personality with certain self-expectations and needs—the idiographic dimension; and the group, with its own expectations and process—the interactive dimension which mediates between the institutional requirements and expectations, and the individual's expectations and needs.

Since institutions and individuals are embedded in a culture with certain mores and values, the character of the institutional roles, group processes, and individual personalities will all be related to the particular ethos or social class of the culture and the specific expectations and need-dispositions to its values (Getzels, Lipham, & Campbell, 1968).

Changing Expectancy and Learning Performance

For some time, academic sociologists and psychologists have been interested in studying the phenomenon of how performance can be affected by changes in expectancy level. From a sociological point of view, Getzels (1963) notes that performance, termed social behavior in his model, is affected by conflicts between or among role expectations of different individuals and/or groups. In psychology, studies of level of expectancy, or level of aspiration, have been focused on how and why the consequences of behavior alter beliefs or anticipations of future success or failure. Researchers have come to these three tentative conclusions:

1. Past success conditions students to make realistic increases in their expectations.
2. Past failures, over a period of time, condition students to lower their expectancies almost as if to guard themselves against failures by never expecting success.
3. Some students unrealistically raise their expectancies almost as if the hope of success alone would bring success (DeCecco, 1968).

Gurin and Gurin (1970) noted that research on changing expectancies has obvious implications for current social problems, such as poverty and the education of the disadvantaged. DeCecco (1968) feels that the above research conclusions support the importance of the teacher expectancy function:

"The student's every effort does not have to meet with success, but he must experience success to keep his wagon hitched to a star of reasonable height. By modifying students' expectations in accordance with these findings, teachers can increase the vigor [motivation] of student efforts" (p. 167).

Reports by Rosenthal (1968), Rist (1970), Katz et al. (in press), and others indicate how detrimental teacher expectancies of failure or unrealistic success—usually unconscious—can be to the learning performance of the poor and disadvantaged learner.

Plan of Part Two

Articles in Part Two will elaborate the perspective of this chapter concerning the interest in, importance of, and application of expectancy theory. Articles in chapter 3 provide the reader with a sociological, psychological, and methodological context for further understanding the expectancy phenomenon. Articles in chapter 4 elaborate the controversy surrounding research on teacher expectations. Finally, articles in chapter 5 focus on different types of expectations as delineated in Getzels' social system model: student, teacher, and community.

Chapter Three
Expectations: Context

The articles in this chapter were chosen to elaborate the discussion of chapter 2 on expectation from a psychological, sociological, and methodological point of view. These articles indicate or imply that expectation is a functional component in person-environment interactions.

Rosenthal's research started with the methodological question: Why and how does one person's bias affect the performance of another, whether it be person or animal? In quest of these answers Rosenthal has done an extensive review of the literature and interprets the results from over one hundred studies in seven research areas. This excerpt from Rosenthal is representative of the research reported in Rosenthal's (1966) book on experimenter bias effects.

Getzels' article portrays a comprehensive model for understanding and explaining social behavior in institutions such as schools. Getzels' model is heuristic in that at least one hundred studies have used this model, or some form of it, as a theoretical base. Getzels' equation, based on the sociology of Parsons and Shils, that "behavior is a function of personality times role expectation" is in marked contrast to Lewin's "behavior is a function of personality times environment" and other similar psychological interpretations. When Getzels' formula for social behavior is elaborated in an institutional setting such as the school, it appears that to study only the interaction of two persons is quite inadequate. On the other hand, when the two persons are studied in terms of their roles and role expectations, plus other institutional and cultural expectations, the research seems more accurate and the results more meaningful. Implied in Getzels' model is that learning performance is a function of the congruence and/or conflict between the various expectations.

Gurin and Gurin have provided an excellent, albeit very theoretical, review of the literature on expectancy as it relates to motivational theory. Unlike Rosenthal's basic query, the motivation psychologist starts with the question: How and why does behavior change? Gurin and Gurin's article is a rather representative indication of the work of socially conscious academic psychologists who are concerned about contemporary social problems and their amelioration. The reader will note that the research conclusions of the Gurins, as well as those summarized by DeCecco (reported in chapter 2), hint at possible teaching strategies to alleviate the expectancy of failure.

The article by Gephart and Antonoplos was included to orient the reader to the methodological issues and assumptions that accrue to research on certain aspects of the person-environment model. The authors have performed a noble service to the research community by their careful delineation of five research-biasing factors in psychological and sociological research. Furthermore, this paper serves as a transition to the main topic of chapter 4.

The reader may want to peruse Robert Merton's (1957) classic article, "Self-fulfilling Prophecy," which is alluded to in Rosenthal's article. Elaboration of Getzels' model and research evidence may be found in Getzels, Lipham, and Campbell (1968). Theoretical essays which further support Rosenthal's point of view may be found in Rosenthal and Rosnow (1969).

Experimenter Expectations
Robert Rosenthal

The particular expectation a scientist has of how his experiment will turn out is variable, depending on the experiment being conducted, but the presence of some expectation is virtually a constant in science. The independent and dependent variables selected for study by the scientist are not chosen randomly, but are selected because the scientist expects a certain relationship to appear between them. Even in those less carefully planned examinations of relationships called "fishing expeditions" or more formally, *exploratory analyses,* the expectation of the scientist is reflected in the selection of the entire set of variables chosen for examination. Exploratory analyses of data, like real fishing ventures, do not take place in randomly selected pools.

The expectations of the scientist are likely to affect the choice of the experimental design and procedure in such a way as to increase the likelihood that his expectation or hypothesis will be supported, which is as it should be. No scientist would select intentionally a procedure likely to show his hypothesis in error. If he could too easily think of procedures that would show this, he would be likely to revise his hypothesis. If the selection of a research design or procedure is regarded by another scientist as too *biased* to be a fair test of the hypothesis, he can test the hypothesis employing oppositely or less biased procedures by which to demonstrate the greater value of his hypothesis. The designs and procedures employed are, to a great extent, public knowledge, and it is this public character that permits relevant replications to serve the required corrective function.

The major concern of this section will be with the effects of the experi-

From "Teacher Expectations and Their Effects upon Children." In *Psychology and Educational Practice* by Gerald S. Lesser. Copyright © 1971 by Scott, Foresman and Company. Reprinted by permission of the publisher.

menter's expectation on the responses he obtains from his subjects. The consequences of such an *expectancy bias* can be quite serious. Expectancy effects on
subjects' responses are not public matters. It is not only that other scientists
cannot know whether such effects occurred in the experimenter's interaction
with his subjects, but the investigator himself may not know. Moreover, there is
the likelihood that the experimenter has not even considered the possibility of
such unintended effects. That is not so different from the situations wherein
the subject's response is affected by any attribute of the experimenter. Later,
the problem will be discussed in more detail. For now it is enough to note that
while other attributes of the experimenter may affect the subject's response,
they do not necessarily affect these responses differentially as a function of the
subject's treatment condition. Expectancy effects, on the other hand, always do.
The sex of the experimenter does not change as a function of the subject's treatment condition in an experiment. The experimenter's expectancy of how the
subject will respond does change as a function of the subject's experimental
treatment condition.

That one person's expectation about another person's behavior may contribute to a determination of what that behavior will actually be has been suggested
by various theorists. Merton (1948) elaborated the very useful concept of *self-
fulfilling prophecy.* One prophesies an event and the expectation of the event
then changes the behavior of the prophet in such a way as to make the prophe-
sied event more likely. The late Gordon Allport (1950) applied the concept of
interpersonal expectancies to an analysis of the causes of war. Nations expecting
to go to war affect the behavior of their opponents-to-be by the behavior which
reflects their expectations of armed conflict. Nations who expect to remain out
of wars, at least sometimes manage to avoid entering into them.

Drawn from the general literature, and the literatures of the healing profes-
sions, survey research, and laboratory psychology, there is considerable evidence
for the operation of interpersonal self-fulfilling prophecies. This evidence, while
ranging from the anecdotal to the experimental, with emphasis on the former,
permits us to begin consideration of more recent research on expectancy effects
with some fairly strong prior probabilities (Mosteller & Tukey, 1968). The
literatures referred to have been reviewed elsewhere (Rosenthal, 1964a, b, 1965,
1966; Rosenthal & Jacobson, 1968), but it may be of interest here to give one
illustration from the literature of experimental psychology. The case is one
known generally as a study of an artifact in animal research. It is less well
known, however, as a study of the effect of experimenter expectancy. While
the subject sample was small, the experimenter sample was very large indeed.
The case is that of Clever Hans (Pfungst, 1911). Hans was the horse of Mr. von
Osten, a German mathematics teacher. By means of tapping his foot, Hans was
able to add, subtract, multiply, and divide. Hans could spell, read, and solve
problems of musical harmony. To be sure, there were other clever animals at the
time, and Pfungst tells about them. There was Rosa, the mare of Berlin, who performed similar feats in vaudeville, there was the dog of Utrecht, and the reading
pig of Virginia. All these other clever animals were highly trained performers
who were, of course, intentionally cued by their trainers.

Mr. von Osten, however, did not profit from his animal's talent, nor did it seem at all likely that he was attempting to perpetrate a fraud. He swore he did not cue the animal, and he permitted other people to question and test the horse even without his being present. Pfungst and his famous colleague, Stumpf, undertook a program of systematic research to discover the secret of Hans' talents. Among the first discoveries made was that if the horse could not see the questioner, Hans was not clever at all. Similarly, if the questioner did not himself know the answer to the question, Hans could not answer it either. Still, Hans was able to answer Pfungst's questions as long as the investigator was present and visible. Pfungst reasoned that the questioner might in some way be signaling to Hans when to begin and when to stop tapping his foot. A forward inclination of the head of the questioner would start Hans tapping, Pfungst observed. He tried then to incline his head forward without asking a question and discovered that this was sufficient to start Hans' tapping. As the experimenter straightened up, Hans would stop tapping. Pfungst then tried to get Hans to stop tapping by using very slight upward motions of the head. He found that even the raising of his eyebrows was sufficient. Even the dilation of the questioner's nostrils was a cue for Hans to stop tapping.

When the questioner bent forward more, the horse would tap faster. This added to the reputation of Hans as brilliant. That is, when a large number of taps was the correct response, Hans would tap very rapidly until he approached the region of correctness, and then he began to slow down. It was found that questioners typically bent forward more when the answer was a long one, gradually straightening up as Hans got closer to the correct number.

For some experiments, Pfungst discovered that auditory cues functioned additively with visual cues. When the experimenter was silent, Hans was able to respond correctly thirty-one percent of the time in picking one of many placards with different words written on it, or cloths of different colors. When auditory cues were added, Hans responded correctly fifty-six percent of the time.

Pfungst himself then played the part of Hans, tapping out responses to questions with his hand. Of twenty-five questioners, twenty-three unwittingly cued Pfungst as to when to stop tapping in order to give a correct response. None of the questioners (males and females of all ages and occupations) knew the intent of the experiment. When errors occurred, they were usually only a single tap from being correct. The subjects of this study, including an experienced psychologist, were unable to discover that they were unintentionally emitting cues.

Hans' amazing talents, rapidly acquired by Pfungst too, serve to illustrate the power of the self-fulfilling prophecy. Hans' questioners, even skeptical ones, expected Hans to give the correct answers to their queries. Their expectation was reflected in their unwitting signal to Hans that the time had come for him to stop his tapping. The signal cued Hans to stop, and the questioner's expectation became the reason for Hans' being, once again, correct.

Not all of Hans' questioners were equally good at fulfilling their prophecies. Even when the subject is a horse, apparently, the attributes of the experimenter make a considerable difference in determining the response of a subject.

On the basis of his studies, Pfungst was able to summarize the characteristics of those of Hans' questioners who were more successful in their covert and unwitting communication with the horse. Among the characteristics of the more successful unintentional influencers were those of tact, an air of dominance, attention to the business at hand, and a facility for motor discharge. Pfungst's observations of sixty years ago seem not to have suffered excessively for the lack of more modern methods of scaling observations. To anticipate some of the research findings turned up much later, it must be said that Pfungst's description seems also to fit those experimenters who are more likely to affect their human subject's responses by virtue of their experimental hypothesis.

In summarizing his difficulties in learning the nature of Clever Hans' talents, Pfungst felt that he had been too long off the track by focusing his attention on the horse instead of the man. Perhaps, too, when we conduct research in the behavioral sciences we are sometimes caught looking at our subjects when we ought to be looking at ourselves. It was to this possibility that much of the research to be summarized here was addressed.

Animal Learning
A good beginning might have been to replicate Pfungst's research, but with horses hard to come by, rats were made to do (Rosenthal & Fode, 1963a).

A class in experimental psychology had been performing experiments with human subjects for most of a semester. Now they were asked to perform one more experiment, the last in the course, and the first employing animal subjects. The experimenters were told of studies that had shown that maze-brightness and maze-dullness could be developed in strains of rats by successive inbreeding. Sixty laboratory rats were equitably divided among the twelve experimenters. Half the experimenters were told that their rats were maze-bright while the other half were told their rats were maze-dull. The animal's task was to learn to run to the darker of two arms of an elevated T-maze. The two arms of the maze, one white and one gray, were interchangeable; and the correct or rewarded arm was equally often on the right as on the left. Whenever an animal ran to the correct side he obtained a food reward. Each rat was given ten trials each day for five days to learn that the darker side of the maze was the one which led to the food.

Beginning with the first day and continuing on through the experiment, animals believed to be better performers became better performers. Animals believed to be brighter showed a daily improvement in their performance, while those believed to be dull improved only to the third day and then showed a worsening of performance. Sometimes an animal refused to budge from his starting position. This happened eleven percent of the time among the allegedly bright rats; but among allegedly dull rats it happened twenty-nine percent of the time. When animals did respond, and correctly so, those believed to be brighter ran faster to the rewarded side of the maze than did the correctly responding rats believed to be dull.

When the experiment was over, all experimenters made ratings of their rats and of their own attitudes and behavior vis-à-vis their animals. Those experimenters who had been led to expect better performance viewed their animals as brighter, more pleasant, and more likeable. These same experimenters felt more relaxed in their contacts with the animals and described their behavior toward them as more pleasant, friendly, enthusiastic, and less talkative. They also stated that they handled their rats more, and more gently, than did the experimenters expecting poor performance.

Similar observations have been made in other experimental studies of animal learning (e.g., Rosenthal & Lawson, 1964). In addition to the differences in handling as a function of the experimenters' beliefs about their subjects, there were differences among experimenters in the reported intentness of their observation of their animals. Experimenters who believed their animals to be brighter watched them more carefully, and this more careful observation of the rat's behavior may very well have led to more rapid and appropriate reinforcement of the desired response. Thus, closer observation, perhaps due to the belief that there would be more promising responses to be seen, may have made effective teachers of the experimenters expecting good performance.

Human Subjects

So far we have given only the results of studies of expectancy effect in which the subjects were animals. Most of the research available, however, is based on human subjects and it is those results we now consider. In this set of experiments at least twenty different specific tasks have been employed, but some of these tasks seemed sufficiently related to one another that they could reasonably be regarded as a family of tasks or a research area. These areas include human learning and abilities, psychophysical judgments, reaction time, inkblot tests, structured laboratory interviews, and person perception.

Learning and Abilities. Larrabee and Kleinsasser (1967) employed five experimenters to administer the Wechsler Intelligence Scale for Children (WISC) to twelve sixth-graders of average intelligence. Each subject was tested by two different experimenters; one administering the even-numbered items and the other administering the odd-numbered items. For each subject, one of the experimenters was told the child was of above-average intelligence while the other experimenter was told the child was of below-average intelligence. When the child's experimenter expected superior performance, the total IQ earned was over seven points higher on the average than when the child's experimenter expected inferior performance. When only the performance subtests of the WISC were considered, the advantage to the children of having been expected to do well was less than three IQ points and could easily have occurred by chance. When only the verbal subtests of the WISC were considered, the advantage of having been expected to do well, however, exceeded ten IQ points. The particular subtest most affected by experimenters' expectancies was "Information." The results of this study are especially striking in view of the very small sample size employed.

Structured Laboratory Interviews. A number of experiments have been conducted in which the experimenters conducted a structured interview with their research subjects. One of these (Raffetto, 1968) was addressed to the question of whether the experimenter's expectation for greater reports of hallucinatory behavior might be a significant determinant of such reports.

Raffetto employed ninety-six paid, female volunteer students from a variety of less advanced undergraduate courses to participate in an experiment on sensory restriction. Subjects were asked to spend one hour in a small room that was relatively free of light and sound. Eight more-advanced students of psychology served as the experimenters, with each one interviewing twelve of the subjects before and after the sensory restriction experience. The preexperimental interview consisted of factual questions such as age, college major, and college grades. The postexperimental interview was relatively well structured, including questions to be answered by "yes" or "no" as well as more open-ended questions, e.g., "Did you notice any particular sensations or feelings?" Postexperimental interviews were tape-recorded.

Half the experimenters were led to expect many reports of hallucinatory experience and half were led to expect few reports. Obtained scores of hallucinatory experiences ranged from zero to thirty-two with a grand mean of 5.4. Of the subjects contacted by experimenters expecting more hallucinatory experiences, forty-eight percent were scored above the mean on these experiences. Of the subjects contacted by experimenters expecting fewer hallucinatory experiences, only six percent were scored above the mean.

Person Perception. The basic paradigm of these investigations has been sufficiently uniform that we need only an illustration (Rosenthal & Fode, 1963b).

Ten advanced undergraduates and graduate students of psychology served as the experimenters. All were enrolled in an advanced course in experimental psychology and were already involved in conducting research. Each student-experimenter was assigned as his subjects a group of about twenty students of introductory psychology. The experimental procedure was for the experimenter to show a series of ten photographs of people's faces to each of his subjects individually. The subject was to rate the degree of success or failure shown in the face of each person pictured in the photos. Each face could be rated as any value from -10 to +10, with -10 meaning extreme failure and +10 meaning extreme success. The ten photos had been selected so that, on the average, they would be seen as neither successful nor unsuccessful, but quite neutral, with an average numerical score of zero.

All ten experimenters were given identical instructions on how to administer the task to their subjects and were given identical instructions to read to their subjects. They were cautioned not to deviate from these instructions. The purpose of their participation, it was explained to all experimenters, was to see how well they could duplicate experimental results which were already well established. Half the experimenters were told that the "well-established" finding was such that they could expect their subjects to rate the photos as being of successful people (ratings of around + 5) and half the experimenters were told that their subjects should rate the photos as being of unsuccessful people (ratings of around −5). Results showed that experimenters expecting "successful" ratings obtained higher photo ratings than did experimenters expecting "unsuccessful" ratings.

Table 1 Experimenter Expectancy Effects in Seven Research Areas

Research Area	Number of Studies	Combined z	Percentage of Studies at $p < .10$	at $p < .05$
Animal Learning	9	+8.64	100%	89%
Human Abilities	10[a]	+2.86	40%	20%
Laboratory Interviews	6[b]	+5.30	83%	33%
Person Perception	64[a,b]	+4.09	36%	23%
Psychophysics	9[a]	+2.55	33%	33%
Reaction Time	3	+1.93	67%	33%
Inkblot Tests	5	+4.77	80%	80%
All Studies	103[c]	+9.94	48%	34%
Binomial test z (N = 103)			+12.55	+13.27

[a]Indicates a single experiment represented in each of three areas.
[b]Indicates a second experiment represented in each of two areas.
[c]Three entries were nonindependent and the mean z across areas was used for the independent entry.
Robert Rosenthal, "Teacher Expectation and Pupil Learning" in Robert D. Strom, Ed., *Teachers and the Learning Process,* © 1971. Reprinted by permission of the author and Prentice-Hall, Inc., Englewood Cliffs, New Jersey.

Many other studies have been reported on expectancy effects on human subjects, including experiments on psychophysical judgments (e.g., Zoble, 1968), reaction time (e.g., Silverman, 1968), and inkblot tests (e.g., Marwit, 1968).

An Overview of Experimenter Expectancy Effects
To summarize the results of studies of experimenter expectancy effects, Table 1 indicates that for each of the seven research areas considered, the number of studies summarized is listed in the second column, the standard normal deviate associated with that number of studies is listed in the third column (all sufficiently large to make it unreasonable to attribute the results to chance), and the percentage of studies having an associated p level of .10 or .05 is listed in the final two columns. By chance we expect the percentages of the fourth column to cluster about the value of ten percent and we expect the percentages of the final column to cluster about the value of five percent. We find, however, about five times too many results at $p < .10$ and about seven times too many results at $p < .05$ to allow us seriously to entertain the hypothesis of chance results.

Magnitude of Experimenter Expectancy Effects. So far we have discussed the results of studies of the effects of the experimenter's expectancy only in terms of their statistical significance or the probability (p) that the results might be attributed to chance. By itself such information does not tell us how large the effects of expectancy tend to be. We want, therefore, to have some estimates of the magnitude of expectancy effects quite apart from the question of the "reality" of the phenomenon. On the basis of analyses reported elsewhere (Rosenthal, 1969), it can be estimated that about two out of three research subjects and about two out of three experimenters will give or obtain responses in the direction of the experimenter's expectancy.

Though we have been able to arrive at some estimate, however crude, of the magnitude of expectancy effects, we will not know quite how to assess this magnitude until we have comparative estimates from other areas of behavioral research. It is possible to suggest that in the bulk of the experimental literature of the behavioral sciences, the effects of the experimental variable are not impressively "larger"—either in the sense of magnitude of obtained p's or in the sense of proportion of subjects affected—than the effects of experimenter expectancy. The best support for such an assertion would come from experiments in which the effects of experimenter expectancy are compared directly, in the same experiment, with the effects of some other experimental variable believed to be a significant determinant of behavior. Fortunately, there are two such experiments to shed light on the question.

Burnham (1966) had twenty-three experimenters each run one rat in a T-maze discrimination problem. About half the rats had been lesioned by removal of portions of the brain, and the remaining animals had received only sham surgery which involved cutting through the skull but no actual damage to brain tissue. The purpose of the study was explained to the experimenters as an attempt to learn the effects of lesions on discrimination learning. Expectancies were manipulated by labeling each rat as lesioned or nonlesioned. Some of the lesioned rats were labeled accurately, but some were falsely labeled as unlesioned. Some of the really unlesioned rats were labeled accurately, but some were falsely labeled as lesioned. The results showed that animals that had been lesioned did not perform as well as those that had not been lesioned, and animals that were believed to be lesioned did not perform as well as those that were believed to be unlesioned. Of special interest is that the effects of experimenter expectancy were actually greater than the effects of the removal of brain tissue.

Burnham's comparison of the effects of experimenter expectancy with some other experimental variable employed animal subjects. Cooper, Eisenberg, Robert, and Dohrenwend (1967) used human subjects to compare the effects of experimenter expectancy with the effects of effortful preparation for an examination on the degree of belief that the examination would actually take place. Each of ten experimenters contacted ten subjects; half of the subjects were required to memorize a list of symbols and definitions that were claimed to be essential to the taking of a test that had a fifty percent chance of being given, while the remaining subjects, the "low effort" group, were asked only to look over the list of symbols. Half of the experimenters were led to expect that "high effort" subjects would be more certain of actually having to take the test, while half of the experimenters were led to expect that "low effort" subjects would be more certain of actually having to take the test. Results showed that there was a very slight tendency for subjects who had exerted greater effort to believe more strongly that they would be taking the test. Of surprising magnitude was the finding that experimenters expecting to obtain responses of greater certainty obtained such responses to a much greater degree than did experimenters expecting responses of lesser certainty. The effects of the experimenters' expectancies were ten times greater than the effects of preparatory effort.

References

Allport, G. W. "The Role of Expectancy." In *Tensions That Cause Wars*, edited by H. Cantril. Urbana, Ill.: University of Illinois Press, 1950. Pp. 43-78.

Burnham, J. R. Experimenter Bias and Lesion Labeling. Unpublished manuscript, Purdue University, 1966.

Cooper, J., L. Eisenberg, J. Robert, and B. S. Dohrenwend. "The Effect of Experimenter Expectancy and Preparatory Effort on Belief in the Probable Occurrence of Future Events." *Journal of Social Psychology*, 1967, 71, 221-226.

Larrabee, L. L., and L. D. Kleinsasser. The Effect of Experimenter Bias on WISC Performance. Unpublished manuscript, Psychological Associates, St. Louis, 1967.

Marwit, S. J. An Investigation of the Communication of Tester-bias by Means of Modeling. Unpublished doctoral dissertation, State University of New York at Buffalo, 1968.

Merton, R. K. "The Self-fulfilling Prophecy." *Antioch Review*, 1948, 8, 193-210.

Mosteller, F., and J. W. Tukey. "Data Analysis, Including Statistics." In *The Handbook of Social Psychology*, vol. 2, edited by G. Lindzey and E. Aronson. 2nd ed. Reading, Mass.: Addison-Wesley Publishing Co., Inc., 1968.

Pfungst, O. *Clever Hans (the Horse of Mr. von Osten): A Contribution to Experimental, Animal, and Human Psychology.* (Translated by C. L. Rahn.) New York: Holt, Rinehart & Winston, Inc., 1911. (Republished: New York: Holt, Rinehart & Winston, Inc., 1965.)

Raffetto, A. M. Experimenter Effects on Subjects' Reported Hallucinatory Experiences under Visual and Auditory Deprivation. Paper presented at the meeting of the Midwestern Psychological Association, Chicago, May 1968.

Rosenthal, R. "The Effect of the Experimenter on the Results of Psychological Research." In *Progress in Experimental Personality Research*, vol. 1, edited by B. A. Maher. New York: Academic Press, Inc., 1964. Pp. 79-114. (a)

Rosenthal, R. "Experimenter Outcome-orientation and the Results of the Psychological Experiment." *Psychological Bulletin*, 1964, 61, 405-412. (b)

Rosenthal, R. Clever Hans: A Case Study of Scientific Method. Introduction to O. Pfungst, *Clever Hans (the Horse of Mr. von Osten).* New York: Holt, Rinehart & Winston, Inc., 1965. Pp. ix-xlii.

Rosenthal, R. *Experimenter Effects in Behavioral Research.* New York: Appleton-Century-Crofts, 1966.

Rosenthal, R. "Interpersonal Expectations: Effects of the Experimenter's Hypothesis." In *Artifact in Behavioral Research*, edited by R. Rosenthal and R. L. Rosnow. New York: Academic Press, Inc., 1969. Pp. 181-277.

Rosenthal, R., and K. L. Fode. "The Effect of Experimenter Bias on the Performance of the Albino Rat." *Behavioral Science*, 1963, 8, 183-189. (a)

Rosenthal, R., and K. L. Fode. "Three Experiments in Experimenter Bias." *Psychological Reports*, 1963, 12, 491-511. (b)

Rosenthal, R., and L. Jacobson. *Pygmalion in the Classroom: Teacher Expectation and Pupils' Intellectual Development.* New York: Holt, Rinehart & Winston, Inc., 1968.

Rosenthal, R., and R. Lawson. "A Longitudinal Study of the Effects of Experimenter Bias on the Operant Learning of Laboratory Rats." *Journal of Psychiatric Research*, 1964, 2, 61-72.

Silverman, I. "The Effects of Experimenter Outcome Expectancy on Latency of Word Association." *Journal of Clinical Psychology*, 1968, 24, 60-63.

Zoble, E. J. Interaction of Subject and Experimenter Expectancy Effects in a Tone Length Discrimination Task. Unpublished AB thesis, Franklin and Marshall College, 1968.

Conflict and Role Behavior in the Educational Setting
Jacob W. Getzels

Not only are there more demands and constraints upon the educator than upon most other occupational groups, but there are more *contradictory* demands and constraints. Although the teacher is expected to be a good citizen, he is barred from many of the roles which are the marks of good citizenship. Outspoken participation in a political party, for example, to say nothing of a socially controversial (even though legal) movement is prohibited. Partisanship in local politics can be a cause for dismissal.[1]

Although the teacher is expected to be a mature person—indeed a model of maturity for his students—his personal behavior is often circumscribed by rules and regulations prescribed for him by others, who, incidentally, need not, in fact do not, themselves abide by the same rules. As one teacher reports, "I don't lead a natural life. I wouldn't dare smoke or drink. When I go to public meetings where the parents and guests smoke, I have to say no. If the parents can smoke, why can't I?"[2]

Even in school matters, presumably the sphere of his own particular competence, the educator is liable to cross-pressures in opposition to his own best judgment. For example, the School Executive Studies found that twenty percent of the superintendents reported facing incompatible demands from their religious and educational affiliations.[3] The members of their church wanted them to act one way, other people in the community in another way. One Catholic superintendent—and he speaks for other denominations as well—said he faced these situations constantly:

"Sometimes, the situation gets pretty touchy. I want to keep my good relations with the Church. Don't forget—most of my school committee members and the local politicians belong to my church. Take this example: one of the Catholic

---

[1] W. B. Brookover, *A Sociology of Education* (New York: American Book Company, 1955), pp. 230-262.
[2] Ibid., p. 245.
[3] N. Gross, "Some Contributions of Sociology to the Field of Education," *Harvard Educational Review*, 1959, 29, pp. 275-287.

groups wanted to let the kids out early from school. They were having some special meetings, and they wanted the kids to be there. I knew that wouldn't be right. It wasn't fair to the other kids. So what did I do? I refused to give an official O.K. to the request, but at the same time I simply winked at it [letting them out early]. I would have offended them if I'd stopped the kids from going, and I just couldn't afford to do that. It really left me bothered."[4]

In all the instances cited (and more could have been given) what was at issue was one form or another of *conflict*—conflict between one position the educator occupied and another, conflict between the educator's needs and the expectations held for him by his "patrons," conflict among the values of the patrons themselves, and so on. These conflicts are a matter of vital concern not only to the educator who must somehow cope with them but also to the community which may be quite unaware of what it is doing and of the effect the conflicts are having upon the education of its children.

In short, the problem of conflict in the educational setting is a crucial issue for conceptual clarification, empirical investigation, and practical solution. What, for example, are the various types of conflict, for clearly not all conflicts are of the same kind? What are the sources of the different kinds of conflict? What is the relationship among them? What are the consequences of conflict? Can a framework be formulated to handle the various issues of the problem within a single set of terms and relationships? Although numerous separate studies have been done on various aspects of the problem, they are quite sundry in point of view and language, and the findings cannot readily be related to each other without at least an attempt to integrate the diverse phenomena into a single conceptual scheme.

Accordingly, the purpose of the present paper is twofold: (1) to describe a model of social behavior—for conflict is of course a social phenomenon—that attempts to integrate within a single framework many of the phenomena bearing on the problem of conflict; and (2) to generate from the model a classification of the kinds and sources of conflict, and to cite a number of research studies to illustrate these types of conflict.

The General Model

The framework we are proposing has already been elaborated elsewhere,[5] and only those dimensions of immediate relevance to the issue of conflict will be sketched here. The framework presumes interpersonal or social behavior as func-

---

[4] Ibid., p. 284.

[5] The same general set of concepts and categories have been applied to other areas of the educational setting, and portions of this paper are drawn from: J. W. Getzels, "A Psycho-sociological Framework for the Study of Educational Administration," *Harvard Educational Review*, 1952, 22, pp. 234-246; J. W. Getzels and E. G. Guba, "Social Behavior and the Administrative Process," *School Review*, 1957, 55, 423-441; J. W. Getzels, "Administration as a Social Process," in A. W. Halpin (Ed.), *Administrative Theory in Education* (Chicago: Midwest Administration Center, University of Chicago, 1958), pp. 150-165; J. W. Getzels and H. A. Thelen, "The Classroom as a Unique Social System," in N. B. Henry (Ed.), *The Dynamics of Instructional Groups* (Chicago: University of Chicago Press, 1960), pp. 53-82. Our debt to the work of Talcott Parsons will be evident.

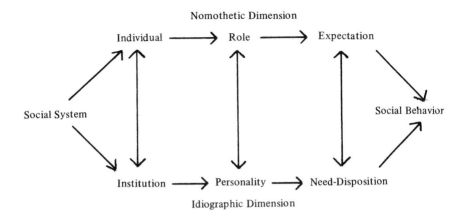

tioning inevitably within the context of a social system. It conceives of the social system (whether a single classroom, a whole school, or a community) as involving two classes of phenomena, the publicly mandatory and the privately necessary, which are viewed in this paper as conceptually independent and phenomenally interactive. There are on the one hand institutions with certain roles and expectations that will fulfill the goals of the system. There are on the other hand individuals with certain personalities and need-dispositions inhabiting the system, whose interactions comprise what is called social behavior. This behavior can be understood as a function of two major analytic elements, (1) institution, role, and expectation, which together refer to the *nomothetic* or normative dimension of activity in a social system, and (2) individual, personality, and need-disposition, which together refer to the *idiographic* or personal dimension of activity in a social system. We represent these dimensions and variables pictorially in the above diagram. To comprehend the nature of social activity and conflict, we must understand the nature and relationship of these elements.

The term *institution* has received a variety of definitions. For our purposes it is sufficient to say only that all social systems have certain imperative functions that are to be carried out in certain routinized patterns. The agencies established to carry out these functions for the social system may be termed institutions. In this sense, we may think of education as an institution fulfilling certain requirements of the social system of which it is a part.

The most important analytic units of an institution are the roles, which, to use Linton's phrase, are the "dynamic aspects"[6] of positions and statuses, and may be defined by the expectations (the rights, privileges, and obligations) to which any incumbent of the role must adhere. A crucial characteristic of roles is that they are complementary. Each role derives its definition and meaning from other related roles. Thus, the role of teacher and the role of pupil cannot be understood or implemented except in relation to each other. In

---

[6] R. Linton, *The Study of Man* (New York: Appleton-Century-Crofts, Inc., 1936), p. 14.

performing the role behavior expected of him, the teacher "teaches" the pupil; in performing the role behavior expected of him, the pupil "learns" from the teachers.

But roles are of course implemented by flesh and blood individuals, and no two individuals are alike. Each stamps a particular role with the unique style of his own personality. Social behavior is not only a function of public mandate but of private necessity, and of course public mandate and private necessity may not coincide. Not all teachers "teach," not all pupils "learn"—at least not in the same way. It is not enough to know only the nature of the roles and expectations within an institution—although, to be sure, institutional behavior cannot be understood apart from these—but we must know also the nature of the individuals inhabiting the roles, and how they perceive and react to the expectations. Just as we analyzed the institutional dimension into the component elements of role and expectation, so we may analyze the individual dimension into the component elements of personality and need-disposition.

The term *personality*, like the term *role*, has received a variety of definitions. For our purposes it is sufficient to conceive of it as the dynamic organization within the individual of those need-dispositions that govern his unique perceptions and reactions to the environment and to its expectations. The central analytic units of personality are the need-dispositions which we may define with Parsons and Shils as "individual tendencies to orient and act with respect to objects in certain manners and to expect certain consequences of these actions."[7] In order to understand the behavior of *specific* role-incumbents in *specific* institutions, we must know both the role-expectations and the need-dispositions involved.

Within this framework then, a given act is conceived as deriving from the interaction between the nomothetic and idiographic dimensions of our model. When the nomothetic axis is maximized—as in the case of rigid expectations for the military man—behavior still retains some personal aspects because no role is ever so closely defined as to eliminate all individual latitude. When the idiographic axis is maximized—as in the case of the less rigid expectations society has for the artist—social behavior still cannot be freed from some role prescription. Indeed, the individual who divorces himself entirely from such prescription is said to be autistic and his behavior a-social and paratactic.

Like all theoretical formulations, the present framework is an abstraction from reality. Certain factors and relationships have been brought into the foreground, others relegated to the background.[8] By focusing on the sociological

---

[7] T. Parsons and E. A. Shils, *Toward a General Theory of Action* (Cambridge: Harvard University Press, 1951), p. 114.

[8] D. O. Hebb says, "To deal with behavior at present, one must oversimplify. The risk, on the one hand, is forgetting that one has oversimplified the problem; one may forget or even deny those inconvenient facts that one's theory does not subsume. On the other hand is the risk of accepting the weak-kneed discouragement of the vitalist, of being content to show that existing theories are imperfect without seeking to improve them. We can take for granted that any theory of behavior at present must be inadequate and incomplete. . . ." *The Organization of Behavior* (New York: John Wiley & Sons, Inc., 1949), p. xiii.

dimension with the central concept of role and the psychological dimension with the central concept of personality, we have omitted other dimensions and variables of social behavior. We should like to mention one other set of concepts, those deriving from the anthropological dimension.

Institutions and individuals are embedded in a culture with certain mores and values. The character of institutional roles and individual personalities is related to the particular ethos of culture, and the specific expectations and need-dispositions to its values. The educator, for example, cannot devote himself effectively to a classical education when that kind of education is no longer supported by the ethos. The pupil cannot ordinarily be expected nor will he want to learn for the sake of learning when learning is not a cultural value. In this sense, we must bear in mind that interacting with the sociological and psychological dimensions is the cultural dimension. By way of summary, we may present the dimensions and central concepts of the framework pictorially as in the diagram above.

In pointing to certain general fulcra of conflict in role behavior, this model, we believe, can help clarify and systematize the nature and sources of strain in the educational setting as a specific case.

Fulcra of Conflict: Some Derivations from the Model

We shall identify for illustrative purposes five major types and sources of conflict, although these do not necessarily exhaust the list.

Conflicts Between Cultural Values and Institutional Expectations

We may mention first an obvious and, in the educational setting, prominent type of conflict, the conflict between the expectations of the specific institution and the values of the general culture. Consider the following instance. It is expected by the school (or at least we assume it is expected or should be expected) that the child will work hard in order to achieve to the fullest extent of his intellectual potentiality and creativity. Accordingly, the child must be motivated to sacrifice immediate ease for ultimate attainment. Recent commentaries suggest, however, that our cultural values are coming to prize ease and sociability more than intellectual independence and achievement.[9] In this sense, the criteria of worth in the classroom and in society at large are incongruent, and to the extent of such incongruence, both teacher and pupil are subject to conflict.

Or consider the following data in relation to potential conflict for the so-called gifted or creative child, and indeed for the gifted or creative teacher, if not for all pupils and all teachers. Spindler [10] analyzed the responses of some 328 graduate education students to such open-ended statements as "The individual is . . . ," "Intellectuals should . . . ," and to paragraphs they wrote describing their concepts of the "Ideal American Boy." From the open-ended sentences, results like this were obtained: "Artists are . . . ," "queer," "perverted," "nuts," "effeminate" (a negative-hostile category of 38 percent), "different," "people," "few," (a neutral category of 35 percent), "creative," "smart," "original," "interesting" (a positive category of 25 percent); "Intellectuals should . . . ," "be more sociable," "be more practical," "get down to earth" (a mildly derogative category of 36 percent), "keep it under cover," "drop dead," "shut up" (an openly hostile category of 20 percent), "apply their intellect," "study," "create," "think" (a neutral to positive category of 40 percent).

Spindler also asked the graduate students to describe the "Ideal American Boy." A content analysis of this technique revealed that the desirable features of character are ranked in the following order, from highest number of mentions to lowest number:

"He should be *sociable,* like people, and get along well with them; he must be *popular,* be liked by others; he is to be *well-rounded,* he can do many things quite well, but is not an expert in anything in particular; he should be athletic (but not a star), and healthy (no qualifications); he should be *ambitious* to succeed, and have clear goals, but these must be acceptable within limited norms; he must be *considerate of others,* ever-sensitive to their feelings about him and about events; he should be a *clean-cut Christian,* moral and respectful of God and parents; he should be patriotic; and he should demonstrate *average academic ability* and *average intellectual capacity.* "[11]

Leadership, independence, high intelligence, high academic ability, individuality, are mentioned relatively infrequently (in about 20 percent of the paragraphs). As Spindler points out, introspective behavior is devaluated (even intellectuals are held in suspicion by many). Deviancy is to be tolerated only within

---

[9] See, for example, D. Riesman, et al., *The Lonely Crowd* (New Haven: Yale University Press, 1950); A. Wheelis, *The Quest for Identity* (New York: W. W. Norton & Co., 1958); W. H. Whyte, *The Organization Man* (New York: Simon and Schuster, Inc., 1956). The problem of conflict among the values of subcultures is of course important but will not be dealt with here.

[10] G. D. Spindler, "Education in a Transforming American Culture," *Harvard Educational Review,* 1955, 25, pp. 145-146.

[11] Ibid., pp. 147-148.

the narrow limits of sociability, of general outwardness, and of conformity ("Artists are perverts").[12]

But it is exactly these culturally devalued characteristics—independence, high intelligence, high academic ability, creativity—that education is supposed to foster. In the strain between cultural values and institutional expectations is one type and source of role conflict in the educational setting.

Conflict Between Role-Expectations and Personality Dispositions

Conflicts of this type occur as a function of discrepancies between patterns of expectations attaching to a given role and patterns of need-dispositions characteristic of the incumbents of the role. Typical of this kind of conflict are the army sergeant with high need for submission, the lighthouse keeper with high need for affiliation, the authoritarian teacher in a permissive school, the administrator with a high need for abasement, and so on. In all these cases there is a mutual interference between nomothetic expectations and idiographic dispositions, and the individual must choose whether he will fulfill individual needs or institutional requirements. If he chooses to fulfill requirements (it is not, of course, always a matter of conscious choice) he is in a sense shortchanging himself, and is liable to unsatisfactory personal adjustment; he is frustrated and dissatisfied. If he chooses to fulfill his needs, he is shortchanging his role and is liable to unsatisfactory role performance; he is inefficient and ineffective.

Lipham[13] recently studied this problem in the educational setting. On the basis of the present model and preceding work in the area, he argued that the role of school administrator could be defined in terms of a number of crucial expectations. The administrator is expected, for example, to exert himself energetically, to strive for higher status, to relate himself successfully to other people, etc. He hypothesized that persons having a basic personality structure characterized by such needs and dispositions will suffer less strain in fulfilling the administrator role and will therefore be more effective than persons whose needs and dispositions are in conflict with the role expectations.

Accordingly, he assessed by interview and personality instruments (including the Adjective Check List and Sentence Completion techniques) the personality structure of two samples of 21 principals each within a single school system, one sample having been rated highest in effectiveness by the superintendent and his staff, the other sample, lowest. The results confirmed the hypothesis; the more effective principals tended to score significantly higher in activity drive, social ability, emotional control, mobility drive, and so on, than did the less effective principals. The less effective principals tended to score higher on such needs as abasement, which are in conflict with the expectations for the principal role.

---

[12] Ibid., p. 148.

[13] J. M. Lipham, *Personal Variables Related to Administrative Effectiveness,* Unpublished doctoral dissertation, University of Chicago, 1960.

Conflicts Between Roles and Within Roles
There is a range and variety of conflicts that occur when a role incumbent is required to conform simultaneously to a number of expectations which are mutually exclusive, contradictory, or inconsistent so that performance of one set of requirements makes performance of the other set of requirements impossible, or at least difficult. These role conflicts are evidence of dislocations in the nomothetic dimension of the social system and may arise in several ways.

Disagreement Within the Reference Group Defining a Given Role. There are numerous instances of this type of conflict in the school setting. The principal of the school may, for example, be expected by some teachers to visit them regularly to give constructive help, and by others to trust them as professional personnel not in need of such supervision. Or, the pupil may be expected by some teachers to emphasize the mechanics of writing, the substance being useful only for the practice of correct form. Other teachers might emphasize the content and substance, the form being merely a vehicle for the communication. Or, perhaps at a more fundamental level, the entire purpose of school and of education (and therefore of the various roles in the school) may be defined differently by different educators even within the same school system.

Prince,[14] for example, asked the question: Are there differences in the basic beliefs and values among educators of different age groups? To answer the question, he constructed a forced-choice questionnaire containing 64 pairs of items, one item in each pair representing a "traditional" value, and the other an "emergent" value, respondents being required to choose the more desirable alternative. Here are some sample pairs:

14A. Feel that "right" and "wrong" are relative terms.
14B. Feel that I should have strong convictions about what is right or wrong.
30A. Feel that discipline in the modern school is not as strict as it should be.
30B. Feel that the change from strict discipline in the modern school is a good thing.
31A. Feel that the most important thing in school is to gain knowledge useful to me in the future.
31B. Feel that the most important thing in school is to learn to get along with people.
64A. Strive to be an expert in something.
64B. Do many things quite well but not be an expert in anything.

The instrument was administered to 98 teachers varying in age from the twenties to the sixties. It was found that the younger the teacher, the more frequent was the tendency to choose the emergent belief as desirable; the older the teacher, the more frequently he tended to choose the traditional belief as desirable. The same effect was found for principals. Prince compared the re-

---

[14] R. Prince, *A study of the Relationships Between Individual Values and Administrative Effectiveness in the School Situation,* Unpublished doctoral dissertation, University of Chicago, 1957.

sponses of ten principals under 47 years of age with the responses of ten principals over 47 years of age. There was a statistically significant difference (at the
.01 level) in the responses of the two groups, the younger principals being consistently more emergent than the older principals.

*Disagreement among Several Reference Groups, Each Defining Expectations
for the Same Role.* To illustrate with an example somewhat outside the immediate context of the public school, the university faculty member may be expected by his department head to emphasize teaching and service to students but
by his academic dean to emphasize research and publication. Although these two
sets of expectations for the same role are not necessarily opposed to each other,
it is clear that the time given to implementing the one set can be seen as taking
time from implementing the other set, and to this extent they conflict.

Or, consider the definition of the superintendent role as viewed by superintendents and their board members and of the school board member role as
viewed by superintendents and school board members. Gross, Mason, and
McEachern[15] studied the agreement and disagreement of these two groups
of "role definers." The instrument used was a series of statements, e.g., "Read
most of the professional journals," to which 105 superintendents and 508
school board members were required to choose one of the following responses:
(A) Absolutely must; (B) Preferably should; (C) May or may not; (D) Preferably
should not; (E) Absolutely must not. The investigators found that on 63 percent
of the items there were statistically significant differences (at least at the .05
level) between the distributions of responses given by the two groups.

Here, for example, are some sample results adapted from the more detailed
and precise analysis of the original report. With respect to expectations for
the superintendent role, the board members and superintendents differed on
such expectations as: "Keep a watchful eye on the personal life of his subordi-
nates" (66 percent of the board members gave "Absolutely must" or "Preferably should" responses, 26 percent of the superintendents gave such responses);
"Defend his teachers from attack when they try to present the pros and cons of
various controversial social and political issues" (70 percent of the superintendents gave "Absolutely must" responses, 29 percent of the board members gave
such responses); "Help teachers to get higher salaries" (46 percent of the superintendents gave "Absolutely must" responses, 8 percent of the school board
members gave such responses). With respect to expectations for the school board
member role, the groups differed on such items as: "Appoint only teachers
nominated by the superintendent" (50 percent of the superintendents gave
"Absolutely must" responses, 23 percent of the school board members gave
such responses); "Concern itself with administrative problems" (56 percent of
the board members gave "Absolutely must" or "Preferably should" responses,
27 percent of the superintendents gave such responses); "Allow the superintendent to spend as much as a day a week away from his own school system
engaging in professional activities not directly related to his job" (56 percent

[15] N. Gross, W. S. Mason, and A. W. McEachern, *Explorations in Role Analysis: Studies
of the School Superintendent Role* (New York: John Wiley & Sons, Inc., 1958).

of the superintendents gave "Absolutely must" or "Preferably should" responses, 24 percent of the board members gave such responses).

Contradiction Between the Expectations of Two or More Roles Which an Individual Is Occupying at the Same Time. It is here that we have the problems arising from the fact that role incumbents in the educational institution are inevitably also role incumbents in other groups and institutions which may have opposing expectations. Conformity to one set of expectations may involve nonconformity to the other set of expectations.

Consider, for example, the adolescent attempting simultaneously to be an outstanding student and a popular member of the "gang." In a recent study Coleman[16] found that only 5.3 percent of 3830 high school students felt that their friends "would envy and look up to them" for being appointed an assistant in the biology laboratory because of their good work; 50 percent felt that their friends "would kid them about it, but envy them." Coleman suggests:

"The ambivalent response illustrates the conflicting feelings of adolescents about scholastic success; privately wanting to succeed and be recognized themselves, but (in most adolescent groups) publicly making fun of the success of others, and disowning interest in scholastic success. Thus it is not only that scholastic success counts little in the adolescent culture; extra effort devoted to scholastic matters often counts negatively and is discouraged."[17]

He makes the following generalization:

"The result of these norms produces in students a conflict of motivation; put very simply, to be one of the fellows and not work too hard in school, or to work hard in school and ignore the group. Different teenagers resolve the conflict in different ways. Whichever way it is resolved, it sets an artificial dilemma. On the one hand are sociable average students (who could do better); on the other hand are a few academically oriented, highly competitive isolates. A boy or girl can be oriented to academic achievement *or* to being popular, but it is hard to be both."[18]

Getzels and Guba[19] studied certain aspects of the teacher role. They posed the following questions: What are the expectations held for teachers as reported by the teachers themselves? How do these expectations accord with the expectations of other roles the teacher occupies? More specifically, in what ways are the several sets of expectations inconsistent? How do these inconsistencies, i.e.,

---

[16]J. S. Coleman, "Academic Achievement and the Structure of Competition," *Harvard Educational Review,* 1959, 29, pp. 330-351. See also pp. 87-94 of *Readings in the Social Psychology of Education,* edited by W. W. Charters and N. L. Gage. (New York: Allyn and Bacon, Inc., 1963).

[17]Ibid., p. 340.

[18]Ibid., p. 345.

[19]J. W. Getzels and E. G. Guba, "The Structure of Roles and Role Conflict in the Teaching Situation," *Journal of Educational Sociology,* 1955, 29, pp. 30-40.

role conflicts, vary from one teaching situation to another? What are the effects of such conflicts on the teacher?

Their initial attempt to answer these questions was based on extensive interviews with 41 teachers drawn from four school systems in two states. Three major areas of conflict were identified, each stemming from a central role a teacher occupied in addition to the teacher role.

1. The socioeconomic role. Teachers are usually assumed to be members of at least a quasi-professional group for whom middle class standards of living are expected. But in comparison with persons for whom similar standards are expected, the teacher receives a salary inadequate for implementing the expectations. Many of the strains felt by teachers arise not only because they are underpaid, but because they are expected to maintain standards of taste and living which are out of their financial reach.

2. The citizen role. Most adults in a community are assumed to be responsible citizens whose judgment regarding their own conduct can be trusted. But the teacher is often not granted the same confidence. He may, for example, be required to participate with more vigor in church affairs than his neighbors, but with less vigor in political matters than his own beliefs dictate. Although the teacher resides in the community, his citizenship may be only second-class, since the expectations placed upon him in his role of teacher restrict the freedom of his role as citizen.

3. The professional role. The teacher is expected to be a specially trained person with expertness in a particular field. Certification of this professional training and competence is required by the community, and persons without such professional certification would not be hired as teachers. In practice, however, the teacher's professional standing and prerogatives may be challenged by almost anyone who has succeeded only in becoming a parent or paying a tax bill. Not only may the school administrator encroach upon the teacher by prescribing more or less minutely what he may or may not do, but the community itself may dictate classroom content and procedures in direct opposition to the teacher's best professional judgment. Thus, conflict ensues. The teacher is expected to be a professional person with special competencies, but he is simultaneously expected to submit to others at crucial points in his own field of competence.

On the basis of the interview material, a group questionnaire was developed, and the responses of 166 teachers in six school systems analyzed. Among the results with respect to the distribution of role conflicts and the effects of role conflict on the teacher, the following findings may be noted.

a. Some role conflicts seem to be *situationally independent.* They have equal impact in all teaching situations sampled, and appear to be independent of local conditions. For example, on a six-point scale from "practically no teacher would agree" (scale score 0) to "very many teachers would agree" (scale score 6), the item, "Although the community expects a teacher to maintain the same standard of living as, say, a minor executive or a successful salesman, the salary typically paid a teacher is too small to make this possible," received a total mean scale score of 2.7 with a range of 2.0 for the low scoring school and 3.2 for the high scoring school.

b. Some role conflicts seem to be *situationally variant.* They have some impact in all teaching situations but may be substantially aggravated or ameliorated by local conditions. For example, the item, "While the average person is usually free to experiment with places of amusement and entertainment, making his selection from among them in terms of his own choice, the teacher can go only to 'nice' places, i.e., approved by the community at large," received a total mean score of 2.1 with a range of 1.4 for the low scoring school and 3.1 for the high scoring school.

c. Some conflicts seem to be *situationally specific.* They are unrecognized in most teaching situations, but seem to have considerable impact in particular localities. For example, the item, "Even though dancing may be an accepted form of social recreation in the community, the teacher who dances is often thought of as somewhat immoral," received a negligible total mean score of 0.4, but it had a mean score of 2.6 in one school.

Regarding the effect of role conflict on the teacher, the data were analyzed as to what kinds of teachers were "more troubled" or "less troubled" by the conflicts. Among the groups who were "more troubled" (at least at the .05 level of significance) were:

"Male teachers, as compared with female teachers; younger married teachers trying to set up appropriate standards of living, as compared with unmarried teachers or older teachers; teachers who come from communities they perceive as different from the community in which they teach, as compared with teachers from communities they perceive as similar to the one in which they teach; teachers who have fewer friends than they would like to have in the community in which they teach, as compared with a sufficient number of friends; teachers who feel that their relationship with the administration is not adequate and satisfying, as compared with those who feel that it is."

Conflicts Deriving from Personality Disorder

If the preceding types of conflict derive from certain dislocations between cultural and institutional dimensions, between institutional and individual dimensions, and from within the institutional dimension itself, there is a type of conflict that occurs as a function of certain dislocations within the individual himself. The effect of such personal instability or maladjustment is to keep the individual at odds with the institution either because he cannot maintain a stable relationship to a given role or because he misperceives the expectations placed upon him. Existential objects and events have minimal representation in his private world, and there is little correspondence between his private world and the worlds of other role incumbents with whom he must interact. In a sense, no matter what the situation, the role is detached from its institutional setting and function and used by the individual to work out his personal needs and dispositions, however inappropriate these may be to the goals of the social system as a whole. It is exactly this type of conflict that selection procedures for potential role incumbents attempt to circumvent when they screen out individuals characterized by one form or another of psychopathy.

Conflict in the Perception of Role Expectations

Opposition among role incumbents as to their mutual rights and responsibilities is not solely a function of personality disorder, and the broader issue may be stated as follows: How is it that some teachers and some pupils, or some superintendents and some board members—or to generalize the case, some complementary role incumbents—seem to apprehend at once their reciprocal obligations and privileges, while others take a long time to reach such understanding, if they reach it at all?

The relevant concept we should like to apply here is "selective perception." We may conceive of any publicly prescribed role relationship as enacted simultaneously in two separate private situations, one embedded in the other. On the one hand is the prescribed relationship as perceived and organized by the one role incumbent in terms of his goals, experiences, and information. On the other hand is the same relationship as perceived and organized by the other role incumbent in terms of *his* goals, experiences, and information. These private situations are related through those aspects of the existential objects, symbols, values, and expectations that overlap in the perceptions of both individuals. When we say two complementary role incumbents understand each other, we mean that the area of this overlap in perception is maximal; when we say that the two complementary role incumbents misunderstand each other, we mean that the area of such overlap is minimal.

In a recent study of the perception of expectations for the superintendent role by superintendents and by various reference groups (teachers, parents, school board members, businessmen, etc.), three specific patterns of conflict relevant to the present general formulation were identified.[20] One tendency was for the superintendent to perceive the expectations of a reference group accurately but not to concur with their views. A second tendency was for the superintendent to believe there was no difference in his view of the expectations and the views of the reference group, when, in reality, significant differences did exist. A third tendency was for the superintendent to believe there was a difference in his view of the expectations and the views of the reference group, when, in reality, significant differences did not exist.

An item from the pilot study may serve as an illustration. The item was "I expect the superintendent to: Choose his friends from people who are important in social, civic, and business affairs." Three types of responses on a five-point scale from "strongly agree" (scale score 1) to "strongly disagree" (scale score 5) were obtained. One response was the superintendent's expression of his own expectations; a second response was the superintendent's estimate of the expectations of the reference group; a third response was the actual expectation given by the reference group. Among the findings was that although the superinten-

[20]S. P. Hencley, *A Typology of Conflict Between School Superintendents and Their Reference Groups,* Unpublished doctoral dissertation, University of Chicago, 1960.

dent scored 2.0 when he expressed his own expectations, and he estimated 3.0 for the school board reference group and 3.5 for the business reference group, the school board actually scored 3.5 (tendency one above) and the business group actually scored 2.4 (tendency three above).

Whatever the kind of conflict (and the specific effects of these different types of conflict need systematic examination), it seems clear from recent research that the proper functioning of certain role relationships in the educational setting depends on the degree of overlap in the perception of expectations by the several complementary role incumbents. Stated in extreme terms, the basic hypothesis underlying these investigations was that when the perception of expectations overlap, the participants in the relationship feel satisfied with the work achieved, no matter what the actual behavior or accomplishment; when the perception of the expectations does not overlap, the participants feel dissatisfied.

Ferneau[21] studied the interaction of consultants and administrators in a school setting. A problem-situation instrument was constructed in which varying expectations for the consultant role could be expressed. The instrument was given to 180 administrators who were known to have had the services of educational consultants and to 46 consultants who were known to have provided this service. Each administrator and each consultant was also asked to evaluate the outcome of the consultation. It was then possible to compare the expectations for the consultant role held by the consultant himself and by the consultee, and to analyze the effect of the congruence or discrepancy of these expectations on the evaluation of the actual interaction.

The results confirmed the hypothesis. When an administrator and a consultant agreed on the expectations, they tended to rate the actual consultation favorably; when they disagreed, unfavorably. And apparently the evaluation of success or failure was in measure independent either of the particular expectations or of the manifest behavior—provided that the participants' perception of the expectations, whatever their character, overlapped.

Moyer,[22] in a study along similar lines, investigated by a Q-sort technique the relationship between the expectations of teachers and of administrators for leadership in the educational setting and the effect of congruence or discrepancy in these perceptions upon teacher satisfaction. Again, the results were consistent with the hypothesis: the greater the agreement between teacher and principal on the expectations for leadership, the more favorable the attitudes toward the work situation.

Summary and Conclusion

Attention has often been called to the abundance of constraints and demands— and of *contradictory* constraints and demands—in the educational setting. The present paper attempted to systematize the relevant issues and phenomena within a single framework, and to illustrate a number of the pertinent role

[21] E. Ferneau, *Role-Expectations in Consultations,* Unpublished doctoral dissertation, University of Chicago, 1954.
[22] D. C. Moyer, *Teachers' Attitudes Toward Leadership as They Relate to Teacher Satisfaction,* Unpublished doctoral dissertation, University of Chicago, 1954.

behaviors and types of conflict by reference to specific empirical studies. We should like to add several comments by way of conclusion. First, we should like to make clear that we have nowhere intended to imply that conflict is inevitably an evil. On the contrary, certain types of conflict, like certain types of necessity, give rise to productive transformations and inventions. And second, because of limitations of space, we have not been able to say anything about conflict resolution, although this is clearly a crucial issue. Certain modes of attenuating strain are implied in the theoretical framework and in the empirical studies, and further work in this area is indicated. Finally, we should like to point out that the present model of social behavior (and the classification of conflict and role behavior derived from it) is not the only possible formulation, or indeed that it is even in some ultimate sense the "right" one. We would suggest that it does seem useful at this time in clarifying various phenomena bearing on the subject, and we would hope that ensuing theoretical and empirical work would make the needed additions and revisions in the present effort.

Expectancy Theory in the Study of Poverty
Gerald Gurin and Patricia Gurin

Much of the literature on poverty, historical as well as contemporary, follows one of two general interpretative approaches. One approach focuses on the institutional aspects of the problem—on the current realities that the poor must deal with. The other focuses on the problems "in" the poor—on pathologies that are the residue of past disadvantage.

At times the distinction between these two approaches has been quite subtle and not sharply delineated. Rainwater, in earlier articles as well as in this issue (1970), has pointed out manifestations of these two approaches in sociological analyses of poverty and disadvantage—some approaches stressing the subcultural distinctiveness of the poor and others their limitations in the opportunity structure. Rainwater further notes that the distinction between these two approaches has not been adequately recognized or discussed in the theoretical sociological literature, and he indicates some of the negative consequences of this neglect on our understanding of the problems of poverty.

For psychologists who have been interested in problems of poverty this bifurcation has also had some negative consequences, although for converse reasons: the distinction between these two approaches has often been too sharply drawn. Psychological and situational approaches are sometimes considered antithetical and even mutually contradictory. Approaches that have focused

From *Journal of Social Issues*, 1970, 26 (2), 83-104. Reprinted by permission of the Society for the Psychological Study of Social Issues.

on reality problems have often assumed that motivational and psychological problems would disappear if basic changes in our institutions and opportunity structures were effected. In parallel fashion, those concerned with psychological and motivational issues have also often separated "psychology" and "reality." They have conceptualized the psychological problems of the poor in terms of "basic" personality dispositions that are the product of early socialization— motives, values, and behavior patterns that have become self-perpetuating and do not necessarily reflect current realities.

This excessively psychological point of view has sometimes led to a search for "deep" pathologies in motivation to interpret behavior that can be more simply explained as reaction to current situational constraints. For example, many of the motivational problems that arise in intervention programs for the poor—problems of commitment and dropout—might be explained more simply and meaningfully by relating them to the limited payoffs from these programs, rather than by analyzing the personality deficits of the poor. This psychological bias has also sometimes distorted the perspective and emphasis of programs attempting to deal with problems of poverty. For example, retraining programs for the hard-core unemployed, particularly the early programs of four or five years ago, often expended more energy and resources on "resocialization" than on meaningful skill training, job development, and job placement.

However, not all psychological and motivational approaches to poverty depend on concepts that are divorced from current reality issues. This point of view was probably more prominent in earlier literature than it is today. For example, the shift in psychological approaches to poverty is typified by the way ideas about social class differences have changed over the past generation. Historically this approach focused on differences in basic motivational and personality dispositions between middle and lower class populations, tracing these back to differences in parent-child relationships and early socialization patterns. In current literature the focus has shifted somewhat. Psychological analyses of class differences now place more emphasis on concepts such as "powerlessness" and "unmet expectations" which to some extent overcome the dichotomization of psychological and reality approaches by pointing to the psychological problems that spring from reality constraints. But there has been little effort to systemize these integrative approaches or to highlight the theoretical and practical issues arising from the confrontation and attempted integration of reality and psychological orientation.

Expectancy as an Integrating Concept

Over the past few years, we have attempted to conceptualize and analyze some of these issues in several studies of groups disadvantaged by poverty or minority status (Gurin, P. & Katz, D., 1966; Gurin, G., 1968; Gurin G., 1970; Gurin, P., et al., 1969). We have found it helpful to focus on the concept of *expectancy* that has been central to motivational theorists such as Atkinson (1964) and Rotter (1954). According to these theorists, motivation of behavior depends not only on a generalized disposition to approach or avoid a given class of objects (the "motive") and the incentive value of the particular goal or object at issue, but also on the expectancy or estimate of the probability that the behavior will lead to the goal. The expectancy orientation forces one to integrate the psychological and reality aspects of the problems of poor people since it ties motivation directly to the question of situational payoffs and constraints.

The expectancy approach has obvious implications for the psychologist inclined to approach problems of poverty by focusing on internal psychological dynamics of the poor. It forces him to relate motivational analysis to realistically available rewards and limitations.

It is less clear how such a framework also forces those who emphasize reality issues to consider individual factors. One might argue that the expectancy construct so points up the extent to which motivational problems are dependent on reality that when changes in realities and opportunity structures occur, these expectancies should change and the problems disappear. However, the issues are far more complex. Although expectancies are affected by immediate objective rewards and constraints and are thus subject to changes as the situation changes, they also are residues of the past. Expectancies are to some extent generalized dispositions that develop, like other personality dispositions, out of an individual's life history of relevant success and failure experiences; these generalized expectancies in turn influence the way an individual reacts to his current realities and to changes in these realities. Viewed in these general *dispositional* terms, expectancies may present problems of resocialization and relearning as serious as those of other personality dispositions; subjective expectancies do not automatically change to conform with changes in objective expectancies. Thus, some of the most interesting theoretical psychological issues begin rather than end when realities and objective expectancies change.

In this paper we will address ourselves to a discussion of some of these issues. Hopefully we are living in a period when opportunities are increasing and at least some attempts are being made to affect situational constraints, particularly for blacks and other minorities in poverty. Concern with psychological issues that are relevant during such changing conditions should be of practical as well as theoretical interest.

To help clarify and delineate some of these issues, we will draw on the motivational literature on expectancy. Since this literature is based mainly on experimental laboratory studies of white middle class college subjects, there are obvious problems in translating it to problems of the poor. The literature has served primarily to point up and highlight problems and issues; it is to these, rather than to suggested solutions, that most of our comments will be addressed.

Within an expectancy framework, two sets of psychological problems are critical for poverty groups. One is the problem of *low* expectancy—the feeling that one has little chance of attaining one's goal. The other, following Rotter's (1966) concept of internal-external control, is the problem of *externally based* expectancies—the feeling that one does not control one's own chances. Although these tend to be related—for example, the feeling of powerlessness reflects both low and externally based expectancies—they are not the same and pose different issues and problems.

In a previous paper we discussed a number of issues that arise when the concept of internal-external control is applied to problems of race and poverty (Gurin, P., et al., 1969). Therefore, we will focus here on the issue of low expectancy. We begin with two sets of questions especially relevant to our interest in affecting the problems of poor people:

1. *What are the possibilities for changing expectancies?* What is the relationship between change in objective probabilities and change in subjective expectancies? What does the expectancy literature tell us about the ease or difficulty of changing expectancies and the stability and generalizability of these changes? Do poverty groups have special problems in learning new expectancies?

2. *What are the possibilities of affecting performance by changing expectancies?* Since we are ultimately interested in affecting behavior that may help poor people deal with their problems, we are interested in changing expectancies only if they affect behavior. What are the relationships among change in objective probabilities, change in subjective expectancies, and change in behavior? Again, the literature will point up complexities that contradict any simplistic assumption of a linear "automatic" relationship whereby changes in objective probabilities bring about congruent changes in subjective expectancies which, in turn, bring about congruent changes in behavior.

Changing Expectancies

The Ease of Changing Expectancies
Many studies, either with children (Crandall, Good, & Crandall, 1964; Crandall, 1963; Mischel & Staub, 1965), or with adults (Feather, 1963, 1965, 1966, 1968; Rychlak & Lerner, 1965; Heath, 1961, 1962; Diggory & Morlock, 1964; Zajonc & Brickman, 1969; Brickman, 1968; Phares, 1957) demonstrate how easily personal expectancies can be altered by changing objective probabilities of success. All use the same kind of experimental setup. Subjects are asked their expectancies of success on reaction-time tasks, solving anagrams or mathematical puzzles, or other skill-based tasks. They are then asked to perform a block of trials on which they are given feedback indicating that they succeeded or failed on most of the trials. Without exception, these studies show that this success-failure feedback vitally affects subsequent expectancies of success on the same task. In fact, the realistic assessment of future chances of success and failure following a reinforcement sequence that is primarily positive or primarily negative is striking. Following success, most subjects alter their original expectancies upward; following failure, most subjects alter downward.

Dissonance Theory—An Opposing View
Still, despite this consistent, large main effect of success-failure feedback, another set of experimental studies, following the dissonance tradition of Festinger (1957) and his students, questions the ease of modifying personal expectancies. The argument, developed and tested first by Aronson and Carlsmith (1962), asserts that people, motivated by the need for self-consistency, may, as one mode for handling dissonance, reject feedback that disconfirms their initial expectancies. It is hardly surprising that people who expect to succeed may act to avoid,

deny, or "undo" failure experiences, since a simple outcome or incentive model would make the same prediction. Success is clearly a more positive outcome and failure a more negative outcome in American society. More striking, therefore, is the dissonance prediction that people who hold low expectancies of success will prefer to "undo" success experiences rather than change their expectancies to correspond with the disconfirming feedback. If true, this would have serious implications for work with poor people who are likely to hold low personal expectancies.

Because of these implications, the data relevant to the dissonance prediction are of particular interest. The Aronson and Carlsmith results, which support the dissonance-avoidance hypothesis, have not always been replicated in subsequent studies that use a similar experimental approach (Lowin & Epstein, 1965; Silverman and Marcantonio, 1965; Frentzel, 1965; Cottrell, 1965, 1967; Zajonc & Brickman, 1969). The most thorough replication attempt is reported by Brock, Edelman, Edwards, and Schuck (1965) who performed several experiments to test the dissonance theory prediction and alternative explanations. The first two of these experiments were exact replications of the Aronson-Carlsmith procedure and obtained similar results. In the four subsequent experiments, Brock et al. varied how frequently the subject was given feedback about his performance. When feedback was clear and frequent, low expectancy subjects did not behave as dissonance theory would predict. Instead, they seemed more motivated by trying to do well than by trying to maintain consistency with their earlier self-conceptions.

In a recent study, Brickman (1968) argued that the inconclusiveness of some of these earlier dissonance experiments may have resulted from two common procedures: (1) inferring, rather than measuring, the state of dissonance that is presumed to follow receipt of discrepant information, and (2) failing to account for the revision of expectancies that should follow from strictly rational responses predicted from an information-processing model. Correcting for both problems, Brickman demonstrated that people, even those with low expectancies, do report more discomfort when their expectancies are disconfirmed than when they are supported by performance feedback. But his data do not show that this discomfort is handled by avoiding expectancy change. Instead, groups receiving the most discrepant feedback revise their expectancies more than a Bayesian formula suggests is optimal, not less as dissonance theory would predict.

The data that Baron presents in his paper in this issue are also relevant to this point (1970). Although Baron does not follow dissonance theory, his SRS approach at times leads to similar consistency predictions. Baron notes that his early theoretical formulation applied his consistency hypothesis to people with a low as well as a high history of reinforcements. However, some of his results have led him to feel that the consistency hypothesis holds mainly for people with a high SRS, while people who have had a history of low reinforcements tend to bias their SRS's upward.

Although dissonance predictions, especially the critical hypotheses regarding low expectancy people, are not always supported, this tradition of research does pose some significant issues for intervention strategies that depend on changing the objective probabilities of poor people.

Different Ways of Responding to Change
First, the dissonance tradition highlights the fact that low expectancy people can handle discrepant success feedback in a variety of ways. In dissonance terminology, they may choose among different, if not alternative, modes of resolving the discomfort produced by this discrepancy. They may change their behavior to undo the successful performance; they may distort feedback to avoid its dissonance implications; they may make cognitive (expectancy) changes to match their new performance. To date we know very little about what kinds of people, under what kinds of conditions, will choose behavioral rather than cognitive modes. It is clear that Aronson and Carlsmith's experimental procedure tried to rule out the possibility of easy cognitive change in order to test the behavioral modification prediction. The critical question in an expectancy-based approach to poverty intervention is what people with low expectancies will do when both cognitive and behavioral change are equally allowable in the situation. Central to dissonance theorists is the implicit assumption, made explicit by Baron in this issue, that cognitive change, involving as it must the possibility of change in not one cognition but in the whole cognitive structure, is more unlikely than behavioral change. But data to support that assumption are generally lacking. We need to know much more about multiple and alternative responses to unexpected successes.

Stability and Generalizability of Expectancy Change
Second, the questions raised by dissonance theory force us to examine the kinds of expectancies that have been so easily modified in typical psychological experiments. By and large, they deal with limited, task-specific expectancies. They may have little to do with the more basic cognitive structure and self-concept that interests both dissonance theorists and us. It is not sufficient to change an expectancy that is limited in time and does not involve the more basic sense of self. Rather, we want to develop new expectancies that will generalize beyond a specific experimental task to other types of situations and, hopefully, eventually to the person's *generalized* feelings about himself. In addition, we are not interested in expectancy change that maintains little stability over time or needs constant reinforcement. Instead, we hope to effect more permanent change.

What do we know about the issues of generalizability and stability of expectancy changes from previous research? They have only rarely been examined, although what literature exists suggests that expectancy change produced in the laboratory may be very limited indeed.

Some studies show that expectancies altered in a single experimental or training session are very unstable. Following a number of training trials in which expectancies are heightened by success and lowered by failure, even a relatively short delay of just twenty-four hours results in decided reversals to pretraining expectancies (Phares, 1966; Schwarz, 1966; Rychlak & Eacker, 1962). The fewer the training trials and the longer the delay after training, the more numerous the reversals. Schwarz's work also suggests that the pattern of success-failure experiences may be even more important than the sheer number in inducing both larger and more stable expectancy change. Controlling for number of successes, expectancies are more heightened when success experiences occur together than when they are more evenly or randomly interspersed by failures. Stability also seems to be affected by the size of the discrepancy between the original expectancy and the feedback. When successes and failures are so numerous that they appear highly discrepant with initial expectancy, change is even less enduring (Schwarz, 1966). This may well result from the incredulity effect of large discrepancies (Baron, 1970). Subjects seem very realistic about modifying expectancies to conform with objective feedback, even when it markedly contradicts what they expect; but the feedback effect may not last beyond the training situation if its credibility is dubious because it is simply too much better or worse than was originally expected.

Since these studies that examine factors affecting stability of expectancy change are few, their suggestions about timing, patterning, and size of discrepancy are by no means conclusive. Yet they do imply that intervention programs designed to alter objective probabilities of the poor must also be concerned with highly complicated techniques if objective changes in the situation are to produce stable changes in poor people's estimates of personal chances of success.

Generalization of expectancy change is even more rarely investigated. Many factors affecting generalization of other kinds of learning may also apply to expectancy change, but too few studies have explored this possibility. What little data we have suggest that certain types of people—those with initially very low expectancies (Mischel & Staub, 1965) and those who believe in internal control—and certain kinds of situations—those based on skill rather than chance (Rotter, 1966)—do show generalization beyond the training task. Still, we know very little about the conditions that will promote generalization to other kinds of tasks or, even more importantly, to the person's generalized expectancy or self-concept.

Special Problems for Poverty Groups
in Learning New Expectancies

Another major question for us is whether the effects of success and failure differ depending on the person's initial expectancies. Specifically, if the expectancy problems of poor people involve both low and externally based expectancies, is there evidence that their responsiveness to changing situations should differ from people with high and internally based expectancies? Extrapolating from the research literature, would we expect poverty groups to have special problems in learning new expectancies as their objective probabilities change?

Conditioner Effects of Low Expectancies. The issue of whether people of low and high expectancies differ in their responses to success and failure has been explored in a few expectancy studies. Most support the hypothesis that sensitivity to success and failure is conditioned by initial generalized level of expectancy. One group of studies supports what might be termed a "noncongruent" hypothesis, namely, that expectancies will change most in reaction to experiences that are particularly discrepant.[1] These studies indicate that people entering a skill situation with a low generalized expectancy will show a greater rise in their success expectations as a result of success experiences than will people with high initial expectancies. Conversely, high expectancy people will decrease their expectation of success more than low expectancy people as the result of failure experiences (Crandall, 1963; Crandall, Good, & Crandall, 1964; Mischel & Staub, 1965;[2] Feather, 1966).

If we wish to raise the low expectancies of poverty groups, these studies are encouraging, since they suggest that low expectancy people may be particularly reactive to success experiences. However, one major limitation of these studies should be noted. Since all the expectancy-change studies demonstrate the large main effect of success-failure and the strong tendency for all people to change their expectancies to conform to the objective probabilities in the feedback, the amount of change tends to become an automatic consequence of "room to move" from the original position. Not all experiments have attempted to control for initial expectancies, and those that have are of questionable adequacy. Thus, the evidence on responsiveness of low expectancy groups to success experiences remains somewhat inconclusive.

Evidence is also scarce on the important questions of whether initial expectancies affect the stability and generalization of newly learned expectancies. Some relevant data appear in an interesting study by Mischel and Staub (1965), which suggest that people with low expectancies tend to overgeneralize to dissimilar as well as similar tasks. This seems to reflect an unusual sensitivity to success and failure experiences and an overdependence on the immediate environment. Such dependence could inhibit the development of stable, realistic expectancies. For people with low expectancies, the unusually heightened expectancies that follow successes could easily be deflated by later failures.

Again, this is an area where research is urgently needed. If the few hints from the literature were to hold up under further investigation, expectancy-based interventions might be highly successful in changing the low expectancies of poor people. However, available data should also make us cautious against undue optimism because the very receptivity of low expectancy people to situational

---

[1]This "noncongruent" hypothesis may help explain why most studies have shown that, while both failure and success feedback affect expectancies, failure has been somewhat more effective, i.e., decrements after failure are generally greater than increments after success (Crandall, 1963; Crandall, Good, & Crandall, 1964; Rychlak & Eacker, 1962; Rychlak & Lerner, 1965; Feather, 1966, 1968).

In general, most studies have investigated middle class populations who have had success experience with the types of tasks presented in the experiments, and who, therefore, might be expected to approach these tasks with generally high expectancies. For such people failure would be more discordant than success. It is interesting that the one exception to this general finding appears in a study by Zajonc and Brickman (1969) that uses a reaction-time task; previous experience would have provided a more ambiguous basis for expectancy evaluations in that task. This finding on the greater efficacy of failure feedback exemplifies how our findings may be dependent on the nature of our typical subjects, and how replication of such studies on poverty groups, with lower initial expectancies, might lead to very different results.

[2]Change in expectancy was not measured directly in the Mischel and Staub study, but was implied in changes in DEL (readiness to delay gratification).

cues might also result in overgeneralization and quick deflation of increased expectancies if the "real" world failed to reinforce their new views of themselves.

Conditioner Effects of Externally Based Expectancies. Although Rotter developed the concept of internal-external control a number of years ago, its great popularity is a recent phenomenon. In the recent upsurge of interest in poverty and race, internal-external control has been widely used as an operationalization of concepts like efficacy and powerlessness. Generally it has been forgotten that Rotter's interest in the concept developed from his theoretical involvement in the question of how new expectancies are learned. Looking at this internal-external concept both as a characteristic of a situation and as a personality orientation, Rotter hypothesized that where control of reinforcements is external—that is, based on chance forces over which the individual has no control rather than on his own internal resources of ability, skill, and effort—the person will learn less predictably from reinforcement. In simple terms, if a person feels that his success or failure in a given situation is determined by chance rather than his own actions, there is no reason for him to utilize this experience in estimating his future chances of success.

Rotter and his associates have tested this hypothesis by comparing people in chance and skill situations and by comparing people defined as holding internal rather than external beliefs. Generally, data on acquisition and realism of learning new expectancies support Rotter's hypothesis. Subjects in skill situations, and those who believe their own actions determine the rewards they receive, show greater increases and decreases in expectancies following success and failure, and they reach a given level of expectancy with fewer successes or failures (Rotter, Liverant, & Crowne, 1961; Phares, 1957; Bennion, 1961). Moreover, they change expectancies more typically and realistically, i.e., increase expectancies after success and decrease them after failure (Phares, 1957; James, 1957; Feather, 1968). In contrast, people in chance situations, or those who believe that external forces generally determine their rewards, change their expectancies less, and less realistically, as a function of success and failure. The issue of how generalization or stability of expectancy change may be conditioned by these factors has rarely been examined. The one study directed to this issue (James, 1957) indicates that generalization is greater in skill than in chance situations and for internally rather than externally oriented subjects.

These results, assuming they are supported by further research on noncollege populations, suggest that the meaning of holding an externally based expectancy may be very different from holding a low expectancy of success. Low expectancy people may be unusually responsive to success, while people who believe their expectancies are determined by forces beyond their control may be especially unresponsive to success. Therefore, the implication of this line of research for poverty programs depends greatly on the connection between level and basis of expectancy among poor people. If poor people suffer from both problems, poverty interventions may face a complex mix of expectancy orientations, some facilitating and some minimizing the possible impact of situational changes and success experiences.

Behavioral Consequences of Expectancy Change

Those who believe that opportunity and situational changes are sufficient strategies in the war on poverty assume either that personal motivation is an unimportant element in behavior or that personal expectancies will automatically follow objective changes, and that these expectancy changes will automatically result in heightened performance. We, too, assume that performance can be enhanced through the motivational significance of increasing expectancies. However, several different theoretical models disclose complexities that contradict a simplistic assumption of a linear or automatic relationship whereby changes in objective probabilities bring about congruent changes in subjective expectancies, which, in turn, bring about congruent changes in behavior.

Does Increase in Expectancy Heighten Performance
for Low Expectancy People?
One approach stresses the motivational significance of simply stating one's expectancy of success on getting commitment and involvement in the task at hand. Improvement in performance is then expected to follow because of the greater involvement. If stating an expectancy is the causally significant factor, performance should improve regardless of a high or low expectancy posture. Data from an experiment by Zajonc and Brickman (1969) support this hypothesis.

The Atkinson model also questions simplistic assumptions about behavioral consequences from heightening expectancies. By assuming that expectancies and incentives are inversely related in an achievement situation, Atkinson predicts that both approach and avoidance achievement motivation are maximally aroused when success probabilities are intermediate, approximately 50-50. Thus, the implications of using success experiences to increase very low expectancies through this intermediate range to a much higher level depend on the person's motive characteristics. If low expectancy people also suffer from high fear of failure—a relationship supported by some studies (Feather, 1963, 1965) but not others (Rychlak & Lerner, 1965; Feather, 1966)—they may well try to avoid performance challenge as their success expectancies increase into an intermediate range. For instance, using an expectancy approach in job-training programs might result in increased dropout or absenteeism among trainees as their expectancies increase, provided: (a) they have both low expectancy and fear of failure problems, and (b) their motivation fits the model suggested by Atkinson. Of course even if there were conclusive support for this model, other sources of motivation, such as desire for money, affiliation, or power, could be used to compensate for the hypothesized avoidance of achievement as low expectancy-high fear of failure trainees experience job success. But it would require considerable sensitivity to all these motive issues to know when to arouse other kinds of motives in order to keep trainees in a skill-training situation that depends primarily on enhancing expectancies through success.

Actually, studies testing predicted performance, motive, and expectancy interactions have produced contradictory results. Most relevant is the work of Feather in which expectancy change plays an important role. Persistence at an insoluble task does seem to follow the interaction model (Feather, 1961, 1963), but performance data do not support it as well (Feather, 1966, 1968). Certainly the performance results do not warrant conclusive pessimism about what would happen if intervention programs attempt to increase the expectancies of the poor. Still this model does raise provocative questions for such programs.

Dissonance theorists also make two assumptions that question whether success experiences will necessarily produce positive performance effects for low expectancy people. First, dissonance can be reduced by making rewards that disconfirm initial expectancies less attractive than those that support expectancies. Brickman (1968), however, finds little evidence that dissonance was handled by reducing the incentive value of outcomes that disconfirmed expectancies. Both anticipated and actual satisfaction with achievement rewards representing success were high, regardless of personal expectancies.

Second, however, dissonance theory predicts that low expectancy subjects will not try to achieve rewards based on success even if they are attractive, because they will find the dissonance created by success too uncomfortable to tolerate. Therefore, performance will be best facilitated by feedback that contradicts initial expectancies very little, if at all. This hypothesis is examined in numerous experiments reported by Baron, with contradictory results. The burden of the dissonance experiments summarized in the preceding section of this paper also questions this hypothesis. In most of the replications of the Aronson-Carlsmith study (1962), low expectancy subjects given success feedback appeared to be motivated more by desire to do well than to avoid dissonance.

Finally, it is important to note that performance hypotheses based on dissonance theory depend largely on the interrelationships of cognitive and behavioral modes of resolving dissonance. Let us assume, for the moment, that success experiences are dissonance-producing and unsettling for low expectancy people. If cognitive change either precedes or is more likely than behavioral resolution, performance may well improve subsequent to the cognitive change, in order to match the person's new heightened sense of his potential. If behavioral resolution precedes or substitutes for cognitive change, low expectancy people should perform badly or undo successful performances in order to maintain expectancy consistency. To date we know too little about these interrelationships among modes of resolving dissonance to decide which performance prediction is most reasonable for low expectancy people.

To summarize: Some difficult problems in using expectancy change to enhance the performance of low expectancy people are suggested by following the Atkinson model and dissonance theory. Nevertheless, available data indicate we need not be as pessimistic as these approaches seem to suggest. On the other hand, we should not leap to the opposite conclusion either. Data are just too sparse to start translating research into appropriate action strategies. It is interesting, for instance, that students following Rotter's concern with expectancy as part of social learning theory have given most of their attention to the learning of expectancies. Very few experimental studies in that tradition take the next step and examine ways that newly acquired expectancies may or may not produce congruent changes in learning or performing in achievement or job-related situations.

Problems in Expectancy-Performance Research
Another problem in translating research into action derives from the kinds of studies typical in this area. Most of the data available to us are correlational and, therefore, not very helpful in isolating whether expectancy change will actually heighten performance. Many studies have shown a positive correlation between expectancy and performance. For instance, children with high academic expectancies also achieve higher grades and perform better on IQ and standard achievement tests (Crandall, Katkovsky, & Preston, 1962; Crandall, Good, & Crandall, 1964; Battle, 1965, 1966; Coleman et al., 1966). Yet, except for some support for the hypothesis that expectancies cause greater involvement and persistence in difficult achievement tasks (Crandall, Katkovsky, & Preston, 1962; Battle, 1965), these studies tell us little about the causal connections between expectancy and performance. Similarly, studies of adults give correlational support but little else. Even Feather's studies rarely employ both the expectancy change and performance improvement scores that are so necessary to unravel their interrelationships.

Data from Zajonc and Brickman (1969) illustrate how important this is; as in other studies, subjects who approached the task with high success expectancies performed better on the first block of trials. However, since this study also uses a measure of performance before the actual experimental performance trials and before the subjects state their initial expectancies, Zajonc and Brickman were able to show that this typical relationship between initial expectancy and first trial performance can be explained as expectancy reflecting rather than determining performance. In addition, with this pre-experimental performance measure, they were able systematically to relate changing expectancy to performance improvement. And the results do not support the simple assumption that raising expectancy leads to raising performance and lowering expectancy leads to lowering performance; rather, they show complex interaction effects. One particularly interesting result is the fact that expectancy reaction to failure has critical implications for performance improvement. Subjects who reduced their expectancies greatly after failure also showed less improvement than subjects who resisted the failure feedback and reduced their expectancies only slightly. In contrast, the study showed no improvement implications from expectancy reactions to success. Subjects who changed expectancies slightly and those who changed greatly improved equally, although Zajonc and Brickman were careful to note that subjects in the success condition may have experienced an improvement ceiling.

Summary and Implications

Major Results and Questions from the Literature
Perhaps the overall impression from the expectancy literature we have reviewed is one of complexity, contradiction, and tentativeness of our knowledge in this

area. Nonetheless, two of the conclusions that can be drawn lend hope for intervention programs that are trying to affect problems of poverty through changing
the environment poor people confront. First, success experiences and reality
changes in opportunities probably can be used to raise the expectancies of low
expectancy people. Second, studies consistently stress that this be done under
conditions where a person feels that the successes come from his own skill and
competence. The literature on internal and external control indicates that effects
of success and failure are not very reliable when a person feels they do not
depend on his own actions.

Our review also indicates, however, that an individual's expectancies do not
automatically follow changes in objective probabilities. We have suggested a
number of complexities that qualify the simplistic assumption that increasing
objective success and opportunity will necessarily lead to heightened subjective
expectancies and more effective behavior. Programs trying to cope with these
issues face several important questions:

1. Under what conditions will success experiences and opportunity changes
   increase personal expectancies and under what conditions will they lead
   to denial and avoidance responses?
2. How can success experiences in an intervention program be used to
   affect long-range stable expectancy changes that carry into the world
   beyond the program?
3. How can the effects of a series of specific positive experiences be made
   to affect an individual's general self-confidence and trust in the environment?
4. Under what conditions can positive effects on psychological expectancies also have positive implications for behavior?

A very general implication follows from the fact that the literature raises
more questions than it answers. We have stressed the complexity of expectancy
issues—especially the point that psychological problems of expectancy, though
responsive to reality changes, will not disappear automatically when those
changes occur—not out of an academic interest in complexity. Rather, it is important to recognize this complexity because it has implications for the underlying philosophy one adopts in attempting to deal with problems of poverty.

In our introduction we have noted the tendency for approaches to poverty
to polarize around psychological and reality positions. There is danger in basing
poverty interventions on an overly psychological approach, on the assumption
that the problems are *in* the poor. This view of the problem and tendency to
blame the poor can become too easily a rationalization for our inability to deal
with the tremendous reality issues in poverty. But it is also dangerous to assume
that there are no motivational problems that are not easily solved with situational changes. When change turns out to be complicated and slow, proponents
of a simplistic reality approach may swing to an equally overly simplified, often
prejudiced, psychological approach—appealing out of frustration to concepts of
deep personality deficit and pathology in the poor, and even, in the case of the
blacks, to the argument of genetic inferiority.

Research Implications
The questions we have raised clearly need further research if we are to use expectancy theories to guide intervention programs. In calling for more research, we might also suggest directions to take in examining generalization, stability, and performance implications of expectancy change.

First, we feel it is important to broaden the kinds of determinants that are investigated in research on stability and generalization. For example, the significance of the social relationship between the trainer and trainee (or experimenter and subject), which Kelman (1965) and Raven (1965) link to permanency and generalization of attitude change, is completely untouched in the expectancy literature (an exception is the work of Baron). The expectancy literature, the product of either social learning or cognitive psychologists, focuses too exclusively perhaps on schedules of reinforcement, task difficulty, feedback discrepancy, or cognitive aspects of personality as determinants of the course of expectancy change.[3] Important as these factors may be, poverty programs concerned with expectancy change may also need to consider characteristics of the interpersonal situation in which the low-income, low-skilled person begins to assess his chances for success. Opportunity changes generally are mediated by people—trainers in job training, employment counselors, teachers, job recruiters, political leaders, etc. Characteristics that make these people possible identification figures and credible to the poor may affect expectancy change as much as they affect permanence of other kinds of attitude change (Kelman, 1965), and as much as expectancy change follows from less interpersonal qualities of situations more typically examined in expectancy literature. This research direction connects with the conviction of many activists regarding the desirability, if not necessity, of involving community people as leaders and models in poverty intervention programs.

Second, to clarify what will happen to behavior when success experiences are used to heighten expectancies, we need the kind of experimental designs that can overcome the limitations of previous research and answer some crucial questions. We must know whether expectancy change means anything or whether performance is primarily a function of either earlier skill and ability or current success, independent of the expectancy reaction to it. An obvious approach to answering these questions is to control possible effects of experience to see if expectancy has any independent effect on performance. But that is exactly what we do not want to do in work with the poor. Job retraining, employment placement, adult education, or successful collective action are all experiences that should be meaningful both for changing expectancies and for enhancing performance. We do not want to demonstrate the significance of expectancy by arguing that it affects future performance independent of these experiences. Rather, we need a research design much like the one used by Zajonc and Brickman, so we can see whether an expectancy reaction to a success experience adds anything to the

---

[3] But note Feather's emphasis on achievement motives as possibly mediating the impact of success and failure on expectancy change, and Mischel and Staub's emphasis on the importance of trust between experimenter and subject.

contribution of the experience itself. Over and over in Feather's work we see that success in early trials is positively related to subsequent performance. What we need is a design that lets us see whether this is more true for subjects who respond to success by greatly increasing their personal expectancies than for subjects who have little, if any, expectancy reaction to success. Moreover, the design must also allow us to examine whether the person's initial expectancy conditions his reaction to success and failure and also conditions the effects of his reaction on performance improvement. Does the person with a very low expectancy respond differently to success and failure than one who already has much higher expectancy? And does his reaction to success and failure have different performance implications than it would have if he came to the situation with more self-confidence?

Most important of all is the pressing need to turn to studies of poor people who are likely to have genuinely lower expectancies of success than any group that has been called a "low expectancy group" in previous research. Like most other motivational research, the expectancy studies have relied almost exclusively on college samples, generally college males. A low expectancy person is anyone below the median in initial expectancies for that sample. We are in the peculiar position of trying to extrapolate from research on that limited and much more affluent group to poor people who have faced much harsher social realities. We, therefore, need to replicate some of the more significant studies in a genuinely low expectancy population. As a more challenging step, we should also extend previous research to issues that are not typically examined and select experimental tasks that are probably more relevant to the job skills and interests of the poor.

Some Limitations in Current Theory and Research
We have noted the need in future research to explore some of the issues that have been raised by our review of the expectancy literature and our attempts to apply it to problems of the poor. In doing so, we have stayed within the framework of the existing approaches. But this framework is narrow, covering only selected aspects of expectancy issues in poverty. The studies mainly have used tasks that reflect individual skill, providing success and failure feedback to influence the individual's expectancies about his ability to perform well. Thus, the existing theory and research are relevant to problems of poverty to the extent that the expectancies of the poor are affected by their individual skills and competences. They are most applicable to intervention programs which, like job training, promote the development of individual competence as the way out of poverty.

Without denying the validity and place for such an approach, we nevertheless feel that it has two critical limitations. First, it assumes a benign environment, one in which success in life does follow from individual competence and achievement. This is implicit in the work on internal-external control, where the internal orientation is interpreted as realistic and "healthy" and the external orientation as a primitive belief in chance and fate. In a previous paper (Gurin, P., et al., 1969) we have suggested that, while this approach may be appropriate for the socially advantaged populations that have been the subjects of most of the expectancy research, it is more questionable when applied to poverty groups. Poor people face many external obstacles that have nothing to do with chance, and a sensitivity to the external determinants of their opportunities and expectancies may lead to more effective rather than less effective behavior.

Second, the competence approach to opportunities and expectancies is limited because it is an individual approach. It points to individual mobility as the solution to poverty and neglects the import of collective action. Focusing on individual skill determinants of expectancy, the literature is not relevant to solutions directed against the situational and institutional determinants of expectancies. Such solutions, by their nature, involve group rather than individual action. We need a whole new direction in expectancy research to make it as potentially relevant to issues like community control as it is to job training programs.

Consideration of the external determinants of expectancies and the appropriateness of collective action to deal with them raises a host of further questions for expectancy theory and research. Clearly, the problem of learning new expectancies is no longer one of changing from an external to a more internal orientation. Rather, poor people are presented with the much more difficult problem of learning to make very complex judgments as to when internal and external interpretations are realistic, when an internal orientation reflects intrapunitiveness rather than a sense of efficacy, when an external orientation becomes defensive rather than a realistic blaming of the social system. Moreover, these judgments must be made at a time when objective opportunities are in flux, making an accurate picture of reality all the more difficult to determine.

References

Aronson, E., & Carlsmith, J. M. Performance expectancy as a determinant of actual performance. *Journal of Abnormal and Social Psychology,* 1962, 65, 178-182.

Atkinson, J. W. *An introduction to motivation.* Princeton, N.J.: D. Van Nostrand, 1964.

Battle, E. Motivational determinants of academic task persistence. *Journal of Personality and Social Psychology,* 1965, 2, 209-218.

Battle, E. Motivational determinants of academic competence. *Journal of Personality and Social Psychology,* 1966, 4, 634-642.

Baron, R. The SRS model as a predictor of Negro responsiveness to reinforcement. *Journal of Social Issues,* 1970, 26 (2).

Bennion, R. C. Task, trial by score variability of internal versus external control of reinforcement. Unpublished doctoral dissertation, Ohio State University, 1961.

Brickman, P. Expectancy disconfirmation and search: Cognitive and affective components. Unpublished doctoral dissertation, University of Michigan, 1968.

Brock, T. C., Edelman, S. K., Edwards, D. C., & Schuck, J. R. Seven studies of performance expectancy as a determinant of actual performance. *Journal of Experimental Social Psychology,* 1965, 1, 295-310.

Coleman, J. S. et al. *Equality of educational opportunity.* U.S. Department of

53 Context

Health, Education and Welfare, Office of Education. Washington, D.C.: U.S. Government Printing Office, 1966.

Cottrell, N. B. Performance expectancy as a determinant of actual performance: A replication with a new design. *Journal of Personality and Social Psychology,* 1965, 2, 685-691.

Cottrell, N. B. The effect of dissonance between expected and obtained performance upon task proficiency and self-estimates of task proficiency. *Journal of Social Psychology,* 1967, 72, 275-284.

Crandall, V. C. The reinforcement effects of adult reactions and non-reactions on children's achievement expectations. *Child Development,* 1963, 34, 335-354.

Crandall, V. C., Good, S., & Crandall, V. J. The reinforcement effects of adult reactions and nonreactions on children's achievement expectations: A replication study. *Child Development,* 1964, 35, 485-497.

Crandall, V. J., Katkovsky, W., & Preston, A. Motivational and ability determinants of young children's intellectual achievement behaviors. *Child Development,* 1962, 33, 643-661.

Diggory, J. C., & Morlock, H. C., Jr. Level of aspiration, or probability of success? *Journal of Abnormal and Social Psychology,* 1964, 69, 282-289.

Feather, N. T. The relationship of persistence at a task to expectation of success and achievement related motives. *Journal of Abnormal and Social Psychology,* 1961, 63, 552-561.

Feather, N. T. The relationship of expectation of success to reported probability, task structure, and achievement related motivation. *Journal of Abnormal and Social Psychology,* 1963, 66, 231-238.

Feather, N. T. The relationship of expectation of success to need-achievement and test anxiety. *Journal of Personality and Social Psychology,* 1965, 2, 118-126.

Feather, N. T. Effects of prior success and failure on expectations of success and subsequent performance. *Journal of Personality and Social Psychology,* 1966, 3, 287-298.

Feather, N. T. Change in confidence following success or failure as a predictor of subsequent performance. *Journal of Personality and Social Psychology,* 1968, 9, 38-46.

Festinger, L. *A theory of cognitive dissonance.* Evanston, Ill.: Row, Peterson, 1957.

Frentzel, J. Cognitive consistency and positive self-concept. *Polish Sociological Bulletin,* 1965, 1, 71-86.

Gurin, G. *Inner-city Negro youth in a job training project: A study of factors related to attrition and job success.* Final report to U.S. Department of Labor, Manpower Administration and U.S. Department of Health, Education and Welfare, Office of Education. Ann Arbor, Mich.: Survey Research Center, Institute for Social Research, University of Michigan, 1968.

Gurin, G. An expectancy approach to job training programs. In V. Allen (Ed.), *Psychological factors in poverty.* Chicago: Markham, 1970.

Gurin, P., Gurin, G., Lao, R. C., & Beattie, M. Internal-external control in the motivational dynamics of Negro youth. *Journal of Social Issues,* 1969, 25 (3), 29-53.

Gurin, P., & Katz, D. *Motivation and aspiration in the Negro college.* Final report to the Office of Education, U.S. Department of Health, Education and Welfare. Ann Arbor, Mich.: Survey Research Center, Institute for Social Research, University of Michigan, 1966.

Heath, D. Instructional sets as determinants of expectancy generalization. *Journal of General Psychology*, 1961, 64, 285-295.

Heath, D. Reinforcement and drive level determinants of expectancy generalization. *Journal of General Psychology*, 1962, 67, 69-82.

James, W. H. Internal versus external control of reinforcements as a basic variable in learning theory. Unpublished doctoral dissertation, Ohio State University, 1957.

Kelman, H. C. Compliance, identification and internalization: Three processes of attitude change. In H. Proshansky & B. Seidenberg (Eds.), *Basic studies in social psychology*. New York: Holt, Rinehart and Winston, 1965.

Lowin, A., & Epstein, G. F. Performance expectancy as a determinant of actual performance: Some additional variables. *Journal of Experimental Social Psychology*, 1965, 1, 248-255.

Mischel, W., & Staub, E. Effects of expectancy on working and waiting for larger rewards. *Journal of Personality and Social Psychology*, 1965, 2, 625-633.

Phares, E. J. Expectancy changes in skill and chance situations. *Journal of Abnormal and Social Psychology*, 1957, 34, 339-342.

Phares, E. J. Delay, anxiety, and expectancy changes. *Psychological Reports*, 1966, 18, 679-682.

Rainwater, L. The problem of lower class culture. *Journal of Social Issues*, 1970, 26 (2).

Raven, B. Social influence and power. In Steiner & Fishbein (Eds.), *Current studies in social psychology*. New York: Holt, Rinehart and Winston, 1965.

Rotter, J. B. *Social learning and clinical psychology*. Englewood Cliffs, N.J.: Prentice-Hall, 1954.

Rotter, J. B. Generalized expectancies for internal versus external control of reinforcement. *Psychological Monographs*, 1966, 80, (1, Whole No. 609).

Rotter, J. B., Liverant, S., & Crowne, D. P. The growth and extinction of expectancies in chance controlled and skilled tasks. *Journal of Psychology*, 1961, 52, 161-177.

Rychlak, J. R., & Eacker, J. N. The effects of anxiety, delay and reinforcement on generalized expectancies. *Journal of Personality*, 1962, 30, 123-134.

Rychlak, J. R., & Lerner, J. J. An expectancy interpretation of manifest anxiety. *Journal of Personality and Social Psychology*, 1965, 2, 677-684.

Schwarz, J. C. Influences upon expectancy during delay. *Journal of Experimental Research in Personality*, 1966, 1, 211-220.

Silverman, I., & Marcantonio, C. Demand characteristics vs. dissonance reduction as determinants of failure-seeking behavior. *Journal of Personality and Social Psychology*, 1965, 2, 882-884.

Zajonc, R. B., & Brickman, P. Expectancy and feedback as independent factors in task performance. *Journal of Personality and Social Psychology*, 1969, 2, 148-156.

The Effects of Expectancy
and Other Research-Biasing Factors
William J. Gephart and Daniel P. Antonoplos

". . . 20 percent of the children in a certain elementary school were reported to their teachers as showing unusual potential for intellectual growth. The names of these 20 percent of the children were drawn by means of a table of random numbers, which is to say that the names were drawn out of a hat. Eight months later these unusual or "magic" children showed significantly greater gains in I.Q. than did the remaining children who had not been singled out for the teachers' attention. The change in the teachers' expectations regarding the intellectual performance of these allegedly "special" children had led to an actual change in the intellectual performance of these randomly selected children."[1]

This quotation summarizes the work reported in *Pygmalion in the Classroom*. Reviews of the book in the professional and general literature express differences of opinion about its contribution. One says:

"Pygmalion thoughtfully discusses the problems of experimental interactions, Hawthorne, placebo, and expectancy controls, and the ethical pitfalls of using naïve subjects. The authors honestly criticize their own weaknesses, point out errors in design, question their results, and show their own frustrations with some contradictory evidence.

It may turn the attention of those responsible for administering expensive programs away from the deficiencies of the children toward the contributions of schools and teachers to pupil failure."[2]

Another states:

"The enterprise which represents the core of this document, and presumably the excuse for its publication, has received widespread advance publicity. In spite of anything I can say, I am sure it will become a classic—widely referred to and rarely examined critically. Alas, it is so defective technically that one can only regret that it ever got beyond the eyes of the original investigator! Though the volume may be an effective addition to educational propagandizing, it does nothing to raise the standards of education research."[3]

The publication, *Pygmalion in the Classroom*, is an extension of work done by Rosenthal and others on a concept called the experimenter bias effect. The

---

[1] Robert Rosenthal and Lenore Jacobson, *Pygmalion in the Classroom.* New York: Holt, Rinehart & Winston, 1968, pp. vii, 98.
[2] Robert M. Neurmberger, *Personnel and Guidance Journal,* February, 1969, p. 576.
[3] Robert Thorndike, *American Educational Research Journal,* November, 1968, p. 708.

From *Phi Delta Kappan,* 1969, 50, 579-583. Reprinted by permission of the *Kappan* and the authors.

confusion about the contribution made by *Pygmalion* has recently been joined by confusion about the experimenter bias effect itself. Barber and several others report five unsuccessful attempts to replicate the original Rosenthal work. Barber initiated this set of investigations to explore possible controls for the experimenter bias effect. When he found that the effect could not be detected, he focused his efforts on replication of the earlier work. The report of Barber's work is presented in the *Journal of Consulting and Clinical Psychology*[4] along with a rebuttal by Rosenthal and a rebuttal to the rebuttal by Barber. Barber concludes that "the experimenter bias effect is more difficult to demonstrate than was implied in several recent reviews, and further research is needed to determine what preconditions are necessary to obtain the effect." A careful examination of the arguments presented by Barber and Rosenthal have led to two conclusions. First, the expectancy factor subsumed in the experimenter bias effect is not as pervasive as the earlier work of Rosenthal and the *Pygmalion* manuscript would have us believe. Second, there is a considerable amount of confusion over five concepts important to research design: Hawthorne effect, experimenter bias, demand characteristics, placebo effect, and halo effect.

The first of these conclusions is based on study of the research reports and the several reviews. Thorndike questions the adequacy of the measuring instrument when used at the first and second grades, the levels at which Rosenthal and Jacobson found significant effects. Neurmberger cites the fact that the teachers were told the names of the "special" students at the start of the school year, yet could not remember who they were at the end. Buckley indirectly indicates that the investigators did not systematically examine the nature of the treatment as applied *by* the teachers.[5] Snow cites as problems probable lack of standardization in the administration of the tests, the effects of subject loss as the experiment progressed, and questionable handling of the variance assumptions inherent in the statistical analysis.[6] In examining *Pygmalion,* the interested reader should also consider the fact that the experimental units in the "Oak School" study were the 18 teachers, not the students. The teachers received the experimental treatment. The investigators did not examine the nature in which they in turn applied that treatment to their students. Thus the analysis ought to have used class means as the statistic rather than the individual student's gain score. Interested educators should examine these reviews as well as the book before accepting the conclusion made regarding the power of teachers' expectancies.

The pervasiveness of the experimenter bias effect itself is well questioned in the Barber article and in his and Rosenthal's discussion cited earlier. Resolution of the debate initiated there demands additional data rather than oratory. The remainder of this presentation will focus on the second point above, the confusion over several concepts important to research design. These concepts have a

[4] Theodore X. Barber, et al., "Five Attempts to Replicate the Experimenter Bias Effect," *Journal of Consulting and Clinical Psychology,* Vol. 33, No. 1, 1969, pp. 1-14.
[5] James J. Buckley, "Who Is Pygmalion, Which Is Galatea," *Phi Delta Kappan,* October, 1968, p. 124.
[6] Richard E. Snow, "Review of Pygmalion in the Classroom," *Contemporary Psychology,* Vol. 14, 1969, pp. 197-199.

commonality that has promoted interchangeable usage. At the same time, they have differences that should be known by people who design and conduct research using human subjects. This presentation will first define the several terms, present a logical schema for the display of their similarities and differences, and conclude with a discussion of the degree to which generalizations about them and their effects can be made.

The five concepts are subtle aspects of the interpersonal interaction that goes by the name of behavioral research. Each of them acts in a role that possibly confounds the results of research through influencing the data generated and the conclusions reached. Despite the similarity in role, experimenter bias, demand characteristics, Hawthorne, placebo, and halo effects display differences on two dimensions: the locus of the effect and the nature of the error contribution.

The first of these, the locus of the effect, refers to the apparent place of the biasing factor in the research process. For example, a halo effect notation signals the possibility that valid measures were not recorded on some of the subjects in a study. The factor is located in the measurement task and more specifically in the scoring as done by the measurer. It could be said that the locus of the halo effect is the biased thoughts in the mind of the measurer. The locus for each of the five concepts is clearer when their definitions are understood. Thus further discussion about locus will be deferred until the definitions have been presented.

The nature of the error contributed can also be seen through the halo effect. The error is in the measurement process. Further, it is not a constant error. Rather, it is a bias of the scores of those persons for whom the measurer has some regard, either positive or negative. Again, the complete discussion of the error contribution for the halo effect or for the others is deferred until the definitions are presented.

Rosenthal is recognized for his contribution of the term "experimenter bias effect." His early writings on the topic indicate his growing awareness of the possibility of confounding the results of an experiment through biases held by the experimenter. He has conducted numerous studies and has been cited by his peers in the American Psychological Association for this work. The effect (EBE) centers on the expectations held by the researcher for the nature of the results: What will the data show? The effect is not just the researcher's expectancy. If it were, it would be an inescapable artifact of investigation. All researchers expect their subjects to perform differently under different experimental treatments. The experimenter bias effect goes further than that. It involves the transmission of that expectancy to the subjects in a way that alters the normal functioning of the subject on the dependent variable central to the research being conducted. It should be added that the discussion here focuses on influence that is subconscious. It does not incorporate the research cheat, the individual who falsifies data.

Rosenthal presents an analysis of the EBE phenomenon in his 1966 book.[7] The dimensions of EBE cited there were determined by extensive research and

---

[7]Robert Rosenthal, *Experimenter Effects in Behavioral Research.* New York: Appleton-Century-Crofts, 1966.

should be known by researchers. Barber's work, as indicated earlier, questions the pervasiveness of the effect, not the logic of its existence or its nature. Rosenthal and Barber appear to agree on its definition. In Rosenthal's words, EBE is "the extent to which [the experimenter] himself might be a relevant but uncontrolled variable affecting research."[8]

The Hawthorne effect is an often-cited phenomenon which appears when the results of an experiment are (1) striking, and (2) defy explanation in line with the procedures used and preexisting information. Typically, the Hawthorne effect signals something positive, that is, a performance was observed that is well beyond what was expected. Although it has been recognized for some time, its source is frequently misstated in the literature. These erroneous quotes attribute it to a study of lighting in the Western Electric Plant at Hawthorne, Illinois. It does come from work done at the Hawthorne plant, but is not a direct product of the lighting studies. Cook[9] indicates that two Harvard investigators studying the process of research in the industrial setting were responsible for the term, despite the fact that they did not use it in their report, *Management and the Worker.* Those studies focused on the number of working hours and rest schedules allowed for women working at a relay-winding task. Regardless of the nature of the independent variable (daily work schedule)—and some thirteen variations were tried—the amount of production went up. Rothlisberger and Dickson, the two investigators involved, offered several explanations for the unexpected result: novelty, the women involved were not working in the normal production line; change in the social structure, the women were not observed in their work by the foreman but by a researcher who involved them in decisions about the schedule for the work day; knowledge of participation in an experiment, the subjects knew that they were in an investigation and talked of themselves as something different from the other women winding relays. Still another explanation of the Hawthorne effect has been offered: The workers in the experiments in the Hawthorne plant knew their daily and hourly output. Some observers have interpreted this factor, knowledge of results, as the crux of the Hawthorne effect. Regardless of the interpretation or definition chosen, one thing is clear: an unanticipated outcome of startling proportions was observed. The nature of this phenomenon was the subject of an investigation undertaken by Cook. In that study Cook defines the Hawthorne effect as:

". . . a phenomenon characterized by a cognitive awareness on the part of the subjects of special treatment created by artificial experimental conditions. It becomes confounded with the independent variable under study, with the subsequent result of either facilitating or inhibiting the dependent variables under study and leading to spurious conclusions."[10]

[8] Robert Rosenthal and Edward S. Halas, "Experimenter Effects in the Study of Invertebrate Behavior," *Psychological Reports,* Vol. 11, 1962, pp. 251-256.
[9] Desmond L. Cook, "The Hawthorne Effect in Educational Research," *Phi Delta Kappan,* December, 1962, pp. 116-122.
[10] Desmond L. Cook, *The Impact of the Hawthorne Effect in Experimental Design in Educational Research,* Cooperative Research Project, 1967, No. 1757. Washington, D.C.: U.S. Office of Education.

Martin Orne has contributed importantly to our understanding of another factor in the interpersonal interaction of behavioral research: demand characteristics. Orne was intrigued with the compliance expressed by individuals who had agreed to participate as subjects in an experiment. Through several investigations of this phenomenon, he developed the idea that each experiment creates demands on the subject that are of the subject's own making. This is not to say that there is no contribution to these behaviors on the part of the experiment, but rather that the subject interprets the nature of the experimental procedures and constructs for himself, both consciously and unconsciously, role demands. Orne indicates that these self-imposed demands for performance result from a respect for authority and a high regard for science. In his words, demand characteristics can be defined as:

". . . the totality of cues which convey an experimental hypothesis to the subject and become significant determinants of subjects' behavior. We have labeled the sum total of such cues as the "demand characteristics of the experimental situation." These cues include the rumors or campus scuttlebutt about the research, the information conveyed during the original solicitation, the person of the experimenter, and the setting of the laboratory, as well as all explicit and implicit communications during the experiment proper. A frequently overlooked but nonetheless very significant source of cues for the subject lies in the experimental procedure itself, viewed in the light of the subject's previous knowledge and experience."[11]

The nature of the halo effect has been suggested earlier. It has been defined by several authors writing about the measurement process and about measurement errors that need to be understood. Helmstadter says:

". . . another widely observed error is a tendency on the part of raters to obscure intraindividual differences by rating a given individual in the same way on all behaviors, whether the characteristics seemed to go together or not. This so-called halo effect is attributed to the fact that many raters allow an overall impression of the subject to influence their description of his specific behaviors."[12]

From this definition it can be reasoned that the halo effect is an inconsistent factor in the determination of the nature of the data generated in an experiment. It operates with some of the subjects and not with others. The ones with whom it operates are the subjects with whom the rater has more contact than that involved in the rating task. The halo effect is variable in the direction of its influence on the nature of the data. The rater's perceptions of the individual being rated are the determiners.

---

[11] Martin T. Orne, "On the Social Psychology of the Psychological Experiment with Particular Reference to Demand Characteristics and Their Implications," *American Psychologist,* Vol. 17, 1962, pp. 776-783.
[12] Gerald C. Helmstadter, *Principles of Psychological Measurement.* New York: Appleton-Century-Crofts, 1964, pp. 191-192.

Selltiz, Jahoda, and their colleagues give the following example:

"If a rater considers a person to be shy and he believes shy people to be poorly adjusted, he is likely to rate the person poorly adjusted as well as shy."[13]

If that same rater believed the individual not to be shy he would not rate him poorly adjusted.

The placebo effect is the last of the research biasers to be discussed here. This term has its greatest application in the field of biomedical research. It refers to reaction on the part of the subjects in the control group of an experiment. Rather than compare something with nothing, as is the case in the static control-group study, and to avoid the halo effect on the part of researchers, a blind procedure has been developed in the biomedical field. That is, all of the subjects are given pills, some of which are the drug being tested while others are chemically inert. The changes in physical condition that can only be credited to the chemically inert pills is what is called the placebo effect. Goldstein and others define the placebo effect as:

". . . the therapeutic effect consequent to the patient's belief in the efficacy of the treatment. . . . Chemically speaking, a placebo is inert or at least has no pharmacological effects which are specially efficacious for the condition being treated."[14]

Consistency of the placebo effect is questionable. Subjects are bound to differ in the degree of suggestivity to which they respond. On that basis the contribution of the placebo effect to the nature of the generated data is inconsistent. The positive to negative direction of the effect is set. If an effect exists, it reduces the amount of the gain which is or should be seen on the part of the experimental subjects. For example, consider a situation in which the control group shows a gain of five units from a pre- to posttest measure, three units of which (by definition) are a result of the placebo effect. In the same study, suppose the experimental units showed a gain score of eight units. The observed difference in the two groups is three units, where the actual difference for the effect of the treatment is six units. In such an instance the placebo effect has reduced the apparent effectiveness of the treatment studied. Thus the contribution of the placebo effect to the understanding of the nature of a phenomenon is negative in direction.

The five factors can be displayed on three facets for purposes of comparison. These facets are:

1. The central aspect of the concept. Each of these biasers appears to have a locus of operation, a place in which the activities which create them congeal into the effect.

---

[13]C. Selltiz, M. Jahoda, et al., *Research Methods in Social Relations.* New York: Holt, Rinehart & Winston, 1967, p. 352.
[14]Arnold Goldstein, et al., *Psychotherapy and Psychology of Behavior Change.* New York: John Wiley & Sons, 1966, p. 42.

Facets for Comparison			
	Central Aspects	Location Within the Research Process	Kinds of Error Contributed
Experimenter Bias Effect	Expectancies held by experimenter and their effect on his behavior with subjects	Structuring of procedures and experimenter-subject inter-action	Modification of the treat-ment with subsequent threat to the internal validity of the test of the hypothesis
Hawthorne Effect 1. Novelty	Interaction be-tween subject and research proce-dures	Initial interac-tion between subject and pro-cedures	Modification of the treat-ment with subsequent threat to the internal validity of the test of the hypothesis
2. Awareness of participation	Same	Throughout the research process	Ditto
3. Altered social structure	Interaction be-tween subject, other subjects, and experimenter	Interactions between individ-uals	Ditto
4. Knowledge of results	Interaction be-tween subject and a specific aspect of the research procedure	Follows report-ing of subjects' performance	Ditto
Demand Characteristics	Subject's percep-tion of his role in the experiment	Continuous	Modification of the sub-ject's role with subsequent threat to the external valid-ity of the test of the hy-pothesis
Halo Effect	Rater's reaction to nonrelevant information in rating process	During measure-ment involving ratings	Measurement error not necessarily common across subjects
Placebo Effect	Control subject's interaction with research proce-dures	During experi-mental and con-trol procedures	Alters performance of control subjects, resulting in an inaccurate. compari-son between groups

　　2. The location within the research process. The five concepts deal with aspects of the research process which, if expressed on a time dimension, display differentiation.

　　3. The kinds of error contributed. Common to all of these concepts is the idea of a contribution to a conclusion on the part of the researcher that diverges from truth in an absolute sense. There are many possible kinds of error that can be identified in the research process. Again, the concepts differ. The grid presented above indicates the levels on these three facets which

depict the different biasing concepts. The reader will note that several definitions for the Hawthorne effect are given, in deference to Cook's work.

Experimenter bias effect centers on the expectancies held by the researcher and their effects on his behavior with subjects. This is the locus at which something congeals that incorrectly shapes the conclusion derived from the research.

The various explanations of the Hawthorne effect seem to have an interaction between the subject and aspects of the research procedures as their central point. They differ in terms of the exact involvement of the research procedures. The novelty dimension involves procedures and the subject's prior experiences. Those to which he is accustomed cannot be productive of a novelty effect. Thus, the novelty effect has to be considered as situational. The awareness-of-participation explanation also focuses on the subject-research procedures interaction. If this interaction produces awareness, the bias effect is created. Again it appears situational, depending on the subject's perceptiveness and the research procedures themselves. The social-structure explanation centers in the interpersonal interactions which, due to the investigation, vary from normal for the individuals involved. This includes subject-subject and subject-experimenter interactions. Knowledge of results centers on the interaction of the subject with a specific research procedure, the provision and self-analysis of his performance.

The subject's perceptions of the research effort seem to be the central aspect of demand characteristics. He processes a variety of cues in the development of his role. In contrast, the halo effect resides in the perceptions of the researcher when he is engaged in rating activities. His perceptions of the subject being rated are merged and confounded with other information he has about that subject. The placebo effect has still a third contrasting locus, the control subject's perception of the treatment he experiences.

The five concepts influence the research process at different points. Demand characteristics, experimenter bias, and the awareness explanation of the Hawthorne effect can be shaped at any point in the research procedures in which the subject is involved. All three of them obtain some structure through the research design developed by the investigator. The remaining concepts can be pinpointed: the Hawthorne novelty explanation to the initial stages of the experimental procedures; Hawthorne social structure explanation to the interpersonal interactions; Hawthorne knowledge of results to those points at which subjects receive feedback on performance; halo effect to the rating tasks; and placebo effect to procedures employed with control subjects. It is suggested that awareness of these operation points should facilitate designs which avoid undue bias.

The error contributions from these effects range from broad conclusion-focused error to narrow measurement error. The former is displayed in the concept, demand characteristics. The subject perceives his experimental role as a combination of the tasks he is asked to perform and those other cues from the setting that he has internalized. As a result his behavior vis-à-vis the experimental treatment differs from his behavior in respect to the same stimulus in normal activities. His behavior may be accurately measured but it lacks generalizability outside that experimental setting. The experiment's external validity is threatened. Experimenter bias and the Hawthorne effects present a threat to internal validity. The experimenter has a hypothesis which he has subjected to a test. A treatment is prescribed as the means for that test. But, due either to influences from the experimenter's expectancies or Hawthorne effect interactions with the experimental procedures, the subject experiences a modified treatment. As a result, the test of the hypothesis is not what it set out to be. The error induced by the placebo effect has the same characteristics but on a limited scale. Since it focuses on the control subjects, the error amounts to a reduction of the apparent value of the experimental treatment. Again the internal validity is threatened. Instead of a test of the difference of experiences A and B, the researcher has a test of A and B plus the placebo effect. The error induced by the halo effect is much more limited. It is an error in the measurement process. Instead of assigning numbers to qualities on the basis of rules, the rater assigns them also on the basis of additional information on *some* of the subjects.

What Can Be Said

Conceptually, these are matters that must be considered in the design, conduct, and interpretation of research. Their existence has been documented in methodological research efforts. There are currently very sound questions raised about their pervasiveness. Of particular interest here is the work of Barber on the experimenter bias effect and of Cook on several aspects of the Hawthorne effect. Their findings suggest that the pervasiveness of the remaining concepts should be the subject of systematic study.

Suggestions for the control of some of these concepts in the design of research can be found in the literature. Included here are the suggestions by Rosenthal, Orne, Campbell and Stanley, Kerlinger, Helmstadter, and others. However, the suggestions for controls have not in most cases been evaluated empirically. They are, rather, logical suggestions evolved from careful intellectual examination of the concepts themselves. Research methodologists will find inherent in them fruitful areas of investigation.

Some negatives are clear. The Hawthorne effect is not a general rubric under which researchers can sweep all unexpected results. Cook's work indicates that on a long-range basis only awareness of participation showed an effect. Barber's work clearly indicates that experimenter bias effect is not all pervasive. Certainly the modest amount that we do know about it as a factor in the research process and the rival hypotheses inherent in *Pygmalion* fail to provide justification for generalizing it as a means for effecting greater learning in schools.

Chapter Four
Expectations: Controversy

The articles in this chapter were chosen to elaborate the controversy surrounding Rosenthal's research on teacher expectations. Two critiques follow the Rosenthal and Jacobson article, along with a rebuttal by Rosenthal and a rejoinder by Thorndike. It should be noted that the critics are wary of Rosenthal's research methodology, and not of the expectancy phenomenon itself.

The Rosenthal and Jacobson article is a very brief summary of some data from their study entitled *Pygmalion in the Classroom* (1968). The critiques by Snow and Thorndike need no comment other than that Snow's full report on the reanalysis of the Rosenthal and Jacobson data is eagerly awaited.

In any case, Rosenthal and Jacobson have not provided data nor an adequate explanation for *how* the teacher influences learning performance. Their data indicate that there was no difference in the amount of time teachers spent with the students in the control and experimental groups. Yet they speculated that there was a difference in the *type* of interaction between teacher and student. Rosenthal used the term *interaction quality hypothesis* to describe this difference. At the present time, this research does not offer the teacher specific advice in terms of optimizing learner performance by manipulating the learner's expectations.

It is interesting to note that some attempts to replicate the Pygmalion Effect have failed to find significant differences on main treatments, but have shown significant interaction among the main effects. Could it be that these interactions are *disordinal* (see the Bracht and Glass article in chapter 8) and operative in these expectancy studies? If so, the indication is that our research methods and assumptions about random sampling may be inadequate to support the observations of teachers, new and old, who have observed the effects of teacher expectancy on student learning. The reader will find some help in thinking about these questions in articles and discussions in Parts Three and Four of this book.

The reader may be interested in pursuing critiques of Rosenthal's work on the experimenter bias effect in nonschool settings. See, for example, Barber et al. (1969), which is followed by a rejoinder by Rosenthal.

Teachers' Expectancies:
Determinants of Pupils' IQ Gains

Robert Rosenthal and Lenore Jacobson

Experiments have shown that in behavioral research employing human or animal Ss, E's expectancy can be a significant determinant of S's response (Rosenthal, 1964, 1966). In studies employing animals, for example, Es led to believe that their rat Ss had been bred for superior learning ability obtained performance superior to that obtained by Es led to believe their rats had been bred for inferior learning ability (Rosenthal & Fode, 1963; Rosenthal & Lawson, 1964). The present study was designed to extend the generality of this finding from Es to teachers and from animal Ss to school children.

Flanagan (1960) has developed a nonverbal intelligence test (Tests of General Ability or TOGA) which is not explicitly dependent on such school-learned skills as reading, writing, and arithmetic. The test is composed of two types of items, "verbal" and "reasoning." The "verbal" items measure the child's level of information, vocabulary, and concepts. The "reasoning" items measure the child's concept formation ability by employing abstract line drawings. Flanagan's purpose in developing the TOGA was "to provide a relatively fair measure of intelligence for all individuals, even those who have had atypical opportunities to learn" (1960, p. 6).

Flanagan's test was administered to all children in an elementary school, disguised as a test designed to predict academic "blooming" or intellectual gain. Within each of the six grades in the school were three classrooms, one each of children performing at above-average, average, and below-average levels of scholastic achievement. In each of the 18 classes an average of 20 percent of the children were assigned to the experimental condition. The names of these children were given to each teacher who was told that their scores on the "test for intellectual blooming" indicated that they would show unusual intellectual gains during the academic year. Actually, the children had been assigned to the experimental condition by means of a table of random numbers. The experimental treatment for these children, then, consisted of nothing more than being identified to their teachers as children who would show unusual intellectual gains.

Eight months after the experimental conditions were instituted all children were retested with the same IQ test and a change score was computed for each child. Table 1 shows the mean gain in IQ points among experimental and control

This research was supported by Research Grants GS-177 and GS-714 from Division of Social Sciences of the National Science Foundation.

Rosenthal, R., and Jacobson, L. Teachers' expectancies: determinants of pupils' IQ gains. *Psychological Reports*, 1966, 19, 115-118. Reprinted by permission of the publisher and authors.

Table 1   Mean Gains in IQ

Grade	Controls		Experimentals		Diff.	t	p†
	M	σ	M	σ			
1	12.0	16.6	27.4	12.5	15.4	2.97	.002
2	7.0	10.0	16.5	18.6	9.5	2.28	.02
3	5.0	11.9	5.0	9.3	0.0		
4	2.2	13.4	5.6	11.0	3.4		
5	17.5	13.1	17.4	17.8	−0.1		
6	10.7	10.0	10.0	6.5	−0.7		
Weighted M	8.4*	13.5	12.2**	15.0	3.8	2.15	.02

*Mean number of children per grade = 42.5.
**Mean number of children per grade = 10.8.
†p one-tailed.

Ss in each of the six grades.[1] For the school as a whole those children from whom the teachers had been led to expect greater intellectual gain showed a significantly greater gain in IQ score than did the control children (p = .02, one-tail). Inspection of Table 1 shows that the effects of teachers' expectancies were not uniform across the six grade levels. The lower the grade level, the greater was the effect (*rho* = −.94, p = .02, two-tail). It was in the first and second grades that the effects were most dramatic. The largest gain among the three first grade classrooms occurred for experimental Ss who gained 24.8 IQ points *in excess* of the gain (+16.2) shown by the controls. The largest gain among the three second grade classrooms was obtained by experimental Ss who gained 18.2 IQ points in excess of the gain (+4.3) shown by the controls.

An additionally useful way of showing the effects of teachers' expectancies on their pupils' gains in IQ is to show the percentage of experimental and control Ss achieving various magnitudes of gains. Table 2 shows such percentages for the first and second grades only. Half again as many experimental as control Ss gained at least 10 IQ points; more than twice as many gained at least 20 IQ points; and more than four times as many gained at least 30 points.

An important question was whether the gains of the experimental Ss were made at the expense of the control Ss. Tables 1 and 2 show that control Ss made substantial gains in IQ though they were smaller than the gains made by experimental Ss. Better evidence for the proposition that gains by experimental Ss were not made at the expense of control Ss comes from the positive correlation between gains made by experimental and control Ss. Over the 17 classrooms in which the comparison was possible, those in which experimental Ss made greater gains tended also to be the ones where control Ss made greater gains (*rho* = .57, p = .02, two-tail).

[1] There were no differences in the effects of teachers' expectancies as a function of Ss' initial level of educational achievement; therefore, the three classrooms at each grade level were combined for Table 1. In one of the three classrooms at the fifth grade level, a portion of the IQ test was inadvertently not readministered so that data of Table 1 are based on 17 instead of 18 classrooms.

Table 2 Percentages of Experimental and Control Ss Gaining 10, 20, or 30 IQ Points (First and Second Grade Children)

IQ Gain	Control Ss*	Experimental Ss**	x^2	p†
10 points	49	79	4.75	.02
20 points	19	47	5.59	.01
30 points	5	21	3.47	.04

*Total number of children = 95.
**Total number of children = 19.
†p one-tailed.

Retesting of the children's IQ had been done in classroom groups by the children's own teacher.[2] The question arose, therefore, whether the greater gain in IQ of the experimental children might have been due to the teacher's differential behavior toward them during the retesting. To help answer this question three of the classes were retested by a school administrator not attached to the particular school. She did not know which children were in the experimental condition. Results based on her retesting of the children were not significantly different from the results based on the children's own teachers' retesting. In fact, there was a tendency for the results of her retesting to yield even larger effects of teachers' expectancies. It appears unlikely, then, that the greater IQ gains made by children from whom greater gains were expected could be attributed to the effect of the behavior of the teacher while she served as an examiner.

There are a number of possible explanations of the finding that teachers' expectancy effects operated primarily at the lower-grade levels, including: (a) Younger children have less well-established reputations so that the creation of expectations about their performance would be more credible. (b) Younger children may be more susceptible to the unintended social influence exerted by the expectation of their teacher. (c) Younger children may be more recent arrivals in the school's neighborhood and may differ from the older children in characteristics other than age. (d) Teachers of lower grades may differ from teachers of higher grades on a variety of dimensions which are correlated with the effectiveness of the unintentional communication of expectancies.

The most important question which remains is that which asks how a teacher's expectation becomes translated into behavior in such a way as to elicit the expected pupil behavior. Prior research on the unintentional communication of expectancies in experimentally more carefully controlled interactions suggests that this question will not be easily answered (Rosenthal, 1966).

But, regardless of the mechanism involved, there are important substantive and methodological implications of these findings which will be discussed in detail elsewhere. For now, one example, in question form, will do: How much of the improvement in intellectual performance attributed to the contemporary educational programs is due to the content and methods of the programs and

---

[2] Scoring of the tests was done by the investigators, not by the teachers.

how much is due to the favorable expectancies of the teachers and administrators involved? Experimental designs to answer such questions are available (Rosenthal, 1966) and in view of the psychological, social, and economic importance of these programs the use of such designs seems strongly indicated.

References

Flanagan, J. C. *Tests of general ability: technical report.* Chicago, Ill.: Science Research Associates, 1960.

Rosenthal, R. The effect of the experimenter on the results of psychological research. In B. A. Maher (Ed.), *Progress in experimental personality research.* Vol. I. New York: Academic Press, 1964, pp. 79-114.

Rosenthal, R. *Experimenter effects in behavioral research.* New York: Appleton-Century-Crofts, 1966.

Rosenthal, R., & Fode, K. L. The effect of experimenter bias on the performance of the albino rat. *Behavioral Science,* 1963, 8, 183-189.

Rosenthal, R., & Lawson, R. A longitudinal study of the effects of experimenter bias on the operant learning of laboratory rats. *Journal of Psychiatric Research,* 1964, 2, 61-72.

Unfinished Pygmalion
Richard E. Snow

In his 1966 book, Rosenthal demonstrated the importance of experimenter effects in behavioral research. After lucid discussion of the experimenter as biased observer and interpreter of data, and of the effects of relatively permanent experimenter attributes on subjects' responses, a series of ingenious experiments was reported showing the effects of experimenter expectancy on both human and animal behavior. Many sound suggestions were then offered on the control and reduction of self-fulfilling prophecies in psychological research. To herald the generality and potential importance of such phenomena, the book closed dramatically with a preliminary analysis of data on teacher expectancy effects and pupil IQ gains in elementary school. Those closing pages (pp. 410-413) have since been expanded by Rosenthal and Jacobson for *Psychological Reports* (1966, 19, 115-118) and *Scientific American* (1968, 218(4), 19-23) and now appear as a not quite fully grown, glossy-backed *Pygmalion.*

A review of *Pygmalion in the Classroom: Teacher Expectation and Pupils' Intellectual Development* by Robert Rosenthal and Lenore Jacobson. New York: Holt, Rinehart & Winston, 1968.

From *Contemporary Psychology,* 1969, 14, 197-199. Reprinted by permission of the American Psychological Association and the author.

The first 60 pages of *Pygmalion* recount in interesting and readable form the nature of self-fulfilling prophecies and then introduce the reader to some educational problems of disadvantaged children, including discussion of teachers' possible roles in these problems. The remainder of the book is essentially a report of original research and must be reviewed as such. It is the considered opinion of this reviewer that the research would have been judged unacceptable if submitted to an APA journal in its present form. Despite its award-winning experimental design, the study suffers from serious measurement problems and inadequate data analysis. Its reporting, furthermore, appears to violate the spirit of Rosenthal's own earlier admonitions to experimenters and stands as a casebook example of many of Darrell Huff's (*How to Lie with Statistics.* New York: Norton, 1954) admonitions to data analysts.

The study involved fast, medium, and slow reading classrooms at each grade from first through sixth in a single elementary school, "Oak" School, in South San Francisco. During May 1964, while Ss were in Grades K through 5, the "Harvard Test of Inflected Acquisition" was administered as part of a "Harvard-NSF Validity Study." As described to teachers, the new instrument purported to identify "bloomers" who would probably experience an unusual forward spurt in academic and intellectual performance during the following year. Actually, the measure was Flanagan's *Tests of General Ability* (TOGA), chosen as a non-language group intelligence test that would provide verbal and reasoning subscores as well as a total IQ. TOGA was judged appropriate for the study because it would probably be unfamiliar to the teachers and because it offers three forms, for Grades K-2, 3-4, and 5-6, all of similar style and content. As school began in Fall 1964, a randomly chosen 20 percent of the Ss were designated as "spurters." Each of the 18 teachers received a list of from one to nine names, identifying those spurters who would be in his class. TOGA was then readministered in January 1965, May 1965, and May 1966. In addition to the main comparison between experimental and control Ss within each grade level and reading ability track, contrasts were also planned for sex and Mexican/non-Mexican subgroups. The complete experiment could be characterized as a $2 \times 2 \times 2 \times 3 \times 6 \times 4$ factorial design, with repeated measures on the last factor, but the full analysis of this table was neither planned nor possible, due to incomplete data and empty cells. Rosenthal and Jacobson chose to obtain simple gain scores from the pretest to the third testing, called the "basic" posttest, and to make their primary comparisons with these. The main statistical computations were two- and three-way analyses of variance, using the unweighted means approximation to overcome problems of unequal cell frequencies. Also provided were supplemental analyses of data from the second and fourth TOGA administrations as well as grades in various school subjects, teacher ratings of classroom behavior, and a substudy of achievement test scores. The results were interpreted as showing ". . . that teachers' favorable expectations can be responsible for gains in their pupils' IQs and, for the lower grades, that these gains can be quite dramatic" (p. 98).

A complete methodological critique is impossible from information available in the book, even though an appendix and several extensive footnotes are included, but the authors have cooperated completely in providing the reviewer and his colleagues access to the original data and permission to reanalyze them. While details of the reanalysis cannot be given here, a full report is planned. Many methodological issues can be elaborated here, however, from a review of the book alone.

Problems began with the decision to rely solely on TOGA. The test does not have adequate norms for the youngest children, especially for children from lower socioeconomic backgrounds. It was administered to separate classes by the teachers themselves; this adds considerable uncertainty about standardization of procedure. All computations were based on IQ scores; the more meaningful raw scores were neither used nor provided for reanalysis, even though they would be preferable for most data analysis purposes. These concerns loom large as one examines data tables in the appendix. In Table A-3, pretest reasoning IQ means for Grade 1 (tested in K) are 47.19 and 30.79 for 16 middle and 19 low track control Ss, and 54.00 and 53.50 for 4 and 2 experimental Ss, respectively. The average for all first grade children is 58. Were these children actually functioning at imbecile and low moron levels? More likely, the test was not functioning at this age level. TOGA does not have norms below an IQ of 60. To obtain IQ scores as low as these, given reasonably distributed ages, raw scores would have to represent random or systematically incorrect responding. Presumably the published conversion tables were extrapolated, even into the chance score range. In the original data cards, one S with a pretest reasoning IQ of 17 had posttest IQs of 148, 110, and 112. Another showed reasoning IQs of 18, 44, 122, and 98. In the opposite direction, still another S had successive verbal IQs of 183, 166, 221, and 168 though TOGA does not have norms above 160. Many other IQs are equally strange. Readers should wonder why other mental ability information, already available from the school or obtainable without undue additional effort, was not used along with TOGA.

Tables 7-1, 7-3, and 7-4, the main results, show that the difference between experimental and control groups in mean gain from first to third testing was essentially zero for all grades except the first two, where the experimental group gain apparently did exceed that of the control group. But the authors correlated grade level with mean difference and say, "We find increasing expectancy advantage as we go from the sixth to the first grade" (p. 74). Examining these mean differences for both the total and part scores, and noting the substantially larger standard deviations for reasoning, it is evident that the reasoning subscores in Grades 1 and 2 provided the principal effect. These are precisely the scores whose meaning is most questionable.

Other aspects of the analysis are also troublesome. Although about 20 percent of the initially tested Ss were lost to the experiment, the effect of this loss on IQ averages in various subgroups is not dealt with directly. No mention is made that unweighted means analysis requires homogeneous variances and random cell-size fluctuations. Data provided in appendix tables indicate that at least the variance assumption may well have been violated in many instances.

Heterogeneity is most apparent in the earliest two grades where ratios of variance for experimental and control groups frequently provide F's of 20 or more. Statistical tests are thus sometimes too conservative and sometimes too liberal. In any event, pooled error terms seem generally unjustified. Throughout the book, p values ranging from .20 to .00002 are used fallaciously as if they were a measure of strength of effect. The authors rely on simple gain tests (i.e., tests of the difference between difference scores), even though many mean pretest differences between treatment groups equal or exceed obtained posttest differences. And it is simply not true that ". . . posttest-only measures are less precise than the change or gain scores. . ." (p. 108). The important repeated measures aspect of the design is ignored. There is no hint that the regression of posttests on pretest for different treatment groups should be of interest to anyone or that the four testings should be of equal importance in the analysis. Results for the other testings, incidentally, are markedly different from those obtained with the "basic" posttest. Also, since transfer of Ss between ability tracks is not discussed, the reader is permitted the dubious assumption that no students changed track across the study's two-year span, even though some IQs changed more than 100 points!

Finally, the reporting style is appalling. It is too easy for the unwary reader to pick choice findings and figures from the book, but too difficult for him to verify the data and analyses on which they are based. Comparisons between text and appendix tables are hampered by use of different subgroupings of the data and absence of intermediate analysis of variance tables. Score distributions are not given. Graphs and tables are frequently misleading: some show only differences between difference scores, where basic data are not available in the book (e.g., Table 7-6); some fail to indicate the small sample sizes on which impressive percentages are based (e.g., Figure 7-2); some use microscopic scales to overemphasize practically insignificant differences (e.g., Figure 8-1); and some display floating zero points and elastic scales, making comparisons from one graph to another difficult (e.g., Figures 9-3 through 9-6). Text and tables, as well as different parts of the text, are not always in close agreement. Statements like "When the entire school benefited as in total IQ and reasoning IQ, all three tracks benefited . . ." (p. 78) are used in describing results. In reconciling results with those of other studies, however, statements like "The finding that only the younger children profited after one year from their teacher's favorable expectations helps us to understand better the [negative] results of two other experimenters . . ." (p. 84).

The book closes with three potentially useful, though cursory, chapters. The first takes some glib steps toward meeting specific methodological criticisms. It also offers speculation on possible processes of intentional and unintentional influence between the teachers and students but fails to face the full realization that the teachers could not remember, and reported hardly having glanced at, the names on the original lists of "bloomers." Another discusses more general methodological aspects of Hawthorne and expectancy studies, including helpful design suggestions. The last provides a capsule summary and some general implications. It is here that the abstraction process from basic data to general statements is most apparent, and it is here that the inadequacy of almost any statistical summary of these data should be clearly specified. But it is not. One fears that the experimenters have convinced themselves, in the course of the analysis and of the book, that what they believed all along is true without further question.

The social importance of the problem studied in this book cannot be overestimated. While social and behavioral scientists are always responsible for the proper conduct and reporting of research, nowhere should this responsibility be more keenly felt and exercised than in work bearing directly on urgent and volatile social issues. With these thoughts in mind, the reviewer notes with growing alarm comments in the popular press such as the following:

"Here may lie the explanation of the effects of socioeconomic status on schooling. Teachers of a higher socioeconomic status expect pupils of a lower socioeconomic status to fail" (Robert Hutchins, Success in Schools, *San Francisco Chronicle,* August 11, 1968, p. 2);

"Jose, a Mexican-American boy . . . moved in a year from being classed as mentally retarded to above average. Another Mexican-American child, Maria, moved . . . from 'slow learner' to 'gifted child,' . . . The implications of these results will upset many school people, yet these are hard facts" (Herbert Kohl, Review of *Pygmalion in the Classroom, The New York Review of Books,* September 12, 1968, p. 31);

"The findings raise some fundamental questions about teacher training. They also cast doubt on the wisdom of assigning children to classes according to presumed ability, which may only mire the lowest groups into self-confining ruts" (*Time,* September 20, 1968, p. 62).

Still further comment has appeared in the *Saturday Review* (October 19, 1968) and in a special issue of *The Urban Review* (September 1968) devoted solely to the topic of expectancy, which includes a selection from *Pygmalion.* The inclusion of such selections in books of readings is, of course, also inevitable.

Considering these releases, expecting wider coverage from less responsible news media in the future, and imagining the irate faces at countless school board and PTA meetings, one recalls the words of Huff (p. 45):

"The fault is in the filtering-down processes from the researcher through the sensational or ill-informed writer to the reader who fails to miss the figures that have disappeared in the process."

Teacher expectancy may be a powerful phenomenon which, if understood, could be used to gain much of positive value in education. Rosenthal and Jacobson will have made an important contribution if their work prompts others to do sound research in this area. But their study has not come close to providing adequate demonstration of the phenomenon or understanding of its process.

Pygmalion, inadequately and prematurely reported in book and magazine form, has performed a disservice to teachers and schools, to users and developers of mental tests, and perhaps worst of all, to parents and children whose newly gained expectations may not prove quite so self-fulfilling.

Review of *Pygmalion in the Classroom*
Robert L. Thorndike

The enterprise which represents the core of this document, and presumably the excuse for its publication, has received widespread advance publicity. In spite of anything I can say, I am sure it will become a classic—widely referred to and rarely examined critically. Alas, it is so defective technically that one can only regret that it ever got beyond the eyes of the original investigators! Though the volume may be an effective addition to educational propagandizing, it does nothing to raise the standards of educational research.

Though it may make for a dull review, I feel I must dissect the study to point out some basic defects in its data that make its conclusions (though they may possibly be true) in no sense adequately supported by the data. The general reasonableness of the "self-fulfilling prophecy effect" is not at issue, nor is the reported background of previous anecdote, observation, and research. The one point at which this review is directed is the adequacy of procedures (of data gathering and data analysis) and the appropriateness of the conclusions drawn from the study that constitutes the middle third of the book.

Before we can dig beneath the surface, we must outline briefly on a surface level what was done and what was reportedly found. In May 1964, the SRA-published Tests of General Ability (TOGA) were administered by the classroom teachers to all pupils in kindergarten and all six grades of a school. The test had been presented to the teachers as a test that ". . . will allow us to predict which youngsters are most likely to show an academic spurt." The following September each teacher was given a list of names of pupils (actually selected by a table of random numbers) who were alleged to be the ones likely to show a spurt.

The children were tested again in January 1965, May 1965, and May 1966. The authors assert that the results support the proposition that the teachers' expectancies influenced the mental development of the children.

A review of *Pygmalion in the Classroom* by Robert Rosenthal and Lenore Jacobson. New York: Holt, Rinehart & Winston, 1968.

Thorndike, Robert L., "A Review of *Pygmalion in the Classroom,*" *American Educational Research Journal,* November 1968, pp. 708-711. Copyright by American Educational Research Association, Washington, D.C. Reprinted by permission of the publisher and author.

The main results of testing in May 1965 (from the authors' Table 7-1) are as follows:

| | Control | | | Experimental | | |
Grade	N	Gain		N	Gain	Difference
1	48	+12.0		7	+27.4	15.4
2	47	+ 7.0		12	+16.5	9.5
3	40	+ 5.0		14	+ 5.0	0
4	49	+ 2.2		12	+ 5.6	3.4
5	26	+17.5		9	+17.4	−0.1
6	45	+10.7		11	+10.0	−0.7

Thus, to all intents and purposes, the alleged effect of the "prophecy" appears in 19 children in Grades 1 and 2. If we are to trust the results, and the large edifice of further analysis and speculation built upon them, the findings for these two grades must be unimpeachable. Let us examine them.

TOGA has two subtests, one consisting of oral vocabulary and one of multi-mental ("which one doesn't belong") items. For the K-2 level of the test, the one used in the pretesting and posttesting of Grades 1 and 2, the two parts of the test contain respectively 35 and 28 items. Let us look first at the pretest data for six classrooms, three tested in kindergarten and three in the first grade. The results, from Appendix Tables A-2 and A-3 were (expressed in numbers that are always spoken of by the authors as "IQs"):

| | Experimental | | | Control | | |
Class	N	Mean Verbal "IQ"	Mean Reasoning "IQ"	N	Mean Verbal "IQ"	Mean Reasoning "IQ"
1A	3	102.00	84.67	19	119.47	91.32
1B	4	116.25	54.00	16	104.25	47.19
1C	2	67.50	53.50	19	95.68	30.79
2A	6	114.33	112.50	19	111.53	100.95
2B	3	103.67	102.33	16	96.50	80.56
2C	5	90.20	77.40	14	82.21	73.93

On the Reasoning Test, one class of 19 pupils is reported to have a mean "IQ" of 31! They just barely appear to make the grade as imbeciles! And yet these pretest data were used blithely by the authors without even a reference to these fantastic results!

If these pretest data show anything, they show that the testing was utterly worthless and meaningless. The means and standard deviations for the total first and second grade classes were (calculated by combining subgroups):

	First Grade		Second Grade	
	Mean	S.D.	Mean	S.D.
Verbal	105.7	21.2	99.4	16.1
Reasoning	58.0	36.8	89.1	21.6

What kind of a test, or what kind of testing is it that gives a mean "IQ" of 58 for the total entering first grade of a rather run-of-the-mill school?

Unfortunately, nowhere in the whole volume do the authors give any data expressed in raw scores. Neither do they give the ages of their groups. So it takes a little impressionistic estimating to try to reconstruct the picture. However, it would not be far off to assume an average age of 6.0 for May of a kindergarten year. An "IQ" of 58 would then mean a "mental age" of 3.5. So we go to the norms tables of TOGA to find the raw score that would correspond to a "mental age" of 3.5. Alas, the norms do not go down that far! It is not possible to tell what the authors did, but finding that a raw score of 8 corresponds to an "M.A." of 5.3, we can take a shot at extrapolating downward. We come out with a raw score of approximately 2! Random marking would give 5 or 6 right!

We can only conclude that the pretest on the so-called Reasoning Test at this age is worthless. And, in the words of a European colleague, "When the clock strikes thirteen, doubt is cast not only on the last stroke but also on all that have gone before."

Another look at one of the Appendix tables (A-6) shows that the six pupils in class 2A who had been picked to be "spurters" have a reported mean and standard deviation of posttest "IQ" of 150.17 and 40.17, respectively. This looks a little high! What does it mean in raw score terms? Again, we must turn detective with somewhat inadequate clues. Not knowing pupil ages, let us assume 7½ as probably on the low side for May in the second grade. An "IQ" of 150 implies, then, a mean "M.A." of 11¼. Back to our TOGA norms to find the corresponding raw score. Alas, the highest entry is 10.0 for a raw score of 26! We must once more extrapolate, and the best we can do from the existing data is to get 28+. (Remember, there are only 28 items in this subtest.) The mean of 6 represents a perfect score! But the standard deviation is 40 "IQ" points. What of those who fall above the mean?

When the clock strikes 14, we throw away the clock!

In conclusion, then, the indications are that the basic data upon which this structure has been raised are so untrustworthy that any conclusions based upon them must be suspect. The conclusions may be correct, but if so it must be considered a fortunate coincidence.

Empirical vs Decreed Validation of Clocks and Tests
Robert Rosenthal

In his recent review of *Pygmalion in the Classroom* (Rosenthal & Jacobson, 1968), Thorndike (1968) raises such important questions about our research instrument and our results that answers to these questions must be made available.

At the beginning of the substantive portion of his review, the reviewer reported the results showing that the effects of favorable teacher expectations occurred only in the first two grades as measured by gains in total IQ. To show that none of the data need be taken seriously, the reviewer then tried to demonstrate the invalidity of the IQ measure at these lower grades. Is there, then, a demonstration that the total IQ, the measure for which the effects were significant only at the lower two grades, was poorly measured? No, indeed. We never see reference to total IQ again, apparently because it was too well measured. Instead, we are given a detailed analysis of reasoning and verbal IQ, which together, make up total IQ. What the reader is not told by the reviewer is that *it is not true* that reasoning IQ, which is most criticized, showed expectancy effects at only the lower grades where it appeared to be less well measured. As a matter of fact, 15 of 17 classrooms showed greater reasoning IQ gains among those randomly selected children who had been alleged to their teachers to be potential bloomers (p = .001). What if we drop those "poorly measured" three first grade classrooms? Why, then it's 13 of 14 classrooms that show the hypothesized outcome (p = .001). While we're tossing out "poorly measured" classrooms, why not throw out the three second grade classrooms? That leaves us only 10 of 11 classes showing the hypothesized outcome (p = .006). It should be quite clear that the general results of the effects of teacher expectations on reasoning IQ do *not* depend upon the inclusion of the particular classrooms singled out by the reviewer.

In connection with his critique of the IQ scores reported, the reviewer made reference to a table that has as its upper and lower limits for total, verbal, and reasoning scores, mental age equivalents of 10.0 and 5.3. Such a table exists, it is true, but there is also a table, two pages earlier, that shows limits of MA from 16.5 to 0.5. In all cases IQ was defined, as might be expected, by the quite standard formula of MA/CA, and for the subtests, as well as for the full test, the full range of MAs was employed. Can we, now, explain a mean posttest IQ of 150 for the six children of the fast track classroom of the second grade who had been alleged to be potential bloomers? Indeed, we can! Their mean MA was

Rosenthal, Robert, "Empirical vs Decreed Validation of Clocks and Tests," *American Educational Research Journal,* November 1969, pp. 689-691. Copyright by American Educational Research Association, Washington, D.C. Reprinted by permission of the publisher and author.

simply 1.5 times the magnitude of their mean CA. The MAs were 16.5, 16.5, 10.0, 10.0, 10.0, and 8.9.

Now what can be said about the very low pretest reasoning IQs of the first grade children? Let us first be very clear that these low IQs reflect no clerical or scoring errors. These low IQs were earned because very few items were attempted by many of the children. The fact that *if* the children had attempted all items they would have earned a higher IQ is interesting but not invalidating. On any IQ test, not trying an item is likely to lower the score. If Flanagan (1960), in his development of TOGA, had intended the chance level of performance to be the basal MA level, he would not have tabulated the MA equivalent of a single item (out of 63) answered correctly!

The first grade children were not, of course, pretested by the first grade teachers. Careful reading of the *Pygmalion* book shows that the "first grade" children were pretested by their kindergarten teachers in the spring of the year. These kindergarten teachers were primarily responsible for assigning the children to the fast, medium, or slow track of the first grade on the basis of their kindergarten performance and without access to the IQ scores that Thorndike felt to be "worthless." We take the hypothesis of "worthlessness" seriously and submit it to empirical test. A worthless test cannot predict better than chance how a kindergarten teacher will subsequently assign pupils to the fast, medium, or slow tracks of a school. Yet children scoring higher on the "worthless" reasoning IQ pretest were far more likely to be assigned to faster tracks than were lower scoring children. The F with 2 and 60 df was 24.05 ($p < .001$). When the track variable was split into a linear regression and deviation from regression component, F for linear regression (df 1, 60) was 45.88 ($p < .001$). Linear F and overall F were both associated with a correlation exceeding .65 (Friedman, 1968). For a "worthless" test, that's not too bad a validity coefficient. One can only wonder what tests the reviewer had in mind as examples of tests that were *really* valid!

There is even more dramatic evidence, however, to test the reviewer's hypothesis of "worthless" tests. If the tests are worthless, they ought not to predict what a different teacher will say about the child's likelihood of being successful in the future, one year after the child took the reasoning pretest, and without the teacher's having access to the IQ scores. Unhappily for the hypothesis of "worthlessness," the tests predict fairly well. The correlation between the reasoning IQ pretests taken at the end of the kindergarten year and a different teacher's prediction of the child's likelihood of being a future success, a prediction made one year later, was +.49 ($N = 57, p < .001$). Not a bad predictive validity for a "worthless" test.

The reviewer likened the invalidity of the reasoning IQ subtest to the faulty mechanism of a clock heard to chime more than 12 times. It should be pointed out that not every listener at Teachers College heard those extra chimes. Thus, in their review, Peter Gumpert (Teachers College) and Carol Gumpert (Albert Einstein College of Medicine) said: "The study provides a perfectly satisfactory demonstration that the teacher expectation effects hypothesized do indeed take place." (1968, p. 22). Readers, nevertheless, were advised by Thorndike to throw away the clock. But, in the words of an Asian colleague, "When a demonstrably adequate clock is cavalierly thrown away, we may question how sincerely the discarder wants to know what time it is."

References

Flanagan, John C. *Tests of General Ability: Technical Report*. Chicago: Science Research Associates, 1960.

Friedman, H. "Magnitude of Experimental Effect and a Table for Its Rapid Estimation." *Psychological Bulletin* 70: 245-251; 1968.

Gumpert, P., and Gumpert, C. "The Teacher as Pygmalion: Comments on the Psychology of Expectation." *Urban Review* 3 (1): 21-25; 1968.

Rosenthal, Robert, and Jacobson, Lenore. *Pygmalion in the Classroom*. New York: Holt, Rinehart and Winston, 1968. 240 pp.

Thorndike, Robert L. Review of *Pygmalion in the Classroom*. *American Educational Research Journal* 5: 708-711; November 1968.

But You Have to Know How to Tell Time
Robert L. Thorndike

True enough, there *is* a table of age equivalents of raw scores that goes from 0.5 years to 16.5 years! (It is for the total score on TOGA.) But does one have to be so naïve as to use it? On how many 6-month-old examinees was it based? And if no children were tested below about the age of 5 years, as seems likely, how secure is an extrapolation stretching downward 4 or 5 years?

Age equivalents represent about as unsatisfactory an approach to an equal-unit scale as we have, even during the elementary school years. When extrapolated far beyond the ages or grades in which testing was done, they become arbitrary, insecure, and largely meaningless.

Note that it is the *scale of measurement* that is being questioned, not the validity of the raw scores. The fact that a child did not understand what he was supposed to do, and consequently omitted all or most of the items, could be quite predictive of his academic status at the time or even a year later. However, it would still be nonsense to say that his mental age was 0.5 or 1.0 or 2.0. And it is the scale of measurement that becomes crucial for the authors' argument.

Review of *Pygmalion in the Classroom*. *American Educational Research Journal* 5: 708-711; November 1968.

Thorndike, Robert L., "But You Have to Know How to Tell Time," *American Educational Research Journal*, November 1969, p. 692. Copyright by American Educational Research Association, Washington, D.C. Reprinted by permission of the publisher and author.

Incidentally, information on the number of omitted items seems quite central to any understanding of the effects of the experimental treatment. If there is one thing that extra encouragement by a teacher might readily do, whether given before or during an examination, it would be to lead a pupil to take a shot at two or three more items, whether he knew the answers or not. When score is simply the number of items right, as it is on TOGA and many other tests, normal luck could then produce a measurable if not a substantial increment in average score. At all ages, one would wish to see data on number attempted as well as number correct.

In closing, let me express a very real interest in the notion of the "self-fulfilling prophecy." I would expect the phenomenon to appear most clearly, to the extent that it is in fact effective, in those areas that are most directly teacher-based and school-dependent, such as learning to read, to write, and to cipher. Perhaps others can learn from *Pygmalion's* shortcomings, and carry out research on these problems that is psychometrically and experimentally adequate.

Chapter Five
Expectations: Expectations and Learning Performance

The two articles in this chapter were chosen to increase the reader's awareness of different factors that can influence teacher expectation and student learning performance. These factors are student social class and community expectation for teaching style and curriculum orientation. For a fuller understanding of the interrelationships and implications of these factors, the reader should keep in mind the interaction model of social behavior developed by Getzels.

The article by Hills is an extension of the famous Task of Education Studies which were based on Getzels' formulations about conflict between and among expectations held by different individuals and groups. The reader may find it surprising that the community has the potential for wielding a modicum of control over the teacher. In another study, Sieber and Wilder (1967) found that in two thirds of the cases they studied there was a marked conflict between what the parents expected of the teacher and the actual goals and instructional style of the teacher.

Beez' article reports an attempt to explain how teacher expectancies for a particular child occur. The notion that school records and files bias teacher perception of a student prior to meeting him has been bandied about for years. Now there are experimental data to substantiate this claim, and an impetus to those who advocate the elimination of records of I.Q. and the subsequent suspension of intelligence testing, especially in inner city schools.

In line with this idea, Katz et al. (in press) have collected data that indicate that race and sex of the teacher-tester can greatly influence the performance of students on I.Q. tests. According to Katz, when a black teacher administers an I.Q. test to a black student and tells the student that he is merely working on a puzzle and to have fun doing it, the black student will do as well or better than his white counterpart. However, when the situation is reversed and a Caucasian teacher proctors the test, the black student is more likely to succumb to the expectation of the teacher and the white culture which say that a black's intelligence is inferior, and the same student will test out significantly lower than when he was with the black tester.

Social Classes and Educational Views
R. Jean Hills

Persons of different educational and occupational backgrounds differ in their views regarding education; that much is certain. That they differ in well-defined ways is rather certain also, as the Task of Public Education studies[1] have indicated. So what? Are these differences reflected in the schools that serve different types of communities? Do the views of teachers in a school that serves a working class community differ from those views of teachers in a school that serves a white collar community?

Operating on the assumptions that the views held by teachers within a school cannot conflict radically with those which characterize the community in which the school exists,[2] and that the views of teachers are at least partially formed through contacts with community members, the investigator in the study reported here[3] sought to answer the questions posed above. The basic hypothesis was that the views of teachers in two secondary schools, each of which served a community populated by a different social class group would differ from one another in the same direction as the views of the two predominant social class groups.

The Task of Public Education studies, cited above, indicated that much disagreement regarding educational purposes could be reduced to different emphases upon the intellectual, vocational, and social aspects of education. These differences in emphasis were probed in the present study by means of questionnaire items that related to "curriculum orientation." Items designed to reflect the intellectual orientation stressed the importance of acquiring knowledge and understanding. The vocational orientation items emphasized the importance of acquiring the skills needed to get a job and to earn a living, and the items indicating the social orientation concerned primarily the importance of getting along with others, and being a good citizen.

In addition to curriculum orientation items, the questionnaire included a section containing items designed to determine preferences among the three styles of teaching derived by Getzels and Thelen[4] from their analysis of the

---

[1] Roger C. Seager and Allen T. Slagle, "Sub-Publics View the Task of Public Education," *Administrator's Notebook*, Vol. VIII, No. 4 (December 1959).

[2] J. W. Getzels and Herbert A. Thelen, "The Classroom Group as a Unique Social System," *The Dynamics of Instructional Groups*, Fifty-ninth Yearbook of the National Society for the Study of Education, Part II (Chicago: University of Chicago Press, 1960), pp. 53-82.

[3] R. Jean Hills, "The Relationship Between the Educational Expectations of Social Class Groups and the Role Expectations Within the Public High School" (Unpublished Ph.D. dissertation, Dept. of Education, University of Chicago, 1961).

[4] Getzels and Thelen, "The Classroom Group as a Unique Social System."

R. Jean Hills, "Social Classes and Educational Views," *Administrator's Notebook*, Volume X, No. 2 (October 1961). The *Administrator's Notebook* is published by the Midwest Administration Center of The University of Chicago. Reprinted by permission of the publisher and author.

classroom group as a social system. Their conceptualization of the social system led to the identification of three distinct teaching styles—the nomothetic, the idiographic, and the transactional.

The nomothetic style of teaching emphasizes the requirements of the institution and, accordingly, places greatest stress on the obligations of students to adhere to rules and regulations. This style is based on the assumption that, given the institutional purpose, appropriate procedures can be discovered and incorporated in the role expectations. Hence, the most effective way to attain the purpose is to define roles clearly and to insist that everyone adhere to the role definition.

The idiographic style of teaching represents the polar opposite of the nomothetic; it emphasizes the personality and needs of the individual student and, accordingly, places greatest stress on the personal dimensions of behavior. For the idiographic teacher, individual differences and needs take precedence over orderly procedures and strict role definitions. The underlying assumption is that greatest achievement will result not from rigid adherence to rigorously defined role expectations, but from each individual's contributing what is most relevant and meaningful to him.

The transactional style is not "pure" and, as a consequence, is less amenable to explicit definition. It may be considered intermediary between the two poles represented by the nomothetic and the idiographic styles; yet, it is not a middle-of-the-road position that represents moderation in all things. Rather, it is one which recognizes that the goals of the institution must be achieved by flesh-and-blood people with varying needs and varying degrees of ability. The implication is that roles will be defined as sharply as possible without prohibiting appropriate need-satisfying behavior. Thus, the personality or the role is emphasized as the situation requires for the optimum solution of a particular problem.

Five items were provided for each of the three curriculum orientations (intellectual, vocational, and social), and for each of the three teaching styles (nomothetic, idiographic, and transactional). Participants responded by indicating the importance of each item on a four-point scale. The weighted responses to the five items for a given orientation or style were then summed to provide a single index. The six indices thus derived provided the means of assessing the respondents' preferences among the curriculum orientations and among the teaching styles.

Two communities and the two secondary schools that served them provided the sources of data for this investigation. The communities were selected to represent contrasting situations with respect to social class composition. Community A is an upper-income, residential suburb of approximately 11,500 inhabitants. Community B is a lower-income, semi-industrial suburb of approximately 3500 inhabitants.

The sample from which data regarding social class differences were taken consisted of 389 respondents from the two communities. The size of the social class subsamples ranged from 36 to 103. Forty-four members of the 101-person faculty of School A, and 16 members of the 23-member faculty of School B responded to the teacher form of the questionnaire. Interviews were conducted with the entire faculty of School B and with a random sample of 23 teachers from School A.

Social Class Differences

Prior to a comparison of the expectations of teachers in the two schools, it was necessary to analyze the responses of community members to determine the differences among the expectations of the several social classes.[5] The analysis revealed no major differences among social class groups regarding preferred teaching style. Varying degrees of emphases were apparent, but there was a clear preference for the nomothetic style of teaching at all class levels.

Sharp differences did exist, however, among the several social classes with respect to curriculum orientation expectations. In close accord with the findings of previous studies, the upper, upper-middle, and middle class respondents indicated a strong preference for an intellectually oriented curriculum. Lower-middle class respondents gave almost equal weights to the three orientations. Lower class respondents, however, placed greatest stress on the social orientation, followed by vocational, then intellectual. The differences between the lower class means on the three indices, although significant, were not great. In other words, lower class members, and lower-middle class members to an even greater extent, gave the three orientations almost equal emphasis.

In contrast to the rather moderate expectations of the lower-middle and lower class members, upper and upper-middle class respondents relegated the vocational aspects of the curriculum to a position of relative unimportance. The intellectual index mean scores for the upper and upper-middle classes, respectively, were four and three times greater than the vocational index means. Middle class respondents attached a greater degree of importance to vocational matters but still their mean score on the intellectual index was twice that on the vocational index.

School Differences

Contrary to the hypothesis, the mean scores of teachers in the two schools did not differ in the predicted direction in a significant number of comparisons. On the two indices that revealed the least agreement among the several social classes, the intellectual and the vocational, there were no significant differences in any direction. The limited number of teacher responses from the two schools made it difficult to draw any firm conclusion regarding the existence or nonexistence of differences, and it was determined, therefore, to supplement the questionnaire data by means of interviews.

Teachers' responses in the interview situation tended to confirm not only the differences between social class expectations, but also the lack of differences in the curriculum orientations of the two schools. School A teachers—the upper income community—reported a strong community demand for an academically oriented college preparatory program. School B teachers reported a preference

---

[5] Classification of respondents by social class was based on: August B. Hollingshead, *Two-Factor Index of Social Class Position* (New Haven: Privately printed, 1955).

on the part of community members for a vocationally oriented terminal program. An important difference not revealed by the questionnaire was evident in the amount of Community A interest in, and pressure on, the school. School B teachers reported no similar phenomenon, but rather an almost complete absence of both interest in, and pressure on, the school. School A teachers were impressed and distressed by the emphasis placed by parents on the value of education in achieving and maintaining social status. Again, no similar situation was evident in School B, where teachers reported almost complete freedom from community pressures.

Despite, or perhaps because of, the great differences between the two communities, both schools provided an academically oriented college preparatory program. Although the programs differed widely in the scope and variety of course offerings, the basic orientations were the same. The intellectual orientation was indicated not only in teachers' comments regarding program emphasis, but also in comments concerning the relative prestige of the several departments and the commonly accepted criteria for teacher and student evaluation.

The most important respect in which the two schools differed was found to lie in the distribution of student registrations among the several programs of study. Despite the strong emphasis on college preparatory programs in School B, the percentage of student registrations in business, industrial arts, and home economics courses was substantially greater than in School A. Conversely, the percentage of student registrations in foreign language, mathematics, and social science courses was greater in School A than in School B.

Does this mean that the two initially stated assumptions were erroneous? Not necessarily; the differences in the distribution of student registrations between the two schools provides some support for the assumption regarding the compatability of school and community views and it seems likely that the negative results in this study were due to the influence of other relevant factors. To illustrate, the generalization "if two sticks are rubbed together, then fire will result" holds only if we specify that the sticks be dry. In the present case it may be that the differential importance of education to the several social class levels as a means of achieving their own goals is a factor of similar relevance.

What about the assumption regarding the influence of community contacts on teachers' views? Must it be abandoned? Seemingly not; a more thorough analysis of teacher responses indicated that in School B—the lower income community—those teachers who reported taking an active part in community organizations more closely approximated the expectations of the upper levels of the class system than did their nonparticipating colleagues. Nonparticipants tended toward greater agreement with the lower social class levels. When the percentage of contacts with the several social classes reported by these two groups of teachers were compared, it was evident that the expectation differences between them were accompanied by corresponding differences in social class contacts, participants reported a high percentage of contact with upper, upper-middle, and middle class community members and, as noted above, tended to agree with the expectations of these levels. Nonparticipants reported a significantly greater percentage of contact with lower-middle and lower class residents and their expectations more nearly coincided with those levels. A similar, but less pronounced, result was apparent in School A which served the more homogeneous upper income community

Thus it would appear that it was not the assumptions regarding community influences that were erroneous, but the implicit assumption that these influences would be sufficiently parallel and of sufficient strength to be readily apparent. While these findings are based on a very limited sample and are necessarily tentative, it appears that differences in teachers' views are associated with differences in social contacts and that the direction of these differences coincides with the teachers' point of greatest contact in the social structure of the community. This is not to say that some teachers in School B were integrated into the lower levels of the class system. The high percentage of contact reported by non-participants may mean that they were not integrated into the community at all. As a consequence, their community contacts may have occurred through the school about school business, and inevitably reflected a greater percentage of contacts with the predominant lower social class levels.

Must one conclude with Counts[6] and his followers that public schools are dominated by the upper levels of the class system? Lacking evidence to the contrary, one might assume that the boards of education in these two communities are composed of members of the upper class levels. But there is evidence to the contrary in this case; the board of education in Community B is comprised of four persons of lower-middle class rank and three persons of middle class rank.

It may be significant to note that the mean scores of the Community B board of education on the six indices are almost identical to those of School B teachers. The contrast with Community A, where all seven board members are of upper class rank, is striking. In this case the mean scores of the board of education and the mean scores of teachers diverge widely. One might hypothesize, pending further investigation, that the views of the lower-middle class board members in Community B have shifted away from the position of their social class peers toward the position of professional school personnel.

Implications
One may draw direct implications for the practice of administration from a study of this kind only at the risk of straining his own imagination, the reader's credulity, or both. Certainly there are insights to be gained regarding the differences that exist in the educational expectations of the several social class levels, and some administrators may wish to speculate about the possible effect of encouraging teachers to participate widely in community affairs. The interesting implications, however, are clearly for further research. A few of these will be mentioned in closing. What changes, if any, in the educational views of an individual occur during incumbency on a board of education? Would a larger sample

---

[6]George S. Counts, *The Social Composition of Boards of Education,* Supplementary Educational Monographs (Chicago: University of Chicago Press, July 1927).

and refined measurements produce more conclusive evidence regarding the association between differences in teachers' views and community contacts? Is divergence of educational views between teachers and community, particularly the student community, associated with a high dropout rate?

The most marked differences in the views of teachers were found to be associated with teaching field affiliation. The views of industrial arts, home economics, commercial, and guidance personnel tended toward decreasing conflict with the views of lower class levels, while the views of teachers of academic subjects, e.g., mathematics, English, and foreign language, tended toward increasing conflict with the views of persons at these levels. Is there greater rapport between lower class students and nonacademic teachers than there is between these same students and academic teachers?

Influence of Biased Psychological Reports on Teacher Behavior and Pupil Performance
W. Victor Beez

Experimental research in the area of effects of expectancies (Rosenthal, 1964a, 1964b, 1966) indicates that the experimenter's orientation and expectation can influence the data. As Rosenthal (1964a) has demonstrated, expectancies of this sort can be communicated in very subtle ways. A variety of cues, so-called demand characteristics, unintentionally communicate to the subject something of what the experimenter is after (Orne, 1962). Communication can be subtle, unintentional, and differential depending upon the subjects or the expectations the experimenter holds for them. Even in highly standardized situations, a subject can be influenced by another person's expectations (Rosenthal, 1966).

That expectancies also influence behavior outside the laboratory has in recent years been demonstrated in educational research (Cahen, 1965; Rosenthal & Jacobson, 1966, 1967, 1968). The findings of these investigators raise serious questions as to present practices in our educational system, and make further investigation imperative. It appears that teacher-pupil interaction operates similarly to laboratory interaction between experimenter and subject.

While Rosenthal and Jacobson investigated changes in IQ due to differential information given to teachers, the present study was mainly concerned with changes in teaching behavior and performance by pupils. It also attempted to

Adapted from a paper read at the American Psychological Association meetings, San Francisco, 1968. This study is based upon a dissertation submitted by the author as a partial requirement for the Ph.D. degree at Indiana University.

From *Learning in Social Settings* by Matthew B. Miles and W. W. Charters, Jr. Boston: Allyn and Bacon, Inc., 1970. Reprinted by permission of W. Victor Beez.

investigate the question raised by Rosenthal's work as to how a teacher's expectation becomes translated into behavior in such a way as to elicit the expected pupil behavior (Rosenthal & Jacobson, 1966).

Method

Subjects

Sixty children from the summer Head Start program in Bloomington, Indiana participated in this study. They ranged in age from 5 years, 7 months to 6 years, 6 months, and had IQs on the Peabody Picture Vocabulary Test from 55 to 127, with a mean of 91. IQ assessment was made *after* completion of the experimental study, so that at the time of experimentation the actual IQ was not known. Children were randomly assigned to either a "low ability" or a "high ability" group. With the exception of name and age nothing was known about a particular child prior to assignment to one of the groups. The names of the children were taken from the list of children attending the Head Start program and none of the children was discussed with either the principal or the regular teacher. Each of the two groups consisted of 15 boys and 15 girls. None of the children in the study had previously attended regular classes.

Sixty "teachers" served as the actual subjects of this study. *S*s were graduate students in the School of Education of Indiana University during the summer of 1967. *S*s ranged in age from 19 to 51 years (*M* = 28-9) and had from 0 to 22 years teaching experience (*M* = 4-6). *S*s were assigned at random to one of the two groups.

Experimenters

Two graduate students in English served as experimenters. Although *E*s were not given details of the study they did guess the general idea. However, throughout the study they did not know what group a particular child was in nor what *S*s had been told about the child's intellectual prospects. Instructions were given in writing to *E*s.

Procedure

Experimentation took place in separate rooms in the elementary school which was used for the Head Start program. Of the school personnel, the principal alone was aware of the purpose of the study. Each *S* worked individually with one child. *S* was told that the purpose of the study was to see how well Head Start children would perform on a number of experimental tasks. Prior to seeing the child, *S* was given a folder containing a faked "psychological evaluation" of the child (see Figures 1 and 2).

All reports were identical for the children belonging to the same groups, with the exception of name and age of child. Reports included "background information," "testing behavior and clinical observation," and "recommendations." The fake IQ data described all children as falling within the average range of intelligence. The reports for the "low ability" children, however, (Figure 2)

Figure 1   Psychological Evaluation

Name: James Carpenter   Date: June 27, 1967
Sex: Male
Birthdate: 8-3-61
Age: 5-11
Examiner: R. L. Simons   C o n f i d e n t i a l

REASON FOR TESTING:

Intelligence Testing for Special Project in Educational Research, summer 1967.

BACKGROUND:

James lives with his parents in Bloomington, Ind. Mr. Carpenter is employed at a local department store as a stock clerk and has completed the eighth grade. Mrs. Carpenter is a housewife and completed nine years of school. There are two younger siblings in the family.

TEST BEHAVIOR AND CLINICAL OBSERVATION:

James was an open and friendly boy who related well to the examiner. He smiled readily and seemed to enjoy adult attention. He frequently initiated conversation and reported at length about things he liked, his home, his play activities, etc.

The boy responded freely to the questions asked him and seemed to be interested in most all the tasks. He responded well to encouragement, was quite attentive and seemed to be well motivated.

Both the Peabody Picture Vocabulary Test, Form A, and the Stanford-Binet, Form L-M, were administered to James. On the PPVT he obtained an IQ of 102, and he received an IQ of 105 on the Stanford-Binet. The two IQ scores are quite similar, and one can classify James as falling within the normal range of intelligence in comparison to children his age.

RECOMMENDATIONS:

Although James comes from a culturally disadvantaged home he has, nevertheless, very good potential for school related tasks and activities. He seems highly motivated and well adjusted to learning situations. It is expected that he will experience little or no difficulty in his school work and should do quite well on the proposed project tasks.

---

called the IQ score "low average," and interpreted the results negatively, stressing negative aspects of cultural deprivation, and predicted that school adjustment would be difficult. The reports for the "high ability" group children (Figure 1) interpreted the IQ information positively, terming it "normal," stressed positive aspects in the child's fictional behavior, and suggested that despite cultural deprivation the child should do well in school. These reports were given in closed folders to Ss so that Es would not know what they contained. Ss were also told not to discuss the "case" with Es.

After S had read the report, the child was brought into the room and given the first task. This task (symbol learning) consisted of a series of 20 signs printed on individual cards (e.g. "STOP," "WALK," "GO," "BOYS," "GIRLS," "DANGER," etc.). S was told to teach as many signs as he could in a standard order within a ten-minute period, using whatever technique or strategy he wanted to use. E unobtrusively recorded the time spent on each sign, the number of signs covered, and tallied S's responses, such as the number of times a word was read

Figure 2 Psychological Evaluation

Name: Richard Walters   Date: June 27, 1967
Sex: Male
Birthdate: 10-28-61
Age: 5-8   C o n f i d e n t i a l
Examiner: R. L. Simons

REASON FOR TESTING:

Intelligence Testing in connection with Special Project in Educational Research, summer 1967.

BACKGROUND:

Richard is a member of a family of 7, living in a two-room house. The owner of the house is currently adding one room which will be used as a bedroom. His father is employed in Martinsville as a truck driver, and his mother is a full time housewife. Both parents were born in Gary, Ind., and moved to Bloomington eight years ago. Both parents have an eighth grade education.

When Richard appeared for testing he was somewhat carelessly dressed. He was sulky, appeared unresponsive, and it was difficult to engage him in any lengthy conversation. It is the feeling of the examiner that the boy disliked the testing situation and, in general, feels uncomfortable in adult company.

TEST BEHAVIOR AND CLINICAL OBSERVATION:

Despite the examiner's attempts to establish good rapport with Richard the boy did not appear to feel comfortable. It was often difficult to elicit a response from him, or at times he even remarked that he did not like the test and it was "dumb." It was necessary to ask him repeatedly to sit up and to pay attention. He was quite fidgety, asking how much longer it was to last, yawned and put his head on the table. It would appear from this that motivation for school related tasks is lacking in Richard.

Richard was first administered the Peabody Picture Vocabulary Test, Form A, on which he obtained an IQ of 95. On the Stanford-Binet Intelligence Scale, Form L-M, he obtained an IQ of 94. The results of the two tests are quite similar and it is suggested that they can be taken as a fairly good estimate of Richard's intellectual abilities. This would place the boy in the "low average" range of intelligence in comparison to children his age. Richard, coming from a culturally disadvantaged home, lacks many of the experiences of normal children his age, and shows a lack of motivation toward learning tasks.

RECOMMENDATION:

Richard's present level of intellectual functioning would suggest that school adjustment will be difficult for him, and there are serious doubts that he will profit from average learning tasks. This might be due in part to a lack of motivation but mainly also because of a lack of previous experience. It is doubtful that he will be able to perform satisfactorily on the proposed learning tasks of the project.

---

to the child, the child was asked to say the word, the child was asked to identify the word from the card, the meaning of the word was explained or demonstrated, etc.

After the ten-minute teaching period, the signs were removed and *S* was asked to present a series of five jigsaw puzzles to the child for a five-minute period, in a standard order. Each puzzle had to be successfully completed before the next could be given. *S* was told to present it any way he wished and that he could interact with the child. *E* again recorded the time spent on each puzzle and number of times S gave clues to the child. After this task the child was moved to a different room, where he was retested by E for recall of the signs covered in the first task.[1]

Finally, after E returned to record Ss' estimates of their children's intelligence test performance level, S was asked to complete a questionnaire, rating the child as to expected achievement level, social competency, and intellectual ability, as compared with children in the regular classroom. S also had to indicate on a rating scale how difficult he thought the sign task was for the child.[2]

Results and Discussion

1. Teachers who had been given favorable expectations about a pupil tried to teach more symbols than did the teachers given unfavorable expectations ($p <$ .001). The mean for the "high ability" group was 10.43 words, the mean for the "low ability" group was 5.66 words attempted. The difference in teaching effort was dramatic. Eight or more symbols were taught by 87 percent of the teachers expecting better performance, but only 13 percent of the teachers expecting poorer performance tried to teach that many words ($p <$ .0000001).

2. The two groups differed significantly ($p <$ .001) in the number of symbols learned by the children. While the mean for the "high ability" group was 5.9, the "low ability" group had a mean of only 3.1 symbols. Most (77 percent) of the children alleged to have better intellectual prospects learned five or more symbols but only 13 percent of the children alleged to have poorer intellectual prospects learned five or more symbols ($p <$ .000002).

3. Ss' ratings of achievement, social competency, and intellectual ability were made on 5-point scales. On achievement, the "low ability" group received a mean of 1.93 as compared with 3.50 for the "high ability" group ($p <$ .001). The difference for social competency is smaller, but still significant beyond the .01 level. The "low ability" group had a mean of 2.57 and the "high ability" group a mean of 3.33. Ratings of intellectual ability gave the "low ability" group a mean of 1.93 and the "high ability" group a mean of 3.43 ($p <$ .001).

4. There was also a difference between the groups in the number of times the meanings of the symbols were explained and, of course, the time spent on each symbol. Ss in the "low ability" teaching group explained the meaning of a word significantly more often, gave more examples, and spent more time on non-teaching activities than did Ss in the "high ability" teaching group ($p <$ .01).

5. All children, except one, completed the puzzles within the permitted

---

[1] During this time, S made an estimate of the level of performance the child would achieve on the French Pictorial Test of Intelligence (one of four levels of difficulty into which the French cards had been sorted). In the "low ability" group, only four children were judged by Ss to be able to master the test above the second level of difficulty; in the "high ability" group, twenty-two children were judged as performing above the second level.

[2] Ss also indicated whether they liked or disliked working with the child (all reported liking it); rated the helpfulness of the psychological report (all but three subjects felt they were "very" or "somewhat" helpful, with no differences across treatments); and rated how comfortable they had felt with the tasks (the majority of the Ss felt comfortable, with no significant differences across treatments).

time. No significant difference was found between the groups in the number of clues given by *S*s.

6. Only one *S* evaluated the symbol-learning task as too difficult for the pupil in the "high ability" group (3.3 percent) whereas 63 percent of *S*s felt that it was too difficult for children in the "low ability" group.

The results strongly support findings by others (e.g., Rosenthal & Jacobson, 1966) that pupils are influenced by their teachers' expectations and have a tendency to behave accordingly. Teachers also act differently depending upon their expectations for the child. When they expect the child to do poorly they attempt to teach less, spend more time on each task, give more examples of meaning, are more likely to engage in nonteaching activities, and repeat the task more often than when they expect better performance from the child. It needs to be pointed out that in this study *S* had practically no time to get acquainted with the child prior to the start of the teaching task and, therefore, relied heavily on the faked "psychological report." However, the data of the evaluation and rating of the child by *S* would support the hypothesis that even in the face of successful performance on the puzzle tasks, *S*'s expectation is not changed.

Some anecdotal material is of interest. One child in the "high ability" group whose actual IQ was 71 (measured *after* the experiment) was taught fourteen signs and learned seven; another child in the "low ability" group with a tested IQ of 127 was taught only five signs and learned three.

After the total experiment was over, the author reported to the groups of *S*s on the actual intent of the experiment. While the "high ability" teachers were rather pleased, the "low ability" teachers seemed more inclined to argue ("but my child *really* was retarded"). Two teachers, in fact, believed that the report had given the IQ as falling within the retarded range.

Mismatches between the report and the events of the teaching situation occurred, but did not seem to affect *S* expectations. One child did not speak, though the report had described him as "frequently initiating conversation." *S* nevertheless rated the report as "most helpful." In another case, a boy was misidentified as a girl in the report; *S* found the report "most helpful" and proceeded with "high ability" expectations.

Conclusions

Results of this sort have serious implications for present practices in educational settings. Even if we consider that this was a somewhat artificial situation and that normally the teacher has a much better knowledge of the child, we are, nevertheless, overwhelmed by the data suggesting drastic effects of expectancies. School children are frequently evaluated throughout their school years in terms of IQ tests, psychological reports, labeling through special classes, etc. For example, a child who is labeled a "slow learner" or "mentally retarded" is automatically expected to do less well than a "normal" child. This expectation might, in fact, retard the performance of the child even more than is necessary. The findings would suggest that one should be very careful as to what information a teacher should receive about a child. On the other hand, the findings may be applied in a constructive way; that is, positive aspects in a child's behavior or ability should be stressed.

References

Cahen, L. S. An experimental manipulation of the "halo effect": A study of teacher bias. Unpublished manuscript, Stanford University, 1965.

Orne, M. T. On the social psychology of the psychological experiment: With particular reference to demand characteristics and their implications. *American Psychologist,* 1962, 17, 776-783.

Rosenthal, R. The effect of the experimenter on the results of psychological research. In N. A. Maher (Ed.), *Progress in experimental personality research.* Vol. I. New York: Academic Press, 1964, pp. 79-114. (a)

Rosenthal, R. Experimenter outcome-orientation and the results of the psychological experiment. *Psychological Bulletin,* 1964, 61, 405-412. (b)

Rosenthal, R. *Experimenter effects in behavioral research.* New York: Appleton-Century-Crofts, 1966.

Rosenthal, R. and Jacobson, L. Teacher expectancies: determinants of pupils' IQ gains. *Psychological Reports,* 1966, 19, 115-118.

Rosenthal, R. and Jacobson, L. Self-fulfilling prophecies in the classroom: teachers' expectations as unintended determinants of pupils' intellectual competence. Paper read at the American Psychological Association meetings, Washington, D.C., 1967.

Rosenthal, R. and Jacobson, L. *Pygmalion in the classroom: teacher expectation and pupils' intellectual development.* New York: Holt, Rinehart and Winston, 1968.

Part Three
Learning Style

Chapter Six
Learning Style: An Introduction

This chapter will further introduce the reader to the concept of learning, or cognitive style. The meaning and relationship of cognitive style to other psychological mechanisms associated with the process of learning will be discussed. A brief history of the theory and research in cognitive style and the relationship between learning style and learning performance will be presented, followed by a model of learning style, its components, and its relationship to instructional style and learning performance. Finally, an introduction to other chapters of Part Three will complete this chapter.

Definitions and Meanings
Learning style and cognitive style have been used synonymously in the literature, although cognitive style appears to be the preferred term. Learning styles are defined by DeCecco (1968) as personal ways in which the learner processes information in the course of learning new concepts. Kagan, Moss, and Siegel (1963) use the term to refer to stable individual preferences in modes of perceptual organization and conceptual categorization of the external environment. Similarly, Messick (1969) sees cognitive styles as information processing habits which represent the learner's typical mode of perceiving, thinking, problem-solving, and remembering. Ausubel (1968) uses the term to refer to both individual differences in cognitive organization and various self-consistent personal tendencies that are not reflective of human cognitive functioning in general.

Related Psychological Terms
Davis (1967) states that various terms such as cognitive control, cognitive systems principles, and perceptual attitude have been used synonymously with cognitive style. But closely related in function to cognitive style are other parameters associated with learning: cognitive structure, learning abilities and learning set, readiness, personality, and motivation and emotion. Since these terms are used frequently in a number of the following articles of Part Three, the reader may find it helpful to refer to this section for definitions.

Cognitive structure, according to Ausubel (1963), is the learner's organization, stability, and clarity of knowledge in a particular subject-matter field at any given moment. If existing cognitive structure is clear, stable, and suitably organized, learning and retention of new material is facilitated. Otherwise, learning and retention, as well as transfer, are inhibited. Learning abilities, according to Jensen (1960), are the various abilities and processes by which the learner acquires new performances. Learning set, on the other hand, refers to the capabilities the learner possesses at any given stage in the learning of a task (Gagné & Paradise, 1961). Readiness is defined by Ausubel (1959) as the adequacy of the learner's existing capacity in relation to some instructional objective. Lazarus (1963) defines personality as the hypothetical structures and processes within the learner that dispose him to act in certain ways. For Ausubel (1968), cognitive style reflects differences in personality organization as well as cognitive functioning and organization. Furthermore, cognitive style mediates between motivation and emotion on one hand and cognition on the other.

A Brief History of Cognitive Style
Historically, cognitive style has been a fledgling consideration in the study of cognitive processes. Before the turn of the century, psychologists like Cattell and Jastrow were measuring individual differences in perceptual characteristics. But when their simple perceptual measurements proved not to be good indicators of general intelligence and learning performance, interest in this phenomenon diminished. Nonetheless, some typologies of perception were described by Vernon, Eysench, and others: analyzers v. synthesizers; color reactors v. form reactors; and so on.

During the 1940's, a series of factor analytic studies initiated by Thurstone, and later by Guilford, delineated a number of factors having to do with perceptual speed, which appeared to be related to cognitive abilities. These studies also pointed with increasing clarity to two closure factors, speed and flexibility, which researchers thought were related to personality and temperament.

Yet the greatest amount of interest and research on cognitive styles was to emanate from three different sources: the Brooklyn group, the Menninger group, and the Fels Institute group.

During the years following World War II, Asch and Witkin and their colleagues at Brooklyn College isolated a perceptual trait, *field dependence-independence,* and showed it to be related to personality structure and certain physical traits. Later studies led to an expansion of the general notion of field dependence-independence, which refers to an individual's ability to perceive and manipulate a figure with or without a ground. In time, the designation *analytic-global* was used to represent a broader dimension of human behavior which could account for not only perceptual functions but also cognitive functions. As the work of the Brooklyn group expanded, Witkin et al. (1962) began to believe that an individual's perceptions were but one component of a larger constellation of interrelated components which together reflected the individual's level of *psychological differentiation.*

Perhaps the broadest and most comprehensive attack on the problem of individual differences in cognitive style has been conducted by the staff of the Menninger Foundation. In a series of experiments, Holzman, Gardner, and their colleagues identified a number of *control principles:* leveling v. sharpening; equivalence range; tolerance for unrealistic experiences; flexible v. restricted control; and differentiation v. undifferentiation. The central theme of the Menninger research was that personality organization, called cognitive control, accounts for an individual's mode of perceiving, remembering, and thinking. For the Menninger group, cognitive style is viewed as a composite of cognitive controls.

Developmental studies of cognition had been carried out by both the Brooklyn and Menninger groups, but the studies by Kagan and his associates at the Fels Institute are perhaps the most widely known. Kagan focused his research on analytic styles of thinking. He found two styles of conceptualization mediating thinking and problem-solving—analytic and nonanalytic. Later research by the Fels group in 1964 led to the conclusion that the analytic-nonanalytic style of responding was related to two major variables: *reflection*—the tendency to analyze and differentiate a complex stimulus configuration into its component parts; and *impulsivity*—the tendency to make immediate, and often inaccurate, responses. Since 1965, Kagan's research has placed less emphasis on individual differences in the degree of stimulus differentiation.

Davis (1967) noted that there is one characteristic common to the work of all three groups. On the one hand is the active analysis by the learner of the entire stimulus: field-independence for Witkin, differentiation for Gardner, and reflection for Kagan. On the other hand, the more passive, global acceptance of the stimulus: field-dependence for Witkin, undifferentiation for Gardner, and impulsivity for Kagan. In all three cases, the primary concern was with the individual differences involving the way in which information was processed.

Nonetheless, a number of problems exist if one attempts to compare, integrate, and generalize data and results from these three sources. The primary problem is that a variety of criterion tests were employed to identify the same cognitive style, and often one finds little correlation between these criterion measures. The most often used criterion tests are: the Embedded Figures Test (EFT), the Rod and Frame Test (RFT), and the Body Adjustment Test (BAT) for Witkin; the Object Sorting Test (OST) and Color Word Test (CWT) for the Menninger group; and the Conceptual Styles Test (CST) and Design Recall Test (DRT) for Kagan. When Witkin and Gardner employed the EFT and RFT to test cognitive styles, Kagan would use the CST. And since analytic performance on the CST was not correlated with performance on the EFT, there was difficulty generalizing results. Because of this and other difficulties, Wallach (1962) advocated the use of a multidimensional, rather than unidimensional, approach to measuring cognitive style.

Others have contributed to the growing literature in cognitive style. Among them are Bruner, Goodnow, and Austin (1956), who described various strategies that the individual employs to form concepts. Rokeach (1960, 1968) and Zagona and Zurcher (1965) have studied the effects of such intraindividual differences as *belief congruence, intolerance,* and *closed mindedness.* Paul (1959) and Uhlmann and Saltz (1965) have studied differences in long-term memory or *retention styles.*

Learning Style and Learning Performance

Today, the popularization and application of research and theory in learning style is being promoted by at least two groups: those concerned with the disadvantaged and the disordered learner (e.g., Riessman, 1964; Shumsky, 1968; Bateman, 1966; Cuban, 1970; and Fantini & Weinstein, 1968); and those concerned with improving individualized instruction (e.g., Cronbach, 1967; Messick, 1969; Rhetts, 1970; and Lesser, 1971).

On the other hand, the educational research establishment has been quite hesitant to endorse the idea that individual differences in aptitude, especially learning style, can and do interact with instructional method to affect learning performance. In fact, the idea of this Aptitude-Treatment Interaction (ATI) hypothesis is alien to many. Bracht and Glass (1968) reflect this attitude that there is little, if any, evidence for an interaction of curriculum treatments and personological variables. For all practical purposes, these individuals see a place in the psychology of learning for basic research in cognitive styles, but little more, at this time.

A Model of Learning Style
as It Relates to Instructional Style

Woodruff (1967), a cognitive theorist, has offered a heuristic model of the behaving-learning cycle that may be helpful in delineating the components of learning style and its relation to instructional style.

Woodruff's model is composed of five stages: stimulation, perception, concept-formation and storage, problem-solving or decision-making, and action. He suggests that there are four sources of stimulation inherent in the meaningful situation: symbolic media; environmental referents; adjustment status or feeling; and verbal communicant interactors. The perceptual stage has three functions: collecting data from all the channels of the stimulation-sensation input; serving as a short-term memory storage area; and selectively filtering by reducing the incoming stimulation and sending it to the concept-formation storage area. This next stage has two functions: concept-formation, often called thinking; and storage, or long-term memory. Stage four, decision-making and problem-solving, refers to concept utilization. Woodruff employs the construct *decision making* to refer to the use of concepts in familiar situations at the intuitive and verbalized level, while employing the construct *problem-solving* to refer to concept utilization in unfamiliar situations. It should be noted that Woodruff distinguishes concept-formation from problem-solving, while others use the terms synonymously or refer to them as having overlapping functions (Ausubel, 1968). The last stage, action or performance, can be of three types—perceptual; adjustive; or communicative—and serves a feedback function to the other stages.

Woodruff suggests that in order to accomplish the learning task most efficiently, the instructor—live or automated—must influence the behavior-learning cycle at four stages: perception; concept-formation; problem-solving and decision-making; and trials of concepts in new forms. This model of instruction, with its assumptions, will be discussed at length in chapter 10.

An Overview of Part Three

The chapters in Part Three elaborate the perspective of this introduction in terms of the current status and dimensions of theory and research in learning styles. Articles in chapter 7 indicate the current interest and commitment of the advocates—both practitioners and theoreticians—of learning styles. The articles in chapter 8 serve to focus the controversy about ATI and the usefulness of learning styles in educational planning and research. Articles in chapter 9 detail research on four of the most well-known dimensions of cognitive style.

Chapter Seven
Learning Style: Context

The articles in this chapter provide an overview of recent interest and developments, both theoretical and practical, in the study of learning styles. The Riessman and Shumsky articles provide a practical viewpoint concerning the importance of recognizing and teaching in terms of the learner's idiosyncratic style, while Messick's article is a more theoretical argument for the importance of including personological variables in instructional research.

Messick's paper was originally read at a symposium entitled "The Evaluation of Instruction" in 1967. A critique of Messick's paper by Cahen (see chapter 8) suggests that the consideration of individual differences in the learner is premature and is only a tangential consideration for instructional planners and theorists. Messick, of course, argues that learning styles and strategies are perhaps the crucial considerations in education, and must be studied and researched in terms of their methodological, as well as value, dimensions. In fact, when individual differences are being discussed, it is impossible to get around the value question.

Riessman, the author of *The Disadvantaged Child* and *New Careers for the Poor,* has also written extensively on individual differences of disadvantaged learners. His parsimonious characterization of the learner as being primarily physical, aural, or visual when receiving and processing information has much appeal and face validity. The reader may want to compare Riessman's observations on the disadvantaged learner with Kagan's characterization of the *impulsive* learner.

Shumsky offers a rather accurate and simple assessment format for discerning differences in learning styles among elementary school children. Furthermore, her suggestions for then teaching in terms of those differences are poignant and sound. Shumsky's suggested questions can help the teacher to develop a whole new perspective on the teaching-learning process. Her message is simple: If the teacher will but learn to observe the learner and his environment—that is, how he struggles to receive, analyze, and retain information—the teacher can then know the best ways to help guide that learner.

The reader will find additional commentary on the usefulness of learning styles in the following sources. Cuban (1970) insists that all young children are basically physical learners, regardless of social class and race, and that even though most schools continue to gear instruction to aural learning and visual learning, the middle class child can learn in spite of this incongruity, while the lower class child fails. Cronbach (1967) offers four possible approaches for dealing with individual differences in the process of instruction. The reader will note that the present book deals with only one of these approaches. Eckstrand (1962) details the reasons why individual differences have always been talked about, but never implemented in psychology and education. Finally, two chapters from Lesser (1971) should be noted: Kogan's chapter is actually an elaboration of Messick's article, and Bissell, White, and Zivin's chapter offers further support for Riessman's assertions.

The Criterion Problem in the Evaluation of Instruction: Assessing Possible, Not Just Intended, Outcomes
Samuel Messick

This paper will discuss cognitive styles and affective reactions as two major classes of criterion variables that should be taken into account in the evaluation of instruction. These two types of variables are emphasized because of their bearing upon questions that should be asked in evaluation studies—questions that stem from particular views about the diversity of human performance and about the role of values in educational research.

Individual Differences in Response to Educational Treatments
Traditional questions in education and psychology have frequently spawned answers that are either wrong since they summarize findings "on the average" in situations where a hypothetical "average person" does not exist, or else are seriously lacking in generality because they fail to consider the multiplicity of human differences and their interactions with environmental circumstances.

Consider the kind of "horse race" question typical of much educational research of the past: Is textbook A better than textbook B? Is teacher A better than teacher B? Or, more generally, is treatment A better than treatment B? Such questions are usually resolved empirically by comparing average gains in specific achievement for students receiving treatment A with average gains for students receiving treatment B. But suppose treatment A is better for certain kinds of students and treatment B better for other kinds of students. Depending upon the mix of students in the two groups, the two treatments might exhibit

The preparation of this paper was supported in part by the National Institute of Mental Health under Research Grant MH-4186.

negligible differences on the average while producing wildly different effects upon individuals. An entirely different evaluation of the treatments might have resulted if some other questions had been asked, such as "Do these treatments interact with personality and cognitive characteristics of the students or with factors in their educational history or family background to produce differential effects upon achievement? Do certain student characteristics correlate with gains in achievement differently in one treatment than in the other?"

From the vantage point of differential psychology, it would appear that educational researchers frequently fail to take proper account of consistent individual differences. They tend to assess treatment effects on the average, presuming that variations in performance around the average are unstable fluctuations rather than expressions of stable personal characteristics. Developmental psychologists, on the other hand, survey essentially the same arena with their own limited purview. They not only frequently make the same assumption about individual variation but also the obverse concerning environmental variation. They seek to uncover for the generic human being general laws of learning and cognition–at best a small number of different laws for assorted idealized types of individuals– and to delineate mental development *on the average,* where the average is taken over all the differential educational experiences and environmental impacts that might interact with current psychological status to moderate change.

To evaluate educational treatments in terms of their effects upon individual students requires not only the assessment of variables directly related to specific treatment goals, such as achievement level, but also the assessment of personal and environmental variables that may moderate the learning. Similarly, to formulate the psychology of the development of cognitive or personality characteristics over a fixed period may require information not only about individual differences in the trait in relation to other traits at different times, but also about the educational treatments and environmental variations accompanying the change. Information about the trait's previous development and the personal, social, and environmental factors associated with prior growth may also be necessary.

If concerns about personal, social, and environmental characteristics were systematically combined with concerns about the effects of educational treatments, a conceptual framework for educational and psychological research would result, stimulating questions about interactions among these components, such as "What dimensions of educational experience are associated with growth on dimensions of cognitive functioning or with changes in attitude or affective involvement, and what social and environmental factors moderate these effects?" The need for such a multivariate interactional approach derives from the view that in education and psychology we are dealing with a complicated *system* composed of differentiated subsystems; even in research on presumably circumscribed issues it is important to recognize the interrelatedness of personal, social, environmental, and educational factors. In such a system it is possible that compensating trade-offs among variables will occur under different conditions to produce similar effects, and that particular outcomes will frequently be multiply determined. This is not to say that overall main effects due to specific educational treatments will not occur or that no personal characteristics will prove to be general over situations, but rather that interactions between treatment variables and personal or environmental factors are probable and should be systematically appraised in evaluating treatment effects.

The major thrust of this approach is that evaluations of the significance of changes in performance or attitude over a given time period as a presumed function of a specific instructional program should consider other changes in human characteristics and environmental influences active at the same time. Educational growth should not be viewed as independent of human growth, and the effects of instructional experiences should not be viewed as independent of other life experiences.

These multiple influences upon behavior should not only be considered at the level of systems analysis, but also at much simpler levels, such as in developing and evaluating a measure of academic achievement, where we sometimes forget that even specific responses are frequently complexly determined and buffeted by many environmental influences. Consider a researcher who attempts to assess quantitative reasoning in a lower class, culturally disadvantaged child by inquiring, "If you had seven apples and I asked you for two, how many would you have left?" The answer comes quickly and triumphantly—"Seven!" Hopefully, of course, we would never use such loose phrasing in our questions, but the example illustrates the point. We often fail to appreciate the extent to which the respondent's affect will be engaged by the content of a question and the extent to which personal, social, and economic factors will focus his attention upon problems quite different from the ones we thought we had posed.

When the efficacy of instruction is evaluated in such a multivariate framework, cognitive styles and affective reactions assume particular interest: (a) as personal characteristics that may interact with treatment variables to moderate learning, retention, and transfer; (b) as dispositions to be monitored to detect any possibly undesirable side effects of instruction; and (c) as qualities to be fostered either directly as specific objectives of the instructional program or indirectly as by-products of other efforts. This latter possibility of fostering stylistic and affective qualities appears to be consonant with general educational aims and the desirability of developing positive attitudes toward school, learning, subject matter, or self. But with respect to cognitive styles there is much less consensus, for we are not sure whether to emphasize particular styles or flexibility in the use of multiple styles, nor are we sure what the options are for changing styles. This problem will be discussed in more detail after we have considered the nature of cognitive styles and some reasons why individual differences in characteristic modes of cognition are relevant to educational practice.

The Role of Values in the Science of Education

To suggest that cognitive styles and affects might serve as additional criteria in the evaluation of instruction is a value judgment; but value judgments abound in the evaluation process, and appear to be made with hesitancy only at the end of the enterprise when a decision about the worth of the program is required. Value judgments are usually made explicitly when the specific goals of the in-structural program are outlined and when particular standards of excellence are accepted for judging success; but they are also made, usually implicitly, when criterion instruments are selected to assess the intended outcomes, when additional criterion measures are chosen to appraise side effects, when particular teaching methods, media, or materials are scrutinized during the course of instruction, and when certain types of transactions between the student and other persons are observed (Stake, 1967)—in short, whenever a subset of the possible alternatives is marked for special attention.

The selection of a subset from the range of possibilities implies priorities—that some things are more important to assess than others. But it is not enough to label such decisions "value judgments" and then proceed with the assessment. If it were, evaluation would be a straightforward affair indeed: we could specify the goals of the instructional program as we intend them and select criterion measures to assess those outcomes that seem directly relevant to the stated objectives. This is what Scriven has called "estimation of goal achievement" in contradistinction to evaluation proper. All appraisal in this case is relative to the stated goals, and the concern is with how well the program achieves its intended objectives. In addition, however, we should inquire to what extent the objectives are worth achieving and, in general, should endeavor to include in the evaluation process provisions for evaluating the value judgments, especially the goals (Scriven, 1967).

An important step in this direction is to be concerned with *possible* as well as *intended* outcomes. Evaluation comprises two major functions—to ascertain the nature and size of the effects of the treatment and to decide whether the observed effects attain acceptable standards of excellence. These two components have been termed *description* and *judgment* by Stake (1967). The point here is that the descriptive phase of evaluation should be as complete as our art and resources allow. In this instance the evaluation specialist should be, in Bruner's words (1966), a "diviner and delineator of the possible"—he should "provide the full range of alternatives to challenge society to choice." This attempt to describe the full range of possible effects of instruction is an important prerequisite for the judgmental phase of evaluation, since it might unearth alternatives that ought to be weighed in reaching the final appraisal. As Henry Dyer (1967, pp. 12-24) has emphasized, "Evaluating the *side* effects of an educational program may be even more important than evaluating its intended effects." Dyer (1967) also pointed out that such broad assessment of the possible effects of an educational program should contribute to an evaluation of its goals. Inverting the customary prescription that one must determine the objectives of instruction before developing measures of instructional outcomes, Dyer suggested that it may not be possible to decide what the objectives ought to be until the outcomes are measured.

In practice, of course, evaluation studies rarely approach completeness. We include in any feasible assessment program only a selection of criterion variables—those that reflect our current view of priorities or our attempt to represent several diverse viewpoints. Again it is not enough just to admit that practical considerations demand selectivity. To develop a science of evaluation, we should endeavor to justify these value judgments on rational grounds in terms of the specific objectives of the instructional program in question and of goals of education that transcend the particular course (Scriven, 1967). It is important not only to explicate the separate value judgments implicit in the choice of each criterion variable, but also to consider interrelations among them. Values rarely exist in isolation. They are typically part of ideologies that provide characteristic ways of thinking about man and society. In considering the assortment of variables to be assessed in a particular evaluation study and the goals that the instruction might serve, we should inquire to what extent do the possible outcomes reflect divergent value systems that "need to be reconciled or compromised and to what extent do they represent simply different frames of reference for compatible goals" (Proposal for a Research and Development Center, 1965).

Incidentally, the particular teaching methods chosen for an instructional program should also be evaluated for their compatibility with multiple goals and values. Even though two goals are reasonably compatible, the method of instruction may foster one aim and hinder the other. Wallach, for example, is concerned that modern methods of teaching, especially those using programmed materials and teaching machines, so emphasize accuracy of responding that the student is likely to acquire a generalized intolerance of error and consequent decline in his originality of thinking. Some other method or combination of methods might be used to develop facility in the analysis of logical implications without diminishing fluency in the generation of conceptual possibilities (Wallach, 1967, pp. 36-57).

Since educational values derive from broader systems of social values, it is appropriate to evaluate goals and criteria for instruction not only in terms of specific educational implications but also in terms of more general social implications. The suggestion that cognitive styles and affective reactions be used as criterion variables in the evaluation of instruction, for example, should be upheld in precisely such terms, but a consideration of the educational and social implications of these dimensions must await a more detailed discussion of the nature of the variables themselves.

Cognition, Affect, and Personality

In recent years we have seen the isolation of several dimensions of individual differences in the performance of cognitive tasks that appear to reflect consistencies in the manner or form of cognition, as distinct from the content of cognition or the level of skill displayed in the cognitive performance (Thurstone, 1944; Witkin et al., 1954; Witkin et al., 1962; Gardner et al., 1959; Gardner et al., 1960). These dimensions have been conceptualized as *cognitive styles,* which represent a person's typical modes of perceiving, remembering, thinking, and problem solving. Some examples of these dimensions are:

1. *Field independence versus field dependence*–"an analytical, in contrast to a global, way of perceiving (which) entails a tendency to experience items as discrete from their backgrounds and reflects ability to overcome the influence of an embedding context" (Witkin et al., 1962).

2. *Scanning*–a dimension of individual differences in the extensiveness and

intensity of attention deployment, leading to individual variations in vividness of experience and the span of awareness (Holzman, 1966; Schlesinger, 1954; Gardner & Long, 1962).

3. *Breadth of categorizing*—consistent preferences for broad inclusiveness, as opposed to narrow exclusiveness, in establishing the acceptable range for specified categories (Pettigrew, 1958; Bruner & Tajfel, 1961; Kogan & Wallach, 1964).

4. *Conceptualizing styles*—individual differences in the tendency to categorize perceived similarities and differences among stimuli in terms of many differentiated concepts, which is a dimension called *conceptual differentiation* (Gardner & Schoen, 1962; Messick & Kogan, 1963), as well as consistencies in the utilization of particular conceptualizing approaches as bases for forming concepts—such as the routine use in concept-formation of thematic or functional relations among stimuli as opposed to the analysis of descriptive attributes or the inference of class membership (Kagan, Moss, & Sigel, 1960; Kagan et al., 1963).

5. *Cognitive complexity versus simplicity*—individual differences in the tendency to construe the world, and particularly the world of social behavior, in a multidimensional and discriminating way (Kelly, 1955; Bieri, 1961; Bieri et al., 1966; Scott, 1963; Harvey, Hunt, & Schroder, 1961).

6. *Reflectiveness versus impulsivity*—individual consistencies in the speed with which hypotheses are selected and information processed, with impulsive subjects tending to offer the first answer that occurs to them, even though it is frequently incorrect, and reflective subjects tending to ponder various possibilities before deciding (Kagan et al., 1964; Kagan, 1965).

7. *Leveling versus sharpening*—reliable individual variations in assimilation in memory. Subjects at the leveling extreme tend to blur similar memories and to merge perceived objects or events with similar but not identical events recalled from previous experience. Sharpeners, at the other extreme, are less prone to confuse similar objects and, by contrast, may even judge the present to be less similar to the past than is actually the case (Holzman, 1954; Holzman & Klein, 1954; Gardner et al., 1959).

8. *Constricted versus flexible control*—individual differences in susceptibility to distraction and cognitive interference (Klein, 1954; Gardner et al., 1959).

9. *Tolerance for incongruous or unrealistic experiences*—a dimension of differential willingness to accept perceptions at variance with conventional experience (Klein et al., 1962).

Stylistic consistencies have also been observed in the differential tendencies of individuals to err by omission or by commission on memory tasks (McKenna, 1967). In addition, several dimensions deriving from the work of Thurstone, Cattell, and Guilford, which are usually considered to fall within the purview of intellectual abilities, also reflect such potential exemplars of style or mode of cognition as speed, flexibility, divergence, convergence, and fluency.

Cognitive styles, for the most part, are information-processing habits. They are characteristic modes of operation which, although not necessarily completely independent of content, tend to function across a variety of content areas. Before considering some possible implications of cognitive styles for educational practice, let us discuss one in more detail to illustrate its generality and breadth of operation. For this purpose the dimension of analytic versus global attitude offers the best example, since it has been extensively studied in various forms by H. A. Witkin and others.

Witkin's early work emphasized individual differences in the characteristic ways in which people perceive both the world and themselves. One of the test situations used was a tilted room in which the subject, seated in a tilted chair, must adjust his body to the true upright. Reliable individual differences were found in this ability; that is, some individuals were reliably more susceptible than others to the influence of the surrounding tilted room. In another test, the subject was seated in a completely dark room and confronted with a luminous rod surrounded by a luminous picture frame; his task was to set the rod to the true vertical position while the frame was set aslant. Again, reliable individual differences were found in this ability, and a substantial correlation was noted between the two tests; the subjects who had difficulty withstanding the influence of the surrounding room while adjusting their body to the upright also had difficulty withstanding the influence of the surrounding frame while adjusting the rod to the upright. These individual differences were initially conceptualized in terms of a differential reliance upon visual cues obtained from the external field as opposed to kinesthetic cues obtained from the subject's own body.

This interpretation of field versus body orientation was extended to a more general dimension of perceptual analysis, however, when it was found that subjects who had difficulty overcoming the influence of the tilted room and the tilted frame also had difficulty overcoming the influence of superimposed complex designs when asked to find hidden simple forms in an embedded-figures test. This extended conception of the dimension was now termed "field dependence vs. field independence": The perception of relatively field-dependent subjects is dominated by the overall organization of the field, whereas relatively field-independent subjects readily perceive elements as discrete from their backgrounds. Sex differences have been repeatedly obtained on the measures of this dimension, with females being relatively more field dependent and males relatively more field independent (Witkin et al., 1954).

Since many correlates for these perceptual scores have been subsequently uncovered in several areas of intellectual and personality functioning, field independence versus field dependence is now viewed as the perceptual component of the broader dimension of *articulated versus global cognitive style.* For example, when the possible relation of field independence to intelligence was investigated, substantial correlations were obtained with some subtests of the Wechsler intelligence scales but not with others. The subtests of the Wechsler scales cluster into three major factors—a verbal dimension composed of the Vocabulary, Information, and Comprehension subtests; an attention-concentration dimension composed of the Digit Span, Arithmetic, and Coding subtests; and an analytic dimension, composed of the Block Design, Object Assembly, and Picture Completion subtests. The measures of field independence were found to correlate substantially with the dimension of analytic intelligence but not with the other two. Thus field-independent subjects exhibited a marked advantage on analytical intelligence tasks, but they could not be characterized as being superior in verbal intelligence or, in a meaningful way, as being superior in general intelligence (Goodenough & Karp, 1961; Witkin et al., 1962).

Children with a relatively articulated mode of cognitive functioning have also been found to have relatively articulated body concepts, as inferred from figure drawings; that is, when asked to draw human figures, these children display more realistic body proportions, more details, and more sex and role characteristics than children with a relatively global mode of functioning. Global subjects also tend to lack a developed sense of separate identity, as reflected in their relative reliance upon others for guidance and support, the relative instability of their self-view, their suggestibility and their susceptibility to social influence in forming and maintaining attitudes and judgments (Witkin et al., 1962; Linton & Graham, 1959).

Developmental studies have indicated that mode of cognitive functioning becomes progressively more articulated, and perception more field independent, with age up to late adolescence. At the same time, however, a child's relative level of articulation vis-à-vis his peers is quite stable. From age 10 to 14, the test-retest reliability of the perceptual index score of field independence was .64 for a group of thirty boys and .88 for a group of thirty girls, and from age 14 to 17 it was .87 for the boys and .94 for the girls (Witkin et al., 1962; Witkin et al., 1967).

In an effort to uncover the possible origins of this cognitive style, Witkin and his colleagues studied patterns of maternal child-rearing practices and mother-child relations. On the basis of interview data, the mothers were classified into two groups: those who fostered the child's differentiation from themselves and who helped him develop a sense of separate identity, and those who did not. In general, this classification of the mothers was found to be significantly related to the performance scores of the children, with the children of the mothers judged to have fostered differentiation being more field independent and cognitively articulated (Dyk & Witkin, 1965).

Differences have been noted in the type of defense mechanisms likely to be adopted by subjects at the two extremes of articulated and global cognitive styles when confronted by conflict and stress. Articulated subjects are more likely to utilize specialized defenses, such as intellectualization and isolation, while global subjects are more likely to utilize primitive defenses, such as denial and repression. No general relation has been found, however, between the degree of articulation of the cognitive style and the degree of personal adjustment or psychopathology. Rather, as with the defenses, when psychological disturbances occur, there are differences in the kinds of pathology that are likely to develop at the two extremes of the styles. Psychopathology in articulated persons is more likely to involve problems of overcontrol, overideation, and isolation; in severe pathological states, delusions are more likely to develop. Pathology in global persons, on the other hand, is more likely to involve problems of dependence, with symptoms such as alcoholism, obesity, ulcers, and asthma; in severe states hallucinations are much more likely to develop (Witkin, 1965). Such findings highlight the fact that styles of intellectual and perceptual functioning are part of the total personality and are intimately interwoven with affective, temperamental, and motivational structures. In some cases, for example, "The general style of thinking may be considered a matrix . . . that determines the *shape* or *form* of symptom, defense mechanism, and adaptive trait" (Shapiro, 1965). In other cases the form-determining matrix may not be a mode of cognition but perhaps a type of temperament or character structure or neurosis—the cognitive style would then be more derivative and would reflect but one component of a broader personality structure that permeates several areas of psychological functioning.

Although in most of this discussion one probably gets the impression that articulated, field-independent subjects have the advantage over their field-dependent peers, situations do exist where a more dependent reliance upon the external field, and particularly a reliance upon social stimuli for guidance and support, is profitable in the accrual of incidental information. Field-dependent subjects have been found to be significantly better than field-independent subjects, for example, in their memory for faces and social words, even though, on the other hand, their incidental memory for nonsocial stimuli is not generally superior (Messick & Damarin, 1964; Fitzgibbon et al., 1965). The fact that certain types of problem situations and certain types of subject matter favor field-dependent subjects over field-independent subjects and vice versa (just as other types of problems might favor broad categorizers over narrow categorizers or levelers over sharpeners, and vice versa) is extremely important, since it highlights the relativity of value of the opposing extremes of each cognitive style. Unlike conventional ability dimensions, one end of these stylistic dimensions is not uniformly more adaptive than the other.

The perceptual and intellectual consistencies just discussed have been interpreted in stylistic terms, which implies, for example, that an individual spontaneously and habitually applies his particular degree of analytic or articulated field approach to a wide variety of situations. Even though a relatively global individual may appear typically global in most situations, it is conceivable that when confronted with a situation that patently demands analysis he might be able to analyze with acceptable skill. Yet in the measurement of this cognitive style, it is usually presumed that subjects who characteristically display an analytic approach will in fact perform better on tasks requiring analysis (such as finding a simple figure in a complicated one) than will subjects who characteristically display a more global approach. Accordingly, most measures of analytic attitude are cast in an ability or maximum-performance framework; if a subject does well at the task, he is assumed to have performed more globally (or to be inadequately applying an unfamiliar, atypical analytic approach). In order to buttress the stylistic interpretation, it would be of interest to relate such maximum performance scores to measures of the spontaneous tendency to articulate the field in a task that ostensibly does not demand analysis.

In one attempt to develop such a task, subjects were required to learn to identify by name (a nonsense syllable) ten complex visual designs, each consisting of a large dominant figure, composed of elements, against a patterned background. In learning to identify these designs, the subject does not have to articulate the component parts, although the instructions do encourage analysis. The subjects are then told that each design was a member of a family of similar designs and that the names they had learned were family names. They are now presented with variations of the original designs (such as the element alone, the form alone, and the form composed of different elements) and asked to identify them in terms of the appropriate family name. In this strategy of test design, it was assumed that subjects who spontaneously articulated the designs during the learning process would be able to identify more variations than subjects who learned to identify the designs in a more global fashion. The total number of variations correctly identified, however, did not correlate significantly with the embedded-figures test. But this was because individuals differed consistently not only in the degree to which they articulated the original designs but in the type of figural component articulated, and the articulation of only one of these components was associated with embedded-figures performance. A factor analysis of variation scores uncovered two major dimensions representing two distinct modes of stimulus analysis, one emphasizing the articulation of discrete elements and the other of figural forms. A third mode reflecting the utilization of background information was substantially correlated with the other two. A significant relation was obtained between embedded-figures performance and the element articulation factor but not the form articulation factor. Although on the one hand element and form articulation are distinct dimensions of stimulus analysis and exhibit different personality correlates, on the other hand they are significantly correlated with each other and combine, along with the background information factor, to form a second-order dimension (Messick & Fritzky, 1963, pp. 346-370).

These findings underscore the fact that the generality of the articulated versus global cognitive style appears at a higher-order level in the factor-analytic sense. Another illustration of this point occurs in a study that attempted to extend Thurstone's perceptual closure factors into the verbal and semantic domains. Thurstone's factor of flexibility of perceptual closure, which is measured by tests like embedded figures, deals with the ability to break one closure in order to perceive a different one and thereby depends upon the capacity to analyze a highly organized perceptual field. Thurstone's factor of speed and perceptual closure deals with the ability to assemble discrete parts into an integrated, meaningful whole and thereby reflects the capacity to structure a relatively unorganized perceptual field (Thurstone, 1944). The concept of an articulated mode of perception implies facility in both analysis and structuring (Dyk & Witkin, 1965), thereby requiring that the two closure factors be correlated, which usually tends to be the case. When several experimental closure tests were constructed using single words and meaningful discourse as the stimulus fields, factors were also uncovered for both speed and flexibility of verbal closure and for both speed and flexibility of semantic closure, in addition to the two perceptual closure factors. The concept of a general articulated versus global cognitive style requires that all of these closure factors be mutually intercorrelated, which also tends to be the case, although the level of correlation is certainly not uniform. Indeed, some limitation on the generality of the style appeared in a second-order factor analysis, which revealed two relatively independent articulation dimensions, one involving the analysis and structuring of figural materials and the other the analysis and structuring of symbolic materials. In addition, a separate second-order factor of general analytical reasoning was also obtained (Messick & French, 1967).

Studies of other cognitive styles, particularly scanning and breadth of categorizing, have revealed a similar range of involvement in areas of personality and psychopathology. Silverman, for example, found that paranoid schizophrenics exhibited significantly more extensive scanning behavior and utilized significantly narrower categories than nonparanoid schizophrenics (Silverman, 1964). Gardner and Long (1962) reported that extreme scanning was marginally related to ratings of isolation, projection, and generalized delay on the Rorschach. This latter finding that scanning behavior tends to be associated with two different defense mechanisms suggests the possibility that extensive scanning may serve different purposes under different circumstances or, perhaps, that there may be two distinct types of scanning. The association with isolation, which is a preferred defense mechanism of obsessives, suggests that the scanning may occur in the service of information seeking, as reflected in the obsessive's concern with exactness to offset doubt and uncertainty. The association with projection, which is a preferred defense mechanism of paranoids, suggests that the scanning may occur in the service of signal detection, particularly danger-signal detection, as reflected in the paranoid's concern with accuracy to offset suspicion and distrust. Some current research at Educational Testing Service attempts to differentiate empirically between these two possible types of scanning. This is done by use of perceptual search tasks in which the subject is required to locate stimuli (signals) embedded in meaningfully organized visual fields, for example, to locate faces camouflaged in pictorial scenes or four-letter words embedded in sentences. Upon completion of the search task, the stimulus materials are removed, and the subject is then asked specific questions about the content of the scenes or the meaning of the set of sentences. Subjects who incidentally acquire information about the field in the process of scanning can thus be differentiated from those whose concern is apparently limited to detecting the signals.

With this brief characterization of cognitive styles in mind, let us now consider some of their possible implications for educational practice and evaluation. To begin with, cognitive styles, by embracing both perceptual and intellectual domains and by their frequent implication in personality and social functioning, promise to provide a more complete and effective characterization of the student than could be obtained from intellectual tests alone. These stylistic dimensions offer for our appraisal new types of process variables that extend the assessment of mental performance beyond the crystallized notion of achievement levels to a concern with patterns of cognitive functioning. These stylistic characteristics should have relevance, although direct research evidence is admittedly very scanty, not only for the course of individual learning in various subject matter areas, but also for the nature of teacher-pupil interactions and of social behavior in the classroom, the family, and the peer group.

Thus, cognitive styles, by virtue of their widespread operation, appear to be particularly important dimensions to assess in the evaluation of instruction. Yet the very pervasiveness that underscores their importance at the same time interferes with the measurement of other important personal characteristics, such as dimensions of specific aptitude. This is because cognitive styles operate in testing situations as well and frequently interact with test formats and test conditions to influence the examinee's score. Consider, for example, the possibility that the five-alternative multiple-choice form of quantitative aptitude tests may favor subjects who prefer broad categories on category-width measures. Initial, rough approximations to the quantitative items might appropriately be judged by these subjects to be "close enough" to a given alternative, whereas "narrow range" subjects may require more time-consuming exact solutions before answering. Significant correlations between category preferences and quantitative aptitude tests have indeed been found, but the level of the correlation turns out to vary widely as a function of the spacing of alternatives on multiple-choice forms of the quantitative items. Scores for breadth of categorizing were found to be substantially correlated with quantitative aptitude scores derived from a multiple-choice form having widely spaced alternatives, marginally correlated with scores on a free-response quantitative test, and negligibly correlated with scores derived from a narrowly spaced form. This suggests that wide spacing of alternatives enhances, and narrow spacing disrupts, the "approximation" strategy that broad categorizers tend to employ on multiple-choice quantitative tests (Messick & Kogan, 1965). Such findings suggest that we should consider the "fairness" of our aptitude and achievement tests not only for different cultures and different sexes, but for individuals having different stylistic propensities. Thus, it is quite possible that cognitive styles are already being reflected in standard evaluation devices; however, their operation under these circumstances is not being assessed for evaluation purposes but serves to contaminate the interpretation of other measures.

Information about cognitive styles offers several possibilities for instructional practice, but choices among them depend upon the results of much needed empirical research. For example, as soon as we are able to assess the cognitive styles of students, we have the possibility of placing them in classrooms in specified ways, perhaps in homogeneous groupings or in particular mixes or combinations. At this point it is by no means clear that particular placements will foster learning for individuals, just as it is by no means clear that homogeneous ability grouping is uniformly beneficial. Similarly, if we can assess the cognitive styles of students, we can also assess the cognitive styles of teachers and consider the possibility of assigning teachers to students to obtain particular combinations of styles that would optimally foster learning. We could also consider selecting particular teaching methods that would be especially appropriate for certain cognitive styles and certain subject matters. As yet, of course, there is very little research to guide us on these points. But even in considering the possibility of matching the student to the teacher or the teaching method, and remembering that with our present assignment procedures some students are in effect so matched while others are not, we should ponder what the criterion of success in this enterprise should be. Should it be the maximal learning of content skills and information?

Consider a possibility that, in the sciences at least, students with an articulated field approach, and perhaps reflective students as well, might learn better with an inductive or "discovery" method of teaching, since it would probably capitalize upon their propensities for analysis and careful consideration of alternatives. More global and more impulsive students, on the other hand, might learn content information better with a directed method of teaching in which rules and principles are specified rather than induced. Consider the likelihood, however, that in our efforts to optimize the learning of subject matter we may so solidify the global child's cognitive style that he may never learn to discover anything in his entire school career. This possibility suggests that teaching to produce maximal learning of subject matter is not enough. We should also be concerned with the student's manner of thinking. One possibility here is that we should attempt to foster alternative modes of cognition and multiple stylistic approaches to problem solving.

Such a goal will not be easily attained, however, since there are many cognitive and personality dimensions that could interact with properties of teaching methods to produce negligible or adverse results. It makes a difference, for example, when and to whom and to what subject matter an inferential discovery method of teaching is applied. Kagan warns us, as an instance, that "impulsive children are apt to settle on the wrong conclusion in the inferential method and become vulnerable to developing feelings of inadequacy. . . ." Since these impulsively derived hypotheses are apt to be incorrect, the impulsive child encounters a series of humiliating failures and eventually withdraws involvement from school tasks (Kagan, 1967; Kagan et al., 1966).

The success of attempts to develop multiple modes of cognition in the individual will depend to a large extent upon the degree to which cognitive styles are malleable. Cognitive styles, as usually conceived, are habits that are spontaneously applied without conscious choice in a wide variety of situations. The possibility being considered here is that through manipulation of educational experience we might convert cognitive styles into cognitive strategies, by which I mean to imply a conscious choice among alternative modes of perceiving, remembering, thinking, and problem solving as a function of the conditions of particular situations. If the cognitive styles are relatively mutable, such efforts at change and multiple development might be feasible at all levels of the educational sequence. If the cognitive styles, or at least some of them, are relatively immutable, it may be necessary to focus attention on the early years and attempt to foster multiple modes of cognition before particular styles crystallize and become predominant. This latter possibility of predominant cognitive styles may be inevitable, regardless of our educational efforts, but we might at least be able to increase somewhat the power of alternative cognitive modes in the hierarchy, thereby reducing to some extent the preemptiveness of habitual thought. As always, however, we must also consider and evaluate the potential dangers in such an enterprise: our efforts to foster multiple modes of cognition in a child may prevent him from soaring in the unfettered application of his preferred style in a particular field.

I have not discussed affective variables at length because most educators, at least when pressed, affirm the importance of enhancing curiosity and of implanting in the student massive and enduring positive affects toward learning and subject matter. Most of us would agree, therefore, that even when an instructional program does not attempt to enhance positive attitudes directly, these variables should still be monitored if possible in the evaluation of the program to guard against unintended decreases in interest or involvement. In the measurement of these affective reactions, however, it seems to me unfortunate that evaluation studies rely so heavily upon the engineering model, which relates inputs and outputs, for there is a marked tendency to assess student achievement and attitudes only at the beginning and the end of the course. As Scriven has emphasized, the medical model is the appropriate paradigm for educational research (Scriven, 1966, pp. 33-49), and one derivative from that model should be an explicit attempt in evaluating a program to take account of the student's attitudes and feelings about the course of the treatment and not just the end result.

I wish to close by underscoring the importance of affect for learning and hence the importance of assessing affect in the evaluation of instruction. This point has been elegantly summarized by John Barth (1964, p. 17) in his novel, *The Sot-Weed Factor:*

". . . of the three usual motives for learning things—necessity, ambition, and curiosity—simple curiosity was the worthiest of development, it being the "purest" (in that the value of what it drives us to learn is terminal rather than instrumental), the most conducive to exhaustive and continuing rather than cursory or limited study, and the likeliest to render pleasant the labor of learning. . . . This sport of teaching and learning should never become associated with certain hours or particular places, lest student and teacher alike . . . fall into the vulgar habit of turning off their alertness, as it were, except at those times and in those places, and thus make by implication a pernicious distinction between learning and other sorts of natural human behavior."

References

Barth, J. *The sot-weed factor.* New York: Grosset and Dunlap, Inc., 1964.

Bieri, J. Complexity-simplicity as a personality variable and preferential behavior. In D. W. Fiske & S. R. Maddi (Eds.), *Functions of varied experience.* Homewood, Ill.: Dorsey Press, 1961.

Bieri, J., Atkins, A. L., Scott, B., Leaman, R. L., Miller, H., & Tripodi, T. *Clinical and social judgment: The discrimination of behavioral information.* New York: John Wiley & Sons, Inc., 1966.

Bruner, J. S. *Toward a theory of instruction.* Cambridge, Mass.: Harvard University Press, 1966.

Bruner, J. S., & Tajfel, H. Cognitive risk and environmental change. *Journal of Abnormal Psychology,* 1961, 62, 231-241.

Dyer, H. S. The discovery and development of educational goals. *Proceedings of the 1966 Invitational Conference of Testing Problems.* Princeton, N.J.: Educational Testing Service, 1967, 12-24.

Dyk, R. B., & Witkin, H. A. Family experiences related to the development of differentiation in children. *Child Development,* 1965, 36, 21-55.

Fitzgibbons, D., Goldberger, L., & Eagle, M. Field dependence and memory for incidental material. *Perceptual and Motor Skills,* 1965, 21, 743-749.

Gardner, R. W., & Long, R. I. Control, defense, and centration effect: A study of scanning behavior. *British Journal of Psychology,* 1962, 53, 129-140.

Gardner, R. W., & Schoen, R. A. Differentiation and abstraction in concept formation. *Psychological Monographs,* 1962, 76, No. 41.

Gardner, R. W., Jackson, D. N., & Messick, S. Personality organization in cognitive controls and intellectual abilities. *Psychological Issues,* 1960, 2, No. 8.

Gardner, R. W., Holzman, P. S., Klein, G. S., Linton, H. B., & Spence, D. Cognitive control: A study of individual consistencies in cognitive behavior. *Psychological Issues,* 1959, 1, No. 4.

Goodenough, D. R., & Karp, S. A. Field dependence and intellectual functioning. *Journal of Abnormal and Social Psychology,* 1961, 63, 241-246.

Harvey, O. J., Hunt, D. E., & Schroder, H. M. *Conceptual systems and personality organization.* New York: John Wiley & Sons, Inc., 1961.

Holzman, P. S. The relation of assimilation tendencies in visual, auditory, and kinesthetic time-error to cognitive attitudes of leveling and sharpening. *Journal of Personality,* 1954, 22, 375-394.

Holzman, P. S. Scanning: A principle of reality contact. *Perceptual and Motor Skills,* 1966, 23, 835-844.

Holzman, P. S., & Klein, G. S. Cognitive system principles of leveling and sharpening: Individual differences in assimilation effects in visual time-error. *Journal of Psychology,* 1954, 37, 105-122.

Kagan, J. Reflection-impulsivity and reading ability in primary grade children. *Child Development,* 1965, 36, 609-628.

Kagan, J. Personality and the learning process. In J. Kagan (Ed.), *Creativity and Learning.* Boston: Houghton Mifflin Company, 1967, pp. 153-163.

Kagan, J., Moss, H. A., & Sigel, I. E. Conceptual style and the use of affect labels. *Merrill-Palmer Quarterly,* 1960, 6, 261-278.

Kagan, J., Moss, H. A., & Sigel, I. E. Psychological significance of styles of conceptualization. In J. C. Wright & J. Kagan (Eds.), Basic cognitive processes in children. *Monograph of Society for Research in Child Development,* 1963, 28, No. 2, 73-112.

Kagan, J., Pearson, L., & Welch, L. Conceptual impulsivity and inductive reasoning. *Child Development,* 1966, 37, 583-594.

Kagan, J., Rosman, B. L., Day, D., Albert, J., & Phillips, W. Information processing and the child: Significance of analytic and reflective attitudes. *Psychological Monographs,* 1964, 78 (Whole No. 58).

Kelly, G. A. The psychology of personal constructs. Vol. 1. New York: W. W. Norton & Company, Inc., 1955.

Klein, G. S. Need and regulation. In M. R. Jones (Ed.), *Nebraska symposium on motivation.* Lincoln, Neb.: University of Nebraska Press, 1954, pp. 225-274.

Klein, G. S., Gardner, R. W., & Schlesinger, H. J. Tolerance for unrealistic experiences: A study of the generality of a cognitive control. *British Journal of Psychology,* 1962, 53, 41-55.

Kogan, N., & Wallach, M. A. *Risk taking.* New York: Holt, Rinehart and Winston, Inc., 1964.

Linton, H. B., & Graham, E. Personality correlates of persuasibility. In I. L. Janies (Ed.), *Personality and persuasibility.* New Haven, Conn.: Yale University Press, 1959.

McKenna, V. *Stylistic factors in learning and retention.* Princeton, N.J.: Educational Testing Service, Research Bulletin, 1967.

Messick, S. Cognitive interference and flexible control. Princeton, N.J.: Educational Testing Service, Research Bulletin (In preparation).

Messick, S., & Damarin, F. Cognitive styles and memory for faces. *Journal of Abnormal and Social Psychology,* 1964, 69, 313-318.

Messick, S., & French, J. W. Dimensions of closure in cognition and personality. Paper delivered at the American Psychological Association, Washington, D.C., 1967.

Messick, S., & Fritzky, F. J. Dimensions of analytic attitude in cognition and personality. *Journal of Personality,* 1963, 31, 346-370.

Messick, S., & Kogan, N. Category width and quantitative aptitude. *Perceptual and Motor Skills,* 1965, 20, 493-497.

Messick, S., & Kogan, N. Differentiation and compartmentalization in object-sorting measures of categorizing style. *Perceptual and Motor Skills,* 1963, 16, 47-51.

Pettigrew, T. F. The measurement and correlates of category width as a cognitive variable. *Journal of Personality,* 1958, 26, 532-544.

Proposal for a research and development center for measurement in education. Princeton, N.J.: Educational Testing Service, 1965.

Schlesinger, H. J. Cognitive attitudes in relation to susceptibility to interference. *Journal of Personality,* 1954, 22, 354-374.

Scott, W. A. Conceptualizing and measuring structural properties of cognition. In O. J. Harvey (Ed.), *Motivation and social interaction.* New York: The Ronald Press Company, 1963.

Scriven, M. Student values as educational objectives. *Proceedings of the 1965 Invitational Conference on Testing Problems.* Princeton, N.J.: Educational Testing Service, 1966, 33-49.

Scriven, M. The methodology of evaluation. In R. W. Tyler, R. M. Gagné, & M. Scriven (Eds.), *Perspectives of curriculum evaluation,* Skokie, Ill.: Rand McNally and Company, 1967, pp. 39-83.

Shapiro, D. *Neurotic styles.* New York: Basic Books, Inc., 1965.

Silverman, J. Scanning-control mechanism and "cognitive filtering" in paranoid and nonparanoid schizophrenia. *Journal of Consulting Psychology,* 1964, 28, 385-393.

Stake, R. E. The countenance of educational evaluation. *Teachers College Record,* 1967, 68, 523-540.

Thurstone, L. L. A factorial study of perception. *Psychometric Monograph No. 4.* Chicago: University of Chicago Press, 1944.

Wallach, M. A. Creativity and the expression of possibilities. In J. Kagan (Ed.), *Creativity and learning.* Boston: Houghton Mifflin Company, 1967, pp. 36-57.

Witkin, H. A. Psychological differentiation and forms of pathology. *Journal of Abnormal Psychology,* 1965, 70, 317-336.

Witkin, H. A., Goodenough, D. R., & Karp, S. A. Stability of cognitive style from childhood to young adulthood. *Journal of Personality and Social Psychology,* 1967, 7, 291-300.

Witkin, H. A., Dyk, R. B., Faterson, H. F., Goodenough, D. R., & Karp, S. A. *Psychological differentiation.* New York: John Wiley & Sons, Inc., 1962.

Witkin, H. A., Lewis, H. B., Hertzman, M., Machover, K., Meissner, P. B., & Wapner, S. *Personality through perception.* New York: Harper & Row, Publishers, 1954.

The Strategy of Style
Frank Riessman

I would like to discuss a concept which I think has been ignored a good deal in teaching and guidance. It is the concept of style—in particular, the style of learning. I believe a crucial element in the development of the individual's learning relates to a careful understanding of the idiosyncratic style elements in the learning process. Students of learning have focused a good deal on rather abstract, molecular concepts of learning derived from pigeons and rats via B. F. Skinner and Clark L. Hull. I am not suggesting that these concepts of learning are not useful, but I think that we have missed the possible value of a more wholistic (molar) or global dimension of learning, operative at the phenomenal level, which I am referring to as style.

An Illustrative Model
One index of style relates to whether you learn things most easily through reading or through hearing or whether you learn through doing things physically, whether you learn things slowly or quickly, whether you learn things in a one-track way or whether you are very flexible in your learning. These examples are not to be conceived as separate from one another. There can be such combinations as a visual-physical learner who learns in a slow, one-track fashion. As a matter of fact, this last pattern is quite characteristic of the disadvantaged child. He learns more slowly; he learns through the physical (that is, by doing things, touching things); he learns visually, and he functions in a rather one-track way in that he doesn't shift easily and is not highly flexible in his learning. This is, of course, an ideal statement—a model.

Let me cite just a few other dimensions of style so that different aspects of it can be seen. For example, some people like to work under pressure; they like a deadline, and they like tests. (Low-income youngsters do not like such conditions.) Some people like to leave a lot of time for their work, enjoying a slow tempo. Some people like to think or even read while walking. Some people

From *Teachers College Record,* 1964, 65, 484-489. Reprinted by permission of the publisher and author.

like to work in a cold room, some in a warm one. Some people like to work for long periods of time without a break; some people like to shift and take frequent breaks. Some people take a long time to warm up, whereas others get into their work very quickly. Some people like to have all of the facts in front of them before they can do any generalizing, and others prefer to have a few facts. Some people like "props," some people do not.

Typically, people do not know their own style nearly well enough. What I am really concerned about is how one can use this concept to improve one's manner of work—whether it be teaching or guidance, social work or psychiatry. Although I am mainly concerned with working with lower socioeconomic groups, I do not mean to imply that the concept of style must be limited to these social strata.

Cognition vs. Emotion

Guidance workers have focused far too much on the categories of emotion, motivation, and personality rather than on the cognitive categories of learning and thinking. There has been much too much emphasis on the emotional approach in attempting to understand why a child doesn't learn. Little careful analysis is given to how the child's learning might improve simply by concentrating on the way that he works and learns, rather than on his affective reasons for not learning. This thesis is almost directly counter to the current view. Today if a child doesn't learn (and if he has intellectual ability), it is quickly assumed that his difficulties must be due to some emotional block or conflict. I am trying to suggest a different way of looking at the problem. He may not be learning because his methods of learning are not suited to his style, and hence he cannot best utilize his power. I would be willing to argue that even where his troubles are, in part, emotional or due to conflict, it still may be possible to ignore this particular focus and concentrate profitably on the specific expression of the difficulty itself—his learning pattern. Even if one rejects my premise that the emotional causes have been overemphasized, one may still give a willing ear to the possibility of dealing with crucial problems of learning in nonemotional, nonpsychodynamic terms. Unfortunately, teachers too often have behaved like psychologists and social workers. It seems to me that they do not sufficiently stress learning processes and styles of learning, apparently preferring motivational categories. One way to build up appropriate prestige in the teaching profession is *not* simply to borrow from psychologists and sociologists, but to concentrate on the development of what education is most concerned with, learning and teaching. When one does borrow from psychology, it may be better to concentrate on learning and cognition rather than personality and motivation.

Animals and Men

If we examine the outcomes of teacher-education courses in learning, educational psychology, and the like, we typically are forced to the suspicion that they amount to very little. Borrowing heavily from animal learning experiments (which by itself is not necessarily bad), such courses are victimized by the fact that the particular concepts and formulations developed in the animal literature have not been easily applicable to human learning problems—whether a child learns slowly, whether he is a physical learner, or whether it takes him a long time to warm up. Although these problems are nearer to our subjective experience, the psychological literature and animal experiments have not really helped us very much to deal effectively with them. When educational psychology courses have actually studied human learning, the focus has not been on the significant problems that I think are related to style. When they attempt, for example, to deal with study habits, they are entirely too general. There is a great deal more to study habits than meets the eye of the introductory psychology textbook. The typical suggestions in the chapter on study habits are based upon various experiments which seem to indicate that distributive learning is better, that one should survey material first, etc. But very little is directed toward the *idiosyncratic* factors that are involved.

For example, some people simply can't tolerate surveying a chapter first. They become so anxious, so disturbed, by being asked to look at the overall view of the chapter that they can't function. These people want very much to read a chapter atomistically. This is their style. It won't help simply to tell such a person that he is not proceeding in the right way and that he really ought to read the chapter as a whole first. The same is true in terms of the general recommendation that one should have a quiet place to study. Strangely enough, some people study quite well in a noisy place, or with certain kinds of noise, and completely quiet places are not best for them. Some people take a long time to warm up; consequently, a great deal of spacing (or distribution) of learning would not be useful for them. This is their style. But the textbook does not tell you this because, in general, over a large number of cases, spaced learning is best.

The same argument applies to examinations or tests. For some people, a test operates as just the right mild anxiety to stimulate the integration of a great deal of material that needs to be learned. On the other hand, there are large numbers of people for whom tests are terrible because they disorganize them, make them too anxious, and thus prevent them from working. Tests are not conducive to the style of these individuals. When it is argued that tests are educationally undesirable because they produce too much anxiety for learning, the arguments refer to such people. When others argue that tests are marvelous because they aid pupils by providing corrections and criticism, they are referring to persons with a different style. Undoubtedly, tests work happily for some pupils, but there are others who forget their wrong answers on tests because it disturbs them so much to remember them.

As a matter of fact, there is a great deal of controversy in the traditional literature on the very question of whether repression of wrong answers occurs or whether "punishment" for giving the wrong answers on tests helps to produce better recall. I am suggesting that two different kinds of styles are involved here. For some people, the information that they gave wrong answers is extremely useful and challenging. If this information is called to their attention in a definite and stimulating way, it makes the wrong answer the figure in the ground. It draws the incorrect responses productively to their attention. For other people, knowing that they have made a mistake is extremely disturbing, destructive of their morale, and leads to a repressing of this material. Therefore, depending upon one's style and one's way of dealing with these problems, tests may be useful or not useful.

Strategies of Modification

My main task is to try to formulate the possible ways in which the strengths of the individual's style can be utilized and its weaknesses reduced or controlled. At this stage in our discussion, I mean the more fundamental, underlying characteristics—for example, the physical style already discussed. This style is laid down early in life and is not subject to fundamental change, although it is possible to *bend* it and to *develop* it. Another aspect of style may be much more malleable and may be more related to habit or set; that is, it may be a derivative or secondary expression of style.

Let us take as an example, what I call the "games" focus of low-income youngsters. They like to learn things through games rather than through tests. To put something in the forms of games is an excellent transitional technique for winning their interest. But I do not know how basic a habit this is. It may be much more changeable than the underlying physical style. Such questions are obviously open to further investigation and research. I am simply trying to provide a general framework by means of which to deal with the issue. I am not sure which elements are more or less changeable, but I do believe that some are quite unchangeable and quite basic, whereas some are more susceptible to intervention. A person who likes to learn by listening and speaking (aural style) is unlikely to change completely and become, say, a reader. I am not suggesting that such a pupil will not learn to read and write fluently, but his best learning, the long-lasting, deep learning that gets into his muscles, is more likely to derive from speaking and hearing.

Now let me return to the problem I am essentially trying to deal with— the strategy of style, the strategy of producing basic changes in people through understanding and utilizing their styles. I want to develop the idiosyncratic strengths, find ways of employing the unorthodox, the specific, the unique, and in some ways limit the weaknesses in the person's style. Under certain conditions, one can overcome some of the weak elements of the style pattern through compensatory efforts and through special techniques. I think, however, that weaknesses in learning are more likely to be alleviated when they are at the level of sets and habits.

Awareness and Utilization

In approaching our problem, the first aim is to have the person become aware of the strengths and potentials in his style—because this is going to be the source of his power. Thus, if an individual has a physical style, he has to learn the special attributes of this style and how to use them. The guidance counselor or teacher will have to help him overcome the invidious interpretations of this style that are prevalent in our society.

Let us take an illustration of a different type. A youngster tells us that he sits down to work but cannot concentrate. It is extremely important at this point (and this is crucial in the diagnosis of style) to ascertain as precisely as possible exactly what takes place in this youngster's routine. For example, when does he study? What time does he come home from school? What does he do first when he comes into the house? He may say,

"I come home, throw down my books, and then I start to remember that I have to do some work. So I get out my books. I try to work. I take out the book, but my mind wanders. I look at the book; I look away. I can't get into the work, and after a few minutes of trying this, I begin to feel discouraged; I begin to feel bad. I feel I can't work. I'm not interested, I'm no good. I get very worried, panic builds up, and then I run away from the work."

There are many possibilities operating in this pattern. One possibility is that this youngster has a slow period of warm up. He does not easily get into something new; he does not shift from whatever he's been doing before (whether he's been outside playing ball or inside listening to the radio). This may be due to a number of reasons. He may be a physical learner. If one is a physical learner, one generally must be involved physically in the work process. One has to get one's muscles into it, and this takes time. If this is our student's pattern, then he must come to understand that although he is slow to warm up, this is not necessarily a negative quality; it is simply a different way of approaching work.

As a matter of fact, it may very often be connected to perseverance, once he gets involved! Once he is immersed, he may go deeper and deeper and not be able to shift away from the work easily. The inability to shift doesn't then operate as a negative feature but as a positive element in his style. But the youngster I described here rarely gets to this point. It's not that he doesn't persevere somewhere, in baseball or somewhere else. But in his school work, he's never gotten past the point of the slow warm up. In order to use his pattern effectively, he has to schedule work accordingly. He cannot schedule his time so that he works for one hour. That's no good because it takes him a half hour to warm up. Even if he were to be successful and stick with it for the half hour as a result of a teacher's or guidance worker's support and stimulation, the problem would remain at the end of the half hour of only having a short time left to work. Consequently, he has to plan a larger time period of work and recognize in advance that it will take him about a half hour to warm up. In other words, the person who would help him must give him a definition of his work pattern in order to realize the positive potentialities in it.

Strength over Weakness
When this new definition is provided, it is probable that a number of consequences will follow if I'm right about the diagnosis. Over a period of time, the warm-up period will shorten because part of the difficulty in the long warm up is the anxiety that emerges as he tries to get into the work and fails. Thus, by getting into the work, his anxiety decreases, and his interest has a chance, concomitantly, to increase.

Now let us take another example, one in which the person's strengths can be used to deal with his weaknesses. How do you teach a person how to read when reading is not his basic style? Everyone is going to need reading ability and writing ability regardless of his style. In order to teach reading to youngsters for whom it is stylistically uncongenial, one may want to use role-playing, which is more related to the physical style of the individual. He can read about something that he just role-played, or he can read about a trip he has recently taken. While teaching reading under these conditions, the teacher must remember that he is not developing a reading style; he is developing a skill, a *balance* in the pupil's style. He is developing minimal efficiency in an area which is not rooted in the learner's style. In a sense, the teacher is going after his Achilles' heel, his weakness, the reading difficulty, by developing it through his strength, whether it be visual, physical, or whatever. This is a basic tactic for defeating or limiting the weakness by connecting it and subjecting it to the strengths.

Minimal Goals
There are some other things one can do in employing the strategy of style. Various transitional techniques can be used, for example, for overcoming some of a pupil's educational weaknesses. Illustratively, low-income youngsters come to the school situation ordinarily with a very poor auditory set. They're not accustomed to listening to people read stories to them. I suggest that this kind of pattern can be limited quite a bit and can be overcome up to a point. I don't think that the school can develop a basic aural style in such children, but effective teachers can teach them to learn through listening even though this isn't their *best* mode of learning. One of the techniques for doing this was developed by a man who worked with schizophrenic children. The technique was simply to make a game out of the auditory problem. He would say, for example, What is six and five? Everybody in the class would have to answer many different times. The pupil cannot fall asleep in such a class. Answering once doesn't leave him free because he may be asked the same question (or somewhat different ones) often. This is an excellent technique for waking up youngsters, and it has been effective with low-income students who are not used to listening. The objective is to bring them up to minimal listening ability, up to grade level. I want to bring low-income youngsters far beyond grade level in most areas, because I think they have considerable creative ability; but in their areas of weakness, I would be happy to bring them simply up to grade level. In areas of weakness, our primary aim should be functioning on a minimal level of adequacy so that weaknesses will not destroy strengths. Techniques of the kind described may be useful in reversing habits and sets which have grown out of the negative aspects of the person's style.

To sum up: In everybody's style, there are certain strengths, and each of us has his own Achilles' heel. The issue in developing a powerful change in a person is related to how one gets to the Achilles' heel and how one utilizes the strengths. This is the central problem of the strategy of style, especially in its application to the low-income pupils of our urban schools.

Individual Differences in Learning Styles
Adaia Shumsky

Variations in Approach to Learning
Children in a given classroom may vary not only in the things they know and in their capabilities for learning, but also in the ways in which they approach and deal with a given task. These variations are usually a function of the way in which they approach most life situations. The timid child will probably approach a new learning task with greater timidity than the bold, assertive kind of child. The highly intense, energetic child will approach a new learning task with more zest than the child who is usually passive and indifferent.

An attempt will be made in the following pages to describe a number of ways in which children show diversity in their handling of learning tasks in the classroom. The examples are by no means inclusive. Rather, they serve the purpose of demonstrating a way by which teachers may observe children to get further insight into the learning process.

Tempo in Learning
The child's individual rate of learning is often confused with capacity. A child may respond very *slowly* but learn no less than one who reacts and absorbs very quickly. Slow tempo is sometimes associated with cautiousness, sometimes with sluggishness. Rapid reactions may be due to impulsiveness and may be accompanied by either inaccuracies or high quality comprehension. In other words, rate or tempo as such can be highly individualistic or can be associated with a wide range of learning behavior.

In attempting to clarify the role of learning pace in different individuals, the teacher may ask the following questions:

Does the child work slowly, cautiously, and accurately? Or does he work slowly and inaccurately?
Does he work quickly with good quality outcome?
Or does he wish to "get it over with"?
Is he the kind of child who works at a variable pace depending on the nature of the task?

The failure to recognize that children differ in the amounts of time they need to function in the learning process poses a major threat to growth. When we expect all children to complete an assignment or master a task in a given length of time, we not only ignore the fact that people move at different rates, we actually force certain children into adopting undesirable ways of learning.

Johnny, who usually takes long to do a job, is a careful and rather profound thinker. He is not satisfied with one solution but may attempt to look at a problem from more than one point of view. He may find, on second thought, that he

From *In Search of Teaching Style* by Abraham Shumsky. Copyright © 1968. Reprinted by permission of Appleton-Century-Crofts, Educational Division, Meredith Corporation.

needs to qualify, correct, or add to something he had previously thought about. By forcing Johnny into a preset time limit, we may encourage him to take short-cuts and cut corners; thus, we may be encouraging a lower level of operation.

David needs a great deal of time because his responses are deliberate. He will not take a step unless the total plan or concept is conceived. He does not plunge into trial and error. By imposing time pressures on David, we are indeed violating a highly desirable way of thinking. We are encouraging him to be more dependent on guesswork than on reason.

Another child may move slowly because he finds the process of thinking, problem solving, and doing, laborious. This type of child generally stands to gain nothing from speeding up his tempo. Some children need to be prodded to move faster because their attention to meticulous detail is excessive and because they derive little learning benefit from dwelling on insignificant details. Others need prodding because they tend to lose sight of the goal they set out to achieve. They need to be reminded of the goal and the ways to get closer to it.

Some children move so fast they need to be slowed down. They may be satisfied with superficial achievements or they may tend to react impulsively without preplanning.

To enable each child to learn at the pace which would result in optimal learning, flexibility in scheduling, and allowances for individual tempo, variations need to be made in the classroom. This requires flexibility in class organization, curriculum development, and the guidance of the teaching-learning process.

Independence in Work

A teacher may want to know how children differ in their capacity to work independently. Who are the children who can work with a minimum of adult direction and prodding? Who are those who need quite a bit of help at the initial stage of a given assignment or task and can later proceed on their own? The teacher needs to know who are the children who need intermittent help (including those who do not ask for it vocally) and who are those who consistently need assistance.

Being aware of variation in children along this dimension can help a teacher make appropriate decisions in the area of grouping. She needs to know which children can make use of self-directed activity while the teacher is busy working with a small group or with an individual. The teacher has to plan in such a way that she will be able to get to those children who may need more help and direction when the group as a whole is working on a given project or assignment.

In assigning homework the teacher may need to know who may or may not be able to complete the work without her presence, how to vary homework assignments so that the children who are more dependent may not have to resort to excessive parental help or complete helplessness. While the teacher is working along with the present levels of development in her class, and adjusting instruction to the needs of the dependent child, she also has to work with this child toward achieving increasing independence.

If independent learning is a major educational goal, then the *ability to plan* becomes one of the major tools to achieve this goal. As children vary in their capacity to plan, it becomes an important educational responsibility to help them in this direction.

Some children have a good sense of inner organization and can therefore plan better. They may need less direct help in planning. They can also be helpful in working in groups with other children, where they can help others acquire a more adequate capacity to plan. Others may need a great deal of teacher assistance and direction in learning how to distribute time, how to decide what they should do first and what they should postpone.

The teacher may thus find it necessary to identify those children who can plan long-range work with appropriate time distribution and those who leave things to the last moment. She needs to know who are the children who know how to assign priority to different tasks and those who become confused when expected to attend to more than one responsibility at a time.

In trying to help the children who have difficulty with planning, the teacher must remember that while they are being helped to acquire a better sense of organization, the change may not come easily. They will need to have support in organization and timing provided from the outside by teachers, other adults, and even peers.

Attentiveness

Children vary in their attentive capacities. Some can be fully attentive for long periods of time, others for short periods of time. Some are more distractable than others; some show various levels of attention at different times. In order to be aware of individual variations in the capacity to be attentive, a teacher may keep in mind the following questions:

Who are the children persistent in their capacity to attend, and who are the highly distractable children (either by external factors such as noise, or by inner factors such as daydreams)?

Are there children who have adequate attention in nonacademic activities and poor attention in academic work?

Are there children who demonstrate good attention capabilities only in areas of special interest to them?

Information of this nature can help the teacher become aware of the child's contact with her instruction. A teacher may thus know whether she needs to stop at intervals and check whether Johnny is still "with it," see that Pam, who is easily distracted, works in a spot where distraction is kept at a minimum; watch Sandy's tendency to get lost in daydreams and call her back to reality by asking a question and probing her attention to a certain topic.

Awareness of individual variations in attention span can also help the teacher determine the length of assignments she should give to different youngsters in her room. Paul, who has the capacity for a long attention span, may be given a long assignment, while Josh, who tends to be distracted every few minutes, may need an assignment broken down into smaller units.

In conclusion, attentiveness is an important factor in learning, as it affects the child's capacity to attend to what is said in class by either teacher or other students. It also affects his ability to remain attentive to a given task, which he is expected to fulfill independently. The teacher's awareness of variations in attention may help her adjust instruction to the specific attention style of an individual child, and when needed, attempt to help the child gradually change in a more positive direction.

Reactions to New Situations

An important way in which children differ is in their reactions to new situations. A child's characteristic response to newness may affect his initial adjustment to a class at the beginning of each year, may affect a move from one school to another and even from one classroom activity to another. In order to become more keenly aware of the different ways in which children respond to new situations, a teacher may observe the children in her class in view of the following questions:

Does the child tend to accept new situations and new learning as a challenge? Is he slow to warm up only at the very initial stage but usually comes around to handle the task with confidence? Or does he "panic" with the introduction of most new materials and situations?

At the beginning of every new school year Lisa has difficulty in getting to school. She complains about frequent headaches or stomachaches. When Lisa gets to school she enters the classroom shivering and remains very anxious most of the time. She does not seem to make much academic headway because she is too anxious to listen and work. A teacher who does not know that Lisa is having her usual reaction to a new class and a new teacher may label Lisa as "problematic" or "neurotic." The teacher may not know that she can help Lisa by introducing into the new situation as much of the familiar old as she can. She may seat Lisa close to an old friend. She may permit Lisa to begin working on some of the books she had last year. She may find out about a favorite interest Lisa has at home and structure a small group activity around it. She may try to bridge the new experience to the familiar one and thus help Lisa overcome her initial dread of the new classroom.

Burt seems comfortable in new social situations but tends to "freeze" when a completely new subject matter is introduced. His initial reaction to new learning is pessimism and avoidance. Although Burt is a capable youngster he tends to believe he would not get it right. Knowing that Burt tends to react in this manner, the teacher should give him more support during the initial stages of learning new material. She may work with him individually a few times when first introducing long division. This teacher knows that if Burt is helped to face the new concept with less trepidation, he will sail smoothly in a short time.

Teachers are often impressed by the initial enthusiasm of a few children and assume that other children should be equally enthused. If they are not, the teacher takes it to mean that these children are perhaps intellectually less able or even incapable of dealing with the new task. Sensitivity to children's reactions to new situations may often change the teacher's evaluation of the child, may help prevent unnecessary difficulties, and may facilitate learning.

Chapter Eight
Learning Style: Controversy

The articles in this chapter were chosen to elaborate the controversy surrounding the Aptitude-Treatment Interaction (ATI) for the planning and prediction of learning performance. Although this controversy has ideological connotations, it appears that the main issue is methodological for the theorist ("We don't have the statistical techniques and measurement devices to do things this way") and financial for the practitioner ("We can't afford to do things this way").

Cahen's article is a direct commentary on Messick's paper appearing in chapter 7. It provides a rather accurate reading of the majority of the research community and their "wait and see" attitude toward ATI and cognitive styles, at least at the time when Messick's paper was presented in 1967. The reader will note that articles cited in Cahen's article—Witkin, Cronbach, and Kagan—appear later in this book. It may also be of interest for the reader to note that Cahen has authored two articles recently which give a much different impression of the potential of ATI. One of the articles describes techniques, such as the Johnson-Neyman procedure, which surmounts a number of the design problems that have been encountered in research on individual differences. In any case, Cahen's optimism over the future of ATI is evident.

The excerpt from Bracht and Glass provides an excellent description of how ATI is an example of a person-environment interaction. The authors' comments are apt and appropriate, even though their conclusion that ATI is a fruitless effort is a bit pessimistic.

Comments on Professor Messick's Paper
Leonard Cahen

In his paper Samuel Messick covers many important aspects of evaluation, and especially emphasizes cognitive styles and affective reactions as they pertain to instructional research. In addition to the commonly assessed areas of pupil achievement, cognitive styles and affective reactions are suggested as further areas of possible assessment in evaluation studies. Among the major themes of Dr. Messick's paper are the need for assessing multiple dimensions of instructional outcomes, the importance of value judgments in instructional systems and their evaluation, and the role that individual differences in cognitive styles and information processing may play in future instructional research.

The idea of assessing the possible and not just the intended outcomes raises some important issues for the evaluator. At a first glance the term *intended* (the counter term *unintended)* poses a difficulty. It takes a great deal of wisdom on the part of the evaluator to anticipate the unintended outcomes of instruction and to make the necessary plans for their assessment. In one sense the unintended outcomes may be conceived as unsought "side effects." In a hypothetical example a high school district adopted a new tenth-grade science curriculum. The objectives of the curriculum, among others, were to foster scientific thinking and to develop laboratory skills and an understanding of the scope of science. At the end of the year, the pupils performed satisfactorily on tests designed to measure these objectives. A negative "side effect," however, was seen in the fact that only a small proportion of these tenth-grade pupils elected an eleventh-grade science course the following year. The proportion of these students electing the eleventh-grade science course was significantly smaller than the proportion of eleventh-grade students taking science courses over the preceding years.

The curriculum builders and school administrators felt that there was a cause-and-effect relationship in the situation and decided that it was important to learn more about why the students generally failed to elect an eleventh-grade science course. This negative "side effect" or unintended outcome was assessed by student interview.

A second form of the unintended outcome occurs when the curriculum developer explicitly attempts to develop a certain set of behaviors but not other behaviors. For this example let us assume that he is attempting to develop behaviors A, B, and C but not D. In this case the intended outcomes are A, B, and C where D becomes explicitly stated as an unintended outcome. An example might be found in one of the modern mathematics curricula developed in the early 1960's. Behaviors A, B, and C might be represented by three sophisticated mathematics behaviors such as understanding of different number systems, the

From *The Evaluation of Instruction: Issues and Problems* edited by M. C. Wittrock and David E. Wiley. Copyright © 1970 by Holt, Rinehart & Winston, Inc. Reprinted by permission of Holt, Rinehart & Winston, Inc.

development of heuristics in problem solving, and an understanding of mathematical algorithms. Behavior D (the unintended outcome) might be represented by a traditional mathematical skill such as accuracy in routine computations or competence in translating Roman numerals. In the mathematics curriculum, the developer of the instructional program has in part exposed his value system.

The example of the mathematics curriculum represents a common problem that faced evaluators in the 1960's. The problem is manifested in the area of instrumentation where the instructional system or curriculum developer felt that standardized testing instruments failed to measure the dimensions he was interested in—A, B, and C (his intended outcomes)—but measured dimension D (his unintended outcome) with relative precision and validity. The mathematics curriculum suggested has led to considerable debate about the role of comparing outcomes across competing curricula or instructional systems when the competing systems have different intended outcomes.

Michael Scriven (1967) has introduced the terms formative and summative evaluation. Formative evaluation is the gathering of information in the early phases of developing a system of instruction. It is used for immediate feedback in modification of the materials. Summative evaluation provides information to the potential consumers of the instructional product. However, as Scriven has pointed out, the distinction between the two terms is not always clear. If curriculum is to be an ongoing activity, a summative evaluation will serve as a first stage of a formative evaluation for the second wave of innovation. In the example of the mathematics curriculum developed above, the evaluator would be asked to provide information on dimension D as well as dimensions A, B, and C if the evaluation were summative.

The two examples of unintended outcomes are developed to show that an outcome may be an unsought side effect, unplanned by the innovator, or may reflect an a priori value judgment by the innovator to exclude certain dimensions from the instructional system.

Dr. Messick has urged evaluators to include psychological as well as achievement dimensions in the evaluative act. He has proposed that, in addition to assessing the face-value components of achievement, instructional systems must also focus on processes and psychological variables as outcomes.

The issue of value judgments in evaluation cannot be overemphasized. Dr. Messick has pointed out that value judgments are made at many phases in the development and assessment of instructional systems. Judgments determine what the anticipated behavioral outcomes are, how they are to be reached, the components and constructs to be measured, and the selection of instruments or techniques to measure or assess the components and constructs and, at a later stage, are used to reach decisions from the outcome data matrix. Too frequently value judgments, at least explicitly, are faced only at the decision-making stages, if at all.

Scriven (1967) has taken the position that the evaluator must play a key role in the incorporation of value judgments in the evaluative process. This is not an easy task for the curriculum evaluator, and because he may not represent the specific discipline underlying the curriculum innovation he has felt that the judgmental processes must be left to the curriculum innovator who does represent the field. Robert Stake (1967) has hypothesized that the evaluator might have less access to data if he became identified with the judging of an instructional program. Stake also poses the problem involved in judging the merit of a program from multivariate data where some of the outcomes are positive and supportive while other outcomes from the same program may reflect negative findings.

If we are to follow Scriven's suggestion that evaluators play active roles in the establishment and utilization of value judgments, we will probably have to give thought to the future sources of evaluators and careful thought as to their training. In addition, the need for identifying methods to analyze values reflected in a program or instructional system (and across competing instructional systems) will hopefully be given more emphasis in evaluation enterprises of the future.

A proposal is made here that might complement methodologies in evaluating and assessing values in instructional research. The proposal states that outcomes at any stage of instruction can be assessed in terms of how well the instruction has prepared the students for future learning. An assumption is made here that learning is a continuous process and that school curricula will eventually reflect a continuity of experiences rather than inarticulated segments of curricula, that is, elementary school math, junior high school math, and so forth. The success of an instructional program at any level could then be evaluated, in part, in terms of pupils' increased aptitudes for future learning.

I would now like to turn to the problem of utilizing individual difference data as elements in the process of placing groups of students in the most appropriate learning treatment. By most appropriate I mean the assignment of pupils to a learning situation or treatment where the pupil has the highest probability of maximum output or achievement. Dr. Messick has carried his suggestions past the initial stages of evaluation to the stage of implementation.

The model using the interaction of treatment or instruction and selected individual differences of learners has received a great deal of attention recently (Cronbach & Gleser, 1965; and Cronbach, 1966). While there is not always agreement about the results of such an interaction model, the conceptualization does form interesting and explicit hypotheses and requires a major change in the application of quantitative strategies to education. It was not too many years ago that behavioral scientists hoped for nonsignificant statistical interactions in their analysis of factorial designs. Nonsignificant statistical findings at the interaction level allowed them (so they believed) to move on to the clear testing of major effects. Similarly, statistical textbooks frequently emphasized techniques for pooling the lower-order interaction mean squares with the error mean square so that more stable-error terms would be available for testing main effects. This technique of pooling reduced type two errors at the expense of potentially destroying the "nuisance" relationships displayed in interactions.

Dr. Messick has stated that interaction models may be useful in the examination of relationships between teacher and pupil characteristics on cognitive dimensions and in determining how these factors might interact to effect pupil learning. One may also wonder about the possible relationships between different organizations of the teaching act with pupil and teacher characteristics and how these would jointly effect pupil learning. Lastly, one may consider the relationship of individual differences on cognitive dimensions (teacher and pupil) and the structuring of the content of instruction. Might there be ways of organizing and presenting the content of instruction so that it interacts with individual differences of pupils and teachers and teaching methods?

The use of individual difference interaction models will require concentrated efforts by evaluators to develop measures with minimal errors of measurement at the critical positions on the individual-difference scales where decisions are made to assign pupils to learning experiences.

The technique of developing evaluation instruments for reliably measuring individual differences has recently given ground to the development of techniques to assess and evaluate group performance. Evaluation studies will need to determine both the important research questions and what mixture or combination of individual versus group assessments reflect the most appropriate techniques for answering the crucial questions underlying assessment and evaluation of a specific instructional system. The item or matrix sampling model developed by Frederic Lord (Lord & Novick, 1968) is a valuable technique for estimating group performance on many dimensions. Additional sampling combinations of items and subjects (successive matrix samplings) would provide a better estimation of the total covariance structure of the set of behaviors under investigation. However, as Dr. Messick points out, there are limitations and potential dangers in inferring performance of individuals from "averaged" or group assessments. This danger is probably more severe in assessing personality dimensions than in assessing achievement output.

It becomes apparent to the evaluator that there is an almost infinite number of possible dimensions to assess and evaluate. The innovator-evaluator must decide which dimensions have the greatest potential for providing information for himself while also providing multidimensional outcome measures for the potential consumer. Value judgments again must play an important role. Explicit statements from the innovator-evaluator concerning priorities assigned to measures, and facts relating to which evaluative dimensions are not included in the study are crucial.

I would now like to consider a few problems that lie ahead in the utilization of individual difference measures in the cognitive style (nonachievement) areas in curriculum research. The study of individual differences in cognitive styles is in its infancy. Dr. Messick encourages use of longitudinal methods to study the long-term interactions between achievement and such psychological processes as cognitive styles. It would be possible and highly desirable to readminister achievement and cognitive batteries over a long period of time and to study the covariance patterns over time within and between the achievement and cognitive domains. The processes underlying achievement and cognitive functions may both be changing, thus making the analyses themselves and the understanding of the analyses very difficult. Witkin and his colleagues (Witkin, Goodenough, & Karp, 1967) have recently reported longitudinal and cross-sectional data on measures of cognitive style. More research of this nature will be needed if we are to utilize and understand cognitive styles and their potential for curriculum research.

Dr. Messick has called to our attention three other aspects related to the role of cognitive styles and curriculum research. He has told us that school experiences should foster an increase in the repertoire of styles for individuals rather than increase the competencies of an individual on a limited set of styles at the expense of other styles. The latter possibility is an inherent danger in the individual-difference interaction model. It might be possible to structure an educational experience so that groups of students develop or increase their cognitive abilities along one dimension while failing to incorporate other styles into their repertoire. The educator must be very careful in structuring these experiences. If we take the dimension of tempo outlined by Jerome Kagan (1966), analytic versus impulsive styles, it is easy to let the semantics of analytic over impulsive determine what appears to be the obvious treatment—and desirable outcome. We must learn to know under what conditions it is favorable for a specific student to act analytically, under what conditions it is best for him to act impulsively, and then to determine a course of instruction that will foster both. It would also be important to teach the student to decide when one style or the other is more appropriate or beneficial.

Dr. Messick has hypothesized that there may be some very important stages in the development of conceptual or cognitive styles, possibly in the very early years, prior to the organism being exposed to formal education. A great deal of research will undoubtedly be devoted to this area in the future.

My final point concerns the difficulty of administering nonachievement batteries in the evaluation of instructional programs. By nonachievement I refer to measures of personality, cognitive style, attitude, and so forth. The problem of invasion of privacy must be considered. In addition, how do students respond to tests not perceived as achievement measures? Students and school administrators will not see the relevance of nonachievement type tests to the evaluation of instructional outcomes.

We will need to convince ourselves first of the utility of individual differences such as cognitive style for instructional research, and then help the innovator to see the value of including these and other process variables in the instructional "package."

References

Cronbach, L. J. "How Can Instruction Be Adapted to Individual Differences?" In R. M. Gagné (Ed.), *Learning and Individual Differences*. Columbus: Charles E. Merrill Publishing Co., 1966, pp. 23-39.

Cronbach, L. J., and Gleser, G. C. *Psychological Tests and Personnel Decisions*. 2nd ed. Urbana: University of Illinois Press, 1965.

Kagan, J. "Developmental Studies in Reflection and Analysis." In A. H. Kidd and J. L. Rivoire (Eds.), *Perceptual Development in Children*. New York: International Universities Press, Inc., 1966, pp. 487-522.

Lord, F. M., and Novick, M. *Statistical Theories of Mental Test Scores.* Reading,
Mass.: Addison-Wesley Publishing Co., Inc., 1968.

Scriven, M. *The Methodology of Evaluation.* American Educational Research
Association Monograph Series on Curriculum Evaluation, no. 1. Chicago: Rand
McNally & Co., 1967.

Stake, R. E., "The Countenance of Educational Evaluation." *Teachers College
Record,* 1967, 68, 523-540.

Witkin, H. A., Goodenough, D. R., and Karp, S. T. "Stability of Cognitive Style
from Childhood to Young Adulthood." *Journal of Personality and Social
Psychology,* 1967, 7, 291-300.

Interaction of Personological Variables and Treatment
Glenn H. Bracht and Gene V. Glass

Generalization is the ability to make general statements about the effect of some
treatment. Interactions between the treatment variable and characteristics of the
subjects, however, may limit the generality of the inference, depending on the
type of interaction. Lubin (1961) has distinguished between ordinal and disordinal interactions for the purpose of determining whether one treatment can
be prescribed for all subjects in the target population or whether different treatments should be prescribed for subjects who possess different measures of some
personological variable. A statistically significant interaction, such as the one
reported in Table 1, is ordinal when the lines which represent the effect of the
various treatment levels across the levels of the personological variable do not
cross (cf. Figure 1). Although such interactions lend to the meaningfulness of
interpreting the data, they do not limit generalizability, i.e., one treatment can
be prescribed for all levels of the personological variable.

Table 1 Analysis of Variance for a Fixed Model Two-Way Classification (Two Treatment
Groups by Three Levels of Aptitude)

SV	df	MS	F	P
Treatment	1	605	2.09	N.S.
Aptitude	2	920	3.17	$<.05$
Interaction	2	890	3.07	$<.05$
Within	144	290		

From Bracht, Glenn H., and Gene V. Glass, "The External Validity of Experiments."
American Educational Research Journal, November 1968, pp. 444-452. Copyright by
American Educational Research Association, Washington, D.C. Reprinted by permission
of the publisher.

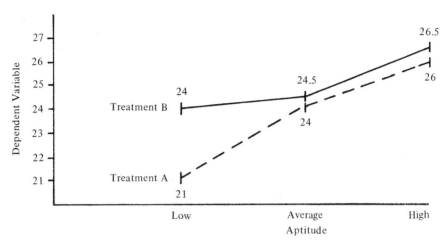

Figure 1   Interaction of Treatments A and B with Three Levels of Ability

When the interaction is statistically significant (cf. Table 2) and the lines cross (cf. Figure 2), further analysis is necessary before it is known if this interaction is ordinal or disordinal, i.e., the crossing of the lines is not sufficient evidence for the existence of a disordinal interaction. There exists an inferential statistical problem for detecting disordinal interactions which Millman (1967) also has discussed. In a two-way fixed model ANOVA design, one tests for the presence of *interaction,* not for *ordinal* interaction *as against disordinal* interaction. The typical *F*-test rejects the null hypothesis of no interaction with high power for either ordinal or disordinal interactions—at the stage of the *F*-test the two types of interaction are not distinguished. Curiously, researchers have divested themselves of their "inferential" scruples and designated a particular significant interaction *disordinal* merely if the lines of the graph cross at any point. The objection we wish to raise against this procedure is apparent in Figure 3. *A statistically significant observed disordinal interaction may be only a chance deviation from an ordinal interaction in the population means.*

What is needed, of course, is a significance test which distinguishes ordinal and disordinal interactions in the population parameters. Such a test is not easily devised, and we can only suggest an imperfect possibility for the 2 × 2 design.

Table 2   Analysis of Variance for a Fixed Model Two-Way Classification (Two Treatment Groups by Three Levels of Aptitude)

SV	df	MS	F	P
Treatment	1	425	1.23	N.S.
Aptitude	2	1215	3.52	<.05
Interaction	2	1325	3.84	<.025
Within	144	345		

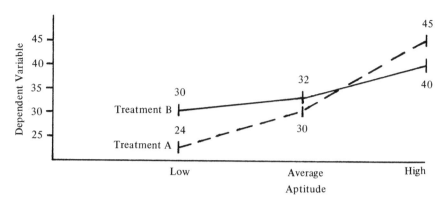

Figure 2 Interaction of Treatments A and B with Three Levels of Ability

Suppose that four population means in a 2 × 2 design are numbered $\mu_1, \ldots, \mu_4$ as in Figure 3. The hypothesis to be tested is that $\mu_1 - \mu_3$ and $\mu_2 - \mu_4$ are both non-zero and differ in algebraic sign. Having observed non-zero differences $\overline{X}_1 - \overline{X}_3$ and $\overline{X}_2 - \overline{X}_4$ which differ in sign (suppose $\overline{X}_1 < \overline{X}_3$ and $\overline{X}_2 > \overline{X}_4$), one could perform individual t-tests of the null hypothesis for the two pairs of means against the alternatives $\mu_1 < \mu_3$ and $\mu_2 > \mu_4$. Assuming these two tests to be independent (which would be only approximately true unless the mean square within was partitioned into two separate parts, one for each test), each directional t-test could be run at a level of significance α_1 which produces the desired level of significance, α, for the pair of tests when substituted into the formula $\alpha = 1 - (1 - \alpha_1)^2$.

To what extent do disordinal interactions (treatments with personological variables) occur in educational settings? Both Cronbach (1966) and Kagan (1966) expressed the belief that the discovery method has more value for some students than for others; some students will perform better with inductive teaching, and some will respond better to didactic teaching. Cronbach (1966, p. 77) contended that generalizations will have to be stated with several qualifications in the form: "With subject matter of this nature, inductive experience of this type, in this amount, produces this pattern of responses, in pupils at this level of development." He also expects discovery to interact more with personality variables than with ability.

Stolurow (1965) also hypothesized the interaction of personological variables with learning strategies and suggested that learning can be optimized by searching out these interactions. He has cited several studies as evidence that such interactions do exist. However, we have reviewed five of these studies (Eigen, 1962; Little, 1934; McNeil, 1962; Reed & Hayman, 1962; and Spence & Taylor, 1951) and found only one (Reed & Hayman, 1962) to contain a statistically significant interaction of treatment with a personological variable. Reed and Hayman found that a high school programed text covering English grammar, punctuation, and capitalization was more effective for high-ability students, but that classroom instruction was better for low-ability students.

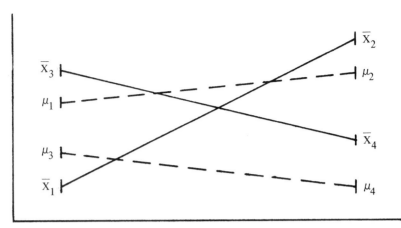

Figure 3 Illustration of an Ordinal Interaction in the Population Means Giving Rise to a Disordinal Interaction in the Sample Means

Unfortunately, Stolurow has interpreted interactions on the basis of a difference in means in the treatment levels and the difference in correlation of the personological variable with the dependent variable in the different treatment groups. This procedure is not legitimate for discovering differentially effective treatments and can lead to a misrepresentation of the data. Treatment groups A and B may differ on dependent variable Y, and the correlation coefficients between Y and a personological variable X may be quite different, though not differing in sign, in groups A and B without there being a disordinal interaction between X and groups A and B.

In his APA presidential address, Cronbach (1957) expressed optimism for discovering interactions between aptitude and treatment. He charged psychologists, both correlational and experimental, to invent constructs and form a network of laws which permits prediction. Interactions between organismic and treatment variables were hypothesized to form a part of this network of laws. Others, including Eckstrand (1962) and Tiedeman and Cogan (1958) feel that research has been devoted primarily to discovering general statements about the teaching-learning process and has failed to account for individual differences in learning. Edwards and Cronbach (1952) have recommended that the most promising organismic variables should be built into the experimental design so that gains can be assessed separately for each variable.

Stern et al. (1956) have suggested an interaction between performance in college and character. It seems likely to them that marked differences between the stereopath and other types of persons would be found in connection with academic performance. They predict that the stereopath will encounter particular difficulties in such areas as the humanities and social sciences where considerable emphasis is placed on abstract analysis, relativity of values and judgment rather than fixed standards, and an intraceptive rather than an impersonal orientation. They also predict that the stereopath is more likely to be found among those entering careers such as law, medicine, business, engineering, etc., and less likely to be among those preparing for academic work or for the expressive arts.

The empirical evidence for disordinal interactions is presently far less convincing than the arguments stated above. Snow et al. (1965) reported that attitude toward instructional films, ascendancy, responsibility, numerical aptitude, verbal aptitude, past experience with entertainment films, and past use of college library instructional films interacted with instructional treatments (film vs. live demonstrations) in a college physics course. Six of these interactions were on an immediate-recall criterion, and the other two were on the delayed recall test. Although the lines crossed for all of these interactions, the authors of this paper have concluded from a further analysis of the data given in the original report (Snow, 1963) that only two of these interactions were disordinal. Our use of one-sided *post hoc* multiple *t*-tests at the 5 percent level of significance to test for differences between the treatment groups at certain levels of the personological variables must be interpreted as very liberal. Thus the probability of the occurrence of these two disordinal interactions is somewhat greater than the obtained level of significance (.05 and .025).

Kress and Gropper (1966) reported a significant disordinal interaction on a retention test (26-27 days after the treatment) of fixed tempo in program instruction and a student's characteristic work rate. When the fixed pace was slow, characteristically slow workers performed better, but when the tempo was fast, the fast workers scored better. The characteristically fast and slow workers were matched on intelligence. It should be noted that the illustration on page 277 of Kress and Gropper's article does not reflect the significant interaction which is shown in their Table 1. The illustration in their Figure 1 is based on two tempos, not four, and on two characteristic work rates, not fourteen. Although a statistical test for the data in Figure 1 was not performed, the authors of this paper feel that, even with a very liberal estimate, a disordinal interaction does not exist.

Hovland et al. (1949) used radio transcriptions to indoctrinate members of the Armed Forces during World War II. One experimental group heard both sides of the argument for some opinion (Program II) while the other experimental group heard only the favorable side of the same opinion (Program I). Program I was more effective for the men who initially favored the opinion, but Program II was more effective for changing the opinion of the men who initially were opposed. Using educational background as a personological variable, they found that Program I was more effective for changing the opinions of the lower educational group (non-high school graduates), but Program II was more effective for the higher educational group (high school graduates). When both initial opinion and educational background were employed as variables in the analysis, the investigators concluded:

"Giving the strong points for the "other side" can make a presentation more effective at getting across its message, at least for the better educated men and for those who are already opposed to the stand taken. This difference in effectiveness, however, may be reversed for the less educated men and, in the extreme case, the material giving both sides may have a negative effect on poorly edu-

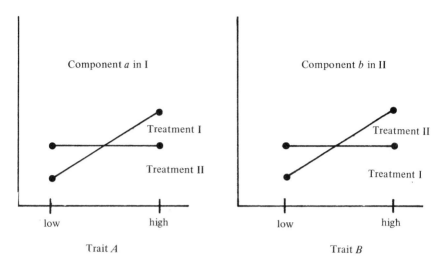

Figure 4   Two Opposing Disordinal Interactions of Traits and Treatment Components Present in the "Same" Personological Variable and Treatments

cated men already convinced of the major position taken by a program. From these results it would be expected that the total effect of either kind of program on the group as a whole would depend on the group's educational composition and on the initial division of opinion in the group. Thus, ascertaining this information about the composition of an audience might be of considerable value in choosing the most effective type of presentation" (p. 215).

Since complete data were not presented, it is not possible to ascertain if these interactions are significantly disordinal.

Cronbach and Gleser (1965) have extended the analysis of the data from Osburn and Melton (1963) to illustrate a disordinal aptitude-treatment interaction. Assuming linear regression and a normal distribution of the personological variable, they estimated the treatment means for various levels of aptitude. The results showed that a modern high school algebra course was superior for students in the upper three fourths of the distribution on *DAT Abstract*, but the traditional course was better for the students in the lower fourth of the distribution. Although a test for the significance of this interaction was not reported, Cronbach and Gleser did conclude that the gain from differential placement would be too small to have much practical value.

Undoubtedly there are other experiments in which disordinal interactions of personological variables with treatment effects have been found, but the authors have no knowledge of them. It is assumed that the frequency of such studies is small. The authors feel that the *molarity* (as opposed to *molecularity*) of both the personological variables and the treatments incorporated into many experiments *may* tend to obscure disordinal interactions which *might* be observable when both the variables and the treatments are more narrowly defined.

Suppose that treatment I contains a component a which facilitates the performance of persons who are high on trait A and interferes with the performance of those low on A. And suppose that treatment II contains a component b which facilitates the performance on persons high on trait B and interferes with the performance of those low on B.

If, in an experimental comparison of treatments I and II, factorially complex measures of the personological variable (containing traits A and B) and the dependent variable are used, the two disordinal interactions in Figure 4 may counterbalance each other and produce no disordinal interaction between the personological variable and treatments I and II. If this supposition is true, one would expect to find personological variable-treatment disordinal interactions more frequently with narrowly defined treatments and variables than in experiments employing broadly defined (complex) variables and treatments, e.g., intelligence and two curricula. Though this observation may suggest where to look for disordinal interactions of personological variables and treatments, it may also suggest that searching for such interactions with treatments as necessarily complex as instructional curricula may be fruitless.

References

Cronbach, L. J. "The Two Disciplines of Scientific Psychology," *The American Psychologist* 12: 671-684; November 1957.

Cronbach, L. J. "The Logic of Experiments on Discovery." In Lee S. Shulman and Evan R. Keislar (Eds.), *Learning by Discovery: A Critical Appraisal.* Chicago: Rand McNally & Company, 1966, pp. 77-92.

Cronbach, L. J., and Gleser, G. C. *Psychological Tests and Personnel Decisions.* Urbana: University of Illinois Press, 1965.

Eckstrand, G. A. "Individuality in the Learning Process: Some Issues and Implications," *The Psychological Record* 12: 405-416; October 1962.

Edwards, A. L., and Cronbach, L. J. "Experimental Design for Research in Psychotherapy," *Journal of Clinical Psychology* 8: 51-59; January 1952.

Eigen, L. D. "A Comparison of Three Modes of Presenting a Programed Instruction Sequence," *The Journal of Educational Research* 55: 453-460; June-July 1962.

Hovland, C. I., Lumsdaine, A. A., and Sheffield, F. D. *Experiments on Mass Communication.* Princeton: Princeton University Press, 1949.

Kagan, J. "Learning, Attention and the Issue of Discovery." In Lee S. Shulman and Evan R. Keislar (Eds.), *Learning by Discovery: A Critical Appraisal.* Chicago: Rand McNally & Company, 1966, pp. 151-161.

Kress, G. C., Jr., and Gropper, G. L. "A Comparison of Two Strategies for Individualizing Fixed-Paced Programed Instruction," *American Educational Research Journal* 3: 273-280; November 1966.

Little, J. K. "Results of Use of Machines for Testing and for Drill upon Learning in Educational Psychology," *The Journal of Experimental Education* 3: 45-49; September 1934.

Lubin, A. "The Interpretation of Significant Interactions," *Educational and Psychological Measurement* 21: 807-817; Winter 1961.

McNeil, J. D. "Programed Instruction as a Research Tool in Reading: An Annotated Case," *The Journal of Programed Instruction* 1: 37-42; 1962.

Millman, J. "Should Differential Treatments Be Used: A Critique of Present Procedures of Analysis and Some Suggested Options." Paper presented at the Annual Meeting of the Educational Research Association of New York State, 1967.

Osburn, H. G., and Melton, R. S. "Prediction of Proficiency in a Modern and Traditional Course in Beginning Algebra," *Educational and Psychological Measurement* 23: 277-287; Summer 1963.

Reed, J. E., and Hayman, J. L., Jr. "An Experiment Involving Use of English 2600, An Automated Instruction Text," *The Journal of Educational Research* 55: 476-484; June-July 1962.

Snow, R. E. *The Importance of Selected Audience and Film Characteristics as Determiners of the Effectiveness of Instructional Films.* Report to the United States Office of Education. Lafayette: Audio Visual Center, Purdue University, 1963.

Snow, R. E., Tiffin, J., and Seibert, W. F. "Individual Differences and Instructional Film Effects," *Journal of Educational Psychology* 56: 315-326; December 1965.

Spence, K. W., and Taylor, J. "Anxiety and Strength of the UCS as Determiners of the Amount of Eyelid Conditioning," *Journal of Experimental Psychology* 42: 183-188; September 1951.

Stern, G. G., Stein, M. I., and Bloom, B. *Methods in Personality Assessment.* Glencoe, Illinois: The Free Press, 1956.

Stolurow, L. M. "Model the Master Teacher or Master the Teaching Model." In John D. Krumboltz (Ed.), *Learning and the Educational Process.* Chicago: Rand McNally & Company, 1965, pp. 223-247.

Tiedeman, D. V., and Cogan, M. "New Horizons in Educational Research," *Phi Delta Kappan* 39: 286-291; March 1958.

Chapter Nine
Learning Style: Learning Style and Learning Performance

The articles in this chapter elaborate on four of the most researched dimensions of cognitive style, and introduce the reader to some of the classic research by the Brooklyn, Menninger, and Fels Institute groups. These four articles will be presented in terms of a simplified version of Woodruff's model—reception, concept-formation and problem-solving, and retention (see chapter 6).

Reception Style. Witkin, Goodenough, and Karp's article presents a resumé of nearly twenty years of research by the Brooklyn group on *psychological differentiation:* the field dependent-independent continuum; the different tests for measuring cognitive style; and some of their notable findings, especially concerning the stability of cognitive styles and their effect on learning performance.

Concept-Formation and Problem-Solving. The article by Bruner, Goodnow, and Austin is excerpted from the classic treatise on thinking by these authors. Bruner contends that after the individual receives information input, he can call on a number of strategies to form concepts. Bruner indicates the advantages and disadvantages of four of these selection or cognitive strategies. The reader should note the similarity between these strategies and Kagan's characterization of impulsivity and reflection.

Kagan's article is representative of the later research efforts of the Fels group. This particular article by Kagan is rather didactic while reporting research data. Kagan provides both a perspective on the dynamics of the reflective-impulsive continuum in terms of the problem-solving process—the reader will note the similarity between Kagan's and Woodruff's models—and the effects of reflectivity-impulsivity on learning performance.

Retention Style. The paper by Holzman and Gardner is indicative of the research interests and methods employed by the Menninger group. Just as the learner has personal or idiosyncratic styles of receiving and analyzing data, so too does he have idiosyncratic ways of retaining it. This is referred to as long-term memory or retention ability and retention style. Individuals who are field-dependent, impulsive, and rather close minded and intolerant of ambiguity will tend to be *levelers;* that is, they tend to blur similar memories and merge perceived objects and events with similar but not identical situations from their past. The obverse is true for the *sharpener,* who tends to be field-independent, reflective, and open minded and tolerant of ambiguity.

A number of tentative conclusions follow from these research efforts. First, all learners do have idiosyncratic ways of perceiving, thinking, and remembering. Second, learning or cognitive style can and does affect learning performance. Third, cognitive style is relatively stable over time. But, fourth, extremes on the continuums of cognitive style moderate with time and can apparently be directly modified, at least to some degree.

The reader will find further research conclusions and educational implications for these and other dimensions of cognitive style in Kogan (1971).

Stability of Cognitive Style
from Childhood to Young Adulthood

Herman A. Witkin, Donald R. Goodenough, and Stephen A. Karp

For a number of years now we have been concerned in our studies with individual consistencies in behavior (Witkin, Dyk, Faterson, Goodenough, & Karp, 1962; Witkin, Lewis, Hertzman, Machover, Meissner, & Wapner, 1954). Starting with observations of individual differences in perception, a variety of other psychological areas was examined for individual differences congruent with those first identified in perception. As the evidence on individual consistencies grew, our concept of them was inevitably modified. With the accumulated evidence now available psychological differentiation has come to serve for us as a construct to conceptualize the particular communality we have observed in a person's functioning in different psychological areas; and we conceive of the individual differences we have found in clusters of interrelated characteristics as differences in extent of psychological differentiation.

Extent of differentiation is reflected in the area of perception in degree of field dependence or independence. In a field-dependent mode of perceiving, perception is dominated by the overall organization of the field; there is relative inability to perceive parts of a field as discrete. This global quality is indicative of limited differentiation. Conversely, a field-independent style of perceiving, in which parts of a field are experienced as discrete from organized background, rather than fused with it, is a relatively differentiated way of functioning. Persons whose field-dependent perception suggests limited differentiation in their experience of the world about them also show limited differentiation in their experience of their bodies. For example, their drawings of the human figure are likely to lack articulation. Further, just as they rely on the surrounding visual

The work described in this paper was supported by a grant (M-628) from the United States Public Health Service, National Institutes of Health. Research Career Development Award MH-K3-16,619, United States Public Health Service, National Institutes of Health, was awarded to the second author.

From *Journal of Personality and Social Psychology*, 1967, 7, 291-300. Reprinted by permission of the American Psychological Association and the authors.

field in their perception of a stimulus object within it, so do they tend to use the social context in which they find themselves for definition of attributes of the self. We have called this a lack of developed sense of separate identity and take it as indicative of a limitedly differentiated self. Finally, persons who perceive in field-dependent fashion are also likely to use such global defenses as repression and denial, suggestive of limited differentiation, whereas field-independent perceivers tend to use specialized defenses, as intellectualization and isolation, suggestive of developed differentiation. Thus, viewed from the standpoint of level of differentiation, people show consistency in their psychological functioning across such diverse areas as perception, body concept, sense of separate identity, and nature of defenses.

The differentiation concept carries a number of implications for problems of development. In this paper we examine two of these implications. One is that during the course of normal development differentiation may be expected to increase with age. The other is that level of differentiation will be relatively stable during development so that the child who at an early age is less differentiated than his peers will tend to occupy a similar position on the differentiation continuum as a young adult as well.

The grounds on which an increase in differentiation with age may be expected are self-evident; and there is already some evidence, now extended in the study to be reported, supporting this expectation. The main ground for predicting relative stability in level of differentiation during development is that formal or structural features of an individual's psychological makeup are likely to show considerable stability over time as compared to content features; differentiation is of course a structural property of a psychological system. Escalona and Heider (1959) have come to a similar conclusion about stability of structural characteristics in their empirical studies of continuity in development. They write:

"Our best predictive successes have occurred in regard to the formal aspects of behavior. With few exceptions we have been better able to forecast *how* a child goes about moving, thinking, speaking, playing, than *what* he is likely to do, think, speak, or play" (p. 73).

Data from several studies with adults have already shown marked stability for several measures of differentiation. In one kind of study attempts were made to alter field dependence experimentally. The methods used have included drugs, such as sodium amytal, dexedrine, chlorpromazine, imiprimine, and alcohol (Franks, 1956; Karp, Witkin, & Goodenough, 1965; Pollack, Kahn, Karp, & Fink, 1960); stress (Kraidman, 1959); training (Witkin, 1948); and electroconvulsive shock (Pollack et al., 1960). The results of the study in which shock was used are particularly striking. Psychiatric patients were tested on the rod-and-frame test prior to shock and again four weeks afterwards. Though on retest they suffered retrograde amnesia for the first test, and so experienced retesting as an entirely new situation, there was no significant change in their rod-and-frame test scores, and the test-retest correlation was very high (.88, $p < .01$). In a more naturalistic study, which examined the effect of important changes in life experiences, Bauman (1951), working with young adults, found no evidence of change in extent of field dependence over a three-year period attributable to marriage, psychotherapy, or psychological trauma (as divorce). Bauman also examined the stability of measures of field dependence and of figure-drawing ratings (reflecting extent of differentiation of body concept). In most cases the test-retest correlations over the three-year period were no lower than test-retest correlations obtained for very short intervals of time, indicating quite striking stability for these measures.

In the studies with adults just reviewed, stability over time was *absolute* in the sense that not only were correlations from test to retest very high, but mean scores were not significantly different. During the growth years, on the other hand, we would expect to find only *relative* stability. Though test-retest correlations for measures of differentiation are again likely to be high, the existence of a general developmental trend toward greater differentiation would make for a change in mean scores. The question of stability during the growth years may be put in this form: How well can we predict a person's adult level of psychological differentiation from the level of differentiation he shows as a child?

In the studies reported here the expectations of increasing differentiation with age and of relative stability have been checked through cross-sectional and longitudinal studies, covering the period from 8 to 24 years of age. Extensive testing has been done in order to examine extent of differentiation in a variety of areas of psychological functioning. This report is limited to the results of perceptual testing, in other words, results on cognitive style. Findings on assessments of differentiation in other areas will be given in later reports.

Of the variety of indicators of psychological differentiation that may be employed in the study of change and stability during development, measures of field dependence are of particular value and have in fact been used most extensively. These measures are not only easily obtained and objective, but the tests from which they are derived can be given in the same form to subjects differing widely in age. The very same tests of field dependence have been used all the way from 8-year-old children to geriatric groups with sufficient variability in performance at each age to permit effective study of individual differences throughout the age range.

For investigations of developmental trends there are obvious methodological advantages in having comparable data from both cross-sectional and longitudinal studies; the data obtained by one method help us deal with problems inherent in the other. In cross-sectional studies there is the inevitable question of comparability of different age samples. This difficulty does not exist in longitudinal studies, of course, where the same sample is used throughout. Accordingly, developmental trends identified in cross-sectional studies may be checked against trends found in longitudinal studies. Longitudinal studies, on the other hand, have their own methodological problems. Chief among these is the confounding effect of repeated measurement on the same individuals, especially when the subject may learn something on one test occasion that may be useful to him on subsequent testing. Cross-sectional studies are free of this difficulty, so that

Table 1 Mean RFT, BAT, and EFT Scores for All Groups

	RFT[a]												BAT				EFT			
	8-13 longitudinal groups[b]				10-24 longitudinal groups				Cross-sectional groups				Cross-sectional groups				Cross-sectional groups			
	M		F		M		F		M		F		M		F		M		F	
Age	M	N	M	N	M	N	M	N	M	N	M	N	M	N	M	N	M	N	M	N
8	17.1	26	20.7	21					17.1	26	21.5	27	17.1	26	15.4	27				
10					14.9	27	16.6	24	14.8	54	17.7	54	13.9	54	14.2	54	137.0	54	156.0	54
11									9.2	21	15.4	24	13.8	21	11.3	24	90.7	21	116.3	24
12									11.2	25	14.1	25	11.3	25	13.0	25	99.1	25	102.0	25
13	10.1	26	13.8	21					7.4	30	10.0	29	10.0	30	8.5	29	57.8	25	78.2	25
14					9.4	27	13.7	24												
15									5.2	25	7.3	25	7.7	25	8.6	25	34.0	25	47.4	25
17									4.5	23	8.6	25	6.0	23	9.4	25	31.2	23	48.1	25
19					7.9	27	12.6	24												
21									7.2	51	12.5	51	8.4	52	10.2	52	39.8	51	57.7	51
24					8.1	27														

[a] RFT and BAT scores are given in mean degrees deviation from upright per trial. EFT scores are given in mean number of seconds to solution per figure. High scores on each test indicate relatively field-dependent performance.
[b] Only subjects tested at all ages are included in the longitudinal data.

to establish the scope of practice effects, longitudinal data may profitably be checked against cross-sectional data.

Subjects and Tests

In the cross-sectional study, the age groups included 8-, 10-, 11-, 12-, 13-, 15-, and 17-year-olds and, in addition, a group of college students (mean age of men, 21.2 years; mean age of women, 19.6 years). Each group consisted of approximately 25 boys and 25 girls, except the 10-year and college groups where the Ns were larger. In the longitudinal study there were two groups: a 10-24-year group and an 8-13-year group. The 10-24-year group consisted of 30 boys and 30 girls when the study began. The girls were seen again at ages 14 and 17, and the boys were seen at both these ages and in addition at age 24.[1] At age 17, 25 of the original group of 30 girls were seen for final testing. At age 24, all but 2 of the original group of 30 boys were seen for final testing. (At age 14, 27 boys and 26 girls were tested and at age 17, 28 boys were tested.) In the 8-13-year longitudinal study there were 26 boys and 27 girls at the outset. Both groups were retested at age 13, at which time 26 boys and 22 girls were seen. The exact number of subjects in each cross-sectional group on each test occasion is given in Table 1.[2]

Every subject in all the groups received the three main tests of perceptual field dependence: the rod-and-frame test, the tilting-room-tilting-chair test, and the embedded-figures test. The subjects in the longitudinal study received, in addition, a number of other tests not considered in this report. These were the Rorschach, the TAT, the figure-drawing test, a miniature-toys-play test (at ages 10 and 14) and the WAIS (at age 17 only); there were also interviews with the children and their mothers. The three perceptual tests used in these studies have been described in detail elsewhere (see Witkin et al., 1962).

In the rod-and-frame test (RFT), the subject is seated in a completely dark-room and adjusts a tilted luminous rod, centered within a tilted luminous frame, to a position he perceives as upright, while the frame remains at its initial position of the tilt. The test consists of three series of eight trials each: In Series 1, body and frame are tilted to opposite sides; in Series 2, body and frame are tilted to the same side; and in Series 3, the body is erect and the frame is tilted. Twenty-eight-degree tilts of the body, frame, and rod are used. The subject's score for each series is the mean degrees absolute deviation of the rod from the true upright.

The tilting-room-tilting-chair test has two parts, the room-adjustment test (RAT) and the body-adjustment test (BAT). In each, the subject sits in a chair,

---

[1] Some of the children were also tested at age 12. Because the sample was very incomplete at that age, with particular attrition at the field-dependent end of the distribution, the results are not included. The fact that some children had this additional testing does not seem to be a problem. As will be seen, the body-erect condition of the rod-and-frame test, the only test of field dependence for which results are considered in the longitudinal study, shows no practice effect.

[2] The 8-year longitudinal groups and the 8-year cross-sectional groups are the same. The 10-year cross-sectional groups include the 10-year longitudinal groups, but have additional cases as well.

which is initially tilted, within a small room, which is also initially tilted. In the eight trials of the room-adjustment test, the room is tilted 56 degrees and the chair 22 degrees, and the subject's task is to adjust the room to the upright while his chair remains tilted. In the six trials of the body-adjustment test, the initial settings of the room and chair are 35 degrees and 22 degrees, respectively; here the subject's task is to make himself straight while the room remains tilted. The subject's score for each of the two tests is again the mean degrees absolute deviation of the item to be adjusted (room or chair) from the true upright when he perceives it as straight.

Finally, in the embedded-figures test (EFT) the subject must locate a previously seen simple geometric figure within a complex figure designed to embed it. The test is composed of 24 pairs of simple and complex figures, and the subject's score for the test is the mean amount of time required to locate each of the simple figures.

As our work developed, and new data accumulated (including data from the present study), it became evident, first, that not all the subtests of this battery of tests provide equally good measures of field dependence, and, second, that some of the tests show practice effects and are therefore not suitable for longitudinal studies which require repeated testing.

Evidence now available from a variety of sources (summarized in Witkin et al., 1962) indicates that the RAT and the two RFT series conducted with body tilted (Series 1 and 2) yield less adequate measures of field dependence. In the RAT, the results of factor analytic studies make it clear that performance is not primarily determined by the field-dependence factor, although the nature of the confounding effect is not yet clear (Goodenough & Karp, 1961; Linton, 1952). In the body-tilted condition of the RFT, performance is partially determined by a tendency to perceive the apparent upright as displaced in the direction opposite to body tilt. This is the E-effect of Müller (1916), which in some subjects is very marked. The presence of individual differences in the E-effect confounds the interpretation of test scores. For these reasons results for the RAT and for RFT Series 1 and 2 are not considered in this paper.

Concerning learning effects, in the EFT knowledge of results is clearly available to the subject during the course of testing; there is accordingly every reason to expect improvement in performance with practice. A clear learning effect has in fact been demonstrated by Witkin et al. (1954) and by Goldstein and Chance (1965). In the present study a comparison between longitudinal and cross-sectional data for subjects of the same age also reveals a learning effect. Subjects in the longitudinal groups who had prior exposure to the EFT tend to do much better than subjects in cross-sectional groups of the same age who were receiving the EFT for the first time. This practice effect limits the usefulness of the EFT for longitudinal studies of development. In the BAT cues as to the location of the upright (and therefore some knowledge of results) may be obtained by the subject as his body is rotated through the objective upright, particularly on trials in which body and field are initially tilted to opposite sides. There is therefore reason to expect a practice effect on this test. Results of past

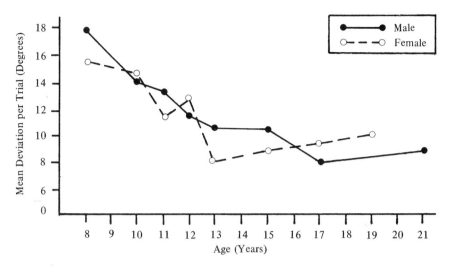

Figure 1   Developmental Curves for Body-Adjustment Test Based on Cross-sectional Data

studies have in fact indicated a practice effect (Witkin et al., 1954). In the present study there was some tendency for longitudinal groups to do better than cross-sectional groups of the same age on the BAT. Although the differences between the two kinds of groups were not as clear-cut for the BAT as for the EFT, the value of the BAT in longitudinal studies is questionable. In the RFT, in contrast to the EFT and BAT, no knowledge of results is available to the subject and evidence from a variety of past studies indicates no learning effect (Witkin, 1948; Witkin et al., 1954). The results of the present study are consistent with the past findings. No learning effect is evident when data from longitudinal and cross-sectional groups of the same age are compared (Table 1).

In view of these findings, for the longitudinal groups data for RFT trials conducted with body erect (Series 3) only will be considered.[3]

Results

The results bear upon three main issues: developmental changes in performance on perceptual tests reflecting extent of differentiation; relative stability of perceptual performance within the context of developmental change; and individual consistency in perceptual functioning at different ages.

Change in Level of Differentiation from Childhood
to Young Adulthood

The data on change in field dependence with age are summarized in Table 1 and Figures 1 through 5. Analyses of variance which bear on the significance of these changes are summarized in Tables 2, 3, and 4.

---

[3] "RFT" will hereafter refer to RFT Series 3.

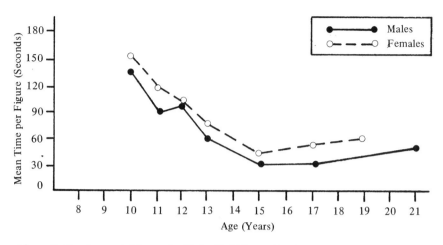

Figure 2   Developmental Curves for Embedded-Figures Test Based on Cross-sectional Data

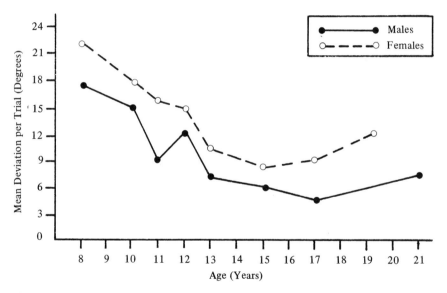

Figure 3   Developmental Curves for Rod-and-Frame Test Based on Cross-sectional Data

In general, a trend toward increasing field independence during development is clearly evident in both the longitudinal and cross-sectional groups. The age effect is significant in both kinds of data (Tables 2 and 3).

Moreover, every single subject in the longitudinal groups went from relatively field-dependent to relatively field-independent performance without significant reversal.

For the most extensively studied longitudinal subjects (males of the 10-24-year group) mean scores on the RFT decline in a regular fashion from 10 to 17

Table 2   Unweighted Means Analysis of Variance[a] for RFT, BAT, and EFT for Cross-sectional Groups

Effect	RFT		BAT		EFT[b]	
	F	df	F	df	F	df
Sex	41.17**	1,499	<1	1,500	13.47**	1,439
Age	30.16**	7,499	15.36**	7,500	44.99**	6,439
Linear trend	154.65**	1,499	91.17**	1,500	230.61**	1,439
Quadratic trend	34.09**	1,499	9.76**	1,500	26.08**	1,439
Higher-order trends	4.48**	5,499	1.32	5,500	3.32**	4,439
Sex X Age	<1	7,499	1.68	7,500	<1	6,439

[a]See Winer (1962, pp. 222-224).
[b]EFT was not given to the 8-year-olds.
**$p < .01$.

Table 3   Analysis of Variance for RFT for Two Longitudinal Groups

Effect	10-17 group[a]		8-13 group	
	F	df	F	df
Sex	4.01	1,49	4.33*	1,45
Age	33.93**	2,98	65.67**	1,45
Sex X Age	2.43	2,98	<1	1,45

[a]In the longitudinal study, started at age 10, boys were followed until age 24 and girls to age 17. To permit a test of sex differences, the data for the 10-17-year period only were considered in this analysis.
*$p < .05$.
**$p < .01$.

years of age and show little change from 17 to 24 years (Table 1 and Figure 4). An analysis of age trends for this group shows significant linear and quadratic components (Table 4). In effect, these significant trend components indicate that there is an overall tendency for children to become less field dependent during development, but the rate of change slows down with increasing age.

The apparent leveling off of the trend toward increasing field independence may indicate that for the average child development of this function is completed by age 17. On the other hand, the leveling off may be an artifact of the RFT test procedure. Specifically, the mean RFT score for the male subjects of the 10-24-year longitudinal group at age 17 is approximately 8 degrees per trial, a value which approaches the minimum possible score of 0 degrees. This may be a limiting factor which in itself produces an apparent leveling off in average scores.

To evaluate this possibility a comparison was made of the seven boys in the 10-24-year group who in their RFT performance at age 10 were most field dependent and the seven who were most field independent. Plots of mean scores at each age for these two groups of subjects are shown in Figure 5. It is evident that the field-dependent group shows at least as much leveling off as the field-independent group, even though the mean scores for the field-dependent group

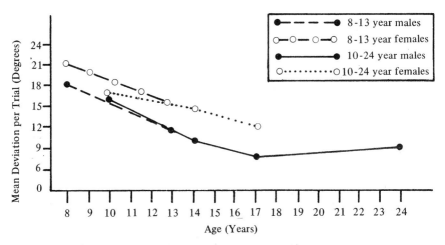

Figure 4   Developmental Curves for Rod-and-Frame Test Based on Longitudinal Data

at the older ages are much farther away from the minimum possible score. These subgroup curves suggest that the leveling off is not entirely a test artifact, but more likely reflects completion of the development process by age 17.

The data for the remaining longitudinal groups and for the cross-sectional groups show similar developmental trends to those just described for the 10-24 male longitudinal group. In the cross-sectional data (Table 1; Figures 1, 2, and 3), although not in the longitudinal data (Table 1, Figure 4), there appears to be a tendency toward a return to more field-dependent performance after age 17, particularly among females. As we will see later, there is reason to believe that this reversal in trend at 17 years in the cross-sectional data is a sampling artifact.

Significant sex differences are found for the RFT and EFT, although not for the BAT, in the cross-sectional data (Table 2). In the data from the longitudinal study the sex difference for the RFT is significant for the 8-13-year group but does not reach significance for the 10-24-year group, although it is in the expected direction (Table 3). The overall tendency for males to be more field independent than females is consistent with the results of many other studies. (See Witkin et al., 1962, for a review of this evidence.)

Table 4   Trend Analysis for RFT for 10-24-Year Longitudinal Males

Effect	F	df
Age	37.09**	3,78
Linear trend	83.52**	1,78
Quadratic trend	26.87**	1,78
Higher order	<1	1,78

**p < .01.

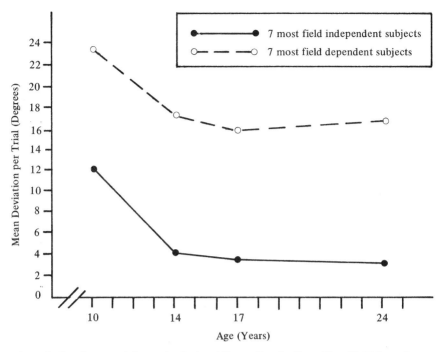

Figure 5   Developmental Curves for Rod-and-Frame Test for Seven Most Field-dependent Males and Seven Most Field-independent Males, at Age 10 in 10-24-year Longitudinal Group

Relative Stability of Level of Differentiation During Development

Evidence on this issue comes from the data on RFT performance of the longitudinal groups, summarized in Table 5. For the 10-24-year groups of males and females test-retest correlations are all significant at better than the .01 level, and range in magnitude from .62 to .92. Even over the longest interval of time for

Table 5   Coefficients of Stability for RFT for Two Longitudinal Groups

Age	Sex	13		14		17		24	
		r	N	r	N	r	N	r.	N
8	M	.76**a	26						
	F	.48*	21						
10	M			.71**	27	.72**	27	.66**	27
	F			.81**	24	.62**	24	—	—
14	M					.92**	27	.84**	27
	F					.76**	24	—	.—
17	M							.90**	27
	F							—	—

aOne-tailed test used.
*p <.05.
**p <.01.

which data are available (from age 10 to 24 for males) the correlation is quite high (.66). For the 8-13-year groups the test-retest correlations are also significant and fairly high.

These findings mean that despite a marked general increase in differentiation in perceptual functioning with age, each individual tends to maintain his relative position among his peers in the distribution of measures of differentiation from age to age. This relative stability is illustrated in the curves for the RFT in Figure 5. In these curves the field-dependent and field-independent groups clearly maintain their positions on the score continuum relative to each other, in the context of a marked decrease in scores for both groups. The evidence thus suggests a high degree of continuity during an individual's development in relative level of differentiation.

Consistency in Perceptual Functioning

The intercorrelations among measures from the various tests of field dependence in the cross-sectional groups at different ages are presented in Table 6. In general, the correlations tend to be in the expected direction (42 of 44 correlations) and significant (33 of 44 correlations). The correlations show no obvious age trend. Individual self-consistency in performance across tests of field dependence is thus evident at all ages examined.

Discussion

The developmental curves derived from both the cross-sectional and longitudinal data show a progressive decrease in field dependence up to age 17. In the period from 17 to young adulthood, however, the longitudinal data show no further

Table 6 Intercorrelations Among RFT, BAT, and EFT Scores for Cross-sectional Groups

Test	Age	BAT				EFT[a]			
		M	N	F	N	M	N	F	N
RFT 3	8	.45*[b]	26	.17	27	—	—	—	—
	10	.42**	54	.40	54	.60**	54	.55**	54
	11	.27	21	.52**	24	.36	21	.60**	24
	12	.26	25	.54**	25	.56**	25	.49**	25
	13	.55**	30	.51**	29	.48**	25	.64**	25
	15	.32	25	.31	25	.56**	25	-.15	25
	17	.29	23	.42*	25	.52**	23	.40*	25
	College	.41**	46	.45**	45	.76**	46	.26*	45
BAT	10					.35**	54	.44**	54
	11					.39*	21	.66**	24
	12					.50**	25	.39*	25
	13					.41**	25	.40*	25
	15					.62**	25	-.18	25
	17					.26	23	.27	25
	College					.54**	46	.58**	45

[a]EFT was not given to 8-year olds.
[b]Correlations are Pearson r's. A 1-tailed test of significance has been used.
*$p < .01$.
**$p < .05$.

change, whereas the cross-sectional data show a clear increase in field dependence. At a time before the longitudinal study had been completed, when we had the cross-sectional data alone, we considered that the rise in the cross-sectional curves after age 17 might signify the beginning of a "return to field dependence." We considered as an alternative possibility that the rise might be the result of a sampling artifact. We looked to the data from the longitudinal study for a choice between these two possibilities. The longitudinal data fail to show a rise and so support the sampling-artifact hypothesis. The manner in which we drew our samples for the cross-sectional study at different ages makes it likely that there was in fact a selection bias in a field-dependent direction in the young-adult sample responsible for the rise. Through age 17, the cross-sectional subjects were drawn from an elementary school and a high school near our laboratory. The young-adult group was drawn from a nearby college. Although a great majority of graduates of primary and secondary schools in this neighborhood do go on to college, some of them go to out-of-town colleges rather than the local college from which our young-adult sample was drawn. Fliegel (1955) has shown that young people who leave home at a relatively early age tend to be more field independent than those who do not, as might be expected from the observation that field-independent persons have a more developed sense of separate identity. The existence in the young-adult college group, as compared to the younger age groups, of a selection bias in the direction of relative field dependence thus seems a reasonable possibility, and would account for the observed rise in the cross-sectional curves after age 17.

Still another possible interpretation of the post-17-year difference between the cross-sectional and longitudinal data is that there is in fact a real tendency for field dependence to increase after age 17, but that this effect is obliterated in the longitudinal data by a counteracting practice effect. This interpretation may clearly be ruled out in view of the absence of a practice effect in the RFT, on which the longitudinal curves are based.

We would conclude from the evidence now on hand that the development of psychological differentiation tends to approach a plateau in young adulthood. This leveling off is clearly evident, as we have seen, when extent of differentiation is assessed in the area of perceptual functioning. It is equally evident in development of differentiation in other psychological areas. Faterson and Witkin, in an unpublished study, have used the figure drawings of the subjects from the longitudinal study to examine differentiation of body concept with age. The body concept of a person may be regarded as differentiated when he experiences it as articulated, that is, when he has a definite sense of parts of the body as discrete yet interrelated and formed into a definite structure. The drawings made by the male subjects of the 10-24-year longitudinal group at all ages were pooled and scored on a 9-point modification of the 5-point sophistication-of-body-concept scale devised in our earlier studies to assess articulation of body concept (Witkin et al., 1962). Placed in Category 1 were highly articulated drawings, that is, drawings showing realistic proportioning, representation of appendages and details in appropriate relation to body outline, and sex differentiation. Drawings placed in Category 9, at the opposite end of the rating scale, showed a low form level (as ovals, rectangles, sticks stuck onto each other), little or no representation of body parts, and an absence of sex identity or role. The developmental curve obtained when mean figure-drawing ratings were plotted against age was identical with the corresponding curve for RFT. Not only was there an increase in differentiation up to age 17, but there was also a leveling off of the curve after that age.

There is clear evidence from studies by Schwartz and Karp (1967), using RFT, BAT, and EFT, and by Comali (1965), using RFT and EFT, that a real "return to field dependence," probably signifying dedifferentiation, does in fact occur, but much later in life. In both studies geriatric groups were found to be extremely field dependent. It seems clear that at some point between 24 years and old age the process of dedifferentiation begins. Results for the intermediate-age-groups studies by Schwartz and Karp and by Comali suggest that this point may be somewhere in the late 30's, on the average, after which the rate of dedifferentiation may accelerate. This conclusion can only be tentative since the number of cases in the intermediate age groups studied was fairly small. Within the general trend toward dedifferentiation at later ages, we may reasonably expect the rate of dedifferentiation to show marked individual differences. Consistent with this expectation Karp, in an unpublished study, found that geriatric subjects who were still actively engaged in regular employment were more field independent than those no longer employed.

The youngest age group in this study was 8 years old. Data on tests of field dependence for younger age groups are, however, available from other studies. Goodenough and Eagle (1963), using a modification of the EFT more appropriate for young children, found a progressive decrease in field dependence in the 5-8-year period. Eagle and Goodenough, in an unpublished study, found the same trend in this age period with children's modifications of the RFT and BAT. Karp and Konstadt (1963) obtained a similar result for the same age period with a slightly different children's modification of the EFT. These observations suggest that 5-year-olds are more field dependent than 8-year-olds. From these earlier findings, taken together with those of the present study, comes the suggestion that the trend toward reduced field dependence is progressive from 5 to 17 years. Caution must however be exercised in simply extending the developmental curves of the present study downward to the 5-year level since the tests used in the 5-8-year period are not identical in format with those used in the present study in the 8-24-year period.[4]

Level of differentiation, as assessed in perceptual functioning, shows high relative stability during the growth years, even over a time span as long as 14 years. This conclusion about stability is strongly supported by the evidence on articulation of body concept. For example, for the 10-24-year longitudinal male

---

[4]The studies by Goodenough and Eagle and by Karp and Konstadt as well as a study by Crudden (1941) suggest that there are no significant sex differences in field dependence in the 5-8-year period. In the geriatric group studied by Schwartz and Karp there were also no sex differences. Thus, the sex differences, found so consistently in older children and adults, appear to be absent in very young children and in the very old.

group, test-retest correlations for figure-drawing sophistication-of-body-concept scores, considered to reflect extent of differentiation in the area of body concept, range from .70 to .92 for the various age comparisons. The correlations between 10-year scores and 24-year scores, involving a 14-year interval, is .81.

In evaluating the high relative stability in level of differentiation we have found, it must be considered that a contributing factor may have been the stability in life circumstances of the particular longitudinal groups we studied. Stability of any psychological characteristic over time—and particularly in the growth years—is likely to depend on stability of the life situation during the period considered. Unstable life situations or important changes in life circumstances may well reduce continuity in relative level of differentiation from one stage of growth to another. The subjects in our longitudinal groups grew up in stable family and overall environmental settings. We do not have the data to say whether or not the high level of stability found in this study would be evident among children from less stable environments. This is an issue for further research.

The 14-year span from age 10 to age 24 covered by our most extended longitudinal study is of course a time of great personal change. This period covers the turbulent events of adolescence, the breaking of close family ties, psychosexual maturation, occupational commitment, and sometimes marriage and the assumption of family responsibility. The psychological impact of all this upon the developing person is of course very great and inevitably contributes to important changes in personal functioning. There is no doubt that many significant psychological changes did take place in our subjects over the 14-year period we studied them. Even with these changes we still find continuity in relative level of differentiation over time.

References

Bauman, G. The stability of the individual's mode of perception and of perception-personality relationships. Unpublished doctoral dissertation, New York University, 1951.

Comali, P. E. Life span developmental studies in perception: Theoretical and methodological issues. Paper presented at 18th annual meeting of the Gerontological Society, Los Angeles, November 13, 1965.

Crudden, C. H. Form abstraction by children. *Journal of Genetic Psychology*, 1941, 58, 113-129.

Escalona, S., & Heider, G. M. *Prediction and outcome.* New York: Basic Books, 1959.

Fliegel, Z. O. Stability and change in perceptual performance of a late adolescent group in relation to personality variables. Unpublished doctoral dissertation, New School for Social Research, 1955.

Franks, C. M. Differences déterminées par le personalité dans la perception visuelle de la verticalité. *Revue de Psychologie Appliquée*, 1956, 6, 235-246.

Goldstein, A. G., & Chance, J. E. Effects of practice on sex-related differences in performance on embedded figures. *Psychonomic Science*, 1965, 3, 361-362.

Goodenough, D. R., & Eagle, C. J. A modification of the embedded-figures test for use with young children. *Journal of Genetic Psychology*, 1963, 103, 67-74.

Goodenough, D. R., & Karp, S. A. Field dependence and intellectual functioning. *Journal of Abnormal and Social Psychology*, 1961, 63, 241-246.

Karp, S. A., & Konstadt, N. Manual for the children's embedded-figures test. Cognitive tests. Brooklyn: Authors, 1963. (P. O. Box 4, Vanderveer Station, 11210)

Karp, S. A., Witkin, H. A., & Goodenough, D. R. Alcoholism and psychological differentiation: The effect of alcohol on field dependence. *Journal of Abnormal Psychology*, 1965, 70, 4, 262-265.

Kraidman, E. Developmental analysis of conceptual and perceptual functioning under stress and nonstress conditions. Unpublished doctoral dissertation, Clark University, 1959.

Linton, H. B. Relations between mode of perception and tendency to conform. Unpublished doctoral dissertation, Yale University, 1952.

Müller, G. E. Uber das Aubertsche Phanoman. *Zeitschrift für Psychologie*, 1916, 49, 109-244.

Pollack, M., Kahn, R. L., Karp, E., & Fink, M. Individual differences in the perception of the upright in hospitalized psychiatric patients. Paper presented at the meeting of the Eastern Psychological Association, New York, 1960.

Schwartz, D. W., & Karp, S. A. Field dependence in a geriatric population. *Perceptual and Motor Skills*, 1967, 24, 495-504.

Winer, B. J. *Statistical principles in experimental design.* New York: McGraw-Hill, 1962.

Witkin, H. A. The effect of training and of structural aids on performance in three tests of space orientation. Technical Report No. 80, 1948, Division of Research, Civil Aeronautic Authority, Washington, D.C.

Witkin, H. A., Dyk, R. B., Faterson, H. F., Goodenough, D. R., & Karp, S. A. *Psychological differentiation.* New York: Wiley, 1962.

Witkin, H. A., Lewis, H. B., Hertzman, M., Machover, K., Meissner, P., & Wapner, S. *Personality through perception.* New York: Harper, 1954.

Selection from *A Study of Thinking*

J. S. Bruner, Jacqueline Goodnow, and G. A. Austin

Ideal Selection Strategies and Their Benefits

We concentrate in this chapter on conjunctive concepts. Let us set before a subject all of the instances representing the various combinations of four attributes, each with three values—specifically, all the instances illustrated in Figure 1—an array of 81 cards, each varying in shape of figure, number of figures, color of figure, and number of borders. We explain to the subject what is meant by a conjunctive concept—a set of the cards that share a certain set of attribute values, such as "all red cards," or "all cards containing red squares and two borders"—and for practice ask the subjects to show us all the exemplars of one sample concept. The subject is then told that we have a concept in mind and that certain cards before him illustrate it, others do not, and that it is his task to determine what this concept is. We will always begin by showing him a card or instance that is illustrative of the concept, a positive instance. His task is to choose cards for testing, one at a time, and after each choice we will tell him whether the card is positive or negative. He may hazard an hypothesis after any choice of a card, but he may not offer more than one hypothesis after any particular choice. If he does not wish to offer an hypothesis, he need not do so. He is asked to arrive at the concept as efficiently as possible. He may select the cards in any order he chooses. That, in essence, is the experimental procedure.

There are four discernible strategies by which a person may proceed in this task. These we label the *simultaneous-scanning strategy,* the *successive-scanning strategy,* the *conservative-focusing strategy,* and the *focus-gambling strategy.* Let us describe each of these briefly and consider the manner in which each bestows upon its users the three benefits mentioned previously.

Simultaneous Scanning

In the present array (Figure 1), composed of instances that may exhibit any of three values of four different attributes, there are 255 possible ways of grouping instances into conjunctive concepts. A first positive card *logically* eliminates 240 of these, and the informational value of any other positive or negative card thereafter presented can similarly be described in terms of the remaining hypotheses that it logically eliminates. Now, simultaneous scanning consists in essence of the person using each instance encountered as an occasion for deducing which hypotheses are tenable and which have been eliminated. This is a highly exacting strategy, for the subject must deal with many independent hypotheses and carry these in memory. Moreover, the deductive process is exacting.

If the subject is able to follow the strategy successfully, his choice of next instances to test will be determined by the objective of eliminating as many

Adapted from Bruner et al.: *A Study of Thinking,* 1956, by permission of John Wiley & Sons, Inc.

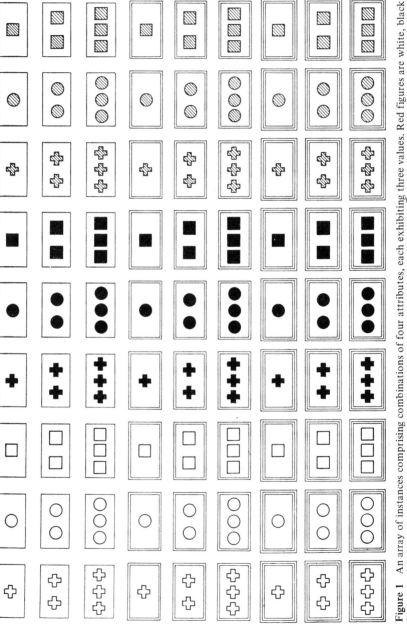

Figure 1   An array of instances comprising combinations of four attributes, each exhibiting three values. Red figures are white, black figures are black, and green figures are shaded. (From Bruner: A STUDY OF THINKING © 1956, John Wiley & Sons, Inc.)

hypothetical concepts as possible per instance chosen. Suppose, for example, that a subject in our experiment has narrowed the possible concepts down to three: the concept must either be all *red* cards, all cards with *circles,* or all cards with *red circles.* Prior choices have eliminated all other hypotheses. Since we are dealing with an ideal strategy here, let us also assume an ideal subject: a subject with perfect rationality and perfect discriminative capacities. Such a subject would certainly know how to avoid choosing redundant instances that eliminated no hypotheses. By choosing a card for testing that contained at least one of the two features, circles or red color, he would guarantee that the next instances encountered contained appropriate information. He would have to decide whether to choose an instance containing *one* of the relevant features or *both* of them: the next instance will contain a circle and no other relevant feature, contain red and no other relevant feature, or it will contain red circles. Consider now the consequences of each of these decisions for each of the three possible concepts, as shown in the table below.

Properties of Instance Chosen for Testing	If Correct Concept Is:		
	Red Only	Circle Only	Red Circle
Red only	Instance positive Eliminates: circle red circle	Instance negative Eliminates: red	Instance negative Eliminates: red
Circle only	Instance negative Eliminates: circle	Instance positive Eliminates: red red circle	Instance negative Eliminates: circle
Red and circle	Instance positive Eliminates: nothing	Instance positive Eliminates: nothing	Instance positive Eliminates: nothing

Such an analysis of the nine possible outcomes should suggest to the subject that his next choice should contain only one of the relevant attributes; at the least, such a choice will eliminate one hypothetical concept, at best two of them. To choose a card containing both relevant attribute values means that no information will be obtained regardless of what the correct concept is.

Now, if the subject can figure out the nine possible outcomes (and has enough time to do so), he will be able to make a wise decision about how next to proceed. The decision is important, for it will determine whether he will be able to solve the problem with one more choice; if these were expensive experiments rather than simple tests of the status of instances, the difference might be critical. But it is quite obvious that most human beings cannot or will not go through such an elaborate analysis of the situation in order to determine their best next step. Indeed, if there had been ten hypotheses still remaining in our example, the paper and pencil work involved in assessing next moves would have been prohibitive. So we can sum up by remarking that while it is possible in principle for the person using simultaneous scanning to plan the best next step, the task of guaranteeing *maximum* informativeness of a next choice is in practice too difficult to accomplish.

With respect to rendering easier the assimilation and retention of information contained in instances encountered, simultaneous scanning has little to recommend it. After each choice the subject must go through the difficult process of deducing which hypothetical concepts have been eliminated and carrying the result of these deductions in memory. There appears to be no means whereby simultaneous scanning can reduce this heavy load on inference and memory.

Nor does simultaneous scanning provide a way of regulating the riskiness of one's next choices—no practical way, at least. We shall leave the matter at that, hoping that it will become much clearer in a later section. The best one can do is to compute the riskiness of a choice by the method just outlined.

Successive Scanning

This strategy consists in testing a single hypothesis at a time. The subject has the hypothesis that *red* is the feature common to all correct cards, and chooses instances containing red in order to test whether they are positive instances. He goes on testing hypotheses until he hits the correct concept. The typical successive scanner then *limits his choices to those instances that provide a direct test of his hypothesis.*

Now it is quite apparent that such a technique for choosing instances cannot assure that the person will encounter instances containing the maximum information possible. That is to say, since instances are chosen only to test one hypothesis at a time, one is likely to choose logically redundant cards some feature of which has been used before to test some previous hypothesis. On this point more will be said later, for it is evident that this is much like discontinuity in learning.

It also follows that the strategy has little worth from the point of view of regulating risk. There is little the user can do either to take bigger gambles or lesser gambles in his choice of instances. His only possible maneuver here is a rather far-fetched one, but one that subjects nonetheless indulge in. This consists really of playing a guessing game with the experimenter in choosing an order of hypotheses to test. For example, subjects will often operate on the assumption that the experimenter is out to "trick" them and that, therefore, the correct concept cannot be a "simple" one, namely, that it will not be a single-attribute concept like "red" or "circles." In consequence, users of successive scanning begin, more frequently than would be expected by chance, by "guessing" that the hypothesis is defined by more than one attribute and choose cards to test such multiattribute hypotheses.

What then is served by the use of successive scanning? The gain is nearly all in the relief of cognitive strain. Limited inference is required and the principal strain on memory is to keep track of what hypotheses have already been tested and found wanting.

A closer examination of the manner in which strain on inference is reduced brings us directly to a most characteristic feature of cognitive activity which we shall encounter on subsequent occasions in analyzing the behavior of subjects in probability situations. It is this. Human subjects—and the same may be true of other species as well—prefer a direct test of any hypothesis they may be working on. To recall the meaning of direct test, a subject is faced with deciding whether a white door or a black door is the correct entrance to a reward chamber and adopts the hypothesis that the white door is correct. There are two ways of testing this hypothesis. The *direct way* is to try the white door. The *indirect way* is to try the black door. In a direct test, as we have noted, the knowledge obtained needs no further transformation for testing the hypothesis. White is either correct or incorrect. The indirect test requires a transformation: if the black door is correct, then the white door was not correct and therefore the hypothesis is wrong; if the black door is wrong then the white door must have been correct and the hypothesis is right. It may be that the reason for the preference for direct test is in the interest of cognitive economy: saving the person from having to transform his knowledge. Another possible explanation, one which does not preclude the first, is that we do not fully accept the possibilities of correctness and incorrectness being mutually exclusive. We have a backlog of experience in which it has not always followed that if white is correct black is wrong or vice versa. We have also experienced situations where more than two alternatives were possible, and only a direct test would be effective.[1]

In any case, when a subject behaves in the typical manner of the successive scanner and limits himself to testing instances directly related to his hypothesis, his behavior appears to follow the principle of direct test. In sum, then, successive scanning has little utility either in guaranteeing maximum informativeness of one's choices or in regulating risk. Its chief benefit is in the reduction of cognitive strain by limiting its user to direct test of hypotheses. As such, its principal utility may be as a procedure that is useful when the cognitive going gets rough or when one has good reason to believe that a particular hypothesis will turn out to be correct.

Conservative Focusing

In brief, this strategy may be described as finding a positive instance to use as a focus, then making a sequence of choices each of which alters but one attribute value of the first focus card and testing to see whether the change yields a positive or a negative instance. Those attribute values of the focus card which, when changed, still yield positive instances are *not* part of the concept. Those attribute values of the focus card that yield negative instances when changed *are* features of the concept. Thus, if the first positive card encountered contains three red circles with two borders (3RO2b), and if the concept is "red circles," the se-

---

[1] It is of interest that the first experiment which drew attention to a preference for direct test—in the form of participant behavior—used a situation where more than two alternatives were possible (E. Heidbreder, "An Experimental Study of Thinking," *Archives of Psychology*, 1924, 11, No. 73).

quence of choices made would be as follows, each choice changing a *single* attribute value of the focus card:

3RO2b (+) focus card*
2RO2b (+) first choice: eliminate "three figures" as a relevant attribute
              value
3GO2b (−) second choice: retain "red" as a relevant attribute value
3R+2b (−) third choice: retain "circle" as a relevant attribute value
3RO1b (+) fourth choice: eliminate "two borders" as a relevant attribute
              value
Ergo: concept is "red circles."

*The symbol (+) denotes a positive instance; (−) a negative instance.

Note one thing. When a subject has changed an attribute value of the focus card and the new card chosen turns out to be positive, this result logically eliminates the attribute in question from consideration. *No* value of such an attribute can be relevant to the concept. The subject need not sample any further values of it.

Several other features of this strategy are especially noteworthy. From the point of view of guaranteeing that each instance encountered be informative, the strategy does just that. By following it, redundancy can be completely avoided. The strategy guarantees, moreover, that each instance encountered will contain a "safe maximum" of information, as we will see when the risk-regulating property of the strategy is examined below.

The benefits in cognitive economy to be gained by using this strategy are striking. The first of these is that by its use the subject is enabled to disregard completely the bewildering business of eliminating possible hypotheses from the domain of 255 possible concepts in terms of which he may group instances. For in fact, the technique is designed to *test the relevance of attributes.* Given an initial positive card, his choices are designed to consider the four attribute values of the focus card one at a time to see which of these may be eliminated. In the present example there are four single attribute values to be considered, much less than the 15 rather complex hypotheses that would have to be considered in simultaneous scanning. A second contribution of this strategy to cognitive economy is that it guarantees that the relevance of all attribute values in the focus card will be *tested relatively directly.* If a change in an attribute value of the focus instance makes a difference, then that attribute value of the focus is relevant; if not, it is irrelevant. A third benefit is more subtle. By choosing a particular positive instance as a focus, the person *decreases the complexity and abstractness of the task* of keeping track of information he has encountered. All subsequent choices and their outcomes can be referred back to this focus instance much as if it were a score card. The attributes of the focus card are ticked off on the basis of subsequent tests.

There is one notable disadvantage to the strategy from the point of view of cognitive economy. Unless the universe of instances to be tested is arrayed in an orderly fashion so that a particular instance may be easily located on demand, the task of search imposed on the user of conservative focusing may become rather severe. We shall see examples of this disadvantage later.

Now for risk regulation. The expression "conservative focusing" has been chosen with good reason. Every choice is safe, safe in the sense that it logically guarantees the presence of information in the instance chosen for testing. This guaranteed information is not the maximum possible. On the other hand, the choice never carries the risk of yielding *no* information. We have already noted that by following the strategy, the subject will never choose a redundant instance, one that carries no new information. To understand fully why it is that a chosen instance almost never contains the maximum amount of information possible, we must turn to a consideration of focus gambling.

Focus Gambling
The principal feature of this strategy is that the subject uses a positive instance as a focus and then changes *more than one* attribute value at a time. In the present array (Figure 1) from which our examples are drawn, the subject might change two or three attribute values at once. This may not seem very different from conservative focusing, but a closer examination will make clear that it is. In particular, several features of focus gambling are of interest from the point of view of the risk-regulating nature of a strategy, and these we shall consider first.

In most tasks involving concept attainment, whether in the laboratory or in everyday life, one objective is to get the job done in as few choices or tests as possible, particularly if choices or tests are costly. It is always possible, given the use of conservative focusing, to complete the job with only as many tests as there are attributes to be tested. Focus gambling provides a way of attaining the concept in *fewer* trials than this limit. But in doing so it also imposes a risk. The risk is this. By using the strategy, one *may* succeed in attaining the concept in fewer test choices than required by conservative focusing. But the strategy also *may* require many more test choices than this. If one is in a position to take such a risk—the risk that solution may be very fast, very slow, or in between—then focus gambling is an admirable procedure. Such a position would be one where, presumably, quick solution paid off very handsomely compared to the losses to be suffered by slow solution.

It can readily be seen how the gambling feature is built into this interesting strategy. Again consider an example. Our subject as before takes as his focus the first positive card given him as an example: three red circles with two borders (3RO2b). Rather than change only *one* attribute value of this focus, he will take a flier and change *three* of them. Let us say then that his next choice is 3G+1b. Now, if the change should "make no difference," i.e., if the instance chosen is still positive, then the concept must be that attribute value shared by the positive focus card and the next card chosen (also positive): namely, "three figures." In one fell swoop, the user of this strategy has eliminated three attributes and attained the concept. Similarly, if two attributes of the focus are changed and a positive instance still results, then the two changed attributes are eliminated. So far, the strategy seems riskless enough.

The difficulty arises when a change in more than one attribute of the focus yields a *negative* instance. For when this happens, the only way in which a person can assimilate the information contained in the instance is to revert to the method of simultaneous scanning: to use the instance as an aid to eliminating possible hypotheses. This has the effect, of course, of diminishing drastically the economical nicety of a focus-gambling strategy. It is now no longer possible to proceed by testing *attributes* for their relevance. Instead, one must deal with *hypothesis elimination* by the method described in connection with simultaneous scanning or throw away the potential information contained in negative instances.

From the point of view of guaranteeing that instances chosen contain new information, focus gambling does not have the feature that makes conservative focusing notable. It does not guarantee that redundant instances will be avoided. For in-so-far as the person using this procedure does not use the information contained in negative instances, he is likely to, and frequently does, choose instances in the course of solution that contain the same information that might have been assimilated from such prior negative instances.

Finally, with respect to making the cognitive task of information assimilation easier, the strategy has most of the features of conservative focusing. One does not have to consider the full array of possible hypothetical concepts (unless one wishes to utilize the information of negative instances). It is geared to the testing of attributes in the focus card rather than to hypothesis elimination in the pure sense. It also provides for direct testing of hypotheses about the relevant attributes. As before, it reduces complexity by the use of a focus instance as a "score card." But it is lacking in economical benefits whenever negative instances occur. The user can do nothing with these unless he shifts strategy. And there is a temptation to do just this. Finally, the strategy also has the fault of requiring a considerable amount of search-behavior if one is to find appropriate instances to test.

Reflection-Impulsivity: The Generality and Dynamics of Conceptual Tempo

Jerome Kagan

The dramatic differences in quality of problem solving among children of the same age or among children of different ages have been attributed primarily to two categories of constructs—motivational variables and/or adequacy of conceptual skills. In effect, differences in quality of cognitive products have been explained by assuming either that one child cared more about his performance, or that one child had more knowledge relevant to the task. However, other cognitive processes are an intimate part of problem-solving activity. One of these processes concerns the degree to which the child reflects over the adequacy of a solution hypothesis.

Some children—and adults—select and report solution hypotheses quickly with minimal consideration for their probable accuracy. Other children, of equal intelligence, take more time to decide about the validity of solutions. The former group has been called impulsive, the latter reflective. The reflection-impulsivity dimension exerts its influence at two places in the problem-solving sequence. A schematic description of the chronology of problem solving includes four phases plus a reporting phase.

Phase 1: Decoding of the problem; comprehension of the problem.

Phase 2: Selection of a likely hypothesis on which to act in order to arrive at solution.

Phase 3: Implementation of the hypothesis (e.g., carry out a relevant arithmetic operation; proliferate a series of synonyms or associates).

Phase 4: Evaluate the validity of the solution arrived at in Phase 3.

Phase 5: Report of solution to an external agent.

The reflection-impulsivity dimension is influential in Phases 2 and 4, the times when the child is selecting a hypothesis to work on mentally or when he is about to report an answer to a teacher, peer, or parent. Previous work has suggested that impulsive selection or reporting of hypotheses is associated with inaccurate performance when adequacy of the child's knowledge repertoire is controlled. Moreover, the tendency to be reflective or impulsive shows intra-individual stability over time and generality across situations involving visual recognition or matching problems (Kagan, in press; Kagan, Rosman, Day, Albert, & Phillips, 1964).

The major purpose of this paper is to explore the relation between the disposition to be reflective or impulsive, and accuracy of performance in a different

This research was supported in part by research grant MH-4464 and MH-8792 from the National Institute of Mental Health, United States Public Health Service. Part of this work was conducted while the author was at the Fels Research Institute.

From *Journal of Abnormal Psychology*, 1966, 71, 17-24. Reprinted by permission of the American Psychological Association and the author.

kind of cognitive task. Specifically, this investigation examines the relation between impulsivity and errors of commission in a series learning task (i.e., reporting words that were never present on the original list). A preliminary study of
third and fourth grade children revealed a positive relation between impulsivity
and errors of commission and this study was a more elegant attempt at replication (Kagan, 1965).

A second purpose of this work is to inquire into the psychodynamics of the
reflection-impulsivity dimension. What are some of the motives, expectancies,
and sources of anxiety that make one child reflective and another impulsive?
The working assumptions are listed below.

Assumption 1. The relation of reflection-impulsivity to quality of performance only obtains for problems that have response uncertainty (i.e., several
response alternatives occur to the child simultaneously, or in close temporal
contiguity, and the child must select the one he judges to be most valid).

Assumption 2. For problems that are difficult and have response uncertainty, the child's tendency to be reflective (i.e., have long decision times) or
impulsive (short decision times) is a function of the balance between the
strengths of the following two standards: produce the answer quickly versus
do not make a mistake. The relation between the positive value of quick success
and the anxiety generated by the possibility of committing an error determines
the child's decision time (i.e., his tendency to be reflective or impulsive).

Assumption 3. If the child's anxiety over a possible error is much stronger
than his desire for quick success, he will be reflective. If his anxiety over committing an error is weak in relation to his desire for quick success, he will be
impulsive.

On the basis of these assumptions it was expected that situations that elicited anticipation of failure would lead to greater anxiety and greater task disrup-
tion in reflective than in impulsive children. Since psychology does not possess
faithful indexes of these two constructs (i.e., desire for success, anxiety over
failure), one possible strategy is to devise experimental interventions that are
expected to elicit these states differentially and examine the differential effect
on children previously classified as impulsive or reflective. The reader should
note that *anxiety over possible failure* is psychologically distinct from *expectation of failure*. A child who has been exposed to chronic failure may enter into
a problem situation with a strong anticipation of failure but minimal anxiety.
Many adolescents who comprise the high school "drop out" group fit this
description. They do not expect to perform with competence yet they appear
to be accepting of this state of affairs. The literature on "fear of failure" has
often failed to distinguish between expectancy of failure and anxiety over
anticipated failure.

The Measurement of Reflection-Impulsivity

Previous research on reflection-impulsivity has used the child's performance
on a visual recognition task (called MFF for Matching Familiar Figures) as the
primary index of the child's position on this dimension. In this test the child

Figure 1   Sample items from Matching Familiar Figures Task (MFF).

is shown a single picture of a familiar object (the standard) and six similar variants, only one of which is identical to the standard. The child is asked to select the one variant that is identical to the standard. Figure 1 illustrates two sample items from the MFF test.

The critical variables scored are response time to the child's first answer and the total number of errors across the 12-item test. Impulsive children in Grades

1-4 have a mean response time between 4 and 10 seconds and make about 15-20 errors. Reflective children have mean response times between 30 and 40 seconds and make between 2 and 6 errors.

In sum, this study tested two hypotheses: (*a*) a positive association between impulsivity on the MFF test and errors of commission on a serial learning task, and (*b*) greater deterioration in serial learning performance for reflective, in contrast to impulsive, children to a communication that suggested the strong possibility of future failure.

Method

Subjects and Procedure
Third-grade subjects (*S*s) (136 boys and 107 girls) from two public schools in neighboring Ohio communities were seen individually for a one-hour session during which the Matching Familiar Figures and WISC vocabulary and informa- tion scales were administered. The *S*s were tested by either a male or female examiner.

Selection of Groups. From this pool of 243 *S*s, smaller groups of reflective or impulsive children were selected. The basis of categorization of an *S* as reflec- tive or impulsive included both response time and errors on the Matching Famil- iar Figures task. The *S*s classified as reflective were above the median of MFF response time and below the median on MFF errors for their sex. Impulsive *S*s were below the median of MFF response time and above the median of MFF errors. The reflective and impulsive *S*s were then assigned to one of three groups —a threat group, a rejection group, and a control group. The reflective and im- pulsive children assigned to these groups were matched on sex and scaled score on the WISC subtests. Thus the mean and range of verbal ability were equal for the reflective and impulsive *S*s across all three experimental groups. Assignment of *S*s in this 2 × 2 × 3 design (12 cells) yielded sample sizes varying from 13 to 24 *S*s in the 12 cells. There were 53 reflective boys and 65 impulsive boys; 45 reflective girls and 40 impulsive girls.

Serial Learning Procedure. Each *S* was seen 3 to 4 months after the initial session by a male experimenter (*E*) for administration of the serial learning task. The detailed procedure follows:

The *E* told the child he was going to test his memory and the child was urged to do as well as he could. The exact instructions were:

"You will hear someone read some words to you on this tape recorder. Try to remember all the words you hear for I will ask you to say the words back to me. The words will be read slowly. Let's listen to a practice list of words."

The *E* allowed the *S* practice with two lists of three and four words each until the *S* understood the nature of the task. The criterion task consisted of four different lists of twelve familiar words each. The lists were recorded at a rate of one word every four seconds using the author's voice. Each *S* was given two trials on each list. The second trial for each list presented the words in an

Table 1 Lists of Words Used in Serial Learning Task

List 1	List 2	List 3	List 4
THUNDER	SHOE	PLATE	CHAIR
DOG	WATER	RIVER	WHEEL
LIGHTNING	COAT	BREAD	COUCH
PENCIL	ROPE	PIPE	BALL
RAIN	SHIRT	SPOON	TABLE
BARN	FLOWER	TREE	FINGER
KNIFE	PANTS	STOVE	BED
STORM	NAIL	CAR	GLUE
LEAF	DRESS	CUP	DESK
WIND	PAPER	DOOR	FIRE
HAMMER	SWEATER	NAPKIN	LAMP
	IRON	SNOW	SOAP

order that was the exact reverse of the first trial. A recall was obtained after each trial, providing two recall scores for each list. Table 1 contains the list of words.

Each of the lists contained six words that belonged to a conceptual category, but each of these conceptually related words was surrounded by a word unrelated to that concept. For example, the List 1 concept included words associated with a "rainstorm" (i.e., thunder, lightning, rain, puddle, storm, wind). The List 2 concept was concerned with "articles of clothing" (i.e., shoe, coat, shirt, pants, dress, sweater). The List 3 concept included words connected with "eating" (i.e., plate, bread, spoon, stove, cup, napkin). The List 4 concept was "furniture" (i.e., chair, couch, table, bed, desk, lamp). The six remaining words in each list were minimally related to each other or to the concept contained in that list.

All Ss were treated alike for the first two lists. The three different experimental treatments occurred following List 2.

The threat group was told:

"O.K., that was fine. These two lists we just finished were really practice lists to give you an idea of what this kind of test is like. The next two lists really count. You will have to do very well on these next two lists. They are hard and children who don't have good memories usually don't do very well, so try and concentrate."

The intent of this communication was to arouse anxiety over possible failure.

The children in the rejection group were told:

"That was poor, you are not remembering enough words. You should do better than that. You should have remembered more words than you did."

The intent of this communication was to arouse anxiety over the examiner's disapproval of the child's performance.

The children in the control group were told:

"O.K., let's take a short rest and then do some more lists."

It is acknowledged that all children may not have reacted to the instructions in the manner hypothesized, for individual differences in response to a communication are always to be expected. However, it is assumed that the majority of Ss in each group experienced thoughts and feelings appropriate to the communication, and that more Ss in the threat and rejection groups experienced anxiety than Ss in the control group.

Following the experimental communication each S was then administered Lists 3 and 4. The major variables scored for both trials of each list were: (*a*) total number of concept words recalled, (*b*) total number of nonconcept words recalled, (*c*) number of intrusion errors, when an intrusion error was defined as the reporting of a word that was not present on the original list read to the child.

Results

Intercorrelation of Recall and Intrusion Scores

Complete intercorrelation matrices were computed for each of the recall and intrusion error scores for the sexes separately and for reflective and impulsive Ss separately for the first two lists, before the experimental interventions.

The relation between recall of concept and nonconcept words (pooling the first two lists) was high for reflective Ss but low for impulsives ($r = .36$ and $.55$ for reflective boys and girls, respectively; $r = .19$ and $.18$ for impulsive boys and girls).[1] Reflective Ss were more consistent in their recall scores for concept and nonconcept words. There was a moderate relation between Lists 1 and 2 for the recall of concept words ($r = .40$, $.24$ for reflective and impulsive boys; $r = .53$ and $.38$ for reflective and impulsive girls). For nonconcept words the corresponding coefficients were $.30$ and $.28$ for boys; $.20$ and $.27$ for girls. There was a low, positive relation between Lists 1 and 2 for intrusion errors ($r = .13$, $.37$ for boys; $.24$ and $.10$ for girls). These correlations were low because the means and standard deviations for intrusion errors were relatively low.

The relationship between recall and intrusion errors was generally negative— the higher the recall score the lower the number of intrusions. The correlations for List 1 were $- .40$ and $- .30$ for reflective and impulsive boys; $.02$ and $.- .37$ for reflective and impulsive girls. For List 2, the corresponding correlation coefficients were $.08$ and $- .40$ for boys and $- .25$ and $.07$ for girls. Thus, the most consistent negative relationships between recall and intrusions for the first two lists held for impulsive boys.

Relation to WISC Scores

The relationship of WISC verbal skills to recall and intrusion scores is of interest. There was no relationship between verbal ability and intrusion errors for either sex or for reflective or impulsive Ss. The coefficients ranged from $- .16$ to $+.12$,

---

[1] The value of r for significance at $.05$ or better (two tailed) is $.27$ for reflective boys, $.24$ for impulsive boys, $.29$ for reflective girls, and $.30$ for impulsive girls.

and none of the coefficients was significant. Thus, as with response time on MFF, an impulsive attitude (in this case measured by intrusion errors) was orthogonal to verbal resources.

Verbal skills were related to recall in a complicated manner. Among boys, there was no relationship to recall of concept related words (r = .10 and .08); but there was a moderately positive relation with recall of nonconcept words (r = .41 for reflective boys and .20 for impulsive boys). Verbal skills facilitated the recall of words having no associative link among them, but had no such facilitating effect on words that were conceptually related to each other. Although this result may appear puzzling, it is not so enigmatic if one views the measure of verbal ability as reflecting, in part, motivation to master intellectual tasks. It is more difficult to recall unrelated words than related words and the greater the motivation to perform well on the learning task the higher this score should be. This increased motivation should also be reflected in higher recall scores for concept words. But the recall score for concept words was considerably higher than that of nonconcept words (a mean of 15 versus 11 for Lists 1 and 2), and it may be that all the children were performing at close to their intellectual capacity for the conceptually related words. As a result, added motivation was less facilitating for these words. It is possible that the brighter boys recalled more nonconcept words because their richer verbal repertoire allowed them to create connections between the unrelated words. However, it is difficult to imagine how a third-grader might quickly connect words like dog-pencil-barn-knife-leaf-hammer as they were being read to him at a relatively fast rate.

Among girls there was no dramatic difference in the association between verbal skills and recall of concept or nonconcept words. The correlations with concept word recall were .59 and .24 for reflective and impulsive girls; the corresponding correlations for nonconcept words were .48 and .47. Thus brighter girls recalled more of both classes of words. This finding is also reflected in the dramatic sex difference in degree of association between verbal skills and total recall for all words for the first two lists. The correlations were high for girls (r = .61 and .46 for reflectives and impulsives), but lower for boys (r = .31 and .18). This type of result is not unusual in our work. It is the rule rather than the exception that verbal ability is typically more highly correlated with a learning or performance measure for girls than it is for boys. Knowledge of a girl's IQ allows one to predict her performance on an intellectual task with greater accuracy than is possible from knowledge of a boy's IQ score. In sum, recall and intrusion scores displayed positive but low generality across the first two lists and recall scores were negatively related to intrusion errors.

The Superiority of Concept Recall
The superior recall of concept over nonconcept words for all Ss for the first pair of lists supports the reasonable assumption that the availability of a mediational link for a group of words facilitates recall of members of the mediationally related class. The differential recall of concept over nonconcept words was assessed for each S for the first and second pairs of lists by subtracting the latter score from the former for each S. The differences for Lists 1 and 2 were dra-

Table 2 Mean Scores on Serial Learning Variables

Variable	Boys						Girls					
	Reflective			Impulsive			Reflective			Impulsive		
	Threat	Reject	Cont.	Threat	Reject	Cont.	Threat	Reject	Cont.	Threat	Reject	Cont.
Concept Recall Lists 1 & 2	15.1	15.8	15.6	14.0	13.6	14.0	15.4	14.8	14.7	13.9	14.4	14.6
Nonconcept Recall Lists 1 & 2	12.8	10.8	12.9	11.0	10.9	11.3	12.2	12.2	11.4	11.2	11.4	11.4
Concept Recall Lists 3 & 4	11.5	12.6	12.6	12.1	13.5	11.1	13.4	13.7	11.2	13.1	13.3	12.3
Nonconcept Recall Lists 3 & 4	11.5	12.2	12.3	10.1	11.8	10.9	12.1	11.9	11.6	10.5	12.4	10.2
Intrusions Lists 1 & 2	1.2	1.1	1.4	1.7	2.0	2.9	1.0	1.2	1.5	1.5	2.1	2.0
Intrusions Lists 3 & 4	5.8	3.2	3.1	4.3	3.9	5.2	3.2	2.3	1.6	3.6	3.3	3.1

matic, for 75 percent of the boys and 80 percent of the girls recalled more concept than nonconcept words ($p < .001$ for each sex). The differences between concept and nonconcept recall were not as dramatic for Lists 3 and 4.

Relationship of Recall and Intrusions
to Reflection-Impulsivity

The mean scores for recall and intrusions for Lists 1 and 2 are presented in Table 2 for each of the 12 groups. The maximal recall score for concept or nonconcept lists for either the first two lists or the second two lists was 24 words.

Analyses of variance were performed for each of the six major variables. In order to expedite these analyses Ss were randomly eliminated from each group containing more than 13 Ss in order to have a constant sample size of 13 for each of the 12 cells. The means and standard deviations for each of the 12 cells were proportional to the parameters derived from the slightly larger samples whose means were presented in Table 2. Summaries of these analyses of variance appear in Table 3.

Recall Data. Reflective Ss recalled more words than the impulsives, especially for Lists 1 and 2. The superior recall of reflective Ss on the first two lists was significant for the nonconcept words ($t = 2.98, p < .01$), and also significant for the nonconcept words ($t = 2.22, p < .05$). The mean recall scores for Lists 3 and 4 were lower for all groups, including the controls. Thus the poorer recall scores on the second pair of lists cannot be attributed to the different experimental communications.

The superior recall of reflective Ss does not appear to be a function of either longer delays before beginning to report words or the character of the initial words reported. There was no significant difference between reflective and impulsive Ss on response latency to begin to report words after termination of the taped list. Moreover, detailed analysis of the first five words recalled by each S did not reveal a greater tendency for reporting concept words by reflective children. The initial five words reported tended to obey the laws of primacy and recency. Thus the superior recall of reflective children seems due to the fact that they persisted longer in their attempt to produce a better cognitive product, suggesting that they were more highly motivated on this task. This suggestion matches other data on reflective and impulsive children which indicate that reflective Ss persist longer with difficult intellectual tasks than their impulsive counterparts with the same verbal ability (Kagan, 1965).

The effect of conditions on recall for Lists 3 and 4 suggested a tendency for the control Ss to have lower recall scores than either the threat or rejection groups. Examination of Table 3 reveals that the "rejection" statement acted as an incentive for most of the Ss.

Intrusion Errors. A major purpose of this study was to replicate an earlier study in which impulsive children produced more intrusion errors than reflectives. These data clearly verified this association for all four lists. The analysis of variance for Lists 1 and 2 revealed a significant F ratio ($F = 7.38, p < .01$) for the reflection-impulsivity dimension, with impulsive Ss producing more

Table 3 Analyses of Variance

Source	df	SS	MS	F	p
Concept words recalled: Lists 1 & 2					
Variable					
Reflection (R-1)	1	73.4	73	7.52	<.01
Sex	1	0.2	0.2		
Error	153	1,485	9.70		
Nonconcept words recalled: Lists 1 & 2					
R-1	1	37.3	37.3	4.78	<.05
S	1	1.2	1.2		
Error	153	1,194	7.8		
Concept words recalled: Lists 3 & 4					
R-1	1	18	18		
S	1	15.4	15.4		
Conditions (C)	2	61.2	30.6	3.03	<.05
R X S	1	5.4	5.4		
R X C	2	6.2	3.1		
C X S	2	17.9	8.9		
R X C X S	2	15.6	7.8		
Error	144	1,459	10.1		
Nonconcept words recalled: Lists 3 & 4					
R	1	45.2	45.2	5.48	<.05
S	1	0.2	0.2		
C	2	57.5	28.7	3.49	<.05
R X S	1	2.1	2.1		
R X C	2	16.7	8.3		
C X S	2	2.6	1.3		
R X S X C	2	0.8	0.4		
Error	144	1,187	8.25		
Intrusion errors: Lists 1 & 2					
R	1	27.1	27.1	7.38	<.01
S	1	2.8	2.8		
Error	153	576	3.7		
Intrusion errors: Lists 3 & 4					
R	1	79.0	79.0	4.97	<.05
S	1	100.1	100.1	6.25	<.05
C	2	9.6	4.8		
R X S	1	8.8	8.8		
R X C	2	80.4	40.2		
C X S	2	18.7	9.4		
R X S X C	2	27.5	14.7		
Error	144	2,290	15.9		

intrusion errors than their reflective counterparts. On Lists 3 and 4, the effect of the reflection-impulsivity dimension was still present ($F = 4.97, p < .05$), and a sex difference occurred, with boys producing more intrusion errors than girls ($F = 6.25, p < .05$). This sex difference is also revealed in the results of an additional analysis. Specifically, the change in intrusion errors from List 2 to List 3 was computed for each S and a constant of 10 added to avoid negative scores. The analysis yielded only one significant F ratio ($p < .01$), with boys displaying larger increases in intrusion errors than girls.

The Effect of Threat on Reflective Ss. There was the suggestion of the predicted association between reflection and the threatening communication when the increase in intrusions from List 2 to List 3 was the score analyzed ($F = 2.56$, $p < .10$ for the interaction between reflection-impulsivity and experimental group). Specifically, reflective children following threat showed the largest increase in intrusion errors, while reflective Ss in the control group produced the smallest increase in intrusions. Moreover, the data in Table 2 reveal that the largest increase in intrusion errors, comparing Lists 3 and 4 with Lists 1 and 2, occurred among reflective boys under threat conditions. These boys showed an increase of 4.6 intrusions, compared with values of 2.1 and 1.7 for reflective boys under rejection and control conditions. A test of the significance of the difference between the threat and rejection groups (4.6 versus 2.1) yielded a t of 1.70 ($p < .10$, two tails). Furthermore, the increase in intrusion errors comparing Lists 3 and 4 with Lists 1 and 2 was greater for the reflective boys under threat than the impulsive boys under threat (4.6 versus 2.6), but this difference was not statistically significant. The frequency data indicated that 60 percent of the reflective boys under threat showed an increase of 3 or more intrusion errors and no reflective boy displayed a decrease. Among the impulsive boys, only 38 percent had an increase of 3 or more intrusions and three boys had fewer intrusions after threat than they did before threat. Although these differences are not statistically significant by conventional standards, they support the notion that reflective boys were more influenced by the instruction that suggested the possibility of future failure.

The differential deterioration in recall also supports these ideas. When concept and nonconcept words were pooled, the reflective boys under threat recalled 4.9 fewer words on Lists 3 and 4 than they did on Lists 1 and 2. This difference compares with a value of 2.8 for impulsive boys under threat. The recall loss of 4.9 words between the first and second pairs of lists is the largest average drop in recall displayed by any of the 12 groups (average loss of 2.0 words for remaining 11 groups). Assuming that a combination of a large increase in intrusion errors and a large decrease in recall would be most indicative of deterioration and, by inference, of anxiety, one final analysis was attempted. Subjects who showed both an increase in intrusion errors of three or more (the median value of all Ss) and a decrease in recall of four or more words were selected. Forty percent of the reflective boys under threat fulfilled this double index of deterioration in performance, in contrast to 27 percent among impulsive boys. Moreover, 4 of the 15 reflective boys under threat deteriorated 12 or more words comparing Lists 3 and 4 with recall in the first two lists. The largest loss in recall among the impulsives was 9 words. Although these differences missed statistical significance, they agree with the notion that telling the child that a task he was about to do was difficult—and failure a likely possibility—had a greater disruptive effect on reflective than impulsive boys.

Discussion and Conclusion

The hypothesis that children classified as impulsive on the visual matching test would make more errors of commission in the serial learning procedure was clearly supported. These data corroborate the results of an earlier investigation and add validity to the postulation of a generalized behavioral tendency to be impulsive (or reflective) in problem situations where the child should consider the validity of his answers. Impulsive children do not pause to consider the probable accuracy of their cognitive products, whether the situation involves visual matching of picture or reporting words in a recall situation.

The hypothesis that reflective Ss are anxious over possible failure received only minimal support, and primarily among boys. The largest increase in intrusion errors and largest loss in recall score occurred among the reflective boys after they were told the lists they were about to hear were difficult. This inference requires the double assumption that the "threat" instruction is likely to generate worry over quality of performance for most of the children and that the sequelae of the anxiety are poor recall and more intrusions. Since there is no independent test of intensity of anxiety this nest of assumptions may be gratuitous. This conceptual problem is pervasive in psychology and indirect inference must often be used.

This interpretation is consistent with the data and current theory but is by no means the only way to interpret the findings.

As noted earlier, anxiety over the possibility of making a mistake is to be distinguished conceptually from expectancy of failure. A child may be so accustomed to failure that he has stopped protecting himself, and as a result, is not highly anxious over possible failure. It is likely that there is a curvilinear relationship between these two variables, with maximum values for the anxiety variable associated with moderate values of expectancy of failure. Children who are maximally or minimally confident of success are apt to be minimally anxious over possible failure.

The major implication of this work is to emphasize the significance of a conceptual tempo variable for cognitive products. Investigators working with "culturally deprived" children believe that one reason for their poor intellectual performance is their impulsive orientation.

The brain-damaged child, as well as the reading-retarded child, is more prone to be impulsive than reflective and his inferior intellectual performances are more often the result of impulsivity than inadequate verbal or knowledge resources. Therapeutic regimes for these children should consider the potential value of training reflection as a specific conceptual habit, independent of the specific substantive content of the material to be mastered.

References

Kagan, J. Impulsive and reflective children. In J. Krumboltz (Ed.), *Learning and the educational process.* Chicago: Rand, McNally, 1965, pp. 133-161.

Kagan, J., Rosman, B. C., Day, D., Albert, J., & Phillips, W. Information processing in the child. *Psychological Monographs,* 1964, 78(1, Whole No. 578).

Leveling-Sharpening and Memory Organization

Philip S. Holzman and Riley W. Gardner

The terms *leveling* and *sharpening* have been used to describe systematic changes in memory organization (Carmichael, Hogan, & Walter, 1932) and the fate of rumors (Allport & Postman, 1947). Omission of inconsistencies, condensation of elements, and general simplification of recalled stories have all been called "leveling." The tendency of a detail of the original structure of a story to dominate its memory organization has been called "sharpening." Wulf (1922) reported analogous processes in the reproduction of geometric figures.

Our use of the terms *leveling* and *sharpening* shares certain features of these meanings, but implies more. We employ the terms to describe opposite poles of a dimensional principle of cognitive control concerning the degree of assimilation between perceptual processes and memory traces (Köhler, 1923; Lauenstein, 1932). The concept of cognitive control is based on the observation that individual differences in cognitive behaviors often reflect habitual, but not necessarily conscious, strategies of adaptation, and the further observation (see Klein, 1954) that the enduring response dispositions represented by such strategies serve to *mediate* the effects of drives upon cognitive behavior. Cognitive controls such as those we have referred to as the leveling-sharpening dimension are presumed to be structural principles of personality organization that give a particular cast to an individual's cognitive behavior.

Generalized leveling-sharpening tendencies have been explored and defined in several prior studies. The assimilation hypothesis just mentioned led to successful prediction of significant relationships between performance in a laboratory test of assimilation-proneness (the Schematizing Test) and the degree of assimilation shown in visual, auditory, and kinesthetic time error (Holzman, 1954; Holzman & Klein, 1954). Extreme leveling has also been shown to be associated with reliance upon repression as a preferred mode of defense (Gardner, Holzman, Klein, Linton, & Spence, 1959; Holzman & Gardner, 1959) and degree of distortion experienced through aniseikonic lenses (Gardner et al., 1959).

The most complete study of the leveling-sharpening control principle to date was done by Gardner et al. (1959). In that study, leveling-sharpening emerged as a clear-cut factor for women, and included test scores used as measures of leveling-sharpening in previous studies, among other measures. This factor was described as pertaining "to differentiation in memory organization as a function of the extent to which successive stimuli assimilate to each other." Apparently because of relatively great assimilation among new percepts and relevant mem-

This study was made possible by Research Grant M-1182 from the National Institutes of Health, Public Health Service.

From *Journal of Abnormal and Social Psychology*, 1960, 61, 176-180. Reprinted by permission of the American Psychological Association and the authors.

ory traces formed earlier, subjects (*S*s) with high factor scores (levelers) formed undifferentiated memory organizations in several tests. *S*s with low factor scores (sharpeners) formed relatively differentiated memory organizations, presumably by virtue of minimal assimilation. A definitive test of the differences in memory schemata in levelers and sharpeners was not, however, undertaken. The present study represents a first such test.

In the earlier studies cited, the criterion of leveling-sharpening has been the Schematizing Test. A complete description of the test may be found in Gardner et al. (1959). Briefly, *S*s are asked to judge in inches the sizes of 150 squares successively projected on a screen. The 14 stimuli range in size from approximately 1 to 14 inches on a side and are projected in a prescribed order that is unknown to the *S*s. The five smallest squares are individually presented (3″ exposure, 8″ interval) in ascending order, then in two random orders. Without *S*'s knowledge, the smallest square is then dropped and one just larger than any seen previously is added. This group of five squares is also presented in ascending order and in two random orders. Subtraction of the smallest square and addition of a larger square is continued in this fashion until all 14 stimuli have been projected.

Several facets of individual difference are apparent in the Schematizing Test. In the present study, we shall deal with only one of these: the accuracy with which *S*s rank the 150 squares presented (computed in terms of ranking accuracy within each series of 15 judgments, a procedure fully described by Gardner et al.). Accurate intraserial ranking requires continuous comparison of the newly exposed square with those presented earlier. If new percepts and memories of earlier squares undergo relatively great change by virtue of assimilation, intraserial ranking accuracy is notably impaired. Thus, discrimination of the relative sizes of temporarily juxtaposed stimuli may be blurred by assimilation.

If our interpretation of the leveling-sharpening principle is correct, *S*s at different points along this continuum should differ predictably in their recall of much earlier experiences, as well as in their registration of temporal sequences of stimulation in the laboratory. Requiring *S*s to retell a story learned long ago, but not purposefully committed to memory, appears to provide a test of the hypothesis that such memory schemata differ in levelers and sharpeners. We would expect young adults who are levelers to have relatively few correct memories of such a story as "The Pied Piper" and to show evidence of relatively great loss and modification of the overall structure of the story. This general hypothesis is, of course, difficult to put to adequate test: some *S*s may have heard the story more frequently during childhood than others, some may have reheard the story more recently than others, etc. These features of their prior experience can obviously not be controlled. Control over other extraneous determinants of recall may have been provided, however, by the following facts: (*a*) the age range of our 41 female *S*s was only 18 to 22, (*b*) their socioeconomic backgrounds were remarkably similar, (*c*) they were all sorority members at one small midwestern university. If age, for example, had been allowed to vary more, the relationships reported here might easily have been obscured.

Method

The Schematizing Test was administered to 41 Ss under the standard conditions described by Gardner et al. For purposes of the present study Ss were divided into groups of 16 levelers and 25 sharpeners on the basis of the mean percentage accuracy of intraserial ranking for five previous samples totaling 175 female Ss.

In a different testing session, each S was asked to tell the story of "The Pied Piper."[1] (Those who reported never having heard it were eliminated.) The stories were recorded.

For purposes of scoring number of elements correct, the story was arbitrarily divided into 11 thematic units:

1. Mention of the town of Hamlin.
2. The town was infested with rats.
3. The townspeople were unable to rid themselves of the rats.
4. The Pied Piper, however, offered to exterminate the rats.
5. If a specified sum of money were paid to him.
6. When he played his pipe, the rats followed him.
7. To a body of water where they drowned.
8. The mayor (or townspeople) refused to pay the Piper.
9. The Piper then played his pipe, which, this time, attracted all the children of the town.
10. The Piper led them out of town into a mountain.
11. Only the lame boy remained behind, because he was unable to keep up with the rest.

Since the story presumably represented "old" memory for most of our Ss, it seemed advisable to scrutinize the preservation of the main outlines of the story, as well as the correct and incorrect responses at the more microscopic level. The two major sections of the story are linked by a key theme: the Pied Piper's leading the children away as *retribution* for the town fathers' refusal to pay him. Each protocol was thus scored for presence or absence of this key theme, without which ellipsis, condensation, or omission of parts of the overall organization must occur.

In addition, the following error scores were obtained by the two experimenters (Es): number of new elements; number of recombinations; number of fragmentations; number of confabulations, i.e., the number of thematic units associatively elaborated. Because of the simplicity of the scoring theme, there were only minor differences in scoring. These were easily reconciled to provide a single set of scores.

---

[1] The use of this story was suggested by David Rapaport.

Results

Quantitative
As anticipated, sharpeners were superior to levelers in their recall of "The Pied Piper." The mean numbers of elements correct were 5.6 for sharpeners, 3.3 for levelers, $t = 2.24, p < .02$, one-tailed test.[2]

The two groups also differed in retention of the key "retribution" theme. Only 26 percent of the levelers retained this theme, whereas 58 percent of the sharpeners' stories were anchored in this central organizational feature of the story.

The stories told by sharpeners were more than half again as long as those told by levelers. Mean number of typed lines in the recall protocols were: sharpeners, 12.9, levelers, 8.3; $t = 1.86, p < .05$, one-tailed test. The two groups were not significantly different in number of new elements, number of recombinations of elements, number of fragmentations, or number of confabulations. The fact that sharpeners produced much longer stories without more errors means, however, that many of their additional elements—those not included in our scoring scheme, which dealt only with correct elements and gross errors—were "sensible" additions that bore a reasonable relationship to the original organization of the story. Since the number-correct score was based only on elements common to various versions of "The Pied Piper," many of these additional elements may represent the particular versions originally heard or read by individual sharpeners.

Qualitative
Qualitative differences in the performances of levelers and sharpeners were perhaps even more impressive than the quantifiable differences just described.

Consider first a performance by one of the levelers that is unique in respect to the core "retribution" theme. This *S* demonstrated her loss of the overall organization of the story by presenting *two* stories—representing the last and then the first parts of the original story. The loss of the key retribution theme showed itself in a fragmentation of the overall structure of the story such that *S* apparently remembered it as two separate and unreconcilable entities.

"Well there was once a man in this village who played a very wonderful, I guess it was a magic flute, and he could walk through the town and all the children would hear him and be so entranced that they would follow him along to listen to him play. And so he, I guess, went through the villages collecting all the children. I [pause], let's see. . . . Oh . . . I think *this* is the, I think *this* is the Pied Piper. This village was full of mice and rats and so in order to get rid of them they loved music and so there was this man that could play a flute and so he went through the village and played the flute and out of the houses came

[2] In a large group of which the present *S*s were a part, the Pearson correlations between ACE scores and leveling-sharpening were not significantly different from zero. Intelligence as traditionally measured, then, is not a significant factor in the differences between levelers and sharpeners on recall of "The Pied Piper."

the mice and rats and they followed him and he led them into the ocean and in
that way the town got rid of all the rodents [laughs]. [*E* asks *S* about first
story.] Oh, I can't answer the first one because I can't remember what he did
with the children, the first story, the one I started and didn't finish."

In the following story, told by a sharpener, the sequence and transition are
much more clearly preserved.

"The people of Hamlin were over-run by rats and they had tried all sorts of
remedies to get rid of the rats and nothing worked. So, one day, they were discussing the rat problem as usual, and this man came to town and the mayor had
just previously offered a bag of gold to anyone who could rid the town of rats,
so this man came to town. His name was Pied Piper and he told the mayor that
he would rid the town of rats for the bag of gold. So, he played on his little pipe
and all the rats followed him out—came down from the houses and followed him
down the street and took them out of town and they disappeared. He came back
for his gold, and the mayor refused to give it to him on the grounds that he never
promised it. So Pied Piper told him he would be sorry if he didn't give him the
gold, that he would take away all the children. Well, the mayor just laughed at
him because he didn't think he could do it. So, he still refused to give him the
gold, so the Pied Piper played the tune again and all the children followed him
out of the town and he took them out into the country where some mountains—
supposedly, the mountains opened up and all the children all went inside to this
paradise, and the children—the mountains closed and the children were never
seen again."

Vagueness was also notable in levelers' recall. Often only an indistinct general
impression of the story could be recovered, with important details missing. The
following story by a leveler seems to highlight these qualities.

"Well, I probably didn't know any facts about it but, well, let's see, didn't he get
rid of the mice or rats or something from the town? I don't remember. But as I
remember, they, they were, they were trying to get rid of them or something,
and he by playing his pipe, or whatever it was, musical instrument, anyway, by
doing that, he drove them out of town, but that's all I've ever known. [*E:* Do
you remember anything else at all?] *S:* Unh uh. [*E:* Do you have the feeling that
there's more to the story?] *S:* Oh, yes, but I probably just don't know."

Discussion
Theories of learning and remembering may be arranged along a continuum of
greater to lesser influence of "personality" factors on these cognitive functions.
In the special theories of Ebbinghaus, for example, the role of general personality
factors enters not at all. Associationistic theories of learning in which the law of
effect plays a crucial role emphasize the part played by affective factors in learning and retention. Gestalt theories of learning and remembering elucidate chiefly
the ways in which structural properties of the material to be learned determine

registration and recall. Others, principally Bartlett (1932), have refined our awareness that memories themselves have organizational properties shaped in part by affects. Psychoanalysis has attempted to take into account the central role of affects in memory in the theory of repression. A complete review and thoughtful critique of these issues has been provided by Rapaport (1950). It may fairly be said that, in general, conceptions of the role of personality in memory have been limited to special effects, such as needs, affects, and specific sets. The concentration on such influences upon memory seems to emerge from an implicit assumption that personality factors are external influences on the learning or recall processes, factors that act either to enhance or to interfere with memory.

Theories of learning and remembering have usually been constructed without reference to individual differences in personality *organization* that shape both registration and recall. The general laws propounded thus far bypass the possibility that Person A and Person B may learn and remember in strikingly different ways, although when their performances are taken together with those of others, the group averages may show conformity to such laws.[3] Recall is a complex process in which details lose or maintain their place within the context of the structural organization of the story as this structure was shaped at the time(s) of the person's exposure to the story.

The cognitive control principles referred to earlier are concepts employed to describe and account for some of the major dimensions along which *personal constants* in thinking, perceiving, remembering, etc., fall. These controls are assumed to represent aspects of the individual's personality organization that determine the nature and quality of such cognitive functions. Leveling-sharpening—a dimension of consistent individual differences in susceptibility to assimilation (process-trace interaction)—is a principle of cognitive organization that affects the registration, and hence recall, of stimuli in a wide variety of situations, here shown to include a test of recall of "The Pied Piper" story. Leveling-sharpening thus seems to be apparent in the organization of old memories, as well as in the organization of memories registered in a current laboratory experiment. This finding implies that leveling-sharpening is a generalized and enduring aspect of cognitive organization. *S*s at the leveling end of this dimension of cognitive organization formed memory schemata for a story heard much earlier that have the following major characteristics: loss of the overall structure of the story, loss of elements as a product of "fusion" in the process of registration, relatively large numbers of elements (considering the number of recallable elements available) contaminated or changed by interaction with other memory-elements-to-be during the registration process.

Repression, one of the special "personality" factors affecting memory, has received considerable clinical attention from psychoanalysts. In previous studies (Gardner et al., 1959; Holzman & Gardner, 1959), we showed that persons who employ repression as a principal defense mechanism tend to be levelers, i.e., that

---

[3] I. H. Paul's (1959) study of individual differences in remembering, however, represents a novel and fruitful approach to understanding individual styles of learning and recall, particularly as these styles affect the "importation" of various kinds of extraneous material in recall.

a major characteristic of the memory apparatus is discernible in both defensive and adaptive uses of memory. In the light of the earlier findings, results of the present study also suggest that a generalized tendency to form undifferentiated memory schemata provides a necessary but not a sufficient condition for the unavailability to intentional verbal expression of ideas that, in psychoanalytic terms, have become drive-cathected. Such generalized clogging in the recall of ideas by levelers is consistent with McGeoch's (1929) demonstration that the higher the degree of the original learning, the less the interference in the reproduction of the material. A further investigation is indicated to determine whether, among levelers, repression occurs in a diffuse fashion, while instances of repression among sharpeners are more discrete and confined to special circumstances.

Experiments now in progress are designed to determine whether or not levelers' undifferentiated initial memory organizations are subject to relatively great "spontaneous" changes after original registration is completed. Although the present study points to a link between registration in the Schematizing Test, earlier registration of "The Pied Piper" story, and subsequent registration of events S experienced as related to the story (at some level of conceptual organization), our results may also be due to postregistration changes that result primarily from lack of differentiation in levelers' memories. A further possibility, pointed to by Gardner et al. (1959), must also be put to the test: that proneness to assimilative phenomena is a function of the intensity with which persons attend to new experiences. Persons who characteristically "cathect" new experiences weakly may be susceptible to assimilation (i.e., may be levelers) because of vagueness and instability in their original percepts.

References

Allport, G. W., & Postman, L. *The psychology of rumor.* New York: Holt, 1947.
Bartlett, F. C. *Remembering: A study in experimental and social psychology.* Cambridge: Cambridge University Press, 1932.
Carmichael, L., Hogan, H. P., & Walter, A. A. An experimental study of the effect of language on the reproduction of visually perceived form. *J. exp. Psychol.,* 1932, 15, 73-86.
Gardner, R. W., Holzman, P. S., Klein, G. S., Linton, Harriet B., & Spence, D. P. Cognitive control: A study of individual consistencies in cognitive behavior. *Psychol. Issues,* 1959, 1, No. 4.
Holzman, P. S. The relation of assimilation tendencies in visual, auditory, and kinesthetic time-error to cognitive attitudes of leveling and sharpening. *J. Pers.,* 1954, 22, 375-394.
Holzman, P. S., & Gardner, R. W. Leveling and repression. *J. abnorm. soc. Psychol.,* 1959, 59, 151-155.
Holzman, P. S., & Klein, G. S. Cognitive system-principles of leveling and sharpening: Individual differences in assimilation effects in visual time error. *J. Psychol.,* 1954, 37, 105-122.
Klein, G. S. Need and regulation. In M. R. Jones (Ed.), *Nebraska symposium on motivation.* Lincoln: Univer. Nebraska Press, 1954, pp. 224-274.
Köhler, W. Zur Theorie des Sukzessivvergleichs und der Zeitfehler. *Psychol. Forsch.,* 1923, 4, 115-175.

Lauenstein, O. Ansatz zu einer physiologischen Theorie des Vergleichs und der Zeitfehler. *Psychol. Forsch.,* 1932, 17, 130-177.

McGeoch, J. A. The influence of degree of learning upon retroactive inhibition. *Amer. J. Psychol.,* 1929, 41, 252-262.

Paul, I. H. Studies in remembering: The reproduction of connected and extended verbal material. *Psychol. Issues,* 1959, 1, No. 2.

Rapaport, D. *Emotions and memory.* New York: International Univer. Press, 1950

Wulf, F. Über die Veränderung von Vorstellungen (Gedächtnis und Gestalt). *Psychol. Forsch.,* 1922, 1, 333-373.

Part Four
Instructional Style

Chapter Ten
Instructional Style: An Introduction

One of the most profitable areas of study in educational research during the past decade has been the scientific study of instructional style. Much of the emphasis of this exploration has been placed on the development of objective, reliable means of systematically observing the process of instruction and classroom interaction. Studies of classroom interaction show that the instructor spends about two thirds of class time on two kinds of communication: handling of information, and the bestowing of rewards and punishments (Flanders, 1965). These different ways of handling information and of applying sanctions are called teaching or instructional styles. Not only can instructional styles be identified, Murphy and Brown (1970) have found them to be consistent over a period of time.

In a similar manner, Gagné (1967a) refers to instructional style as ways in which the instructor controls the external learning situation: with commanding attention, with presenting stimuli, and with the nature and sequencing of verbal directions given the learner. Furthermore, styles of instruction can be thought of in terms of the following dimensions: student v. content oriented; learner v. teacher oriented; authoritarian v. democratic v. permissive; businesslike v. unplanned; discovery v. expository teaching; and so on (Sieber & Wilder, 1967).

In this book, instructional style is synonymous with Lesser's (1971) description of instruction strategy, which is the choice of curriculum, its content, level, sequence, pace, and style of presentation. And since these different ways of handling information and applying sanctions have been found to have differential effects on student behavior, including achievement (Taba, 1967), researchers have become very interested in analyzing and predicting instructional style. This chapter will briefly overview what is called the *systematic observation movement,* pointing out some of the difficulties in studying instructional style, and then indicate attempts to establish a theory of instruction based on individual differences, especially learning style.

The Systematic Observation Movement: Four Orientations[1]

Systematic observation refers to a formalized method or system of classifying, recording, and quantifying different classroom behaviors of either the learner,

---

[1] The structure of the following section has been adapted, in part, from C. K. Murray's (1970) review and that of Flanders (1969).

the instructor, or both. Measurable variables are usually categorized as *presage, process,* or *product.* As Flanders (1969) puts it, measuring an instructor's trait of warmth toward learners is a measure of a characteristic that existed before instruction begins and is called a *presage* variable. The corresponding *process* variable would be some behaviorally specified measure of warm acts while instructing. The *product* variable, then, would be an educational outcome, such as measurement of learner attitude or achievement, that is logically related to instructor warmth. Early studies on *teacher effectiveness* focused primarily on presage variables, while most studies today focus their attention on process variables.

Observation systems themselves can be divided into two types: sign and category. A sign system is comprised of a list of classroom behaviors which the observer checks during a specified period of time, regardless of the number of times the behavior occurred during that period of time. The Taxonomy of Cognitive Behavior, to be described later, is an example of this type of system. A category system, however, consists of a discrete set of categories by which the observer tallies and classifies all the behavior exhibited during a given period of time. Flanders' Interaction Analysis System is such a system.

A number of attempts to systematically observe classroom behavior are recorded in the literature. As early as 1914 Horn developed a system based on the classroom seating chart to determine the extent of learner participation. In the 1930's, Wrightstone used the seating chart method to code instructor responses and stimulations arising from the interactions of the total class, as well as the individual student. Later, Wrightstone developed a learner response instrument. Whereas the instructor response categories were encouragement, discouragement, and questioning, the learning response categories were initiative, responsibility, and memory.

With this background in mind, these four major orientations in the systematic observation movement will be discussed: social-emotional climate, cognitive climate, nonverbal climate, and multidimensional assessment of climate.

Social-Emotional Climate

During the late 1930's, H. H. Anderson measured the *integrative* and *dominative* behavior of instructors as they interacted with learners in the classroom. These measures gave an indication of the classroom's *social climate.* Anderson found that the instructor's remarks influenced the behavior of the learner by either requiring conformity—dominative contacts—or by encouraging participation—integrative contacts. A series of studies in the 1940's indicated that these two types of behavior could be systematically observed (Anderson & Brewer, 1945, 1946).

Research on authoritarian, democratic, and laissez-faire leadership by Lewin, Lippett, and White (1943) extended the work of Anderson. Utilizing the laboratory approach, Lewin and his colleagues studied the effects of these three leadership styles on the behavior of boys participating in after school boys' club programs. They found that adult leaders who behaved in the dominative manner set a general dominative or authoritarian climate and that their boys were more easily distracted and more compliant, while, in reality, more rejecting of leader domination. On the other hand, socially integrative behavior on the part of leaders tended to elicit integrative responses from their boys, who were more spontaneous and showed greater initiative.

In time interest grew in systematically observing group behavior. By 1949 Withall had developed a seven-category system designed in terms of a learner-centered-teacher-centered continuum. In 1950 Bales introduced a timing factor for systematically observing classroom behavior at set intervals.

On the basis of this early work in social-emotional climate, Flanders (1965) developed a summary description of the integrative instructor as one who accepts, clarifies, and supports the learner's ideas and feelings. On the other hand, dominative instructors frequently issue directions and orders, and tend to focus on their own ideas. They criticize the learner and are concerned with justifying their own position and authority.

From these definitions of two instructional styles, Flanders then designated a ten-category system of observation wherein dominative and integrative contacts were integrated in terms of the kind of influence the instructor exerted, direct or indirect. The first seven categories dealt with the instructor's verbal behavior, and the last three with the learner's. To aid the observer in categorizing and sequencing his observations, Flanders added the concept of the matrix (see chapter 11 for an extended discussion of this system).

Since, with as little as four hours of training in the use of this matrix system, observers can make highly reliable judgments of both instructor and learner behavior, Flanders' system has been used to study a number of problems. For example, Moskovitz (1967) found that student teachers trained in Interaction Analysis used more indirect means of influencing their instruction than did those not trained in the technique. Furst and Amidon (1967) found that elementary school teachers tended to be more indirect in the early grades, and more direct in the fifth and sixth grades. Today, the Flanders system is by far the best known, most easily learned, and most widely used system of systematic observation.

A number of other category systems dealing with the social-emotional climate paralleled Flanders'. Hughes (1959) developed a system which focused only on instructor behavior. Although primarily designed to assess the quality of instruction, Hughes' system can be used conjointly with Flanders' to give a fuller description of instructional·behavior. Ober, Soar, and Brown have developed the Reciprocal Categories System (RCS) to give a more adequate consideration to the general dimension of the learner's verbal behavior. The RCS consists of nine categories which are reciprocal to both instructor talk and learner talk, with only a single category for silence and confusion. Hough's Observation System for Instructional Analysis (OSIA), Medley and Mitzels' Observation Schedule and Research (OSCaR), and Amidon and Hunter's Verbal Categories System (VICS) are other examples of more precise instruments that stemmed from the pioneering efforts of Flanders and his predecessors.

Cognitive Climate

The systematic observation movement has been largely directed toward observation of verbal interactions which provide measurement of the social-emotional climate of the instructional-learning act. While this focus has provided valuable information, these data are by definition one dimensional. Since the main task of education is purportedly to promote intellectual activity, the analysis of the cognitive aspects of classroom behavior is of major importance in investigating the educational process, and is indispensable in developing an adequate instructional theory. In particular, three systems that focus on cognitive processes offer potentially valuable methods of understanding classroom interaction. These are the systems developed by Smith and Meux (1963), Gallagher and Aschner (1963), and Brown, Ober, Soar, and Webb (1967).

Working from the perspective of the empirically oriented philosopher concerned with the logic of the instructional process, Smith and Meux (1963) focused their attention on the logical operations that were apparent in classroom interaction. Their comprehensive system described the logical process observed in what they called *episodes* of verbal interaction between instructor and learner. Eight basic categories were described: defining, designating, classifying, comparing-contrasting, conditional inferring, explaining, evaluating, and opinioning. Each of these categories was then elaborated. For instance, Smith and Meux insisted that the observer should be aware of eight different kinds of explanation: normative, empirical-substantive, judgmental, procedural, sequential, teleological, explanation by consequences, and mechanical. Needless to say, using Smith and Meux's system can provide highly specific descriptions of the logical processes that occur in any classroom. Because it is a rigorously empirical approach, Smith and Meux's system has provided much impetus for research. Unfortunately, training in this method is likewise rigorous and time consuming, thus lessening its practical usefulness.

The work of Gallagher and Aschner (1963) was largely based on the psychological research of Guilford's three-dimensional model of intellectual functioning. Gallagher and Aschner have focused their attention on the first dimension, *operations of thinking,* and have developed five categories for analyzing classroom interaction: cognitive-memory, convergent thinking, evaluative thinking, divergent thinking, and routine. Each category was divided into a number of specific categories, the total being twenty-four. An observer can easily be trained in this system of observation in a short time and, because between-observer reliability coefficients are rather high, this system is quite attractive to the researcher for a wide variety of investigations.

The Taxonomy of Cognitive Behavior (TCB) was developed by Brown, Ober, Soar, and Webb (1967) at the University of Florida. This sign system of systematic observation was an attempt to operationalize Bloom's *Taxonomy of Educational Objectives: Cognitive Domain.* The TCB consisted of seven levels of cognitive behavior: knowledge, translation, interpretation, application, analysis, synthesis, and evaluation. Fifty-five items elaborated these seven levels and were arranged in a hierarchical order from simple to complex cognitive activity. Training in the use of this system is simple and short, and high between-observer and within-observer consistency can be achieved in about ten hours of training.

Nonverbal Climate

The preceding sections have dealt with verbal instructions that are characteristic of all instruction. Another characteristic of all instructors no matter where or what they teach is that they send and receive messages without saying or hearing a word. Galloway (1968) felt that in any classroom the exchanges of messages that were nonverbal in character often played a more significant role in student learning than the formal instruction that took place.

Galloway has developed a nonverbal communications continuum ranging from *encouraging* to *restricting,* based on the human communication theory of Reusch-Bateson. Twenty categories elaborated this continuum, and these categories further described each of Flanders' ten categories. With the exception of Flanders' first category, which does not need extension or qualification, there was one nonverbal category for use when the verbal encouraged interaction and one nonverbal category for use when the verbal restricted interaction. This system does not cover all aspects of the instructor's nonverbal communication, but it does give useful information on several important areas. According to Lail (1968), the Flanders and Galloway systems should be used together since the Flanders system provided information on *what* is said and Galloway's systems dealt with *how* things are said. Lail claimed that even at this early stage of development, the use of Galloway's nonverbal categories helped instructors become more sensitive to their learners' attention and interests, and thereby the instructor himself became more encouraging and flexible.

Kounin (1970) has delineated how instructor behavior can affect learner behavior. He concluded that there was a lawfulness to the role of instructor and the dynamics of classroom instruction. Many of Kounin's categories for observing classroom management were of a nonverbal nature and related to an instructor's "with-it-ness," "overlapping," "smoothness," and "momentum."

Strodbeck (1965) has used the term *hidden curriculum* to refer to the attitudes and behaviors that are relatively independent of the subject-matter topics which define the formal curriculum. These attitudes and behaviors are nearly always nonverbal and are acquired by the learner as a consequence of his experiences while interacting in the classroom. In terms of Flanders' point of view, regardless of the subject matter, a learner consistently exposed to an instructor who uses a narrow range of direct influence techniques not only learns a particular subject matter, but may also learn to become compliant and dependent on the instructor. In many respects, it seems then that the consideration of nonverbal behavior and the notion of the hidden curriculum may add a necessary dimension to a more total consideration of instructional style.

Multidimensional Assessment of Climate

It seems quite likely that employing a plurality of systematic observation instrumentation will provide a more fruitful approach toward viewing classroom behavior than by any singular view of the instructional-learning process. Brown

(1970) has remarked that, in a very real sense, an instrument for the systematic observation of classroom behavior is itself a theory of instruction which has been put into a useful and verifiable form. Therefore, the more complete the instrumentation of observation, the more complete the theory of instruction should be. This was in part the rationale for Wood's (1970) study, which used three different dimensions of classroom behavior (see chapter 11 of this book). Wood found that cognitive behaviors, social-emotional climate, and instructional procedures were highly correlated. One of the most interesting findings was the relationship of instructor and learner cognitive levels to learner verbal behavior and instructional method. Wood found that when the instructor based his instruction on the learner's ideas, using information and hypotheses which were learner initiated, there was a close relationship between high level of cognition of instructor as well as learner. When the reverse was true and the instructor was highly directive and did not solicit or use the learner-initiated ideas, the learner remained at the lowest cognitive level while the instructor's level of cognition was considerably higher. And when this discrepancy was present, a differential in achievement was noted. Amidon and Hunter (1967) also discussed a rationale for the multidimensional study of classroom interaction. Bergin (1970) suggested a multistaged, multidimensional model.

Difficulty in Studying Instructional Style and
Developing an Instructional Theory
Until the last few years, the main reasons for the lack of research evidence on what instructors should do in the classroom has been the difficulty of defining the variables associated with the instructional act and measuring them. Measurement of global notions of *teacher effectiveness* were found to be useless, and fifty years of research on this global characteristic yielded almost nothing in the way of conclusions. (See the following reviews of the literature: Morsch & Wilder, 1954; Medley & Mitzel, 1963; Gage, 1965; and Flanders, 1969.) Campbell and Barnes (1969) indicated that there may be at least 100,000 microelements in the instructional act.

However, enormous strides have been made during the last decade in defining and measuring instructional-learning behavior, and a more comprehensive theory of that process is emerging. Kuhn (1962) noted that developing sciences split off from philosophy and became established in their own right when adequate means of measurement were developed. The possibility that systematic observation of instructional interaction is the measurement breakthrough that will permit the development of a science of effective instruction now seems very likely.

Relation of Instructional Style to Learning Style
The development of systematic techniques to measure the process of instruction has had practical significance, in addition to the theoretical significance just mentioned. These observational techniques can serve as self-analysis for the instructor to assess and then modify his instructional behavior in accordance with the variety of requirements necessary to facilitate meaningful learning perfor-

mance. According to Lesser (1971), these requirements include instructional goals and strategies, subject-matter content, and learner characteristics and needs, especially learning style.

Previous discussion of Woodruff's model in chapter 6 indicated the interaction between instructional style and learning style. Woodruff (1967) suggested that, in order for optimal learning to take place, the instructor must influence the behavior-learning at four stages: perception, concept-formation, problem-solving, and trial or implementation. To accomplish this, the instructor must prepare subject matter in light of the learner's idiosyncratic ways of receiving and processing information in order to maximize perceptual input and conceptual organization in the learner. Then the learner's attention must be guided by means of verbal interaction during perception, concept-formation, problem-solving, trial, and trial interpretation. Finally, the instructor must provide trial situations which make realistic demands on the learner for adjustmental reactions, so that the concepts being learned can be subjected to trial, validation, and value-formation.

Plan of Part Four

Chapter 11 includes three articles which describe the current interest and research on systematic observation. The articles in chapter 12 indicate certain ideological and methodological difficulties in studying instructional style. Finally, the articles and reports in chapter 13 give some preliminary evidence for one of the implicit hypotheses of the book, namely that matching instructional style to selective learner individual differences will optimize learning performance.

Chapter Eleven
Instructional Style: Context

Articles in this chapter were chosen to convey a sense of the current interest and research in systematic observation of instructional style. For the researcher, systematic observation has been increasingly used in carefully controlled empirical research designs to study teacher behavior and effectiveness. For the practitioner, systematic observation has provided a self-analytic feedback mechanism which can serve as the basis for modifying behavior in accordance with the variety of requirements necessary to facilitate learning. For the theorist, this research and application will be instrumental in developing a more comprehensive understanding of the instructional process. As Flanders (1963) has put it, "Teaching will always remain an art, but it will [finally] be studied scientifically." And as long as instruction continues to be mediated in a group setting, the promise and utility of this particular person-environment interaction—that is, the instructor interacting with the climate of the instructional group—is limitless.

The article by Flanders is an excellent summary statement of Flanders' vision and instrumentation. As a result of his research efforts, Flanders hopes to modify teacher education programs so that prospective teachers will be helped to discover what their intention (expectations) should be, and then to develop training situations in which behavior gradually matches intention with practice.

The article by Campbell and Barnes reviews twelve research studies involving the most popular systematic observation techniques, Flanders' Interaction Analysis Scale. The author's conclusion seems to be that use of such a scale by a teacher will almost insure increased student learning performance. Rosenshine's article in the next chapter is a measurement specialist's comment on the Campbell and Barnes article.

The article by Wood is unique in its multidimensional approach to the observation, assessment, and consequent planning for the instructional process. Wood has focused on studying the relationship of three different dimensions: knowledge acquisition, personal growth, and reflective thinking. In a personal communication, Wood indicated that recent research has established and clarified even more relationships between and among these dimensions than are reported in his 1970 report. Wood's study is indeed indicative of the future direction of research in instructional style.

The reader may want to check on these additional sources: Amidon and

Hough (1967) have edited a series of social-emotional climate-type articles, many directly related to the work of Flanders. The entire issue of the *Journal of Research and Development in Education*, 4 (1), 1970, is devoted to current topics in systematic observation. Ober, Bentley, and Miller (1971) give complete instructions for measuring classroom social-emotional and cognitive climate, and for developing instructional strategies based on this feedback.

Intent, Action, and Feedback:
A Preparation for Teaching
Ned A. Flanders

The Problem
The point is that much of what is learned in education courses is neither conceptualized, quantified, nor taught in a fashion that builds a bridge between theory and practice. Education students are only occasionally part of an exciting, systematic exploration of the teaching process, most infrequently by the instructor's example. How can we create, in education courses, an active, problem-solving process, a true sense of inquiry, and a systematic search for principles through experimentation? At least one factor favors change and that is the lack of solid evidence that anything we are now teaching is clearly associated with any index of effective teaching, with the possible exception of practice teaching.

A great many factors resist curriculum change in teacher education. Perhaps the most important is that genuine curriculum innovation, to be distinguished from tinkering with content and sequence, would require that existing faculty members, old and new alike, think differently about their subject matter, act differently while teaching, and relate differently to their students. For some this is probably impossible, for all it would be difficult. Yet changes do occur when enough energy is mobilized and convictions are strongly held.

It is a serious indictment of the profession, however, to hear so many education instructors say that their students will appreciate what they are learning *after* they have had some practical teaching experience. What hurts is the obvious hypocrisy of making this statement and then giving a lecture on the importance of presenting material in such a way that the immediate needs and interests of the pupils are taken into consideration. Such instances reveal a misunderstanding of theory and practice. To be understood, concepts in education must be verified by personal field experiences; in turn, field experiences must be efficiently conceptualized to gain insight. With most present practices, the

Flanders, Ned A. "Intent, Action, and Feedback: A Preparation for Teaching." *The Journal of Teacher Education* 14: 251-260; September 1963. Reprinted by permission of the publisher.

gorge between theory and practice grows deeper and wider, excavated by the very individuals who are pledged to fill it.

One stumbling block is our inability to describe teaching as a series of acts through time and to establish models of behavior which are appropriate to different kinds of teaching situations. This problem has several dimensions. First, in terms of semantics, we must learn how to define our concepts as part of a theory. We also need to organize these concepts into the fewest number of variables necessary to establish principles and make predictions. Too often we try to teach the largest number of variables; in fact, as many as we can think of for which there is some research evidence. Second, in terms of technology, we must develop procedures for quantifying the qualitative aspects of teaching acts so that our students will have tools for collecting empirical evidence. Third, in terms of philosophy, we must decide whether our education students are going to be told about teaching in lectures and read about it in books or if they are going to discover these things for themselves. This paper will be devoted to these three issues, in reverse order.

A Philosophy of Inquiry

When Nathaniel Cantor (5) published his nine assumptions of orthodox teaching, there was little evidence to support his criticisms. Must pupils be coerced into working on tasks? In what way is the teacher responsible for pupils' acquiring knowledge? Is education a preparation for later life rather than a present, living experience? Is subject matter the same to the learner as it is to the teacher? The last decade has provided more evidence in support of Cantor's criticism than it has in defense of existing practice.

H. H. Anderson and his colleagues (1, 2, 3, 4) first demonstrated that dominative teacher contacts create more compliance and resistance to compliance, that dominative teacher contacts with pupils spread to the pupil-to-pupil contacts even in the absence of the teacher, and that this pattern of teaching creates situations in which pupils are more easily distracted and more dependent on teacher initiative.

Flanders and Havumaki (8) demonstrated that dominative teacher influence was more persuasive in changing pupil opinions but that such shifts of opinion were not stable since inner resistance was so high.

A research team in Provo, Utah (9) believes that patterns of spontaneous teacher action can be identified and that more effective patterns can be distinguished from less effective patterns. The difference is that more dominative patterns are less effective.

Our own eight-year research program which involved the development of interaction analysis as a tool for quantifying patterns of teacher influence lends further support to Cantor. The generalizations to follow are based on all teachers observed in our different research projects. This total is only 147 teachers, representing all grade levels, six different school districts in two countries; but these teachers came from the extremes of a distribution involving several thousand teachers. The total bits of information collected by interaction analysis are well in excess of 1,250,000.

The present, average domination of teachers is best expressed as the rule of two thirds. About two thirds of the time spent in a classroom, someone is talking. The chances are two out of three that this person is the teacher. When the teacher talks, two thirds of the time is spent by many expressions of opinion and fact, giving some direction and occasionally criticizing the pupils. The fact that teachers are taking too active a part for effective learning is shown by comparing superior with less effective classrooms. A superior classroom scores above average on constructive attitudes toward the teacher and the classwork. It also scores higher on achievement tests of the content to be learned, adjusted for initial ability. In studies (7) of seventh grade social studies and eighth grade mathematics, it was found that the teachers in superior classrooms spoke only slightly less, say 50 to 60 percent of the time, but the more directive aspects of their verbal influence went down to 40 to 50 percent. These teachers were much more flexible in the quality of their influence, sometimes very direct, but on more occasions very indirect.

To describe the classrooms which were below average in constructive pupil attitudes and in content achievement (they are positively correlated), just change the rule of two thirds to the rule of three fourths plus.

The foregoing evidence shows that no matter what a prospective teacher hears in an education course, he has, on the average, been exposed to living models of what teaching is and can be that are basically quite directive. After fourteen or so years he is likely to be quite dependent, expecting the instructor to tell him what to do, how to do it, when he is finished, and then tell him how well he did it. Now it is in this general context that we turn to the question of how we can develop a spirit of inquiry with regard to teaching.

Thelen (10) has described a model of personal inquiry, as well as other models, and the question is whether teacher education can or should move toward this model. He describes this model as follows (ibid., p. 89):

". . . (personal inquiry) is a process of interaction between the student and his natural and societal environment. In this situation the student will be aware of the process of which he is a part; during this process he will be aware of many choices among ways he might behave; he will make decisions among these ways; he will then act and see what happens; he will review the process and study it with the help of books and other people; he will speculate about it, and draw tentative conclusions from it."

Returning to the education course, the student will be aware of the learning process of *that* classroom, he will confront choices, he will make decisions among the choices, he will act and then evaluate his actions, and then he will try to make some sense out of it with the help of books, the instructor, and his peers. This is a tall order, but who knows, it may be the only route to discovery and independence for the prospective teacher.

Occasionally we hear of exciting learning experiences in which education students attain a sort of intellectual spirit of inquiry. A unit on motivation can begin with an assessment of the motivation patterns of the education students.

The same assessment procedures can then be used at other grade levels, permitting comparisons and generalizations. Principles of child growth and development can be discovered by observation and learned more thoroughly, perhaps, than is possible with only lecture and reading. But this is not what is meant by inquiry.

Inquiry in teacher education means translating understanding into action as part of the teaching process. It means experimenting with one's own behavior, obtaining objective information about one's own behavior, evaluating this information in terms of the teacher's role; in short, attaining self-insight while acting like a teacher.

Procedures for obtaining self-insight have been remarkably improved during the last decade in the field of human relations training. Two characteristics of these training methods seem relevant to this discussion. First, information and insights about behavior must become available in a way that can be accepted and in a form that is understood. Second, opportunities to utilize or act out these insights must be provided. Our ability to accept information about ourselves is a complex problem, but it helps if we believe the information is objective, valid, and given in an effort to help rather than hurt. Our understanding of this information will depend a great deal on our ability to organize the information conceptually. Freedom to act at least requires freedom from threat or embarrassment.

From all of these things, a spirit of inquiry develops.

The Technique of Interaction Analysis

Interaction analysis is nothing more and nothing less than an observation technique which can be used to obtain a fairly reliable record of spontaneous verbal statements. Most teacher influence is exerted by verbal statements, and to determine their quality is to approximate total teacher influence. This technique was first developed as a research tool, but every observer we ever hired testified that the process of learning the system and using it in classrooms was more valuable than anything else he learned in his education courses. Since interaction analysis is only a technique, it probably could be applied to teacher education in a fashion that is consistent or even totally inconsistent with a philosophy of personal inquiry. How it is used in teacher preparation is obviously as important as understanding the procedure itself.

The writing of this manuscript followed the completion of a terminal contract report of a U.S. Office of Education-sponsored, in-service training program based on interaction analysis as a tool for gathering information. How we used interaction analysis is illustrated by the conditions we tried to create for the fifty-five participating teachers, most of whom represented about one half of the faculties of two junior high schools:[1]

---

[1] Interaction analysis as a research tool has been used ever since R. F. Bales first developed a set of categories for studying groups. Most of our research results can be found in the references at the end of this paper. Its use as a training device is more recent. Projects have taken place in New Jersey, Philadelphia, Chicago, and Minneapolis. Systematic evaluation is available in only the Minneapolis project.

1. Teachers developed new (to them) concepts as tools for thinking about their behavior and the consequences of their behavior. These concepts were used to discover principles of teacher influence. Both types of concepts were necessary: those for describing actions and those for describing consequences.

2. Procedures for assessing both types of concepts in practical classroom situations were tried out. These procedures were used to test principles, to modify them, and to determine when they might be appropriately applied.

3. The training activities involved in becoming proficient in the assessment of spontaneous behavior, in and of themselves, increased the sensitivity of teachers to their own behavior and the behavior of others. Most important, teachers could compare their intentions with their actions.

4. By avoiding a discussion of right and wrong ways of teaching and emphasizing the discovery of principles of teacher influence, teachers gradually became more independent and self-directing. Our most successful participants investigated problems of their own choosing, designed their own plans, and arranged collaboration with others when this seemed advantageous.

Five filmstrips and one teacher's manual have been produced and written. These materials would have to be modified before they could be used with undergraduate students. Before asking how interaction analysis might be used in teacher preparation, we turn next to a description of the procedures.

The Procedure of Observation

The observer sits in a classroom in the best position to hear and see the participants. At the end of each three-second period, he decides which category best represents the communication events just completed. He writes this category number down while simultaneously assessing communication in the next period and continues at a rate of 20 to 25 observations per minute, keeping his tempo as steady as possible. His notes are merely a series of numbers written in a column, top to bottom, so that the original sequence of events is preserved. Occasionally marginal notes are used to explain the class formation or any unusual circumstances. When there is a major change in class formation, the communication pattern, or the subject under discussion, a double line is drawn and the time indicated. As soon as the total observation is completed, the observer retires to a nearby room and completes a general description of each separate activity period separated by the double lines, including the nature of the activities, the class formation, and the position of the teacher. The observer also notes any additional facts that seem pertinent to an adequate interpretation and recall of the total visit.

The ten categories that we used for interaction analysis are shown in Table 1.

The numbers that an observer writes down are tabulated in a 10 X 10 matrix as sequence pairs, that is, a separate tabulation is made for each overlapping pair of numbers. An illustration will serve to explain this procedure.

Teacher: "Class! The bell has rung. May I have your attention please!" [6]
During the next three seconds talking and noise diminish.[10]
Teacher: "Jimmy, we are all waiting for you." [7] Pause.

Table 1 Categories for Interaction Analysis

Teacher Talk	Indirect Influence	1.* Accepts Feeling: accepts and clarifies the feeling tone of the students in a nonthreatening manner. Feelings may be positive or negative. Predicting or recalling feelings are included. 2.* Praises or Encourages: praises or encourages student action or behavior. Jokes that release tension, not at the expense of another individual, nodding head or saying, "um hm?" or "go on" are included. 3.* Accepts or Uses Ideas of Student: clarifying, building or developing ideas suggested by a student. As teacher brings more of his own ideas into play, shift to category five. 4.* Asks Questions: asking a question about content or procedure with the intent that a student answer.
	Direct Influence	5.* Lecturing: giving facts or opinions about content or procedures; expressing his own ideas, asking rhetorical questions. 6.* Giving Directions: directions, commands, or orders with which a student is expected to comply. 7.* Criticizing or Justifying Authority: statements intended to change student behavior from nonacceptable to acceptable pattern; bawling someone out; stating why the teacher is doing what he is doing; extreme self-reference.
Student Talk		8.* Student Talk–Response: talk by students in response to teacher. Teacher initiates the contact or solicits student statement. 9.* Student Talk–Initiation: talk by students which they initiate. If "calling on" student is only to indicate who may talk next, observer must decide whether student wanted to talk. If he did, use this category.
		10.* Silence or Confusion: pauses, short periods of silence and periods of confusion in which communication cannot be understood by the observer.

There is no scale implied by these numbers. Each number is classificatory; it designates a particular kind of communication event. To write these numbers down during observation is to enumerate, not to judge a position on a scale.

Teacher: "Now today we are going to have a very pleasant surprise, [5] and I think you will find it very exciting and interesting. [1] Have any of you heard anything about what we are going to do?" [4]
Pupil: "I think we are going on a trip in the bus that's out in front." [8]
Teacher: "Oh! You've found out! How did you learn about our trip?" [4]

By now the observer has written down 6, 10, 7, 5, 1, 4, 8, and 4. As the interaction proceeds, the observer will continue to write down numbers. To tabulate these observations in a 10 × 10 matrix, the first step is to make sure that the entire series begins and ends with the same number. The convention we use is to add a 10 to the beginning and end of the series unless the 10 is already present. Our series now becomes 10, 6, 10, 7, 5, 1, 4, 8, 4, and 10.

These numbers are tabulated in a matrix, one pair at a time. The column is indicated by the second number, the row is indicated by the first number. The

Table 2

Category	1	2	3	4	5	6	7	8	9	10	Total
1				1							1
2											0
3											0
4								1		1	2
5	1										1
6										1	1
7				1							1
8				1							1
9											0
10						1	1				2
Total	1	0	0	2	1	1	1	1	0	2	9

first pair is 10-6; the tally is placed in row ten, column six cell. The second pair is 6-10; tally this in the row six, column ten cell. The third pair is 10-7, the fourth pair is 7-5, and so on. Each pair overlaps with the next, and the total number of observations, "N," always will be tabulated by N-1 tallies in the matrix. In this case we started a series of ten numbers, and the series produced nine tallies in the matrix.

Table 2 shows our completed matrix. Notice that in a correctly tabulated matrix the sums of the corresponding rows and columns are equal.

The problem of reliability is extremely complex, and a more complete discussion can be found in two terminal contract reports (6,7) one of which will be published as a research monograph in the 1963 series of the Cooperative Research Program. Education students can learn how to make quick field checks of their reliability and work toward higher reliability under the direction of an instructor.

The Interpretation of Matrices
A matrix should have at least 400 tallies, covering about twenty minutes or more of a homogeneous activity period, before attempting to make an interpretation.

Certain areas within the matrix are particularly useful for describing teacher influence. Some of these areas will now be discussed by making reference to Table 3.

The column totals of a matrix are indicated as Areas "A," "B," "C," and "D." The figures in these areas provide a general picture by answering the following questions: What proportion of the time was someone talking compared with

Table 3 Matrix Analysis

Category	Classification			Category	1	2	3	4	5	6	7	8	9	10	Total
Accepts Feelings	Teacher Talk	Indirect Influence		1											
Praise				2	Area E										
Student Idea				3											
Asks Questions		Direct Influence		4	"Content Cross'							Area I			
Lectures				5											
Gives Directions				6						Area F					
Criticism				7											
Student Response	Student Talk			8	Area G							Area H	Area J		
Student Initiation				9											
Silence				10											
				Total	Area A					Area B		Area C	Area D		
					Indirect Teacher Talk					Direct Teacher Talk		Student Talk			

the portion in which confusion or no talking existed? When someone was talking, what proportion of the time was used by the students? By the teacher? Of the time that the teacher talked, what proportion of his talk involved indirect influence? Direct influence?

The answers to these questions form a necessary backdrop to the interpretation of the other parts of the matrix. If student participation is about 30 or 40 percent, we would expect to find out why it was so high by studying the matrix. If the teacher is particularly direct or indirect, we would expect certain relationships to exist with student talk and silence.

The next two areas to consider are areas "E" and "F." Evidence that categories 1, 2, and 3 were used for periods longer than three seconds can be found in the diagonal cells, 1-1, 2-2, and 3-3. The other six cells of Area E indicate various types of transitions between these three categories. Sustained praise or clarification of student ideas is especially significant because such elaboration often involves criteria for praise or reasons for accepting ideas and feelings. The elaboration of praise or student ideas must be present if the student's ideas are to be integrated with the content being discussed by the class.

Area F is a four-cell combination of giving directions (category 6) and giving criticisms or self-justification (category 7). The transition cells 6-7 and 7-6 are particularly sensitive to difficulties that the teacher may have with classroom discipline or resistance on the part of students. When criticism follows directions or direction follows criticism, this means that the students are not complying satisfactorily. Often there is a high loading on the 6-9 cell under these circumstances. Excessively high frequencies in the 6-6 cell *and* 7-7 cells indicate teacher domination and supervision of the students' activities. A high loading of tallies in the 6-6 cell alone often indicates that the teacher is merely giving lengthy directions to the class.

The next two areas to be considered are Areas G and H. Tallies in these two areas occur at the instant the student stops talking and the teacher starts. Area G indicated those instances in which the teacher responds to the termination of student talk with indirect influence. Area H indicates those instances in which the teacher responds to the termination of student talk with direct influence. An interesting comparison can be made by contrasting the proportion G to H versus the proportion A to B. If these two proportions are quite different, it indicates that the teacher tends to act differently at the instant a student stops talking compared with his overall average. Often this is a mark of flexible teacher influence.

There are interesting relationships between Area E and Area G and between Area F and Area H. For example, Area G may indicate that a teacher responds indirectly to students at the instant they terminate their talk, but an observer may wish to inspect Area E to see if this indirect response is sustained in any way. The same question with regard to direct influence can be asked of Areas F and H. Areas G and H together usually fascinate teachers. They are often interested in knowing more about their immediate response to student participation.

Area I indicates an answer to the question, What types of teacher statements trigger student participation? Usually there is a high tally loading in cells 4-8 and 4-9. This is expected because students often answer questions posed by the teacher. A high loading on 4-8 and 8-4 cells alone usually indicates classroom drill directed by the teacher. The contrast of tallies in columns 8 and 9 in this area gives a rough indication of the frequency with which students initiate their own ideas versus respond to those of the teacher.

Area I is often considered in combination with Area J. Area J indicates either lengthy student statements or sustained student-to-student communication. An above-average frequency in Area C, but not in Area J, indicates that short answers, usually in response to teacher stimulation, have occurred. One would normally expect to find frequencies in Area E positively correlated with frequencies in Area J.

We turn next to concepts and principles of teacher influence before speculating about how this technique can be applied to teacher education.

Concepts and Principles of Teacher Influence

It may be too early to determine what are the *fewest* number of concepts which, if organized into logically related principles, can be used by a teacher to plan how he will use his authority. Surely he will need concepts that refer to his authority and its use. He will need concepts to describe learning goals and pupil tasks. He will need concepts to classify the responses of students. He may also need concepts to characterize class formations and patterns of classroom communication. These concepts are at least the minimum.

Concepts That Refer to Teacher Behavior

Indirect Influence. Indirect influence is defined as actions taken by the teacher which encourage and support student participation. Accepting, clarifying, praising, and developing the ideas and feelings expressed by the pupils will support student participation. We can define indirect behavior operationally by noting the percent of teacher statements falling into categories 1, 2, 3, and 4.

Direct Influence. This concept refers to actions taken by the teacher which restrict student participation. Expressing one's own views through lecture, giving directions, and criticizing with the expectation of compliance tend to restrict pupil participation. We can define direct behavior operationally by noting the percent of teacher statements falling into categories 5, 6, and 7.

Other concepts which we do not have the space to discuss include: flexibility of teacher influence, dominance or sustained direct influence, and intervention.

Concepts That Refer to Learning Goals

Clear Goals. Goal perceptions are defined from the point of view of the pupil, not the teacher. "Clear goals" is a state of affairs in which the pupil knows what he is doing, the purpose, and can guess at the first few steps to be taken. It can be measured by paper-and-pencil tests, often administered at different points in a problem-solving sequence.

Ambiguous Goals. "Ambiguous goals" describes a state of affairs in which a pupil is not sure of what he is expected to do, is not sure of the first few steps, or is unable to proceed for one reason or another. It can be measured as above.

Other concepts in this area include: attractive and unattractive clear goals, pupil tasks, task requirements, and similar concepts.

Concepts That Refer to Pupil Responses

Dependent Acts. Acts of dependence occur when a pupil not only complies with teacher influence but solicits such direction. A pupil who asks a teacher to approve of his work in order to make sure that it is satisfactory, before going on to the next logical step, is acting dependently. This type of response can be measured by observation techniques and by paper-and-pencil tests on which he indicates what kind of help he would like from the teacher.

Independent Acts. Acts of independence occur when the pupils react primarily to task requirements and are less directly concerned with teacher approval. The measurement of this concept is the same as for dependent acts.

Other concepts include: dependence proneness—a trait, compliance, conformity, counterdependence, and similar concepts.

Some Principles That Can Be Discovered

We discovered in our research (7) that, during the first few days of a two-week unit of study in seventh grade social studies and when introducing new material in eighth grade mathematics, superior teachers (as previously defined, page 196)

are initially more indirect, becoming more direct as goals and associated tasks
become clarified. We also suspect that these same teachers are more indirect
when helping pupils diagnose difficulties, when trying to motivate pupils by
arousing their interest, and in other situations in which the expression of pupil
perceptions is helpful. On the other hand, the average or below average teacher
did exactly the opposite.

Now the problem in teacher education is not only to create a situation in
which education students could verify these relationships but could practice
controlling their own behavior so as to become indirect or more direct at will.
One place to begin is to have two, six-man groups work on a task under the
direction of a leader. One task is something like an assembly line; it has a clear
end product and sharp role differentiation. The other task is much more difficult
to describe and does not have clear role differentiation. Now let the class super-
impose different patterns of leader influence. Let them interview the role play-
ers, collect interaction analysis data by some simplified system of categories,
and discuss the results. When undergraduate students first try to classify verbal
statements, it sometimes helps to use only two or three categories. In one instance, the issue was the effect of using broad questions versus narrow questions.
A broad question was one to which it was hard to predict the type of answer. A
narrow question was one to which it was easy to guess at the type of answer.
Which type of question was more likely to increase pupil participation? The
students role-played this and kept a record of broad questions, narrow questions,
and the length of the response. The fact that they verified their prediction correctly for this rather superficial problem was much less important compared
with the experience that they gained. They learned how to verify a prediction
with empirical evidence, and some had a chance to practice control of their own
behavior for professional purposes.

There is no space here to list a complete set of principles that can be investigated by systematic or intuitive data-collecting procedures. The following questions might stimulate useful learning activities. Does dependence always decrease
as goals become clear? Is the final level of dependence determined by the pattern
of teacher influence when goals are first formulated? Are measures of content
achievement related to the pupils' attitudes toward the teacher and the schoolwork? What effects can you expect from excessive and pedantic clarification
of pupil ideas and feelings? And many others.

Applications of Interaction Analysis
to Teacher Education

Suppose that before education students were given their practice teaching assignment, they had been exposed to a variety of data-collecting techniques for assessing pupil perceptions, measuring achievement, and quantifying spontaneous
teacher influence. Suppose, further, that these skills had been taught in a context
of personal inquiry as described earlier. What effect would this have on their approach to practice teaching?

One of their suggestions might be that two students should be assigned as a team to the first assignment. While one took over the class the other could be collecting information; the next day or so, the roles could be reversed. Together they would work out a lesson plan, agree on the data to be collected, go over the results with the help of the supervising teacher who might also have the same data-collecting skills. This situation could approach the inquiry model described earlier. The practice teacher might discover that his failure to clarify the pupils' ideas restricted the development of curiosity or that his directions were too short when he was asked for further help; both of these inferences can be made from an interaction matrix with reasonable reliability and objectivity.

Later on a student may wish to take a practice teaching assignment by himself and turn to the supervising teacher for aid in feedback. In either case, the requirement is that the learner be able to compare his intentions with feedback information about his actions and analyze this information by using concepts which he found useful in his earlier courses in education.

There are some precautions that can already be stated with regard to the use of interaction analysis in such a situation.

First, no interaction analysis data should be collected unless the person observed is familiar with the entire process and knows its limitations.

Second, the questions to be answered by inspecting the matrix should be developed before the observation takes place.

Third, value judgments about good and bad teaching behavior are to be avoided. Emphasis is given to the problem being investigated so that cause-and-effect relationships can be discovered.

Fourth, a certain amount of defensive behavior is likely to be present at the initial consultation; it is something like listening to a tape recording for the first time.

Fifth, a consultation based on two observations or at least two matrices helps to eliminate value judgments or at least control them. Comparisons between the matrices are more likely to lead to principles.

Just how experiences of the type we have been discussing will fit into the present curricula is difficult to know. If activities of the sort described in this paper are valuable, are they to be superimposed on the present list of courses or is more radical surgery necessary?

Perhaps this is the point to risk a prediction, which is that teacher education will become increasingly concerned with the process of teaching itself during the next few decades. Instead of emphasizing knowledge which *we think* teachers will need in order to teach effectively, as we have in the past, we will turn more and more to an analysis of teaching acts as they occur in spontaneous classroom interaction. We are now at the point in our technology of data collecting at which procedures for analyzing and conceptualizing teaching behavior can be developed. Systems for doing this will become available regardless of whether they are similar or dissimilar to the procedures described in this paper. When this fine day arrives, the role of the education instructor will change, and the dichotomy between field and theory will disappear. The instructor's role will shift from talking about effective teaching to the rigorous challenge of demonstrating effective teaching. The process of inquiry will create problem-solving activities that will produce more independent, self-directing teachers whose first day on the job will be their worst, not their best.

These changes will be successful to the extent that the graduates of teacher education can learn to control their own behavior for the professional purpose of managing effective classroom learning. It will be the responsibility of the education instructor to help prospective teachers discover what their teaching intentions should be and then create training situations in which behavior gradually matches intentions with practice. Teaching will remain an art, but it will be studied scientifically.

References

1. Anderson, Harold H. "The Measurement of Domination and of Socially Integrative Behavior in Teachers' Contacts with Children." *Child Development* 10: 73-89; June 1939.

2. Anderson, Harold H., and Brewer, Helen M. *Studies of Teachers' Classroom Personalities, I: Dominative and Socially Integrative Behavior of Kindergarten Teachers.* Applied Psychology Monographs of the American Psychological Association. No. 6. Stanford, California: Stanford University Press, July 1945.

3. Anderson, Harold H., and Brewer, Joseph E. *Studies of Teachers' Classroom Personalities, II: Effects of Teachers' Dominative and Integrative Contacts on Children's Classroom Behavior.* Applied Psychology Monographs of the American Psychological Association. No. 8. Stanford, California: Stanford University Press, June 1946.

4. Anderson, Harold H.; Brewer, J. E.; and Reed, M. F. *Studies of Teachers' Classroom Personalities, III: Follow-up Studies of the Effects of Dominative and Integrative Contacts on Children's Behavior.* Applied Psychology Monographs of the American Psychological Association. No. 11. Stanford, California: Stanford University Press, December 1946.

5. Cantor, Nathaniel. *The Teaching-Learning Process.* New York: Dryden Press, 1953, pp. 59-72.

6. Flanders, N. A. A terminal contract report on using interaction analysis for the inservice training of teachers. To be submitted to the U.S. Office of Education, N.D.E.A., Title VII. Available from the author, University of Michigan, after April 1963.

7. Flanders, N. A. *Teacher Influence, Pupil Attitudes, and Achievement.* Dittoed manuscript to be published in 1963 as a Research Monograph, Cooperative Research Program, U.S. Office of Education. Available from author, University of Michigan, 1962. 176 pp.

8. Flanders, N. A., and Havumaki, S. "Group Compliance to Dominative Teacher Influence." *Human Relations* 13: 67-82.

9. Romney, G. P.; Hughes M. M.; and others. *Progress Report of the Merit Study of the Provo City Schools.* Provo, Utah, August 1958. XIX + 226 pp. See also *Patterns of Effective Teaching: Second Progress Report of the Merit Study of the Provo City Schools.* Provo, Utah, June 1961. XII + 93 pp.

10. Thelen, H. A. *Education and the Human Quest.* New York: Harper Brothers, 1960, pp. 74-112.

Interaction Analysis—A Breakthrough?
James Reed Campbell and Cyrus W. Barnes

Since publication of the Coleman Report, the *Kappan* has published several articles which directly state that research has failed to uncover any superior teaching methodology at any grade level. To quote from Millard Clements' article of October, 1968, "In most schools, the method of instruction, type of teacher, or size of class makes no difference in test performance."[1]

To some extent this contention is true, because no all-encompassing methodology has been discovered. In fact, researchers in this area have long abandoned this fruitless search. It is now apparent that teaching is so amazingly complex that no simple method will ever be found. Instead, researchers have simply attempted to isolate one or more productive microelements of the complex instructional process and, therefore, limit the number of variables to a manageable number which could be measured in some fashion.

The search for the various microelements has been under way in dozens of research centers throughout the country. To date, researchers have isolated about 600 promising microelements in the 26 observational systems developed on the cognitive, psychological, and social levels.

The Flanders interaction analysis observational system is the most thorough-

Table 1

	Teacher Behaviors
Indirect	1. Teacher accepts student's feelings.
	2. Teacher praises student.
	3. Teacher accepts or uses student's ideas.
	4. Teacher asks question.
Direct	5. Teacher lectures.
	6. Teacher gives direction.
	7. Teacher criticizes.
	Student Behaviors
	8. Predictable student response to teacher question.
	9. Student-initiated response.
	Miscellaneous
	10. Silence or confusion.[2]

[1] M. Clements, "Research and Incantation: A Comment," *Phi Delta Kappan*, October 1968, p. 107.

[2] N. A. Flanders, *Interaction Analysis in the Classroom—A Manual for Observers*. Michigan: University of Michigan, 1965, p. 7.

From *Phi Delta Kappan*, 1969, 50, 587-590. Reprinted by permission of the *Kappan* and the authors.

ly developed. This system has isolated the following 10 verbal microelements on the psychological-social level (see Table 1). These categories are each mutually exclusive, so that a researcher is able to select one or more categories every three seconds during a teacher's lesson. In practice, a trained observer is capable of coding as many as 1000 responses during a 45-minute lesson. Once the coding has been completed, the total number of tallies and the percentage of time spent in each category are calculated.

To further reduce the data, the category totals may be added in numerous combinations in order to produce a wide variety of interaction ratios. The two most widely used ratios are determined as follows:

$$\frac{I}{D} = \frac{Indirect}{Direct} = \frac{Sum \ totals \ for \ Categories \ 1 \ to \ 4}{Sum \ totals \ for \ Categories \ 5 \ to \ 7}$$

$$\frac{i}{d} = \frac{Indirect}{Direct} = \frac{Sum \ totals \ for \ Categories \ 1 \ to \ 3}{Sum \ totals \ for \ Categories \ 6 \ and \ 7}$$

Research to date, both at New York University and other centers, has established the fact that average teachers (referred to as "direct") have I/D ratios ratios below .40 and i/d ratios of below 1.00, while a select segment of teachers (referred to as "indirect") have ratios which are .7 and 2.00, respectively. When an indirect teacher has an i/d ratio of better than 2.00, he is spending twice as much time in the use of indirect (i) rather than direct (d) categories; i.e.,

$$\frac{i}{d} = \frac{1000}{500} = 2.$$

Likewise, a direct teacher spends greater amounts of time in direct rather than indirect categories; i.e.,

$$\frac{i}{d} = \frac{750}{1000} = .75.$$

Once the teacher's verbal behavior has been quantified into an interaction ratio (independent variable), then it is possible to determine the effect of such teacher's behavior on achievement and attitude development (dependent variable).

Let us briefly review some of the more productive research studies done on this basis. Flanders[3] conducted a study (1955-1956) involving the classes of 34 eighth-grade social studies teachers. He did another[4] (1957) involving the classes of 34 New Zealand elementary teachers. Both studies showed that classes of the indirect teachers had higher levels of attitude development (.01 level).

---

[3] N. A. Flanders, *Teacher Influence, Pupil Attitudes and Achievement*. Washington, D.C.: U.S. Government Printing Office, 1965, pp. 50-65.
[4] Ibid., pp. 53-65.

In 1960 Flanders[5] conducted another experiment involving 16 eighth-grade math teachers and 16 seventh-grade social studies teachers. It showed that both attitude development and achievement were significantly better for the classes of indirect teachers. During 1961-1962 Flanders and Amidon[6] conducted a study involving 560 eighth-grade math and 480 seventh-grade social studies students, producing the same results with significantly higher achievement and attitude development for the indirect group.

In another study at this grade level, LaShier[7] (1966) found significantly higher achievement and attitude development for eighth-grade biology classes of indirect student-teachers.

On the elementary level, Brown[8] (1960) showed higher achievement in arithmetic among elementary classes of under- and over-achievers for pupil-centered classes. Nelson[9] (1966), in a language arts study, found that first-graders' compositions were superior both quantitatively and qualitatively in terms of total verbal output and vocabulary for the indirect methodology. Bellter, Weber, and Amidon[10] (1966), in a study of 100 culturally deprived kindergarten pupils, showed that indirect teachers produced greater gains from their classes on achievement measures.

Soar[11] (1967), in a study of 16 classes of third-, fourth-, fifth-, and sixth-grade youngsters, found vocabulary growth greater for indirect groups, and reading growth greater for indirect groups in grades three, four, and five. Furst and Amidon[12] (1967), in a study of high- and low-achieving groups of elementary youngsters, found that the high groups tended to have more indirect than direct teachers.

Davidson[13] (1968), in a study of children from grades two to six, found that indirect teachers produced higher levels of critical thinking. Powell[14] (1968) found that indirect classes showed higher scores on SRA achievement tests, but

[5]Ibid., p. 114.

[6]E. Amidon and N. A. Flanders, "The Effect of Direct and Indirect Teacher Influence on Dependent-Prone Students Learning Geometry," *Journal of Educational Psychology,* December, 1961.

[7]W. S. LaShier, "An Analysis of Certain Aspects of the Verbal Behavior of Student Teachers of Eighth-Grade Students Participating in a BSCS Laboratory Block," *Dissertation Abstracts,* June, 1966, pp. 7, 168.

[8]G. I. Brown, "Which Pupil to Which Classroom Climate?," *Elementary School Journal,* February, 1960.

[9]L. Nelson, "Teacher Leadership: An Empirical Approach to Analyzing Teacher Behavior in the Classroom," *Journal of Teacher Education,* Winter, 1966, p. 425.

[10]E. K. Bellter, W. A. Weber, and E. J. Amidon, *Classroom Interaction Newsletter,* December, 1965, p. 9.

[11]R. S. Soar, "Pupil Needs and Teacher-Pupil Relationships: Experiences Needed for Comprehensive Reading," *Interaction Analysis: Theory, Research, and Application.* Massachusetts: Addison-Wesley Publishing Co., 1967, pp. 243-250.

[12]N. Furst and E. J. Amidon, "Teacher-Pupil Interaction Patterns in the Elementary School," *Interaction Analysis: Theory, Research, and Application.* Boston, Mass.: Addison-Wesley Publishing Co., 1967, pp. 167-175.

[13]R. L. Davidson, "The Effects of an Interaction Analysis System on the Development of Critical Reading in Elementary School Children," *Classroom Interaction Newsletter,* May, 1968, p. 13.

[14]E. V. Powell, "Teacher Behavior and Pupil Achievement," *Classroom Interaction Newsletter,* May, 1968, p. 24.

no significant difference in reading achievement. Weber[15] (1968), in a study of 180 third- and fourth-grade youngsters, found that the indirect classes had higher scores on verbal creativity.

Finally, Campbell[16] (1968), in a study of 10 general science teachers and their seventh-, eighth-, and ninth-grade classes, found that the indirect group was significantly better in terms of achievement (STEP Test, .001 level) and scientific attitude development (Scientific Curiosity, Cause and Effect, Suspended Judgment, .05 level).

It is thus apparent that the microelements involved in the indirect/direct ratios (indirectness) do affect achievement and attitude development in almost every subject area at almost every grade level from K-9.

Even though much of this research is very recent and generally unpublished, it is surprising that the educational community appears not to be aware of the contribution being made in this area. In spite of this notable progress, it should be quite clear that no claim is being made for the discovery of a universal panacea for the solution of all our methodology problems. On the contrary, several studies on grade levels 10 to 16 have been unable to isolate any productive microelements within the Flanders system. In the hope of discovering some positive relationship at these levels, researchers at New York University have recently completed two exploratory studies at the senior high level and another at the community college level. Furthermore, within the next two years various members of this research group will conduct a number of cognitive and affective exploratory studies at these levels in order to extend and enlarge preliminary findings.

The research to date seems to indicate that explicit methodologies exist at the elementary, junior, and senior high levels; therefore it is probable that different ratios and combinations will turn out to be specifically productive for each grade level.

However, the isolation of several crucial affective microelements at the elementary and junior high level is one of the most productive achievements of educational research. Finally, after years of failure and discouragement, we have isolated the first of many microelements which will eventually be utilized in a quantified theory of instruction. As an example of what such quantification will bring, let us illustrate how the 10 Flanders microelements can be used in analyzing the following 10 seconds of dialogue:

Time	(Seconds)	*Code*
1	Teacher asks a long question	4
		4
5	Student answers (briefly)	8
	Teacher uses his own opinion at length	5
10		5

---

[15]W. A. Weber, "Teacher Behavior and Pupil Creativity," *Classroom Interaction Newsletter,* May, 1968, p. 31.
[16]J. R. Campbell, "Cognitive and Affective Process Development and Its Relation to a Teacher's Interaction Ratio" (Unpublished Ph.D. Thesis, New York University, 1968).

Table 2   Category 4–Teacher Asks Question (Three-Category Combinations)

Category	1	2	3	4	5	6	7	8	9	10
1	411	412	413	414	415	416	417	418	419	4110
2	421	422	423	424	425	426	427	428	429	4210
3	431	432	433	434	435	436	437	438	439	4310
4	441	442	443	444	445	446	447	448	449	4410
5	451	452	453	454	455	456	457	458	459	4510
6	461	462	463	464	465	466	467	468	469	4610
7	471	472	473	474	475	476	477	478	479	4710
8	481	482	483	484	485	486	487	488	489	4810
9	491	492	493	494	495	496	497	498	499	4910
10	4101	4102	4103	4104	4105	4106	4107	4108	4109	41010

The coded sequence would be 4-4-8-5-5 with the following combinations: 4-4, 4-8, 8-5, 5-5. The combinations are formed by pairing each category with its predecessor and then again with its antecedent. Thus the student's response (8) was caused by the preceding (4) and resulted in the teacher's giving his own opinion (5). One hundred such combinations are utilized in analyzing a teacher's lesson by placing the sequenced data into a 100-cell 10 x 10 matrix. Since the matrix utilizes sequenced data, it can be used to analyze, at any one of 100 points, the incident that caused the category to appear or the incident that immediately followed any coded response. In practice, if a teacher's class suffers from excessive confusion, we can now present a concrete analysis of the teacher's verbal qualities that are causing the confusion. Furthermore, an individual's matrix can be compared cell by cell, column by column, with those matrices derived from the researchers cited above. We can, therefore, compare on the affective level one teacher's lesson with hundreds of direct and indirect teachers on a national basis. By such an analysis we can further determine objectively both the strengths and weaknesses of the lesson and diagnostically outline affective verbal patterns which have proved successful to a vast number of teachers at the same level. The potential productivity of such analysis is presently being widely explored in preservice practice teaching courses and in-service courses.

However, the 100-cell analysis is no simple matter for the observer to interpret fully, and it is even more difficult for the teacher to implement the constructive elements specified. The complexity of such an approach is clearly evident when one category is isolated with its two-combination pairs; i.e., 4-1, 4-2, 4-3, 4-4, 4-5, 4-6, 4-7, 4-8, 4-9, 4-10. Each one of these pairs may be considered a distinct teacher mechanism for asking a question, and the implementation of each may involve a separate set of verbal behaviors and psychological skills. To make matters more complex, the research we have performed to date indicates that these two-category combinations are too narrow and limited for classroom use. Instead, three- and four-category combinations are infinitely more productive in the analysis of instruction. To illustrate, let us limit our analysis to the question (4) category and simply depict the one hundred resulting combinations (refer to Table 2). Each one of these combinations may be a fruitful method of asking a question and may involve a further complexity of human skills. It is probably clear to the reader that the total number of three-category combinations for the 10 interacting microelements is 1000 (a 100-cell matrix for each category). In practice, our research shows that most direct teachers show a surprisingly small number of different patterns, while the indirect teacher shows at least a tenfold superiority in his variety of combinations. However, little research has been performed on these microcombinations; therefore, in the summer of this year the N.Y.U. research staff will attempt to study several of these teaching patterns in the Allen-Gage teach-reteach microteaching technique by video-taping teachers as they isolate one or more of these elements. Perhaps combinations of four or five categories will result in providing the most fruitful approach. Although the resulting complexity would involve the astounding number of 100,000 combinations, a much smaller number will doubtlessly turn out to be productive. The implications of this research are twofold.

First, objective analysis of the teaching process: At long last we can approach objective evaluation instead of the widespread subjective process now in vogue. We can now give a teacher something definite, both in the form of a diagnosis and subsequent prognosis to utilize in improving his teaching, and perhaps we can move away from the hopelessly vague folklore which has come to be known as education.

In the twenty-first century, when the historians of education speak of the present era of supervision, they will doubtless be astounded that any individual could observe a class, see so much, understand so little, and produce a crisp evaluation of the teacher, the process, and the content in so short a time. The resulting superficiality has become apparent both to teachers and their militant spokesmen.

Second, theory of instruction: It is probably clear that the complexity and fruitfulness of even 10 microelements is almost without limit. In the years to come, many of these combinations will be eliminated while others will turn out to be highly productive. It must be further emphasized that our entire discussion has been limited to only 10 microelements on the psychological-social level, and the final process of teaching may involve hundreds or even thousands of distinct nonoverlapping microelements. Out of the 600 elements now under investigation, at least 200 are nonrecurring, and the number of entirely distinct elements will continue to grow. Certainly, the resulting complexity of even a 100-category system with two interacting combinations would involve 10,000 different patterns, while combinations of three elements would involve well beyond a million distinct teaching patterns.

It is probably clear why the old global, head-on, all-inclusive methodology studies of the past have failed to uncover a single, simple method which could be used in K-16 to solve all our educational problems. In fact, such an approach seems to have been a preposterous undertaking in view of our present knowledge of the complexity involved.

What will education be like with such a complex system? What will be the role of the teacher in view of such complexity? Perhaps teachers will rely heavily on specific combinations analyzed and tailored for individual groups by the computer. Perhaps teachers will specialize in one segment of the teaching process, and by means of teams present material to a given group of students. Perhaps the computer will be the only instrument capable of handling such a theory of instruction. Whatever the final result, this quantification process will radically change teaching as we know it today.

A Multidimensional Model
for the Observation, Analysis,
and Assessment of Classroom Behavior
Samuel E. Wood

This study was motivated by the virtual absence of information concerning the relationship of structural properties of observational systems, and is the first research effort to use the three dimensions of classroom behavior studied here simultaneously.

It was theorized that several instruments, each reflecting an explicitly different dimension of classroom behavior, could be used simultaneously to collect observational data; and, following certain analytical procedures, the data would yield information concerning: (1) areas where these systems cross contexts in the reflection and description of classroom behavior, and (2) where they remain unique. It was expected that relationships between student and teacher behavior could be found both within and between the measured dimensions.

It was further theorized that a factor structure could be identified largely in agreement with current classroom behavior theory, but it was expected that some relationships heretofore undefined could be discovered.

The problem was formally stated as follows:

"The purpose of this research was to identify and define the system of interrelationships between and among three observational instruments each built to reflect classroom behavior from an explicitly different theoretical vantage point."

The three instruments used in the study were the following:

1. *The Florida Taxonomy of Cognitive Behavior* (B. B. Brown, R. L. Ober, and R. S. Soar, 1967) is built to measure classroom behavior from the philosophic orientation of Essentialism—"or that combination of realism and idealism which makes the discovery of truth and the acquisition of knowledge the chief aim of education."

From *Journal of Research and Development in Education,* 1970, 4, 84-85, 92-94, published by College of Education, University of Georgia. Reprinted by permission of the publisher and author.

2. *The Reciprocal Category System* (R. L. Ober, 1969), through the analysis of verbal interaction, measures classroom behavior along the philosophic dimension of Humanism—"either the idealistic or existentialist version, which sees the production of adequate, authentic, and well adjusted human beings as the overriding aim of education."

3. *The Teacher Practices Observation Record* (B. B. Brown, 1968) measures classroom behavior from the viewpoint of Pragmatism—"or John Dewey's philosophy of experimentalism, which sees the primary purpose of education to train students in the process of reflective thinking (or intelligent inquiry) and to apply them to the solution of mankind's problems."

Procedures of the Research

Design
In general, the design of the study consisted of classroom observations using the FTCB, RCS, and TPOR simultaneously. Observations were made in each of 117 classrooms by three-member teams of faculty and graduate students in education from the University of Florida.

Prior to "live" observations, team members attended training sessions in which practice data were collected using audio and video taped segments of actual classroom behavior. Training sessions were continued until all observers achieved an acceptable level of reliability using the instrument on which they were to collect data.

Subjects
Subjects for the study were 117 teachers selected randomly from the some 260 teachers of a county school system in North Florida. More broadly, the "unit" of observation was the classroom, with student as well as teacher behavior being considered. Consequently, the number of subjects whose behavior could have entered the observations, at least potentially, was 3600 teachers and students. Subjects were drawn from all of the eleven schools in the county, representing twelve grade levels (1-12) and ten different subject areas.

Although the school district is in close proximity to a metropolitan area, the background generally characteristic of the subjects was perhaps more rural than urban. Informal observation suggested that while most of the span of socioeconomic levels was involved, probably the lower-middle was more heavily represented.

Analysis of the Data
Treatment of raw observational data involved the preparation of 19 x 19 matrices for the RCS, and computing item category, and numerous score totals for the TPOR and FTCB. This reduced raw data to a manageable form from which selected measures could be abstracted and factor analyzed. The initial series of 70 measures derived from the three instruments were subjected to a principal components factor analysis with varimax rotation. The rotated factor matrix was subsequently analyzed for the purpose of identifying clusters of classroom

process measures which tend to go together on the basis of a common dimension or factor. Each measure with a loading of ±.30 or higher was included in the study.

Results and Discussion
Results of the study show a relatively clear twelve-factor structure suggesting that while some reflective overlap exists among the three instruments, and between pairs of instruments, each retains a wide range of descriptive exclusivity.

Implications
Several implications appear to follow from these results. It is clear that teachers should not remain fixed at the two lowest cognitive levels (1.00 Knowledge, 2.00 Translation) if they seek to facilitate higher level student cognition. Neither should they simply move up the cognitive hierarchy. Rather, higher levels of student cognition appear to be facilitated when the teacher recedes to "field" and students become "figure," if one considers this in a preceptual psychology frame of reference.

Among the clearest findings was that higher level student cognition occurred most prominently along with student clarification and extension of ideas, student acceptance of another's behavior and student questions. Notably absent from the above relationships were any directly observable measures of teacher behavior.

This implies that peer group relationships are crucial in the facilitation of high levels of student cognition. In some measure, this implication calls for more training which casts the teacher in the role of a catalyst helping to channel and direct classroom discussion activities without dominating or directly controlling.

There was evidence in the analysis that an informal "tension free" classroom climate, warmed by the teacher, was related to experimental classroom practices. Thus, the implication follows that climate warming is congruent with such experimental practices as the teacher "participating in pupil activities," encouraging "free self-expression," "active pupil participation," and making "pupils the center of attention."

This and other related findings could imply that the direct measures of teacher socioemotional verbal behavior, although similar and compatible, do not always vary in common. In fact, each of the three indirect teacher categories (1. warming the climate, 2. acceptance of ideas, 3. amplifying, extending another's ideas) was found to function within a different set of relationships. Therefore, it appears reasonable to suggest that socioemotional verbal categories which appear to differ in degree when compared only to other verbal categories may be found to differ in kind when coupled with other measurable dimensions of behavior.

Other implications appear to be relevant within the socioemotional dimension of behavior. There were suggestions in the data that teachers who are characteristically warm and acceptant on occasions used critical or climate-cooling behavior but usually in small increments. The same teachers tended to use supportive emotional behavior very frequently but, again, in short units. Teachers considered to be cool and rejectant, on the other hand, rarely ever used warm or acceptant behavior. Their use of rejectant or climate-cooling behavior may have occurred rather infrequently but, when used, continued for rather long periods of time. This seems to imply a basic difference in behavior style suggesting that characteristically "cool," rejectant teachers overreact to what they perceive as inappropriate student behavior, prolong the "criticism," and, thus, focus on the emotional climate aspect of classroom behavior to the exclusion of the other measured dimensions. On the other hand, characteristically "warm," acceptant teachers tend to show a greater frequency of emotional behavior, but use it intermittently. Then, if a warm, informal style is desirable teachers should not be encouraged to focus exclusively upon the socioemotional dimension, but, rather, to weave it in and out of the total behavioral stream at appropriately determined intervals. Thus, the sequencing or purposeful patterning of verbal behavior would become equally as important as the nature of the behavior.

Experimental behavior was found to be related to teacher questions as well as a warm climate. This would seem to imply that teacher questions, more than alternative verbal techniques, tend to promote an experimental classroom scope. But more broadly and of more importance to this study is the implication that single dimension views of student and teacher relationships alone, whether cognitive, experimental, socioemotional, or some other, do not produce a comprehensive enough view of classroom behavior. In fact it might even be misleading to make judgments about the production of student cognitive level by observing verbal behavior alone, or to hypothesize about emotional climate by observing only experimental-nonexperimental behavior.

At any rate, a more widely diversified, and exceedingly more complex system of interrelationships may be identified and analyzed when viewed through the larger, more reflective, and more descriptive contexts of classroom behavior provided by a plurality of instrumentation.

Most of the implications discussed here point toward less direct teacher behavior, less teacher dominance in the classroom, and more student involvement in transactional processes if the quality of student behavior advocated by most educational leaders as desirable is to be facilitated (i.e., higher level student cognition, warm, threat-free, socioemotional climate, classrooms experimental in scope embracing much of Dewey's theory, etc.). Other questions remain, however, if findings from this study and similar studies are to be utilized.

Should teachers be rigidly trained to produce those teaching behaviors that are found to be related to particular student behavior and, as predictability increases, to shape student behavior within a predetermined context? Or, should teachers simply be made aware of teaching behaviors found to be related to certain student behaviors and left to their own judgments concerning the production and control of these behaviors?

Whatever the answer to these questions may be, it appears that systematic observation will play a crucial role in training teachers to use particular behaviors, or make them aware of the nature of their behavior as it relates to facilitating diverse styles, levels, and kinds of student behavior.

Furthermore, it appears that more than one of two dimensions of classroom behavior must be used since certain dimensions, heretofore elusive to direct measure, are being more sharply defined (i.e., cognitive dimensions); and new dimensions in this exceedingly complex domain are falling into focus (i.e., image provoking behavior). Indeed, a number of additional dimensions probably remain undefined.

However, even now the concept of *multidimensionality*, or a plurality of observational systems, provides a more fruitful approach toward viewing classroom behavior than a one-dimension look. The greater the number of vantage points from which classroom behavior can be viewed, the greater the amount of control teachers can bring to bear upon their own behavior and that of their students in the classroom.

In conclusion, it now appears possible to train teachers to:
1. Form multidimensional planning models including as many aspects of classroom behavior as feasible.
2. Utilize interrelated behavioral techniques and patterns which strengthen and support cross-dimensional classroom processes.
3. Employ a plurality of systematic observational instrumentation as reflective and descriptive sources of feedback.
4. Evaluate their own behavior based upon analysis of observational data, and thus modify planning models (step 1) where appropriate.

Efforts continue, through empirical studies, to identify more precisely the system of relationships which consistently cross dimensions within the directly observable category of teacher-student classroom *process* measures. Once a sufficient body of findings can be generated, they can be tied systematically to *presage* and *product* measures with a high degree of confidence. Teachers will become increasingly able to predict the consequences of their classroom behavior and that of their students. Hopefully the *presage* variables, the attitudes, abilities, beliefs, and those unique particularities which teachers and students alike being with them to the classroom situation can be systematically and purposively linked to optimally suitable *process* experiences in individual and group settings. Then, *product* measures will begin to have meaning.

References

Brown, B. B. *The Experimental Mind in Education.* New York: Harper and Row, 1968.

Brown, B. B., Ober, R. L., and Soar, R. *The Florida Taxonomy of Cognitive Behavior.* Gainesville: The University of Florida, 1967.

Ober, R. L. *The Reciprocal Category System.* Tampa: R. L. Ober, 1969.

Wood, S. E. Collecting and Interpreting Data Yielded by the Multidimensional Technique of Classroom Observation. *Research in Education* E.R.I.C., 1970.

Chapter Twelve
Instructional Style: Controversy

Articles in this chapter point out some of the ideological and research biases that have been or continue to be counterproductive to the development of adequate instructional theory and practice. Also evident is the implication that taking an "either-or" position on instructional style, such as authoritarian *or* democratic, direct *or* indirect, didactic *or* discovery oriented, is an unrealistic stance for classroom instruction.

Anderson's article is a review of a number of the classic studies on social-emotional climate. He concludes that the available evidence failed to demonstrate that either democratic or authoritarian leadership has been associated consistently with increase in performance. Furthermore, Anderson questions the adequacy of the authoritarian-democratic construct for educational research and the moralistic implication regarding these two polar adjectives. The reader may recall that many researchers, like Lewin, were appalled by the arbitrary actions of authoritarian leaders in Germany and Italy before and during the Second World War, and their ideological bias apparently influenced their experimental design and data.

In his article Cronbach notes that honest research is hard to do, and that existing research on instructional style has not yet yielded the answers needed to make firm and honest recommendations to the practitioner. Cronbach suggests that more complex experimental research is indicated, and offers a fivefold interaction schema which can reduce some of the bias traditionally associated with the planning of experiments and analysis of data. The time is ripe for implementing such proposals.

While Anderson questions the actual practical significance of a number of studies showing small, but statistical, significance, Rosenshine is concerned with the actual statistical significance of current research which suggests that indirect teacher influence increases student learning performance. Particularly, Rosenshine attacks the Campbell and Barnes article, which is reprinted in chapter 11. In a personal communication, Rosenshine stated that he didn't like writing this "hatchet piece" but felt he had to point out some obvious misinterpretations of data on interaction analysis studies. Rosenshine suggested that the reader look at the original research and draw conclusions, rather than take his or Campbell and Barnes' interpretation.

Other commentary on these topics can be found in the following sources:

Mitchell (1969) analyzes and evaluates research in terms of five criteria for advancing knowledge about person-environment interactions. Soar (1970) comments on the need for the instructor to be capable of using direct or indirect influence in his teaching, depending on student learning style, particular goals of a lesson, and particular subject matter. He offers an interesting interpretation of the criticisms directed at nondirective teaching and the progressive education movement.

Learning in Discussions: A Resume of the Authoritarian-Democratic Studies
Richard C. Anderson

In most teaching methods textbooks you will find reference to two basic teaching styles which can be called teacher-centered and learner-centered. (See, for example, Brandwein, Watson, & Blackwood, 1958; Burnett, 1957; Burton, 1952; Cronbach, 1954; and Grambs, Iverson, & Patterson, 1958.) If you consult a book on industrial management, a book on counseling or psychotherapy, or, indeed, the section on leadership in a textbook on social psychology, you will very likely find a similar statement about leadership. Leadership is universally defined in terms of a hypothetical authoritarian-democratic dimension. Many labels have been applied to this dimension—perhaps it should be called a dichotomy, for such it has been in practice: dominative-integrative, employer-centered–employee-centered, teacher-centered–learner-centered, therapist-centered–client-centered, supervisory-participatory, directive-nondirective; but the idea is basically the same.

As the reader is no doubt well aware, authoritarian-democratic theory and research are the subject of lively controversy in education today. Some educators claim that learner-centered methods are most desirable. For example, Mursell concluded:

"Thus the importance of a 'democratic' classroom situation is no mere fancy, nor is it based on sentimentalism, or on any far-fetched philosophy. It is a highly significant factor in the realistic organization of learning for the sake of authentic results" (1954, p. 146).

Others argue that teacher-centered methods are most satisfactory. Grambs, Iverson, and Patterson (1958, pp. 115-116) have asserted that the average teacher leans toward authoritarian teaching, stating that "the school . . . is by

Anderson, Richard C., "Learning in Discussions: A Resume of the Authoritarian-Democratic Studies," *Harvard Educational Review*, 29, Summer 1959, 201-215. Copyright ©1959 by President and Fellows of Harvard College. Reprinted by permission of the publisher and author.

tradition authoritarian. . . . Teachers who seek more democratic ways sometimes find that a number of their colleagues strenuously oppose their new approach." The critical student of educational method and policy will want to be in a position to assess the validity of claims from these opposing points of view.

This paper hopes to shed some light on issues basic to this controversy by returning to primary sources. Forty-nine experimental studies in which authoritarian leadership has been compared with democratic leadership will be reviewed. Two questions will be asked of this research:

1. Is there sufficient evidence that one of these two styles of leadership is more effective?
2. Does the authoritarian-democratic continuum provide an adequate conceptualization of leadership?

Later it will be suggested that failure to define carefully "authoritarian" and "democratic," or whatever synonyms were used, has been a general shortcoming of leadership research. For the present, rough working definitions of these terms will be attempted. Authoritarian leaders generally act in an impersonal manner; punish members who disobey or deviate; decide what the group will do or talk about; decide upon division of labor; determine how work shall be done; judge the soundness of ideas; do more talking than the other members of the group. Democratic leaders generally act in a friendly, personal manner; allow the group as a whole to plan the agenda; allow group members to choose the tasks they will perform; allow group members to talk with one another without permission from the leader; accept suggestions from the group about how the work shall be done; talk only a little more than the average group member. In short, the authoritarian leader makes most decisions for the group whereas the democratic leader shares decision-making with the other members. Just how the democratic leader handles deviation is a moot question. Proponents of democratic leadership argue that deviation rarely occurs in democratically led groups, maintaining that when it does occur the whole group punishes the offending member. This punishment takes the form of withdrawal of love rather than the aggression and overt hostility which are the rule in autocratically led groups. Observation suggests that people committed to democratic leadership are placed in severe conflict when the situation seems to require open aggression in order to thwart deviation.

This paper will avoid philosophical issues except insofar as they have influenced the kind and quality of research. Rather, authoritarian and democratic leadership styles will be compared in terms of two criteria of effectiveness which can be experimentally investigated. The first criterion is productivity. The definition of productivity varies according to the institutional setting of the experiment. In industrial research, productivity refers to work done or units produced, and also to the quality of the work. In educational experiments, productivity means the amount learned. Learning also has its qualitative aspects, and these will be considered whenever there are data available. In still another type of study "changes in behavior" will be identified with productivity.

Morale is the second criterion of effectiveness. Morale can be defined as the extent to which group members find the group personally satisfying and the extent to which they believe the group is successfully progressing toward its goals.

There is a problem worth noting in connection with these definitions. The actual definitions of productivity and morale have varied immensely from study to study depending partly upon the kind of institutional setting in which the research was done and partly on the authors' judgments about what was important to observe and measure. In addition, the extensiveness and quality of measures of productivity and morale have varied tremendously. In one case the estimation of morale consisted of the impression of casual observers that "the children seemed to be enjoying themselves a great deal." In another case the measure of productivity was the number of comments showing insight into child psychology (Perkins, 1951). In the latter instance the investigator was faced with a type of discussion in which there necessarily was no tangible product. This kind of problem frequently arises. Whether the solution of any one experimenter is adequate remains to be seen. One thing is evident: the solutions differ. It might well be asked whether these diverse studies are comparable and whether generalization from these studies will have any meaning. One reason the present author is willing to review these studies as though they had some measure of generality is that many synthesizers, specifically the writers of educational textbooks, have assumed that quite unqualified generalization is possible. For instance, after reviewing some of the relevant literature, Burton (1952) stated that,

"Learners *accomplished more* with the help of cooperative, democratic teachers, both in subject matter learning and in the development of personal-social-moral traits. The superiority of settings for learning under the guidance of democratic personalities was overwhelming" (p. 297). (Italics in original.)

Review and Critique
The classic research—which had a great effect on subsequent investigation—was conducted by Lewin, Lippitt and White (1953) who studied the effects of authoritarian and democratic leadership on groups of boys whose task was making papier mâché masks. They found that there were least interpersonal conflict, least aggression, least scapegoating, and highest morale in groups with democratic leaders. The largest number of masks was produced by groups with authoritarian leaders, though democratic groups were capable of more sustained work when the leader was not present than were authoritarian groups. Laissez-faire groups showed both low morale and low productivity.

A multitude of studies investigating authoritarian and democratic leadership followed the research of Lewin et al. However, the results have been disappointing. It is still impossible to demonstrate that either of the two styles is more closely associated with high productivity or high morale. After an extensive review of the literature, Hare (1959) offered the conclusion that democratic leadership is associated with low productivity and high morale whereas authoritarian leadership is associated with high productivity and low morale.

This conclusion demands serious qualification, however, on the basis of situational factors. The finding that morale is high in democratic groups holds for such groups as fraternities, sororities, boys' clubs, grade school classes, therapy groups, and temporary groups (Adams, 1943-1946; Anderson, 1937, 1939; Bovard, 1951, 1952; Bills, 1952, 1957; Deignan, 1956; Faw, 1949; Flanders, 1951; Hemphill, 1949; Lewin, 1953; McKeachie, 1951, 1954; Perkins, 1951; Rasmussen, 1956; Roseborough, 1953; Sheldon & Landsman, 1950; Thelen & Whithall, 1949; White & Lippitt, 1953; Wischmeier, 1955; Zeleny, 1940) but does not always hold in military groups, business groups, and college classes (Berkowitz, 1953; Guetzkow et al., 1954; Hemphill, 1949; Heyns, 1949; Krumboltz, 1955; McCurdy & Lambert, 1952; Wispe, 1951). Some of the discrepancy in research findings may be accounted for as follows: Democratic leadership is associated with high morale when a primary group goal is social, as in the case of the recreational and fraternal groups, or emotional catharsis, as in the case of the therapy groups. Morale is higher under authoritarian leadership, however, in groups which are primarily committed to some task goal rather than a social-emotional goal.

The picture is also somewhat cloudy in regard to productivity. There is wide agreement that authoritarian leadership is most effective when the task is simple and concrete (e.g., Adams, 1954). Some investigators claim that democratic groups are most productive when the task is a complex one requiring insightful behavior, and particularly when it requires cooperation among members. This finding has not been supported by all studies, however. For example, McCurdy and Lambert (1952) compared "miniature dictatorships and democracies" on a switching problem involving cooperation and found no difference in number of correct choices.

Some dramatic evidence often cited to support the contention that democratic leadership results in superior productivity compares democratically led discussions with lectures. These studies, which are summarized by Lewin (1953), generally show that after a democratically led discussion there is more change in behavior than after a lecture. In one representative study conducted during World War II, six groups of Red Cross volunteers were asked to increase their use of beef hearts, sweetbreads, and kidneys. Three groups were given "attractive lectures . . . which linked the problem of nutrition to the war effort" and included recipes for preparing "delicious dishes" from the three meats (pp. 287-288). In each of the other three groups a discussion was started in order to get housewives to use the three meats "without attempting any high pressure salesmanship" (p. 288). After the discussions the women were asked to show, by raising their hands, who was willing to try one of these meats within the next week. Women attending lectures were not asked to make a decision. According to the results of a follow-up study, only 3 percent of the women who heard lectures served one of the meats never served before, while of the women who took part in the group discussion and decision, 32 percent served one of them.

This difference in behavior could be due to the discussion, the decision, or both. Lewin himself emphasized the importance of the decision, though he felt that people are "more ready . . . to make a decision after a group discussion than after a lecture" (p. 290). Proponents of democratic leadership techniques have tended to overlook the possible significance of the decision. They choose to believe that this study—and other similarly ambiguous studies by followers of Lewin—demonstrates that democratic methods of leadership are superior to lectures and, by implication, to authoritarian leadership in general.

The relative influence of discussion and decision on changes in behavior has been examined by Bennett (1955). This study, which is fully discussed by Festinger (1957), was concerned with getting students to volunteer to serve as subjects in psychological experiments at the University of Michigan. A third of the subjects heard a lecture which tried to persuade them to volunteer, another third (in groups of thirteen) engaged in discussions about the desirability of volunteering, while the final third was simply reminded that requests would be made for volunteers. One fourth of the subjects from each group was not asked to make any decision about volunteering. The remaining three fourths were asked to make a decision, some anonymously, some publicly. The subjects of the three groups were matched according to their responses to a questionnaire about their attitudes toward volunteering for psychological experiments. Thus one may regard the subjects in each of the experimental groups as having the same initial willingness to volunteer. Shortly after the "treatment" the experimental subjects were sent letters requesting them to come to a certain place at a certain time if they wished to volunteer. The percentages of subjects from the lecture, discussion, and "simple reminder" groups who showed up at the designated time and place were 22, 21, and 19, respectively. In other words, the lecture, discussion, and simple reminder were equally effective in persuading people to volunteer. The data show, however, that 15 percent of the "no decision" subjects (N equals 135) volunteered, whereas 22 percent of the subjects (N equals 338) who had been asked to make a decision showed up. Bennett (1955) reported that this difference was significant at the .07 level of confidence. These data suggest that changes in behavior should be attributed to making a decision rather than engaging in discussion. Perhaps the greater magnitude of change following decision in the Lewin food studies stems from the fact that, unlike the lecture groups, the discussion-decision groups were told that there would be a follow-up study (Lewin, 1953, p. 293).

Research findings from educational investigations are especially contradictory. We cannot state with any certainty that either teacher-centered or learner-centered methods are associated with greater learning. Some researchers claim superior learning for learner-centered groups (Allport, 1950; Bovard, 1952; Brandwein, 1958; Faw, 1949; Flanders, 1951; Neuman, 1957; Perkins, 1951; Peters, 1948; Sheldon & Landsman, 1950; Thompson and Tom, 1957; Zeleny, 1940). In one of the early investigations, Zeleny (1940) conducted a series of five small experiments with college classes in sociology, found a slight advantage for learner-centered groups in each case. Faw (1949) showed that college students in nondirective groups learned more about psychology than did students in directive groups. Similarly, Allport (1950) has reported that students in a college social relations course believed they learned more in permissive than in directive sections. Thompson and Tom (1957) found that students in learner-centered groups acquire and retain significantly more information about dairy farming than do those in teacher-centered groups. Unfortunately, the observed superiority of learner-centered groups in this study cannot be attributed wholly to the classroom behavior of the teacher since elaborate steps were taken to provide students from learner-centered groups with a chance to carry out dairy projects at home, whereas students from teacher-centered groups were insured of no such opportunity. Perkins (1951) has reported that teachers attending in-service classes in educational psychology with permissive instructors made more comments indicative of psychological insight than those in teacher-centered classes. Flanders (1951) found that pupils taught by a learner-centered teacher showed superiority over the students of an autocratic teacher in the acquisition and retention of four principles of human relations. After observing three science classes under autocratic, laissez-faire, and democratic conditions, Brandwein (1958) felt that students in the democratic situation learned more. A study of "nondirective group therapy with students in academic difficulty" (Sheldon & Landsman, 1950) shows marked superiority for the nondirective over the directive method. In the same vein, Neuman (1957) found that students who learned lists of words using their own techniques showed better recall than students directed to use a learning technique developed by a group of psychologists familiar with verbal-learning research.

A number of investigations have found no difference between learner-centered and teacher-centered methods (Bills, 1952; Deignan, 1956; Eglash, 1954; Farquhar, 1955; Haigh & Schimidt, 1956; Landsman, 1950; McKeachie, 1951; Ostlund, 1956; Rasmussen, 1956; Rehage, 1951; Slomowitz, 1955; Smith & Johnson, 1952; Wispe, 1951). In a typical study, Wispe found no overall difference between groups on the objective part of a final examination in an introductory college course in social relations, but did find that students of low ability did better if taught by teacher-centered methods.

Using content analysis of discussion transcripts to measure learning, Ostlund (1956) found slightly greater learning on the part of learner-centered groups; however, the difference was statistically significant for only one index of learning. It may be wondered whether the Ostlund study and other similarly inconclusive investigation would have showed a significant advantage for learner-centered methods if the treatment had lasted longer. With a few exceptions, the longest experiments have run no more than a semester. Many have been only a few weeks in duration. If we are to believe proponents of democratic teaching, our schools are essentially authoritarian, and it may take considerable exposure before students become acculturated to learner-centered methods. A study by Peters (1948) which lasted two years is suggestive in this respect. Peters found a slight advantage for democratic teachers at the end of the first year, which became a marked superiority by the end of the second year. Directly opposed to the Peters' finding is a survey study of 66 history teachers and 1275 students by Brookover (1943), who found a significant negative relationship between student ratings of teachers' permissiveness and mean gains in information on a history test. In Brookover's words, "Apparently the students like the friendly teachers better, but they learn more when taught by the more authoritarian ones" (p. 300).

It is also argued that investigations which use final examinations as a measure of learning and which fail to remove anxiety connected with grades provide an inadequate comparison of teacher-centered and learner-centered methods. It is suggested (McKeachie, 1951) that in a truly democratic situation no external authority would evaluate achievement. Rather, each student would provide his own internal yardstick, evaluating his own progress. Under these conditions, it is argued, learner-centered groups would probably show superiority. A series of experiments at the University of Michigan illustrate this point nicely. In the original experiment Guetzkow, Kelley, and McKeachie (1954) found that students in teacher-centered groups showed slight superiority on a final examination. What is more, morale was higher in teacher-centered groups, and students in these groups expressed more desire to take additional courses in psychology and major in psychology than did students from other groups. Subsequently, McKeachie (1951) conducted an experiment in which an effort was made to reduce grade anxiety. He found no difference on a final examination. In a companion study, Bovard (1952) found that students in the learner-centered groups showed greater insight into psychological processes than students in the teacher-centered groups. Haigh and Schimidt (1956) found that "when students are permitted to choose between a teacher-centered and a group-centered class and when the students in the group-centered class are not required to learn subject matter by the examination-grade system there is no significant difference between these two types of classes at the end of the term" (pp. 301-302). However, reducing the anxiety surrounding grades provides no guarantee that learner-centered groups will do as well or better than teacher-centered. This is evidenced in a study by Asch (1951) in which the instructor-centered group achieved higher grades on both objective and essay portions of a final examination in psychology, despite the fact that the score on the examination was not a basis for grading in the learner-centered group.

One other factor may weigh against discovering possible advantages inherent in the learner-centered method. It may be that the sorts of learning best implemented by teacher-centered methods are measured with relative ease, whereas the more intangible learnings of learner-centered groups elude quantification. A study by DiVesta (1954) is enlightening in this respect. He found greater gains on knowledge and attitude tests for students taught by the instructor-centered method, but superior improvement in leadership skills for students taught by the learner-centered method. Rehage (1951) conducted an investigation of teacher-pupil planning in which he found no difference between groups on measures of learning and attitude change, though the experimental group did much more extra work, seemed to have more insight into the process of group planning, and seemed to have more interest in the subject matter than did the control group. Anderson (1956) found that the group taught by a directive teacher recalled much more information than other groups while the nondirective group scored significantly higher on a measure of interest in the subject studied than did the directive group.

In addition to the studies cited above, Burke (1956), Husband (1951), and Ward (1956) all have reported greater learning in teacher-centered groups.

To summarize the educational research reviewed in this article, eleven studies have reported greater learning for learner-centered groups, thirteen have shown no difference, and eight have found teacher-centered methods superior to learner-centered. It should be noted that while some investigations have reported a *statistically* significant difference favoring one method or other, it is doubtful if any of these differences are of *practical* or *social* significance. Some writers, such as Bills (1957), argue that despite—or because of—the failure to find a striking difference in regard to learning, we should prefer the learner-centered method because of its greater association with high morale and psychological well-being.

It is a rather general finding that morale is higher in learner-centered groups (e.g., Thelen & Whithall, 1949). The only exceptions to this generalization appear to occur in situations in which there is high anxiety about grades which are awarded on the basis of final examination scores (Guetzkow et al., 1954; Krumboltz, 1955; Wispe, 1951).

There are probably several factors, in addition to the suggestions above, which contribute to the confusing and contradictory pattern of research findings. The first of these is lack of methodological rigor and inadequate research design.[1] Furthermore, many experimenters in this field display a surprising lack of familiarity with other research. This is evidenced by bibliographies which fail to list any experimental studies of authoritarian-democratic leadership styles except, of course, Lewin, Lippitt, and White. Study after study has been conducted with basically the same conception and execution and in apparent isolation from other research. The results of twenty years of investigation remain embarrassingly noncumulative.

Another serious defect in this research stems from the fact that operational definitions of leadership styles have lacked precision. Herein lies an important reason for contradictory findings. The present author believes that the lack of precise operational definitions of leadership styles is symptomatic of a larger problem: the authoritarian-democratic construct is an inadequate basis for research because, for one thing, it presumes to summarize the complexity of group life into a single dimension. There are probably many variables of leadership and group life. Hemphill (1949), after analysis of some five hundred existing groups, arrived at sixteen descriptive variables. Factor analyses of Hemphill's variables (Gekoski, 1952), as well as several factor analyses by Carter and Couch (1953), yield three dimensions which the present author likes to interpret as follows:

1. *The Affective area.* Includes degree of interpersonal warmth or coolness, tension or relaxation; degree of antagonism or solidarity. Opposes friendly pleasant exchange to hostility and constraint.

2. *The Procedural area.* Includes statement and control of agenda, control of communication, division of labor. Refers to amount of structure and degree of organization as opposed to degree of disorganization or looseness of structure.

---

[1] For a critical review of some of the authoritarian-democratic studies which pays some attention to methodological problems, see Roseborough (1953). See also McKeachie (1954), who discusses the teacher-centered—learner-centered controversy in an analysis which stresses methodological shortcomings and weak experimental design.

3. The Task area. Includes quantity and quality of work done, units produced, ideas presented, solutions considered. Opposes solution reached, problem
solved, high performance maintained to no solution, problem unsolved, poor
performance. Productivity versus sterility.

No doubt there are other dimensions and subdimensions yet to be conclu-
sively identified. In view of the probable complexity of leadership, the authoritarian-democratic construct appears to be an ill-defined and oversimplified
conception of leadership variables. As such this construct cannot be defended
on functional grounds. To say that a style of leadership is authoritarian does not
adequately describe the behaviors which the leader actually exhibited. Very
likely many studies, all of which labeled leadership styles in the same way,
actually differed a great deal at the concrete level of what the leaders said and
did. These variations in behavior could, of course, lead to variable results. Use of
these simplifying labels tends to limit our thinking about leadership. For example, because we have grown used to thinking of the authoritarian leader as
impersonal, cool, and sometimes hostile, the possibility of a leader who maintains complete control of the decisions of the group and yet is friendly and
personal does not seem very real to us.

Moreover, the words "authoritarian" and "democratic" contain surplus
meanings. The proliferation of synonyms for "authoritarian" and "democratic"
can be interpreted as an effort to escape the normative overtones of the original
terms; in other words, an effort to be "objective." "Authoritarian" and "democratic" have been purposely used in this paper because the present writer believes that behind the facade of objectivity expressed in less-loaded words there
lurks an essentially moralistic interpretation of leadership by many researchers
and theorists and the bulk of the popularizers.

It serves no practical or scientific objective to prove that unreasonably extreme leadership types are ineffective; yet, there is reason to feel that a number
of researchers have been led to this specious demonstration by the moralism
inherent in the authoritarian-democratic conceptualizations. The greatest number of studies in which the "bad" leadership type is overdrawn have a democratic
bias. Cronbach (1954) has put this point very well, stating that,

"When teacher-control was branded as 'autocracy,' and contrasted with so-called
democratic teaching, all the research seemed to be trying to prove that teacher-
control cannot possibly work. These studies are usually made by training some
leaders to use each particular style of leadership, so that different styles can be
compared. Almost without exception, the dominative leaders are taught to be
harsh, to use hostile comments in criticizing students, and to discourage student
initiative. This means that we lack research on friendly, adaptable teacher control, which is the pattern most teachers are presently trying to use" (pp. 455-
456).

It is hard to tell how many investigations have been seriously damaged by the
biased distortion of one of the leadership styles. A handful of studies is clearly
affected, as shown by protocols and incidents reported as well as by descriptions

of leadership behavior. This bias has probably operated to a marked degree in a number of other studies, and to some degree in most investigations.

This leads directly to a further and very serious inadequacy in the authoritarian-democratic conceptualization. Even if, as the present writer contends, "authoritarian" and "democratic" conveys a grossly oversimplified picture of leadership behavior, it would still be possible to defend these concepts if there were some good reason for believing that the complex of behavior which "democratic" or "authoritarian" seem to encompass is likely to be associated with high productivity and high morale. Unfortunately no such mediating body of theory and knowledge exists. This statement is probably true of most areas of applied social science, and it is certainly applicable to educational research. There are no adequate notions of how the authoritarian-democratic construct is related to learning. With the exception of a few clinically derived, *ad hoc* hypotheses emanating largely from the Rogerian school of psychotherapy and *The Authoritarian Personality,* the research on leadership styles seems to flow more from ethical generalization than from scientific hypothesis. Much of the research on teaching methods in the last twenty years seemed bent of discovering whether "The meek shall inherit the earth," or whether, on the other hand, "Nice guys lose."

Whatever the motivation behind it, a principal difficulty of research in teaching methods—and leadership research in general—has been the rather low level of empiricism. Teacher-centered and learner-centered methods have been repetitiously investigated not because there were well conceived ideas as to *how* one would lead to superior learning, but merely to find out *if* one style was superior to the other. We were not fortunate enough to find that one method is consistently better than or even consistently different from the other; thus, we are now forced to explore new avenues. In short, the authoritarian-democratic construct, as far as education is concerned at least, has far outlived its usefulness either as a guide to research or as an interpretation of leadership behavior.

Conclusion

The evidence available fails to demonstrate that either authoritarian or democratic leadership is consistently associated with higher productivity. In most situations, however, democratic leadership is associated with higher morale. But even this conclusion must be regarded cautiously, because the authoritarian leader has been unreasonably harsh and austere in a number of investigations reporting superior morale in democratic groups. In the educational setting, morale appears to be higher under learner-centered conditions, at least when anxiety over grades is reduced.

The authoritarian-democratic construct provides an inadequate conceptualization of leadership behavior. When a satisfactory body of knowledge about learning in social situations is available it will then be possible to describe the behaviors which a teacher can exhibit to achieve a given learning outcome. It seems reasonable to suppose that leadership styles or teaching methods emanating from knowledge about learning will have a higher probability of meeting criteria of effectiveness than do *a priori* styles or methods. At least, studies based on two *a priori* styles have not led to consistent or easily interpretable results.

References

Adams, R. G. The behavior of pupils in democratic and autocratic social climates. *Abstracts of Dissertations,* Stanford University, 1943-1946, 19-21, 83-86.

Adams, S. Social climate and productivity in small groups. *Amer. Soc. Rev.,* 1954, 19, 421-425.

Adorno, T. W. et al. *The authoritarian personality.* New York: Harpers, 1950.

Allport, G. W. How shall we evaluate teaching the social sciences. In Bernice B. Cronkhite (Ed.), *A handbook for college teachers.* Cambridge: Harvard University Press, 1950.

Anderson, H. H. An experimental study of dominative and integrative behavior in children of preschool age. *J. soc. Psychol.,* 1937, 8, 335-345.

Anderson, H. H. Domination and social integration in the behavior of kindergarten children and teachers. *Genet. Psychol. Monogr.,* 1939, 21, 287-385.

Anderson, R. C. Teacher role, personality, and productivity. Unpublished manuscript, available from the author, 1956.

Asch, M. J. Nondirective teaching in psychology. *Psychol. Monogr.,* 1951, 65, 4.

Bennett, E. B. Discussion, decision, and consensus in 'group decision'. *Human Relations,* 1955, 8, 251-273.

Berkowitz, L. Sharing leadership in small, decision-making groups. *J. abnorm. soc. Psychol.,* 1953, 48, 231-238.

Bills, R. E. An investigation of student-centered teaching. *J. educ. Res.,* 1952, 46, 313-319.

Bills, R. E. Personality changes during student-centered teaching. *J. educ. Res.,* 1957, 50, 121-126.

Bovard, E. W. The experimental production of interpersonal affect. *J. abnorm. soc. Psychol.,* 1951, 46, 521-528.

Bovard, E. W. Clinical insight as a function of group process. *J. abnorm. soc. Psychol.,* 1952, 47, 534-539.

Brandwein, P. *The gifted student as future scientist.* New York: Harcourt, Brace, and Co., 1955.

Brandwein, P., Watson, F., Blackwood, P. *Teaching high school science: a book of methods.* New York: Harcourt, Brace, and Co., 1958.

Brookover, W. B. The social roles of teachers and pupil achievement. *Amer. soc. Rev.,* 1943, 8, 391.

Brookover, W. B. *A sociology of education.* New York: American Book Co., 1955.

Burke, H. R. An experimental study of teaching methods in a college freshman orientation course. *Dissertation Abstr.,* 1956, 16, 77-78.

Burnett, R. W. *Teaching science in the secondary school.* New York: Rinehart and Co., 1957.

Burton, W. H. *The guidance of learning activities.* Second Edition. New York: Appleton-Century-Crofts, Inc., 1952.

Carter, L. F. Leadership and small group behavior. In Sherif, M., and Wilson, M. (Eds.), *Group relations at the crossroads.* New York: Harper, 1953.

Cronbach, L. J. *Educational psychology.* New York: Harcourt, Brace and Co., 1954.

Deignan, F. J. A comparison of the effectiveness of two group discussion methods. *Dissertation Abstr.*, 1956, 16, 1110-1111.

DiVesta, F. J. Instructor-centered and student-centered approaches in teaching a human relations course. *J. appl. Psychol.*, 1954, 38, 329-335.

Eglash, A. A group discussion method of teaching psychology. *J. educ. Psychol.*, 1954, 45, 257-267.

Farquhar, W. H. An investigation of the relationship of three teaching methods to student behavior in a how to study course. *Dissertation Abstr.*, 1955, 15, 2442.

Faw, V. A. A psychotherapeutic method of teaching psychology. *American Psychologist*, 1949, 4, 104.

Festinger, L. *A theory of cognitive dissonance.* Evanston, Illinois: Row, Peterson, and Co., 1957.

Flanders, N. A. Personal-social anxiety as a factor in experimental learning. *J. educ. Res.*, 1951, 45, 100-110.

Gekoski, N. Predicting group productivity. *Personnel Psychol.*, 1952, 5, 281-292.

Grambs, J. D., Iverson, W. J., Patterson, F. K. *Modern methods in secondary education.* (Rev. ed.) New York: The Dryden Press, 1958.

Guetzkow, H., Kelley, E. L., McKeachie, W. J. An experimental comparison of recitation, discussion, and tutorial methods in college teaching. *J. educ. Psychol.*, 1954, 45, 193-207.

Haigh, G. V. and Schimidt, W. The learning of subject matter in teacher-centered and group-centered classes. *J. educ. Psychol.*, 1956, 47, 295-301.

Hare, A. P. *Social interaction: An analysis of behavior in small groups.* New York: John Wiley and Sons, Inc., in press.

Hemphill, J. K. Situational factors in leadership. *Ohio State University Educational Research Monographs,* No. 32, 1949.

Heyns, R. W. The effects of variation in leadership on participant behavior in discussion groups. *Microfilm Abstr.*, 1949, 9, Part II, pp. 161-163.

Husband, R. W. A statistical comparison of the efficacy of large lectures versus smaller recitation sections upon achievement in general psychology. *J. Psychol.*, 1951, 31, 297-300.

Krumboltz, J. D. An investigation of the effect of three teaching methods on motivational outcomes in a how to study course. *Dissertation Abstr.*, 1955, 15, 2470.

Landsman, T. An experimental study of a student-centered learning method. Unpublished doctoral dissertation, Syracuse University, 1950.

Lewin, K. Studies in group decision. In Cartwright, D. and Zander, A. (Eds.) *Group dynamics: Research and theory.* Evanston, Illinois: Row, Peterson, and Co., 1953.

McCurdy, H. G., and Lambert, W. E. The efficiency of small human groups in the solution of problems requiring genuine cooperation. *J. Pers.*, 1952, 20, 478-494.

McKeachie, W. J. Anxiety in the college classroom. *J. educ. Res.*, 1951, 45, 153-160.

McKeachie, W. J. Student centered versus instructor centered instruction. *J. educ. Psychol.*, 1954, 45, 143-150.

Mowrer, O. H. Authoritarianism versus self-government in the management of children's aggressive reactions as preparation for citizenship in a democracy. *J. soc. Psychol.*, 1939, 10, 121-126.

Mursell, J. *Successful teaching: Its psychological principles.* (2nd ed.) New York: McGraw-Hill, 1954.

Neuman, S. E. Student versus instructor design of study method. *J. educ. Psychol.,* 1957, 48, 328-333.

Ostlund, L. A. An experimental study of case-discussion learning. *J. exp. Educ.,* 1956, 25, 81-89.

Perkins, H. V. Climate influences on group learning. *J. educ. Res.,* 1951, 45, 114-119.

Peters, C. C. *Teaching high school history and social studies for citizenship.* Coral Gables, Florida: University of Miami Press, 1948.

Rasmussen, G. R. Evaluation of a student-centered and instructor-centered method of conducting a graduate course in education. *J. educ. Psychol.,* 1956, 47, 449-461.

Rehage, K. J. Pupil-teacher planning. *J. educ. Res.,* 1951, 45, 111-114.

Roseborough, M. E. Experimental studies of small groups. *Psychol. Bull.,* 1953, 50, 275-303.

Singer, J. L., and Goldman, G. D. Experimentally contrasted social atmospheres in group psychotherapy with chronic schizophrenics. *J. soc. Psychol.,* 1954, 40, 23-37.

Sheldon, W. D., and Landsman, T. An investigation of nondirective group therapy with students in academic difficulty. *J. Consult. Psychol.,* 1950, 14, 210-215.

Slomowitz, M. A comparison of personality changes and content achievement gains occurring in two modes of instruction. *Dissertation Abstr.,* 1955, 15, 1790.

Smith, H. C., and Johnson, D. An experimental study of attitudes and achievement in the democratic classroom. 1952 meetings of A.P.A.

Thelen, H. A., and Whithall, J. Three frames of reference; the description of climate. *Hum. Relat.,* 1949, 2, 159-176.

Thompson, O., and Tom, F. Comparison of the effectiveness of a pupil-centered versus a teacher-centered pattern for teaching vocational agriculture. *J. educ. Res.,* 1957, 50, 667-678.

Ward, J. N. Group-study versus lecture-demonstration method in physical science instruction for general education college students. *J. exp. Educ.,* 1956, 24, 197-210.

White, R., and Lippitt, R. Leader behavior and member reaction in three 'social climates.' In Cartwright, D. and Zander, A. (Eds.) Group dynamics: Research and theory. Evanston, Illinois: Row, Peterson, and Co., 1953.

Wischmeier, R. R. Group-centered and leader-centered leadership: An experimental study. *Speech Monogr.,* 1955, 22, 43-49.

Wispe, L. G. Evaluating section teaching methods. *J. educ. Res.,* 1951, 45, 161-186.

Zeleny, L. D. Experimental appraisal of a group learning plan. *J. educ. Res.,* 1940, 34, 37-42.

The Logic of Experiments on Discovery
Lee J. Cronbach

In spite of the confident endorsements of teaching through discovery that we read in semipopular discourses on improving education, there is precious little substantiated knowledge about what advantages it offers, and under what conditions these advantages accrue. We badly need research in which the right questions are asked and trustworthy answers obtained. When the research is in it will tell us, I suspect, that inductive teaching has value in nearly every area of the curriculum, and also that its function is specialized and limited (Cronbach, 1963, pp. 378-382). The task of research is to define that proper place and function.

Honest research is hard to do, when learning by discovery is the battle cry of one side in the ardent combat between educational philosophies. We have, on the one hand, the view of education as cultural transmission, which hints strongly that it is the teacher's job to know the answers and to put them before the pupil. On the other, we have the view of education as growth, arguing that the only real and valuable knowledge is that formulated by the pupil out of his own experience. The second position, which appeals to liberal, humanitarian, and instrumentalist biases, has a long history. In the last thirty-odd years the bias favoring do-it-yourself learning has been very strong, as educators and psychologists have united in attacks on teacher dominance and pupil conformity. Consequently, we have had almost none of the cut-and-thrust debate needed to define issues and to expose implications or fallacies of the evidence.

It is time to put aside the polemic question, Is teaching through discovery better than didactic teaching? (*Didactic* is perhaps not the ideal brief label for the pedagogy in which the teacher sets forth knowledge, but among the words that come to mind it has the advantage of being least value-loaded.) We shall have to ask subtle questions and exhibit both patience and ingenuity in unraveling them. How to frame research studies to get the right information is not at all clear; sometimes we can meet one of the supposed requirements of research design only at the expense of another, and if all my recommendations were to be followed, research would become impossibly elaborate. One of the hopes is that discussion among investigators and educational innovators can generate some agreement as to which subquestions and which improvements in research design should have priority in the next stages of investigation.

I propose that we search for limited generalizations of the following form:
> With subject matter of this nature,
> inductive experience of this type,
> in this amount,
> produces this pattern of responses,
> in pupils at this level of development.

Lee J. Cronbach, "The Logic of Experiments on Discovery," in Lee S. Shulman and Evan R. Keislar (Eds.), *Learning by Discovery,* © 1966 by Rand McNally & Company, Chicago, pp. 76-92. Reprinted by permission of the publisher.

Since this sentence constitutes an outline of the remainder of my paper, let me clarify each segment of it before I proceed.

First, the subject matter. Surely we cannot generalize over all educational content indiscriminately, yet the literature on discovery reads as if a general conclusion is sought. Moreover, unless learning tasks are comparable to those of the classroom, they are unserviceable as a basis for educational recommendations.

Second, the type of training. I can amplify this sufficiently for the moment by referring to type and amount of guidance as a significant aspect of the training.

Third, the amount of inductive experience. I have no faith in any generalization upholding one teaching technique against another, whether that preferred method be audiovisual aids, programmed instruction, learning by doing, inductive teaching, or whatever. A particular educational tactic is part of an instrumental system; a proper educational design calls upon that tactic at a certain point in the sequence, for a certain period of time, following and preceding certain other tactics. No conclusion can be drawn about the tactic considered by itself.

Fourth, the pattern of outcomes. Education has many purposes, and any learning experience must be judged in terms of all those goals. To take a simple example, there must exist some method of teaching arithmetic that produces graduates who compute brilliantly—and who hate all work involving numbers. It would be improper to advocate this method on the basis of research that considers only its effect on computational skill. It is no defense for the advocate to say that computation is the only objective that concerns *him*. If he recommends an educational change, it is his responsibility to consider how that change will affect all the outcomes that reasonable men consider important.

Fifth, the pupils. I suspect that inductive teaching is more valuable for some learners than others, and that we should not generalize over all pupils.

As I go on to illustrate wise and unwise research decisions, I am restricted by the content of past studies. In these studies the learner is nearly always to discover some simple connection or, at best, a formula or inductive generalization. When a writer argues that discovery is a thrilling personal experience he seems to have in mind the sort of startling reorganization of interpretation illustrated on the grand scale by Kepler, and on a lesser scale by Kekulé. These "retroductions" (Hanson, 1958) are *D*iscoveries that appear to be quite different psychologically from *d*iscoveries of simple regularities. Big-D *d*iscoveries are infrequent even in the life of the scientist. I doubt that the pupils in today's innovative classroom are having many big-D experiences, and I doubt that the psychologist will be able to arrange conditions so that Discovery will occur while the subject is under his eyes. Hence my account is limited to research on little-d discovery. We should not, however, allow ourselves to think that in these studies we are learning about the effect of retroductive discovery. (E. R. Hilgard draws my attention to the fact that we are equally without research on a "really fine kind of discovery: discovering problems rather than discovering solutions" [Mackworth, 1965]).

Selection of Learning Tasks

Since the question before us is educational, experimental tasks ought to have psychological properties closely similar to those of educational subject matter. Discovery surely becomes more valuable as the linkage between the stimulus and the correct response becomes more rational. Rationality is at a maximum in tasks where the correct response can be deduced from the givens of the problem or from a network of established ideas. For example: finding the number of diagonals from any vertex in a polygon of n sides. Once a child understands the question, he can confirm or infirm any rule he proposes, with no help from an instructor. While the younger child confirms empirically, the older child can see that the rule is a logical necessity. There is a natural (but not necessarily a logical) linkage in tasks where the response has a readily discerned consequence. Do apples taste good? The answer might in principle be deduced from the chemistry of plants and the physiology of taste, but in practice the discovery is made through a provisional try followed by natural reinforcement. At the opposite extreme from rationality are those tasks where the S-R linkage is arbitrary, so that the person can know what is correct only because the experimenter tells him so. An example is Duncan's experiment (1964), where a digit is presented along with three adjectives and the learner has to guess which adjective has been selected randomly as correct. Discovery at this point has been reduced to sheer trial and error.

Learning by discovery is said to teach a sort of intellectual self-reliance. The child who understands the structure of the number system believes that he can work out subtraction combinations for himself, believes that he can check his own answers, believes that the answer to an arithmetic problem is always the same, believes (more broadly) that any new quantitative problem has a discoverable solution. Piaget and Smedslund (Ripple & Rockcastle, 1964) consider intellectual self-regulation—checking the consistency among one's beliefs before converting a belief into action—to be the chief ingredient in operational thought. Where inductive teaching is to promote intellectual self-reliance, is it not obvious that it must use tasks whose answers are rationally determined? Where we want to teach an experimental attitude, must we not use tasks whose solutions are empirically confirmable? Arbitrary tasks cannot possibly generate the important attitudes sought in serious inductive teaching of educational content.

Many experimental tasks that have value for other problems seem too lacking in rationality for the proper study of discovery. The task of Wittrock et al. (1964) where the child selects a picture representing a *la* or *le* French noun is arbitrary; the child's task is primarily to discover what the experimenter has in mind. The rules and codes used by Stacey (1949), Haslerud and Meyers (1958), and others are likewise arbitrary. The subject has to detect a pattern or regularity, but the patterns change from example to example. The patterns are not 'principles' (even though mistakenly given that name), and they do not fit into any system of mutually supporting propositions.

If we are concerned with the implications of discovery for understanding a discipline, the task should be part of a whole system of subject matter. The summation-of-series task of Gagné and Brown (1961) is well chosen. A solution called correct is correct in the eyes of God as well as of the experimenters. The training tasks are representative of series problems and, insofar as one task can be representative, of all mathematics. But we should not generalize from mathematics to other school subjects. If it is proposed, for example, to apply inductive methods in history by requiring pupils to draw conclusions from source documents, then there had better be experiments with such lessons. We might learn, for example, that the pupil who forms his own historical generalizations becomes much too confident of the dependability of his inferences, since social data cannot be counted on to contradict an error unequivocally.

Type of Teaching
With regard to experimental treatment, the first requirement is that each treatment be given a fair chance to show what it can do; by and large, educational innovators have violated this rule. What usually happens is something like this: John Doe contends that programmed presentation of college geology is better than conventional lectures. He assembles a writing team and spends two years drafting material, editing every sentence, trying it on pilot classes, and revising. Then Doe runs a grand experiment in which ten classes are taught with his material, while ten classes take the regular lecture course. Unless his writers were painfully inept the test scores favor the new method, and unless Doe is a very saint of an experimenter, he concludes that programmed instruction is more effective than the lecture method. Doe *has* shown that his programs give better results than the lectures in their casual, unedited, tired old form, but the outcome would very likely to have been reversed if he had put the same two-year effort into tuning up the lectures. Nothing of explanatory value has been learned from his study.

Studies of discovery have rarely given didactic instruction a fair shake. The control group suffers from one or another of the following impediments in nearly every study:

1. *Shorter Training Time.* In the Hilgard-Irvine-Whipple (1953) study with Katona's card tricks, the students who developed the rule for themselves worked with the material two to four times as long as those given the rule; they had to, to reach the criterion. In such a case, differences in transfer scores are interpretable only if the discovery group, with its greater opportunity to learn, *fails* to surpass the contrast group.

2. *Limited Goals.* The nondiscovery group is often led to think that manipulation of a formula is the only goal of instruction. Any insight into the nature of the formula is incidental rather than intentional learning for them, whereas the discovery group is oriented toward the meaning of the formula. Consider the Gagné-Brown experiment. The rule-and-example group practiced substituting numbers in the formulas for summation of various series, and was trained to criterion on that limited decoding skill. The guided-discovery group was taught to look for a pattern relating the terms of a particular series and the corresponding sums, to use a symbolic code for term number, term value, and sum, to translate the pattern into a symbolic formula, and then to substitute numbers into the formula. These students met a fourfold criterion. Gagné and Brown are

right in asserting that instructional effectiveness depends more on what is learned than on method of instruction, but their study is interpreted by them and others as supporting the *method* of guided discovery. For a fair test of the value of discovery, their rule-and-example program should have explicated the structural relationships that the discovery group was led to find for itself, and these relationships should have entered the end-of-training criterion for the rule-and-example group. (Note that my comments on this aspect of the Gagné-Brown study do not agree with those in Wittrock's paper [Shulman & Keislar, 1966], pp. 52-54.)

Mental set is an important variable in the training, as we see in the Hilgard experiment. One of his treatment groups was shown how to find the rule in one card-trick problem after another, but often the student who found a rule set about at once to memorize it. Because no one had conveyed to him that he was supposed to learn the rationale and the rule-finding technique, he put them out of his mind. Rarely is the experimental subject told, even in general terms, what transfer tasks constitute the objectives of instruction. Keeping the objectives of instruction secret from the learner is pedagogically unsound, and an experiment where this is done is an improper base for educational generalizations.

3. *Rote Instruction.* The McConnell (1934) studies of arithmetic and others like it allegedly compare discovery with didactic teaching—but note these excerpts from McConnell's description of the second method: "The [number fact] is identified by the teacher dogmatically and autocratically. There is a studious effort to keep the child from verifying the answers. He will not know why 8 + 5 is 13. [The method] does not tolerate concrete teaching, discovery, or insightful manipulation." Thiele (1938) shows a similar exaggeration; his nondiscovery group was given "isolated facts as though each fact had no relation to any other fact taught." Such experiments with nonrational drill may once have been justified by the challenge of Gestalt theory to that of Thorndike (as it stood before he introduced "belongingness" as a principle in 1932), but they are not pertinent today.

Didactic teaching can and should develop meaning out of concrete experience and lay bare the mathematical structure behind an algorithm. Only comparing that kind of didactic teaching with discovery methods tells us anything of value today. We may note that Forgus and Schwartz (1957) found no difference at all between discovery and meaningful didactic teaching.

4. *Prejudicial data analysis.* As Olson (1965) points out, one of the studies most often cited as supporting discovery attains this result by illogical analysis of the data. Haslerud and Meyers (1958) had the student work with codes, each sentence requiring a different encoding rule. For any one person ten sentences were in this *G* form:

Write each word backwards.
(A) THEY NEED MORE TIME
    YEHT DEEN EROM EMIT
(B) GIVE THEM FIVE MORE
On the *G* rules the subject merely practices encoding. The *D* form for the other ten sentences was the same except that the rule was omitted and had to be in-

ferred from the A example. The G and D sentences were presented alternately in a single list. The G_1 score was the number of sentences correctly encoded from the G list; the D_1 score was the number of D sentences for which the code was found and applied. The transfer measure presented multiple-choice items like this:

THEY CAME AND WENT

a. MNEN ECTE
   ATA HWYD
b. DOBM RGHO
   CKF DEIN
c. YEHT EMAC
   DNA TNEW
d. HPZC OHAT
   RRS FSHZ

One of the four alternatives is a transformation of the given sentence by a rule that was in either the G or D list during training. The G_2 score was the number of items based on G rules where the subject chose the correct alternative, and the D_2 score was similarly based on the ten items involving D rules. The score means were as follows:

G_1 8.6	G_2 7.8	Difference -0.9
D_1 5.4	D_2 8.0	Difference 2.7

The Haslerud-Meyers report gives these facts, but puts all the emphasis on the difference scores. The authors first run a significance test to show that the mean difference for the discovery group departs from zero. This is wrong for many reasons, not the least of which is that with a free-response first test and a multiple-choice second test, one would expect a gain of 2.5 points among persons performing entirely at random. But the more fundamental error is to use difference scores at all. Test 2 is the only measure that is operationally the same for both groups and therefore the only fair basis for comparison. The difference of 0.2 points is trivial and nonsignificant. The much-cited conclusion, based on the difference in difference scores, arises simply because the D_1 task was much harder than the G_1 task, and so there was lots of room for an increase from D_1 to D_2.

I turn now to a pervasive dilemma in experimental design and analysis. Shall we train every subject to criterion under both D and G methods, in which case the D training ordinarily gets more time to produce its effect? Or shall we equate time, and if so, how shall we treat the nondiscoverers? In the latter design an average over the whole D group, while assessing the net utility of the treatment, has no explanatory value. Using a principle one has discovered is one thing; performing on a problem whose principle was not discovered during training is another. We might discard those who fail to discover, but that biases the experiment by throwing out the weaker members of the experimental group. To pair experimental and control subjects and to discard every nondiscoverer along with his opposite number in the control group is better, but places too much faith in our imperfect matching. I am inclined to think that transfer data for all subjects have to be analyzed in a way that takes initial scores into account. One possibility is to treat separately the discoverers in the D group and the non-discoverers, since their transfer scores have different meanings. I am not content with this resolution of the difficulty, however, since there are probably degrees of discovery and nondiscovery (cf. Travers, 1964, p. 498).

One further complication. Surely it is good pedagogy to apply a further treatment to the child who fails to discover. In most studies prior to 1960, the subject who could not discover the answer simply left the problem unsolved. We may contrast this with Baddeley's little study (1963), where, after a minute of effort to unscramble an anagram, the unsuccessful subject was given the answer and went on to another anagram. Interestingly, his subjects later recalled more of the answers given to them than of the answers they had worked out for themselves. The finding, like Kersh's (1958), begins to make a case for learning by trying to discover and failing! Or, at the very least, suggests an aspect of the discovery treatment that has been given very little attention.

The fact that experiments are often loaded against the nondiscovery group leads naturally to a recommendation to make the discovery and didactic treatments alike in every respect but one, but this is too facile a recommendation, as can be seen if we think further about duration of training. Suppose we agree that the discovery instruction is to continue until nearly all the pupils pass a criterion test. Then there is no way to make the treatment uniform even for members of that treatment group. A certain child reaches the criterion early: if we terminate his training we allow him less training time than others; if we have him work on additional relevant problems, he encounters content others in his group do not. It is even less possible to hold constant the experience of different groups. The didactic group can be expected on the average to master the solution earlier. Do we shorten their instruction? Give them more problems on the same rule at the risk of boring them? Take them on to additional rules? Whatever we do, it is clearly impossible to give desirable instruction for each group while keeping all variables constant save one.

I doubt that any recommendation will fit all studies, but my inclination is to fall back on optimization within a fixed time. In education, a certain amount of time is allocated to a particular course, and experimentation should tell us how to use that time (cf. Lawrence, 1954). I would fix a certain period of instruction, say, 400 minutes, and compare two styles of instruction by arranging the two best instructional plans we can within that time limit. For style A, then, we have to select subject matter suited to that style, arrange whatever length and spacing of instruction fits that style, and similarly adjust explanations, reinforcements, etc. Likewise for style B. In the Gagné-Brown summation task, for example, I can imagine that the series problems used to develop insight by a rule-and-example style would differ from the set of problems best suited to the discovery style. If so, not even the content studied would be held constant.

Have I now completely contradicted my criticism of experimenters who confound other variables with discovery? I think not. An educational procedure is a system in which the materials chosen and the rules governing what the teacher does should be in harmony with each other and with the pupil's qualities. If we want to compare the camel with the horse, we compare a good horse and a good camel; we don't take two camels and saw the hump off one of them. My objection is to didactic treatments that do not use sound didactic pedagogy. Wherever we can reasonably predict that giving a concrete experience or explaining clearly or stating the aims of instruction will make the didactic teaching more potent, we should adopt that good procedure. We should likewise optimize the discovery treatment in *its* own terms, though it is impossible to adjust all the parameters experimentally. When the study is finished, and style A produces the better result, a colleague can always argue that a change in another parameter would have reversed the result. That trouble we can never escape. Even after the most highly controlled experiment, our colleague can contend that style B would have been superior if one of the controlled parameters had been held constant at a different level.

On the whole, I would favor more attention to comparisons of different inductive procedures than to further studies with a didactic contrast group. Experiments have shown a good deal about how to optimize didactic procedures, but there has been little analytic work on discovery methods. The study of Hilgard, Edgren, and Irvine (1954) where different groups were led to the solution in different ways is, I think, unique. We have seen useful studies on degree of guidance, but there has been less attention to the character of the guidance. We have some studies where the instructor gives hints about solution of the problem at hand (e.g., Gagné & Brown), others where the instructor gives hints about information-processing technique for solutions (Corman, 1957; Wickelgren, 1964), and, in the Hilgard studies, didactic teaching of an algorithm for generating (discovering?) a solution to a certain type of problem.

An important aspect of the treatment is the extent to which the pupil puts what he discovers into words. The instructor may or may not urge the learner to formulate his generalization in words and may or may not monitor the formulation for correctness. Closely related is the choice of criterion for deciding that a pupil has reached the solution and can go on to new work. A discovery emerges through several stages, and one can solve quite a few similar problems before he consolidates the intellectual basis for the solution. It is hard to say which decision on these points would make for the best inductive teaching; right now the need is to make an explicit decision in the experimental plan and to report it clearly. The Gagné-Smith (1962) study is a model in this respect. It puts considerable substance behind George Stoddard's famous remark that we learn not by doing but by thinking about what we are doing.

I shall draw attention to just one more of the variations in teaching procedure that must be studied. The experimental psychologist has invariably studied discovery by the isolated learner. He arranges conditions so that the learner cannot profit—or be handicapped—by what other members of the class do and say. Educators, however, are concerned with group instruction in which many pupils face a problem together and all of them throw their partial insights into the discussion. The teacher may lead out one pupil Socratically; if so, are the others discovering vicariously or are they learning a solution given to them? Studies of isolated learners tell us nothing about the effect on bystanders or those who share a discussion. There have been some controlled studies of group problem-solving (Lorge et al., 1958) and team-learning (Glaser, Klaus, & Egerman, 1962), but they are rather remote from our present topic. I have seen no studies of inductive teaching that analyze the group process and its effects on pupils who play different roles.

Extent of Inductive Teaching

Educational recommendations seek to optimize the student's development over a long time span. The educator is not nearly so concerned with the mastery of a single principle as with the student's cumulative development of insight and skill. Studies of inductive teaching have generally employed very brief instruction, yet the recommendations apply to whole courses or whole curricula. I am dubious about such extrapolation, and join Carroll (1963) in urging studies of instruction continued over a substantial time span.

Even as small experiments, the discovery studies have been too miniature. Typically, there is an hour of training and one delayed transfer test. But consider the moral of Duncan's study (1964) with five consecutive days of work and a new learning task each day. He found negative transfer from Day 1 to Day 2, and positive transfer thereafter. A study confined to two days would have given a false conclusion. Something like a minimum length for an educational experiment is seen in Kersh's 1964 study with 16 hours of instruction and McConnell's with 35-40 hours (1934).

I am impressed by the possibility that *some* experience in discovering principles in a field of knowledge will radically alter the relation the learner perceives between himself and the knowledge, and his way of behaving when he forgets a solution or encounters an unprecedented problem. I offer the hypothesis, however, that this can be accomplished by devoting only a small fraction of the instructional time to inductive procedures.

To illustrate, let me offer a hypothetical plan for teaching cooking; if nothing else, this will provide relief from too much talk of mathematics and physics. Although recipes can be discovered or invented, I would start by giving experience in following recipes, along with reasons for measuring exactly and following directions. This is didactic teaching. The pudding scorches if not stirred according to directions, and the girl discovers that authority was right in its warnings— but that surely is not what we mean by a discovery approach. Around, perhaps, age 12, my class would experiment. The most elementary experiment might be to vary the amount of water added to one cup of pancake flour and observe the product under standard baking conditions. Trivial as this is, it can float profound enough notions in its wake: optimization, control of experimental conditions, interaction of variables, variation in criterion with the purpose or artistic taste of the judge, etc. While these simple experiments would initiate new thinking about recipes and cooking, I'd guess that six such parametric inquiries could teach nearly as much as six dozen. We might well shift back to prescription and demonstration when we teach the girl to make pie crust. Once she has some experimental background, she should have no difficulty in accepting the teacher's statement about what chilling the crust before rolling does to the texture, particularly if the teacher supports the statement with photographs and samples. We had her make discoveries to establish an attitude. This attitude, once established, can be sustained in subsequent didactic teaching. Later exposition can and should continually hold in view the experimental base of recipes, the legitimacy of adapting them to fit personal criteria, and other such concepts. From time to time there will need to be further experimentation, in inventing recipes, for example. When I propose that some small fraction of the course use discovery methods, I am not saying "and let the rest of the course remain as it was." On the contrary, I want didactic teaching modified to capitalize on the meanings and attitudes that were established through discovery.

Now there may be those who argue that a girl simply cannot fully understand the technique for making pie crust if she is told how to do it. Then what is the right experiment to determine how much discovery is needed? No short-term treatment can provide any evidence. Instead, we need experiments lasting at least a semester, and ultimately extending into studies of long-term growth.

Some of the advantages claimed for discovery in past experiments may arise from its novelty, and would vanish in a long-term treatment. Kersh (1958) had students learn or discover rules for summation of series and found a sleeper effect. Many in the discovery group had not mastered the rules at the end of the training hour, but a month later they outperformed an instructed group. Their side comments at the time of retest convinced Kersh that the discovery method had aroused such interest that they puzzled over the problem on their own time or looked up the answer in the library. Something similar was found in Kersh's 1962 experiment. I have long felt that this result can be attributed to novelty. I doubt that a discovery approach causes typical pupils to work on math for their own satisfaction when further problems are put before them day after day. I was therefore somewhat gratified by Kersh's 1964 experiment. After sixteen training sessions there was no difference between didactic and inductive groups in tendency to use the information outside of class. This supports my argument for reasonably extended studies.

Outcome Variables

Although in general writings we preach that education has many outcomes, this view is not much honored in planning research on educational learning. Only gradually are we moving away from the experimental paradigm in which amount or rate of learning is the sole dependent variable, and into a timid attempt to appraise educational development multidimensionally. Recent studies on discovery usually include both retention and transfer tasks, but even so the dependent variables are few compared to the outcomes that spokesmen claim for discovery methods. If we put together these various claims, we have a list somewhat like the following. To facilitate discussion I have offered a neat label for each class of outcomes, but I do not take the labels as constituting a taxonomy. I make no attempt to list all available illustrations of studies that assess a given outcome.

1. *Time to criterion.* Ordinarily, a criterion of performance on the tasks on which the subject is trained. May require ability to verbalize principle (e.g., Gagné & Brown, 1961; Corman, 1957).

2. *Application.* Ability to solve problems where the discovered rule is relevant, for example, applying the formula for the sum of an arithmetic series to a set of numbers not encountered in training (e.g., Kersh, 1958).

3. *Retention.* Ability to recall a rule or to rediscover or reconstruct the rule (e.g., Ray, 1961). While delayed tests calling for verbal statement or application are common, the experimenter rarely finds out which mode of retention the subject is using.

4. *Conviction.* Adherence to a principle in a confusing stimulus situation where perceptual cues support an answer contrary to the principle. This type of resistance to extinction is best represented in Smedslund's study (1961) of the Piaget plasticine problem, where the tester palms a bit of material and so it seems that the conservation principle has been violated. Evaluation of conviction is also illustrated by the social psychologists' studies of propaganda and counterpropaganda.

5. *Rationale.* Understanding of the consistency between this principle and other concepts in the discipline. This might be exemplified by the child's explaining the equal-angle reflection of a billiard ball in terms of vectors. Interviews used by McConnell to obtain data on how pupils account for number facts are also pertinent.

6. *Epistemology.* Concept of the logic of the field of study, of the criteria of truth in the field; knowing, for example, the relative weight in judicial decisions of *stare decisis,* the election returns, and the judge's digestion.

The foregoing all represent different levels of knowledge of the subject matter.

7. *Specific rule-finding technique.* Ability to find rules for closely similar problems. Gagné and Brown develop this, for sum-of-series problems, by teaching the subject to line up in a table the term number, the term, and the sum to that point, and then to look for patterns. (See also Hilgard et al., 1953.)

8. *Heuristics.* Ability to solve diverse problems in the discipline by having acquired general search and information-processing behaviors (e.g., Kersh's [1964] observations of attack on new problems).

9. *Aptitude.* Ability to learn subject matter in the field, whether by improved motivation or tendency to look for meaning or to criticize preliminary solutions. The changes that increase aptitude for learning from one type of instruction may not be helpful under other instruction. McConnell (1934) had taught number facts; as one measure of effect he presented a silent-reading lesson on two-digit subtraction and tested how well pupils could perform after that instruction. Since the operation took just twenty minutes, it is not a very adequate measure of learning ability (cf. Carroll, 1963, and Cronbach, 1965).

10. *Interest.* Concentration or voluntary effort at the time of training. Represented in Kersh's studies and in an attitude questionnaire of McConnell.

11. *Valuation.* Enduring interest, desire to study in the field, appreciation of the value of knowledge in the field.

12. *Creative urge.* Finding gratification in coping with problems, making efforts to construct knowledge for oneself, being less dependent on authority.

If, in referring to one of these objectives, I have cited no illustrative measurement of that objective, it is because no example in the literature on discovery is known to me. Hence our first conclusion is that many possible consequences of discovery have not been investigated. It seems to me that our interest should concentrate on those wide-ranging objectives that have to do with the pupil's broad educational development, rather than on his mastery of the particular lesson. I believe that inductive teaching is rarely superior to other meaningful teaching for putting across single generalizations, but I share the hope that it has special power to make a practicing intellectual out of the student. I want to see a heightened effort to collect data on theoretical understanding, heuristics, aptitude, valuation, creative urge, and epistemology. These are the variables least considered in the past research, and not surprisingly, since it is scarcely credible that a 50-minute experimental treatment will confer any of these benefits on the learner. Educational development comes through continued instruction with intellectually significant subject matter and that is what we should investigate.

Individual Differences
Discovery surely has more value for some pupils than for others. We should expect an interaction between the discovery variable and pupil characteristics, such that among pupils classified at the same level some respond better to inductive teaching and some better to didactic teaching. Perhaps the simplest question to begin with is the matching of instructional technique to age, or to some subtler measure of general development such as mental age, along the lines suggested by Osler's studies (Osler & Fivel, 1961; Osler & Trautman, 1961).

The interacting variables may have more to do with personality than with ability; I am tempted by the notion that pupils who are negativistic may blossom under discovery training, whereas pupils who are anxiously dependent may be paralyzed by demands for self-reliance. If that were to be found, however, it might imply that those of the latter group especially need training in intellectual independence rather than that they should be allowed to learn passively.

Ultimately, enough knowledge should permit us to say that a fourth-grader with one profile of attainment needs discovery experience, whereas another will move ahead more rapidly on all fronts if teaching is didactic. A pupil who already accepts the meaningfulness of the number system and who has the confidence to look for generalizations on his own will only be delayed, I suspect, by having to figure out his own rules for multiplying decimals. Conversely, for the pupil who has plenty of arithmetic skill and very little understanding of the origin of the rules, nothing could be more important than some experience in discovering such rules.

Conclusions
The educational psychologist is torn between two responsibilities. His responsibility as educational specialist is to give schools advice on matters where the evidence is pitifully limited. His responsibility as scientist is to insist on careful substantiation of claims for each educational innovation. In education, unfortunately, there is great furore about whatever is announced as the latest trend, and the schools seem to career erratically after each Pied Piper in turn. This

giddy chase keeps them almost beyond earshot of the researcher standing on his tiny, laboriously tamped patch of solid ground, crying in a pathetic voice, "Wait for me! Wait for me!"

Knowing that panacea-mongers always have the last word (even though the word changes from year to year), knowing that it will take decades at best for research to catch up with the claims, what stance are we to take? I suggest a judicious blend of these not-incompatible attitudes:

Hospitality to new ideas.

Skepticism about slogans and ill-defined terms, and about doctrines that promise to cure dozens of educational ills out of the same bottle.

Resolution to make research incisive rather than polemic, to clarify what about the new proposal is valid and why, rather than to score points for or against the innovation.

Willingness to advise educators along whatever path we can extrapolate from what we know, but to make clear that this advice is extrapolation and nothing more.

I have indicated a number of reasons why the existing research on inductive teaching has not begun to give the answers needed for firm recommendations to the schools. I have suggested that there will need to be more complex experiments, planned along quite different lines from those of the past literature. We have to explore a fivefold interaction—subject matter, with type of instruction, with timing of instruction, with type of pupil, with outcome. Understanding will be advanced by each experiment, so long as the investigator is open-mindedly curious, and keeps the whole problem in mind while interpreting his exploration of one small corner of it.

References

Baddeley, A. D. A Zeigarnik-like effect in the recall of anagram solutions. *Quart. J. exp. Psychol.,* 1963, 15, 63-64.

Carroll, J. B. A model of school learning. *Teachers Coll. Rec.,* 1963, 64, 723-733.

Corman, B. R. The effect of varying amounts and kinds of information as guidance in problem solving. *Psychol. Monogr.,* 1957, 71, No. 2 (Whole No. 431).

Cronbach, L. J. *Educational psychology,* 2nd edition. New York: Harcourt, Brace and World, Inc., 1963.

Cronbach, L. J. Issues current in educational psychology. In Morrisett, L. N., and Vinsonhaler, J. F. Mathematical learning. *Monog. Soc. Res. Child Develpm.,* (Serial No. 99), 1965. Pp. 109-126.

Duncan, C. P. Learning to learn in response-discovery and in paired associate lists. *Amer. J. Psychol.,* 1964, 77, 367-379.

Forgus, R. H., and Schwartz, R. J. Efficient retention and transfer as affected by learning method. *J. Psychol.,* 1957, 43, 135-139.

Gagné, R. M., and Brown, L. T. Some factors in the programming of conceptual learning. *J. exp. Psychol.,* 1961, 62, 313-321.

Gagné, R. M., and Smith, E. C., Jr. A study of the effects of verbalization on problem solving. *J. exp. Psychol.,* 1962, 63, 12-18.

Glaser, R., Klaus, D. J., and Egerman, K. Increasing team proficiency through training: II. The acquisition and extinction of a team response. Pittsburgh: American Inst. for Res., 1962.

Hanson, N. R. *Patterns of discovery.* New York: Cambridge University Press, 1958.

Haslerud, G. M., and Meyers, Shirley. The transfer value of given and individually derived principles. *J. educ. Psychol.,* 1958, 49, 293-298.

Hilgard, E. R., Edgren, R. D., and Irvine, R. P. Errors in transfer following learning with understanding: Further studies with Katona's card-trick experiments. *J. exp. Psychol.,* 1954, 47, 457-464.

Hilgard, E. R., Irvine, R. P., and Whipple, J. E. Rote memorization, understanding, and transfer: An extension of Katona's card-trick experiments. *J. exp. Psychol.,* 1953, 46, 288-292.

Kersh, B. Y. The adequacy of "meaning" as an explanation for superiority of learning by independent discovery. *J. educ. Psychol.,* 1958, 49, 282-292.

Kersh, B. Y. The motivating effect of learning by directed discovery. *J. educ. Psychol.,* 1962, 53, 65-71.

Kersh, B. Y. Directed discovery vs. programmed instruction, a test of a theoretical position involving educational technology. Final Report, NDEA Title VII. Project Number 907, Grant Number 7-47-0000-165, Oregon State System of Higher Education, 1964.

Kersh, B. Y. Learning by discovery: what is learned? *The Arithmetic Teacher,* 1964, 11, 226-232.

Lawrence, D. H. The evaluation of training and transfer programs in terms of efficiency measures. *J. Psychol.,* 1954, 38, 367-382.

Lorge, I., Fox, D., Davitz, J., and Brenner, M. A survey of studies contrasting the quality of group performance and individual performance, 1920-1957. *Psychol. Bull.,* 1958, 55, 337-372.

McConnell, T. R. Discovery vs. authoritative identification in the learning of children. *Stud. Educ.,* 1934, 9, (5), 13-60.

Mackworth, N. H. Originality. *Amer. Psychologist,* 1965, 20, 51-66.

Olson, D. R. Note on Haslerud and Meyers' transfer-of-principles experiment. *J. educ. Psychol.,* 1965, 56, 107-108.

Osler, Sonia F., and Fivel, Myrna W. Concept attainment: I. The role of age and intelligence in concept attainment by induction. *J. exp. Psychol.,* 1961, 62, 1-8.

Osler, Sonia F., and Trautman, Grace. Concept attainment: II. Effect of stimulus complexity upon concept attainment at two levels of intelligence. *J. exp. Psychol.,* 1961, 62, 9-13.

Ray, W. E. Pupil discovery vs. direct instruction. *J. exp. Educ.,* 1961, 29, 271-280.

Ripple, R. E., and Rockcastle, V. N. (Eds.), Piaget rediscovered. *J. res. sci. teaching,* 1964, 2, (3). And as a separate, Cornell University, 1964.

Smedslund, Jan. The acquisition of conservation of substance and weight in children: III. Extinction of conservation of weight acquired 'normally' and by means of empirical controls on a balance. *Scand. J. Psychol.,* 1961, 2, 85-87.

Stacey, C. L. The law of effect in retained situation with meaningful material.

In Swenson, Esther J. et al., *Learning theory in school situations.* University of Minnesota Studies in Education. Minneapolis: University of Minnesota Press, 1949. Pp. 74-103.

Thiele, C. L. *The contribution of generalization to the learning of addition facts.* New York: Teachers College, Columbia University, 1938.

Travers, R. M. W. *An introduction to educational research* (2nd ed.), New York: Macmillan, 1964.

Wickelgren, W. A. Cues that elicit analytic-deductive methods in concept attainment. *Brit. J. Psychol.,* 1964, 55, 143-154.

Wittrock, M. C., Keislar, E. R., and Stern, Carolyn. Verbal cues in concept identification. *J. educ. Psychol.,* 1964, 55, 195-200.

Interaction Analysis: A Tardy Comment
Barak Rosenshine

The verdict is not in, and is not likely to be in for some time, on the relationship between a teacher's behavior as measured by the Flanders Interaction Analysis (IA) system[1] and pupil achievement. This holds true despite the glowing review of 12 studies presented by Campbell and Barnes[2] in the June 1969 issue of the *Kappan.*

In that review the results of each study were labeled statistically significant, and the overall conclusion was that "the microelements involved in the indirect/ direct ratios do affect achievement and attitude development at almost every grade level from K-9."[3]

However, if one goes beyond the summaries which Campbell and Barnes read and checks the original reports, then one sees flaws in all of the "results" they cited. These flaws include: (1) inappropriate statistical analyses by the investigators, (2) limits in the external validity or generalizability of the study, (3) data omitted from the summary reports, and (4) misinterpretations in reading. A more careful examination shows that not one of these 12 studies provides clear data which can be applied with confidence to a teacher training program. In short, the Campbell and Barnes review, which is based on secondary information, yields conclusions inconsistent with the original data.

---

[1]E. J. Amidon and N. A. Flanders, *The Role of the Teacher in the Classroom.* Minneapolis: Association for Productive Teaching, 1967.

[2]J. R. Campbell and C. W. Barnes, "Interaction Analysis—A Breakthrough?" *Phi Delta Kappan,* June 1969, pp. 587-590.

[3]Ibid., p. 588.

From *Phi Delta Kappan,* 1970, 51, 445-446. Reprinted by permission of the *Kappan* and the author.

Review of Studies

The order in which studies will be cited here is identical to that used in the
original review by Campbell and Barnes. The first "study" is actually four studies
reported by Flanders[4] –two using pupil attitude as the dependent variable, two
using pupil achievement. In all these studies, student scores were used as the unit
of analysis. But the degrees of freedom should have been the number of *teachers*
rather than the number of students, because the teachers were the sampling
unit,[5] and because we wish to generalize the results to the training of teachers.
In a subsequent analysis of the same seventh- and eighth-grade classes, Flanders[6]
corrected this error and reported linear correlations of .47 and .41 between the
i/d ratio of the teachers and the *class mean* achievement scores (adjusted by
regression for aptitude or prior knowledge) for the 15 seventh-grade classes and
the 16 eighth-grade classes respectively. Although these correlations are respect-
able, they miss being statistically significant at the .05 level.

The second study in the review, by Amidon and Flanders,[7] is an acceptable
experiment, but it cannot be generalized to teacher training for two reasons.
First, only one teacher was involved. Second, during indirect teaching the
teacher "accepted student ideas" twice as often as the indirect teachers in the
original studies by Flanders,[8] and during direct teaching the teacher used criticism three times as often as the direct teachers in Flanders' original studies.

The study by LaShier[9] is also of questionable generality, because (1) the
teachers were student teachers, and (2) they were teaching the BSCS curriculum
to eighth-grade pupils. The BSCS curriculum was written for high school biology
students; many teachers believe that the materials are too difficult even for
pupils at the high school level.

The study by Brown[10] is inconclusive on two counts. First, Brown used the
Withall system[11] for observing teacher behavior, not IA. Second, as Medley and
Mitzel have noted, the procedure for calculating the correlation was in error, and

[4]N. A. Flanders. *Teacher Influence, Pupil Attitudes, and Achievement* (U.S. Office of Education Cooperative Research Monograph No. 12, OE-25040). Washington, D.C.: USOE,
1965.
[5]D. T. Campbell and J. C. Stanley, "Experimental and Quasi-Experimental Designs for
Research on Teaching," in N. L. Gage (ed.), *Handbook of Research on Teaching.* Chicago:
Rand McNally, 1963, p. 193.
[6]N. A. Flanders, *Analyzing Teaching Behavior.* New York: Addison-Wesley, 1970.
[7]E. J. Amidon and N. A. Flanders, "The Effect of Direct and Indirect Teacher Influence
on Dependent-Prone Students Learning Geometry," *Journal of Educational Psychology,*
December 1961, pp. 286-291.
[8]Flanders, *Teacher Influence.*
[9]W. S. LaShier, "An Analysis of Certain Aspects of the Verbal Behavior of Student Teachers
of Eighth Grade Students Participating in a BSCS Laboratory Block" (Paper presented at the
meetings of the National Science Teachers Association, April 1966. Also available as an unpublished doctoral dissertation, University of Texas, 1965).
[10]G. I. Brown, "Which Pupil to Which Classroom Climate?" *Elementary School Journal,*
February 1960, pp. 265-269.
[11]J. Withall, "The Development of the Climate Index," in "Experimental Research toward
a Theory of Instruction" (H. A. Thelen, ed.), *Journal of Educational Research,* October
1951, pp. 96-98.

"it is impossible to tell from the published data what the correct values of *r* would be." [12]

The authors were accurate in their report of the short article they read by Nelson:[13] The teacher's i/d ratio was significantly higher when she prepared her class for a pupil-determined writing topic than it was when she prepared her class for a teacher-determined writing topic. But in this study, teacher style and writing assignment are confounded, so that we cannot determine whether the significant differences were due to the method of determining the topic or the teacher's i/d ratio. The use of a single teacher further limits the generalizability of any results. In the complete report, Nelson noted that there were no significant differences in the quality of the essays produced under the two conditions.[14]

The study by Beller, Weber, and Amidon[15] involved a total of four teachers; because of this no statistical tests were run. The report on the study by Soar[16] is an accurate summary. But the short piece by Soar is a *post hoc* analysis of a larger investigation.[17] In this larger study, involving 55 teachers and their classrooms, the factor containing the loadings for indirect teaching *was not* significantly correlated with any of the four class-mean residual gain scores in vocabulary, reading, or arithmetic. Moreover, in the report that was cited by Campbell and Barnes, the use of pupils rather than classes as the unit of measure is questionable.

The description of the study by Furst and Amidon [18] is inaccurate. Their report is purely descriptive of teacher-pupil interaction patterns in the elementary grades; no achievement data were ever collected in that study.

The article by Davidson[19] is incomplete. Davidson conducted an experiment to determine whether he could change the classroom behavior of ten classroom teachers; a modified IA system was used to record the experimental effect. As Campbell and Barnes reported, the experimental group exhibited significantly

---

[12]D. M. Medley and H. E. Mitzel, "Measuring Classroom Behavior by Systematic Observation," in N. L. Gage (ed.), *Handbook of Research on Teaching,* p. 297.

[13]L. N. Nelson, "Teacher Leadership: An Empirical Approach to Analyzing Teacher Behavior in the Classroom," *Journal of Teacher Education,* Winter 1966, pp. 417-425.

[14]L. N. Nelson, "The Effect of Classroom Interaction on Pupil Linguistic Performance" (Unpublished doctoral dissertation, University of California, Los Angeles, 1964). See especially p. 45.

[15]E. K. Beller, W. Weber, and E. J. Amidon, "Teacher Behavior and Intellectual Functioning in Deprived Kindergarten Children" (Paper presented at the annual meetings of the American Educational Research Association, Chicago, February 1966).

[16]R. S. Soar, "Pupil Needs and Teacher-Pupil Relationships: Experiences Needed for Comprehending Reading," in E. J. Amidon and J. B. Hough (eds.), *Interaction Analysis: Theory, Research and Application.* Reading, Mass.: Addison-Wesley, 1967, pp. 243-250.

[17]R. S. Soar, "An Integrative Approach to Classroom Learning" (Final Report, Public Health Service Grant No. 5-R11 MH 01096 and National Institute of Mental Health Grant No. 7-R11-MH 02045). Philadelphia: Temple University, 1966.

[18]N. Furst and E. J. Amidon, "Teacher-Pupil Interaction Patterns in the Elementary School," in E. J. Amidon and J. B. Hough (eds.), *Interaction Analysis,* pp. 167-175.

[19]R. L. Davidson, "The Effects of an Interaction Analysis System on the Development of Critical Reading in Elementary School Children," *Classroom Interaction Newsletter,* May 1968, pp. 12-13.

more "critical thinking responses" than the controls. However, it was only in his dissertation[20] that Davidson added that there were no significant differences between the experimental and control groups on the only achievement measure used in the study, the Stanford Achievement Test in reading.

The results obtained by Powell[21] and Weber[22] are difficult to interpret because of their design[23] and because adjustments were not made for pupil ability or aptitude. Both investigators studied the same teachers and pupils but were concerned with different criterion measures. In both studies, the individual pupil was the statistical unit. In a larger report, Powell concluded, "It seems clear that . . . no clear-cut benefit has been shown to accrue from indirect teaching."[24] Even in the abstracts cited by Campbell and Barnes, Powell[25] and Weber[26] explicitly stated that the significant differences were found only in the third grade, and that in the fourth grade "measured differences in classroom processes were not related to pupil achievement."[27]

The final study, by Campbell himself,[28] is currently unavailable. But if only 10 teachers were studied, as reported, and the results were reported as significant at the .001 level, this implies a correlation coefficient of .87 or higher, something which has never occurred in any of the IA studies. It is possible that students, rather than classes, were used as the unit of measure.

None of the above comments is directed at the IA system or at the results produced using the system. A comprehensive review of the studies relating IA variables to student achievement and attitude remains to be published. There are far more studies, both favorable and unfavorable to IA, than the 12 cited by Campbell and Barnes. If these 12 studies alone are summarized, it appears that teacher "indirectness" has a consistent but low positive correlation with achievement, one which is seldom significant at the .05 level.

---

[20] R. L. Davidson, "The Effects of an Interaction Analysis System on the Development of Critical Reading in Elementary School Children" (Unpublished doctoral dissertation, University of Denver, 1967).

[21] E. V. Powell, "Teacher Behavior and Pupil Achievement" (Paper presented at the annual meetings of the American Educational Research Association, Chicago, February 1968; also available as an unpublished doctoral dissertation, Temple University, 1967).

[22] W. A. Weber, "Relationships Between Teacher Behavior and Pupil Creativity in the Elementary School" (Paper presented at the annual meetings of the American Educational Research Association, Chicago, February 1968; also available as an unpublished doctoral dissertation, Temple University, 1967).

[23] Cf. G. A. Nuthall, "Types of Research on Teaching," *New Zealand Journal on Educational Studies,* November 1968, pp. 125-147; Flanders, *Analyzing Classroom Behavior.*

[24] Powell, "Teacher Behavior and Pupil Achievement" (the AERA paper), p. 4.

[25] E. V. Powell, "Teacher Behavior and Pupil Achievement," *Classroom Interaction Newsletter,* May 1968, pp. 23-25.

[26] W. A. Weber, "Teacher Behavior and Pupil Creativity," *Classroom Interaction Newsletter,* May 1968, pp. 30-33.

[27] Powell, "Teacher Behavior and Pupil Achievement" (in *Classroom Interaction Newsletter*), p. 25. See also Weber, "Teacher Behavior and Pupil Creativity," p. 31.

[28] J. R. Campbell, "Cognitive and Affective Process Development and its Relation to a Teacher's Interaction Ratio" (Unpublished doctoral dissertation, New York University, 1968).

The exact usefulness of IA in predicting pupil achievement remains to be determined. The relationship may not necessarily be linear.[29] It is possible that the major usefulness of IA will be in identifying extremes—those teachers who are most or least effective—and that the scatter in the middle will be too large to fit any type of curve. Perhaps IA will be most useful in telling us, for example, that out of a sample of 50 teachers, those five who are most critical toward their pupils are obtaining significantly less achievement than the others (although there is no significant correlation across the entire sample). Perhaps IA will be able to identify those positive affective variables which appear in significantly greater frequency in the five strongest teachers in this same sample of 50.

This critique is not intended merely as a criticism of the report by Campbell and Barnes. The flaws are representative of a number of such "reviews" on teacher behavior which marshall a number of half-read, half-digested studies into some form of educational truth. In compiling such reviews, the authors usually limit themselves to reading reports abstracted in other reviews or short abstracts of the original investigation. Yet, as my critique attempts to illustrate, such a path is not without obstacles; reviewers and authors of short articles frequently omit details which are critical. There is a need for more comprehensive reviews which are based upon a reading of the original research documents, and such reviews should be acceptable as doctoral dissertations. Without such reviews we may continue to be misled into crying "truth, truth" where there is no truth.

---

[29]R. S. Soar, "Optimum Teacher-Pupil Interaction for Pupil Growth," *Educational Leadership,* December 1968, pp. 275-298.

Chapter Thirteen
Instructional Style: Instructional Style
and Learning Performance

Articles in this chapter reflect the main hypothesis of this book, namely that instruction can and should be fitted to individual differences in learning style as well as self, group, and community expectations. The first article suggests how learning style is actually shaped prior to formal schooling to a great extent by the mother's instructional style. Two other articles report on school-based research that bear out this book's hypothesis. The last article rather appropriately summarizes much of the available research on fitting instruction to individual differences.

The significance of the Hess and Shipman article is that it goes beyond socioeconomic status as an explanation of why the disadvantaged child turns out as he does, and focuses on the actual interaction between mother and child. The more aware one becomes of preschool influences, the easier it is to accept the fact that the mother *is* a teacher. Hess and Shipman's study shows rather clearly that the way a mother communicates not only influences the child's immediate performance, but also shapes his learning style and information-processing strategies. Longitudinal studies are still needed to determine the long-range effects of this interaction.

The school-based research reported by Rhetts, as well as by Taba and Elzey, have been commented on in chapter 1. However, the reader should note that Rhetts uses the phrase *attribute-treatment interaction* rather than aptitude-treatment interaction, since the term *aptitude* connotes constructs measured by conventional aptitude tests. Rhetts suggests that the term *attribute* is broad enough to include an individual difference or learner characteristic variable which proves to be empirically useful. Furthermore, Rhetts suggests that "task" analysis must be involved in any attempt to talk about individualized learning. Thus ATI becomes ATTI.

The Lesser article offers the practitioner an excellent summary of research on adapting instruction to individual differences. He aptly distinguishes between organizational or administrative attempts to modify instructional program planning, such as by systems analysis design, nongrading, computer management, etc., and pedagogical or teacher-oriented attempts to adapt instruction to particular learners.

Research of this type has stimulated some provocative advances in computer-assisted instruction (CAI). Atkinson (1970) reported on the "dialogue" type of

251

CAI. The goal of this approach is to provide the learner with the richest possible interaction between the computer and the learner—a situation in which the student is free to construct natural language questions and responses. In short, the student can exercise almost complete control over the sequences of the instructional-learning process.

The reader will find further information on the above topics in the following sources: A more complete treatment of Hess and Shipman's research is included in Hill (1967). Hoy (1968) suggests that schools are "status-oriented" in the same sense that Hess and Shipman found the lower class mother to respond to her child. Does this indicate that the disadvantaged learner's style is more compatible for school learning than for middle class children whose style is more "person-oriented"? The entire February-March issue of *Education* (1970) is devoted to the PLAN Program. Lesser (1971) summarizes research on organizational variation in modifying instruction in his book on individual differences. Also included are articles on personality, motivation, and moral development.

Finally, although a number of critiques of the main hypothesis of this book have already appeared in chapters 8 and 12, there is one more that should not go unheeded. In the September 1971 issue of *Atlantic Monthly,* Richard Herrnstein reviewed the controversy concerning intelligence and heredity, and concluded that intelligence is inextricably related to social class level and success. And since heredity establishes the limits of intelligence, while environment suggests the possibilities of reaching those limits, Herrnstein suggests then that to the degree the environment becomes more favorable for the development of intelligence, i.e., individual differences and needs are matched by instructional method, then an even larger proportion of the variation in I.Q. will be attributable to heredity. Thus, the average person would have increased learning performance, but, instead of his performance being similar to others', it would be more noticeably different. In short, Herrnstein implies that to the extent we focus on individual differences, the greater we will increase the differences between people, especially in terms of social class and economic status.

Early Experience and the Socialization of Cognitive Modes in Children

Robert D. Hess and Virginia C. Shipman

The Problem

One of the questions arising from the contemporary concern with the education of culturally disadvantaged children is how we should conceptualize the effects of such deprivation upon the cognitive faculties of the child. The outcome is well known: children from deprived backgrounds score well below middle-class children on standard individual and group measures of intelligence (a gap that increases with age); they come to school without the skills necessary for coping with first grade curricula; their language development, both written and spoken, is relatively poor; auditory and visual discrimination skills are not well developed; in scholastic achievement they are retarded an average of 2 years by grade 6 and almost 3 years by grade 8; they are more likely to drop out of school before completing a secondary education; and even when they have adequate ability are less likely to go to college (Deutsch, 1963; Deutsch & Brown, 1964; Eells, Davis, Havighurst, Herrick, & Tyler, 1951; John, 1963; Kennedy, Van de Riet, & White, 1963; Lesser, 1964).

For many years the central theoretical issues in this field dealt with the origin of these effects, argued in terms of the relative contribution of genetic as compared with environmental factors. Current interest in the effects of cultural deprivation ignores this classic debate; the more basic problem is to understand how cultural experience is translated into cognitive behavior and academic achievement (Bernstein, 1961; Hess, 1964).

The focus of concern is no longer upon the question of whether social and cultural disadvantage depress academic ability, but has shifted to a study of the mechanisms of exchange that mediate between the individual and his environment. The thrust of research and theory is toward conceptualizing social class as a discrete array of experiences and patterns of experience that can be examined in relation to the effects they have upon the emerging cognitive equipment of the young child. In short, the question this paper presents is this: what *is* cultural deprivation, and how does it act to shape and depress the resources of the human mind?

This research is supported by the Research Division of the Children's Bureau, Social Security Administration; Department of Health, Education, and Welfare; Ford Foundation for the Advancement of Learning; and grants-in-aid from the Social Science Research Committee of the Division of Social Sciences, University of Chicago. Project staff members who made specific contributions to the analysis of data are Jere Brophy, Dina Feitelson, Roberta Meyer, and Ellis Olim.

The arguments we wish to present here are these: first, that the behavior which leads to social, educational, and economic poverty is socialized in early childhood—that is, it is learned; second, that the central quality involved in the effects of cultural deprivation is a lack of cognitive meaning in the mother-child communication system; and, third, that the growth of cognitive processes is fostered in family control systems which offer and permit a wide range of alternatives of action and thought and that such growth is constricted by systems of control which offer predetermined solutions and few alternatives for consideration and choice.

In this paper we will argue that the structure of the social system and the structure of the family shape communication and language and that language shapes thought and cognitive styles of problem-solving. In the deprived-family context this means that the nature of the control system which relates parent to child restricts the number and kind of alternatives for action and thought that are opened to the child; such constriction precludes a tendency for the child to reflect, to consider and choose among alternatives for speech and action. It develops modes for dealing with stimuli and with problems which are impulsive rather than reflective, which deal with the immediate rather than the future, and which are disconnected rather than sequential.

This position draws from the work of Basil Bernstein (1961) of the University of London. In his view, language structures and conditions what the child learns and how he learns, setting limits within which future learning may take place. He identifies two forms of communication codes or styles of verbal behavior: *restricted* and *elaborated.* Restricted codes are stereotyped, limited, and condensed, lacking in specificity and the exactness needed for precise conceptualization and differentiation. Sentences are short, simple, often unfinished; there is little use of subordinate clauses for elaborating the content of the sentence; it is a language of implicit meaning, easily understood and commonly shared. It is the language form often used in impersonal situations when the intent is to promote solidarity or reduce tension. Restricted codes are nonspecific clichés, statements, or observations about events made in general terms that will be readily understood. The basic quality of this mode is to limit the range and detail of concept and information involved.

Elaborated codes, however, are those in which communication is individualized and the message is specific to a particular situation, topic, and person. It is more particular, more differentiated, and more precise. It permits expression of a wider and more complex range of thought, tending toward discrimination among cognitive and affective content.

The effects of early experience with these codes are not only upon the communication modes and cognitive structure—they also establish potential patterns of relation with the external world. It is one of the dynamic features of Bernstein's work that he views language as social behavior. As such, language is used by participants of a social network to elaborate and express social and other interpersonal relations and, in turn, is shaped and determined by these relations.

The interlacing of social interaction and language is illustrated by the distinction between two types of family control. One is oriented toward control by *status* appeal or ascribed role norms. The second is oriented toward *persons.* Families differ in the degree to which they utilize each of these types of regulatory appeal. In status- (position-) oriented families, behavior tends to be regulated in terms of role expectations. There is little opportunity for the unique characteristics of the child to influence the decision-making process or the interaction between parent and child. In these families, the internal or personal states of the children are not influential as a basis for decision. Norms of behavior are stressed with such imperatives as, "You must do this because I say so," or "Girls don't act like that," or other statements which rely on the status of the participants or a behavior norm for justification (Bernstein, 1964).

In the family, as in other social structures, control is exercised in part through status appeals. The feature that distinguishes among families is the extent to which the status-based control maneuvers are modified by orientation toward persons. In a person-oriented appeal system, the unique characteristics of the child modify status demands and are taken into account in interaction. The decisions of this type of family are individualized and less frequently related to status or role ascriptions. Behavior is justified in terms of feelings, preference, personal and unique reactions, and subjective states. This philosophy not only permits but demands an elaborated linguistic code and a wide range of linguistic and behavioral alternatives in interpersonal interaction. Status-oriented families may be regulated by less individuated commands, messages, and responses. Indeed, by its nature, the status-oriented family will rely more heavily on a restricted code. The verbal exchange is inherent in the structure—regulates it and *is* regulated by it.

These distinctions may be clarified by two examples of mother-child communication using these two types of codes. Assume that the emotional climate of two homes is approximately the same; the significant difference between them is in style of communication employed. A child is playing noisily in the kitchen with an assortment of pots and pans when the telephone rings. In one home the mother says, "Be quiet," or "Shut up," or issues any one of several other short, preemptory commands. In the other home the mother says, "Would you keep quiet a minute? I want to talk on the phone." The question our study poses is this: what inner response is elicited in the child, what is the effect upon his developing cognitive network of concepts and meaning in each of these two situations? In one instance the child is asked for a simple mental response. He is asked to attend to an uncomplicated message and to make a conditioned response (to comply); he is not called upon to reflect or to make mental discriminations. In the other example the child is required to follow two or three ideas. He is asked to relate his behavior to a time dimension; he must think of his behavior in relation to its effect upon another person. He must perform a more complicated task to follow the communication of his mother in that his relationship to her is mediated in part through concepts and shared ideas; his mind is stimulated or exercised (in an elementary fashion) by a more elaborate and complex verbal communication initiated by the mother. As objects of these two divergent communication styles, repeated in various ways, in similar situations and circumstances during the preschool years, these two imaginary children would be expected to develop significantly different verbal facility and cognitive equipment by the time they enter the public school system.

A person-oriented family allows the child to achieve the behavior rules (role requirements) by presenting them in a specific context for the child and by emphasizing the consequences of alternative actions. Status-oriented families present the rules in an assigned manner, where compliance is the *only* rule-following possibility. In these situations the role of power in the interaction is more obvious, and, indeed, coercion and defiance are likely interactional possibilities. From another perspective, status-oriented families use a more rigid learning and teaching model in which compliance, rather than rationale, is stressed.

A central dimension through which we look at maternal behavior is to inquire what responses are elicited and permitted by styles of communication and interaction. There are two axes of the child's behavior in which we have a particular interest. One of these is represented by an *assertive, initiatory* approach to learning, as contrasted with a *passive, compliant* mode of engagement; the other deals with the tendency to reach solutions impulsively or hastily as distinguished from a tendency to *reflect,* to compare alternatives, and to choose among available options.

These styles of cognitive behavior are related, in our hypotheses, to the dimensions of maternal linguistic codes and types of family control systems. A status-oriented statement, for example, tends to offer a set of regulations and rules for conduct and interaction that is based on arbitrary decisions rather than upon logical consequences which result from selection of one or another alternatives. Elaborated and person-oriented statements lend themselves more easily to styles of cognitive approach that involve reflection and reflective comparison. Status-oriented statements tend to be restrictive of thought. Take our simple example of the two children and the telephone. The verbal categoric command to "Be quiet" cuts off thought and offers little opportunity to relate the information conveyed in the command to the context in which it occurred. The more elaborated message, "Would you be quiet a minute? I want to talk on the phone" gives the child a rationale for relating his behavior to a wider set of considerations. In effect, he has been given a *why* for his mother's request and, by this example, possibly becomes more likely to *ask* why in another situation. It may be through this type of verbal interaction that the child learns to look for action sequences in his own and others' behavior. Perhaps through these more intent-oriented statements the child comes to see the world as others see it and learns to take the role of others in viewing himself and his actions. The child comes to see the world as a set of possibilities from which he can make a personal selection. He learns to role play with an element of personal flexibility, not by role-conforming rigidity.

Research Plan

For our project a research group of 163 Negro mothers and their 4-year-old children was selected from four different social status levels: Group A came from college-educated professional, executive, and managerial occupational levels; Group B came from skilled blue-collar occupational levels, with not more than

Table 1   Mean Number of Typed Lines in Three Data-Gathering Situations

	Upper Middle $N = 40$	Upper Lower $N = 40$	Lower Lower $N = 36$	ADC $N = 36$
School situations	34.68	22.80	18.86	18.64
Mastery situations	28.45	18.70	15.94	17.75
CAT card	18.72	9.62	12.39	12.24
Total	81.85	51.12	47.19	48.63

high-school education; Group C came from unskilled or semiskilled occupational levels, with predominantly elementary-school education; Group D from unskilled or semiskilled occupational levels, with fathers absent and families supported by public assistance.

These mothers were interviewed twice in their homes and brought to the university for testing and for an interaction session between mother and child in which the mother was taught three simple tasks by the staff member and then asked to teach these tasks to the child.

One of these tasks was to sort or group a number of plastic toys by color and by function; a second task was to sort eight blocks by two characteristics simultaneously; the third task required the mother and child to work together to copy five designs on a toy called an Etch-a-Sketch. A description of various aspects of the project and some preliminary results have been presented in several papers (Brophy, Hess, & Shipman, 1965; Jackson, Hess, & Shipman, 1965; Meyer, Shipman, & Hess, 1964; Olim, Hess, & Shipman, 1965; Shipman & Hess, 1965).

Results

The data in this paper are organized to show social-status differences among the four groups in the dimensions of behavior described above to indicate something of the maternal teaching styles that are emerging and to offer examples of relations between maternal and child behavior that are congruent with the general lines of argument we have laid out.

Social-Status Differences

Verbal Codes: Restricted Versus Elaborated. One of the most striking and obvious differences between the environments provided by the mothers of the research group was in their patterns of language use. In our testing sessions, the most obvious social-class variations were in the total amount of verbal output in response to questions and tasks asking for verbal response. For example, as Table 1 shows, mothers from the middle class gave protocols that were consistently longer in language productivity than did mothers from the other three groups.

Taking three different types of questions that called for free response on the part of the mothers and counting the number of lines of typescript of the protocols, the tally for middle-class mothers was approximately 82 contrasted with an average of roughly 49 for mothers from the three other groups.

These differences in verbal products indicate the extent to which the mater-

258   Instructional Style

Table 2   Social Status Differences in Language Usage (Scores Are the Means for Each Group)

	Social Status			
Scale	Upper Middle $N = 40$	Upper Lower $N = 42$	Lower Lower $N = 40$	ADC $N = 41$
Mean sentence length[a]	11.39	8.74	9.66	8.23
Adjective range[b]	31.99	28.32	28.37	30.49
Adverb range[c]	11.14	9.40	8.70	8.20
Verb elaboration[d]	.59	.52	.47	.44
Complex verb preference[e]	63.25	59.12	50.85	51.73
Syntactic structure elaboration[f]	8.89	6.90	8.07	6.46
Stimulus utilization	5.82	4.81	4.87	5.36
Introduced content	3.75	2.62	2.45	2.34
Abstraction[g]	5.60	4.89	3.71	1.75

[a]Average number of words per sentence.
[b]Proportion of uncommon adjective types to total nouns, expressed as a percentage.
[c]Proportion of uncommon adverb types to total verbs, adjectives, and adverbs, expressed as a percentage.
[d]Average number of complex verb types per sentence.
[e]Proportion of complex verb types to all verb types, simple and complex.
[f]Average number of weighted complex syntactic structures per 100 words.
[g]Proportion of abstract nouns and verbs (excluding repetitions) to total nouns and verbs (excluding repetitions), expressed as a percentage.

nal environments of children in different social-class groups tend to be mediated by verbal cue and thus offer (or fail to offer) opportunities for labeling, for identifying objects and feelings and adult models who can demonstrate the usefulness of language as a tool for dealing with interpersonal interaction and for ordering stimuli in the environment.

In addition to this gross disparity in verbal output there were differences in the quality of language used by mothers in the various status groups. One approach to the analysis of language used by these mothers was an examination of their responses to the following task: They were shown the Lion Card of the Children's Apperception Test and asked to tell their child a story relating to the card. This card is a picture of a lion sitting on a chair holding a pipe in his hand. Beside him is a cane. In the corner is a mouse peering out of a hole. The lion appears to be deep in thought. These protocols were the source of language samples which were summarized in nine scales (Table 2), two of which we wish to describe here.

The first scale dealt with the mother's tendency to use abstract words. The index derived was a proportion of abstract noun and verb types to total number of noun and verb types. Words were defined as abstract when the name of the object is thought of apart from the cases in which it is actually realized. For example, in the sentence, "The lion is an *animal*," "animal" is an abstract word. However, in the sentence, "This animal in the picture is sitting on his throne," "animal" is not an abstract noun.

In our research group, middle-class mothers achieved an abstraction score

Table 3 Person-Oriented and Status-Oriented Units on School Situation Protocols (Mothers)

A. Mean Number

Social Class	Person-Oriented		Status-Oriented		P/S Ratio	N
Upper middle	9.52	(1-19)	7.50	(0-19)	1.27	40
Upper lower	6.20	(0-20)	7.32	(2-17)	0.85	40
Lower lower	4.66	(0-15)	7.34	(2-17)	0.63	35
ADC	3.59	(0-16)	8.15	(3-29)	0.44	34

B. Mean Percent

Social Class	Person-Oriented	Status-Oriented	N
Upper middle	36.92	27.78	40
Upper lower	31.65	36.92	40
Lower lower	26.43	40.69	35
ADC	20.85	51.09	34

of 5.6; the score for skilled work levels was 4.9; the score for the unskilled group was 3.7; for recipients of Aid to Dependent Children (ADC), 1.8.

The second scale dealt with the mother's tendency to use complex syntactic structures such as coordinate and subordinate clauses, unusual infinitive phrases (e.g., "To drive well, you must be alert"), infinitive clauses (e.g., "What to do next was the lion's problem"), and participial phrases (e.g., "Continuing the story, the lion . . ."). The index of structural elaboration derived was a proportion of these complex syntactic structures, weighted in accordance with their complexity and with the degree to which they are strung together to form still more complicated structures (e.g., clauses within clauses), to the total number of sentences.

In the research group, mothers from the middle class had a structure elaboration index of 8.89; the score for ADC mothers was 6.46. The use of complex grammatical forms and elaboration of these forms into complex clauses and sentences provides a highly elaborated code with which to manipulate the environment symbolically. This type of code encourages the child to recognize the possibilities and subtleties inherent in language not only for communication but also for carrying on high-level cognitive procedures.

Control Systems: Person Versus Status Orientation. Our data on the mothers' use of status- as contrasted with person-oriented statements come from maternal responses to questions inquiring what the mother would do in order to deal with several different hypothetical situations at school in which the child had broken the rules of the school, had failed to achieve, or had been wronged by a teacher or classmate. The results of this tally are shown in Table 3.

As is clear from these means, the greatest differences between status groups is in the tendency to utilize person-oriented statements. These differences are even greater if seen as a ratio of person-to-status type responses.

The orientation of the mothers to these different types of control is seen not only in prohibitive or reparative situations but in their instructions to their

Table 4 Information Mothers Would Give to Child on His First Day at School

Social Status	Imperative	Instructive	Support	Preparation	Other	N
			% of Total Statements			
Upper middle	14.9	8.7	30.2	8.6	37.6	39
Upper lower	48.2	4.6	13.8	3.8	29.6	41
Lower lower	44.4	1.7	13.1	1.2	39.6	36
ADC	46.6	3.2	17.1	1.3	31.8	37
			% of Mothers Using Category			
Upper middle	48.7	38.5	76.9	33.3	87.2	...
Upper lower	85.4	17.1	39.0	19.5	70.7	...
Lower lower	75.0	5.6	36.1	8.3	77.8	...
ADC	86.5	16.2	43.2	8.1	86.5	...

children in preparing them for new experiences. The data on this point come from answers to the question: "Suppose your child were starting to school tomorrow for the first time. What would you tell him? How would you prepare him for school?"

One mother, who was person-oriented and used elaborated verbal codes, replied as follows:

"First of all, I would remind her that she was going to school to learn, that her teacher would take my place, and that she would be expected to follow instructions. Also that her time was to be spent mostly in the classroom with other children, and that any questions or any problems that she might have she could consult with her teacher for assistance."

"Anything else?"

"No, anything else would probably be confusing for her at her particular age."

In terms of promoting educability, what did this mother do in her response? First, she was informative; she presented the school situation as comparable to one already familiar to the child; second, she offered reassurance and support to help the child deal with anxiety; third, she described the school situation as one that involves a personal relationship between the child and the teacher; and, fourth, she presented the classroom situation as one in which the child was to learn.

A second mother responded as follows to this question:

"Well, John, it's time to go to school now. You must know how to behave. The first day at school you should be a good boy and should do just what the teacher tells you to do."

In contrast to the first mother, what did this mother do? First, she defined the role of the child as passive and compliant; second, the central issues she presented were those dealing with authority and the institution, rather than with learning; third, the relationship and roles she portrayed were sketched in terms of status and role expectations rather than in personal terms; and, fourth, her message was general, restricted, and vague, lacking information about how to deal with the problems of school except by passive compliance.

Table 5   Mean Responses to Adult Sigel Sorting Task (Maps)

| | Social Status | | | |
Category	Upper Middle $N = 40$	Upper Lower $N = 42$	Lower Lower $N = 39$	ADC $N = 41$
Total descriptive	3.18	2.19	2.18	2.59
Descriptive part-whole	1.65	1.33	1.31	1.49
Descriptive global	1.52	0.86	0.87	1.10
Relational-contextual	5.52	6.79	7.38	6.73
Categorical-inferential	3.30	3.00	2.23	2.66

A more detailed analysis of the mothers' responses to this question grouped their statements as *imperative* or *instructive* (Table 4). An imperative statement was defined as an unqualified injunction or command, such as, "Mind the teacher and do what she tells you to do," or "The first thing you have to do is be on time," or "Be nice and do not fight." An instructive statement offers information or commands which carry a rationale or justification for the rule to be observed. Examples: "If you are tardy or if you stay away from school, your marks will go down"; or "I would tell him about the importance of minding the teacher. The teacher needs his full cooperation. She will have so many children that she won't be able to pamper any youngster."

Status Differences in Concept Utilization. One of the measures of cognitive style used with both mothers and children in the research group was the *S*'s mode of classificatory behavior. For the adult version (Kagan, Moss, & Sigel, 1963), *S* is required to make 12 consecutive sorts of MAPS figures placed in a prearranged random order on a large cardboard. After each sort she was asked to give her reason for putting certain figures together. This task was intended to reveal her typical or preferred manner of grouping stimuli and the level of abstraction that she uses in perceiving and ordering objects in the environment. Responses fell into four categories: descriptive part-whole, descriptive global, relational-contextual, and categorical-inferential. A descriptive response is a direct reference to physical attributes present in the stimuli, such as size, shape, or posture. Examples: "They're all children," or "They are all lying down," or "They are all men." The subject may also choose to use only a part of the figure—"They both have hats on." In a relational-contextual response, any one stimulus gets its meaning from a relation with other stimuli. Examples: "Doctor and nurse," or "Wife is cooking dinner for her husband," or "This guy looks like he shot this other guy." In categorical-inferential responses, sorts are based on nonobservable characteristics of the stimulus for which each stimulus is an independent representative of the total class. Examples: "All of these people work for a living" or "These are all handicapped people."

As may be seen in Table 5, relational responses were most frequently offered; categorical-inferential were next most common, and descriptive most infrequent. The distribution of responses of our status groups showed that the middle-class group was higher on descriptive and categorical; low-status groups were higher on relational. The greater use of relational categories by the working-class mothers is especially significant. Response times for relational sorts are usually

Table 6   Children's Responses to Sigel Sorting Task (Means)

	Social Status			
Category	Upper Middle $N = 40$	Upper Lower $N = 42$	Lower Lower $N = 39$	ADC $N = 41$
Descriptive part-whole	2.25	0.71	0.20	0.34
Descriptive global	2.80	2.29	1.51	0.98
Relational-contextual	3.18	2.31	1.18	1.02
Categorical-inferential	2.02	1.36	1.18	0.61
Nonscorable verbal responses	5.75	6.31	6.64	7.24
Nonverbal	3.00	6.41	7.08	8.76
No sort	1.00	0.62	2.21	1.05

Table 7   Percentage of Four-Year-Old Children Responding in Each of the Categories

	Social Status			
Category	Upper Middle $N = 40$	Upper Lower $N = 42$	Lower Lower $N = 39$	ADC $N = 41$
Descriptive part-whole	40.0	28.6	18.0	14.6
Descriptive global.	70.0	54.8	53.8	31.7
Total descriptive	80.0	66.7	59.0	39.0
Relational-contextual	77.5	66.7	41.0	43.9
Categorical-inferential	52.5	45.2	30.8	24.4
Nonscorable verbal	85.0	88.1	92.3	85.4
Nonverbal	52.5	66.7	82.0	87.8
No sort	12.5	7.1	25.6	19.5

shorter, indicating less reflection and evaluating of alternative hypotheses. Such responses also indicate relatively low attention to external stimuli details (Kagan, 1964). Relational responses are often subjective, reflecting a tendency to relate objects to personal concerns in contrast with the descriptive and categorical responses which tend to be objective and detached, more general, and more abstract. Categorical responses, in particular, represent thought processes that are more orderly and complex in organizing stimuli, suggesting more efficient strategies of information processing.

The most striking finding from the data obtained from the children's Sigel Sorting Task was the decreasing use of the cognitive style dimensions and increasing nonverbal responses with decrease in social-status level. As may be seen in the tables showing children's performance on the Sigel Sorting Task (Tables 6 and 7), although most upper middle-class children and a majority of the upper lower-class children use relational and descriptive global responses, there is no extensive use of any of the other cognitive style dimensions by the two lower lower-class groups. In looking at particular categories one may note the relative absence of descriptive part-whole responses for other than the middle-class group and the large rise in nonverbal responses below the middle-class level. These results would seem to reflect the relatively undeveloped verbal and conceptual ability of children from homes with restricted range of verbal and conceptual content.

Relational and descriptive global responses have been considered the most immature and would be hypothesized to occur most frequently in preschool children. Relational responses are often subjective, using idiosyncratic and irrelevant cues; descriptive global responses, often referring to sex and occupational roles, are somewhat more dependent upon experience. On the other hand, descriptive part-whole responses have been shown to increase with age and would be expected to be used less frequently. However, these descriptive part-whole responses, which are correlated with favorable prognostic signs for educability (such as attentiveness, control, and learning ability), were almost totally absent from all but the upper middle-class group. Kagan (1964) has described two fundamental cognitive dispositions involved in producing such analytic concepts: the tendency to reflect over alternative solutions that are simultaneously available and the tendency to analyze a visual stimulus into component parts. Both behaviors require a delayed discrimination response. One may describe the impairment noted for culturally disadvantaged children as arising from differences in opportunities for developing these reflective attitudes.

The mother's use of relational responses was significantly correlated with their children's use of nonscorable and nonverbal responses on the Sigel task and with poor performance on the 8-Block and Etch-a-Sketch tasks. The mothers' inability or disinclination to take an abstract attitude on the Sigel task was correlated with ineffectual teaching on the 8-Block task and inability to plan and control the Etch-a-Sketch situation. Since relational responses have been found (Kagan, Moss, & Sigel, 1963) to be correlated with impulsivity, tendencies for nonverbal rather than verbal teaching, mother-domination, and limited sequencing and discrimination might be expected and would be predicted to result in limited categorizing ability and impaired verbal skills in the child.

Analysis of Maternal Teaching Styles

These differences among the status groups and among mothers within the groups appear in slightly different form in the teaching sessions in which the mothers and children engaged. There were large differences among the status groups in the ability of the mothers to teach and the children to learn. This is illustrated by the performance scores on the sorting tasks.

Let us describe the interaction between the mother and child in one of the structured teaching situations. The wide range of individual differences in linguistic and interactional styles of these mothers may be illustrated by excerpts from recordings. The task of the mother is to teach the child how to group or sort a small number of toys.

The first mother outlines the task for the child, gives sufficient help and explanation to permit the child to proceed on her own. She says:

"All right, Susan, this board is the place where we put the little toys; first of all you're supposed to learn how to place them according to color. Can you do that? The things that are all the same color you put in one section; in the second section you put another group of colors, and in the third section you put the last group of colors. Can you do that? Or would you like to see me do it first?"

Child: "I want to do it."

This mother has given explicit information about the task and what is expected of the child; she has offered support and help of various kinds; and she has made it clear that she impelled the child to perform.

A second mother's style offers less clarity and precision. She says in introducing the same task:

"Now, I'll take them all off the board; now you put them all back on the board. What are these?"

Child: "A truck."

"All right, just put them right here; put the other one right here; all right put the other one there."

This mother must rely more on nonverbal communication in her commands; she does not define the task for the child; the child is not provided with ideas or information that she can grasp in attempting to solve the problem; neither is she told what to expect or what the task is, even in general terms.

A third mother is even less explicit. She introduces the task as follows:

"I've got some chairs and cars, do you want to play the game?" Child does not respond. Mother continues: "O.K. What's this?"

Child: "A wagon?"

Mother: "Hm?"

Child: "A wagon?"

Mother: "This is not a wagon. What's this?"

The conversation continues with this sort of exchange for several pages. Here again, the child is not provided with the essential information he needs to solve or to understand the problem. There is clearly some impelling on the part of the mother for the child to perform, but the child has not been told what he is to do. There were marked social-class differences in the ability of the children to learn from their mothers in the teaching sessions.

Each teaching session was concluded with an assessment by a staff member of the extent to which the child had learned the concepts taught by the mother. His achievement was scored in two ways: first, the ability to correctly place or sort the objects and, second, the ability to verbalize the principle on which the sorting or grouping was made.

Children from middle-class homes were well above children from working-class homes in performance on these sorting tasks, particularly in offering verbal explanations as to the basis for making the sort (Tables 8 and 9). Over 60 percent of middle-class children placed the objects correctly on all tasks; the performance of working-class children ranged as low as 29 percent correct. Approximately 40 percent of these middle-class children who were successful were able to verbalize the sorting principle; working-class children were less able to explain the sorting principle, ranging downward from the middle-class level to one task on which no child was able to verbalize correctly the basis of his sorting behavior. These differences clearly paralleled the relative abilities and teaching skills of the mothers from differing social-status groups.

The difference among the four status levels was apparent not only on these sorting and verbal skills but also in the mother's ability to regulate her own be-

Table 8 Differences among Status Groups in Children's Performance in Teaching Situations (Toy Sort Task)

Social Status	Placed Correctly (%)	Verbalized Correctly (%)		N
A. Identity sort (cars, spoons, chairs):				
Upper middle.........	61.5	28.2	45.8[a]	39
Upper lower..........	65.0	20.0	30.8	40
Lower lower.........	68.4	29.0	42.3	38
ADC...............	66.7	30.8	46.2	39
B. Color sort (red, green, yellow):				
Upper middle.........	69.2	28.2	40.7[a]	39
Upper lower..........	67.5	15.0	22.2	40
Lower lower.........	57.9	13.2	22.7	38
ADC...............	33.3	5.1	15.4	39

[a]Percent of those who placed object correctly.

Table 9 Differences among Status Groups in Children's Performance in Teaching Situations (8-Block Task)

Social Status	Placed Correctly (%)	One-Dimension Verbalized (%)		Both Verbalized (%)		N
A. Short O:						
Upper middle.........	75.0	57.5	57.5[a]	25.0	33.3[a]	40
Upper lower..........	51.2	39.0	43.2	2.4	4.8	41
Lower lower.........	50.0	29.0	33.3	15.8	31.6	38
ADC...............	43.6	20.5	22.2	2.6	5.9	39
B. Tall X:						
Upper middle.........	60.0	62.5	64.1[a]	27.5	45.8[a]	40
Upper lower..........	48.8	39.0	42.1	17.1	35.0	41
Lower lower.........	34.2	23.7	26.5	7.9	23.1	38
ADC...............	28.2	18.0	20.0	0.0	0.0	39

[a]Percent of those who placed object correctly.

havior and her child's in performing tasks which require planning or care rather than verbal or conceptual skill. These differences were revealed by the mother-child performance on the Etch-a-Sketch task. An Etch-a-Sketch toy is a small, flat box with a screen on which lines can be drawn by a device within the box. The marker is controlled by two knobs: one for horizontal movement, one for vertical. The mother is assigned one knob, the child the other. The mother is shown several designs which are to be reproduced. Together they attempt to copy the design models. The mother decides when their product is a satisfactory copy of the original. The products are scored by measuring deviations from the original designs.

These sessions were recorded, and the nonverbal interaction was described by an observer. Some of the most relevant results were these: middle-class mothers and children performed better on the task (14.6 points) than mothers

Table 10 Performance on Etch-a-Sketch Task (Means)

	Social Status			
	Upper Middle $N = 40$	Upper Lower $N = 42$	Lower Lower $N = 40$	ADC $N = 41$
Total score (range 0-40)..	14.6	9.2	8.3	9.5
Average number of attempts..........	12.7	17.2	12.2	15.1
Complete figures rejected.............	2.3	3.6	3.5	3.4
Child's total score	5.9	4.0	3.4	4.0
Child's contribution to total score (percent) ...	40.4	43.5	41.0	42.1

and children from the other groups (9.2; 8.3; 9.5; [Table 10]). Mothers of the three lower-status groups were relatively persistent, rejecting more complete figures than the middle-class mothers; mothers from the middle class praised the child's efforts more than did other mothers but gave just as much criticism; the child's cooperation as rated by the observer was as good or better in low-status groups as in middle-class pairs (Table 11); there was little difference between the groups in affect expressed to the child by the mother (Brophy et al., 1965).

In these data, as in other not presented here, the mothers of the four status groups differed relatively little, on the average, in the affective elements of their interaction with their children. The gross differences appeared in the verbal and cognitive environments that they presented.

Against this background I would like to return for a moment to the problem of the meaning, or, perhaps more correctly, the lack of meaning in cultural deprivation. One of the features of the behavior of the working-class mothers and children is a tendency to act without taking sufficient time for reflection and planning. In a sense one might call this impulsive behavior—not by acting out unconscious or forbidden impulses, but in a type of activity in which a particular act seems not to be related to the act that preceded it or to its consequences. In this sense it lacks meaning; it is not sufficiently related to the context in which it occurs, to the motivations of the participants, or to the goals of the task. This behavior may be verbal or motor; it shows itself in several ways. On the Etch-a-Sketch task, for example, the mother may silently watch a child make an error and then punish him. Another mother will anticipate the error, will warn the child that he is about to reach a decision point; she will prepare him by verbal and nonverbal cues to be careful, to look ahead, and to avoid the mistake. He is encouraged to reflect, to anticipate the consequences of his action, and in this way to avoid error. A problem-solving approach requires reflection and the ability to weigh decisions, to choose among alternatives. The effect of restricted speech and of status orientation is to foreclose the need for reflective weighing of alternatives and consequences; the use of an elaborated code, with its orientation to persons and to consequences (including future), tends to produce cognitive styles more easily adapted to problem-solving and reflection.

The objective of our study is to discover how teaching styles of the mothers

Table 11[a]   Mother-Child Interaction on Etch-a-Sketch Task (Means)

	Social Status			
	Upper Middle N = 40	Upper Lower N = 41	Lower Lower N = 39	ADC N = 39
Praises child	4.6	6.9	7.2	7.5
Criticizes child	6.4	5.5	6.4	5.9
Overall acceptance of child	2.2	3.2	3.4	3.6
Child's cooperation	5.6	5.3	4.5	5.1
Level of affection shown to child	4.8	5.4	5.2	5.8

[a]Ratings made by observer; low number indicates more of the quality rated.

induce and shape learning styles and information-processing strategies in the children. The picture that is beginning to emerge is that the meaning of deprivation is a deprivation of meaning—a cognitive environment in which behavior is controlled by status rules rather than by attention to the individual characteristics of a specific situation and one in which behavior is not mediated by verbal cues or by teaching that relates events to one another and the present to the future. This environment produces a child who relates to authority rather than to rationale, who, although often compliant, is not reflective in his behavior, and for whom the consequences of an act are largely considered in terms of immediate punishment or reward rather than future effects and long-range goals.

When the data are more complete, a more detailed analysis of the findings will enable us to examine the effect of maternal cognitive environments in terms of individual mother-child transactions, rather than in the gross categories of social class. This analysis will not only help us to understand how social-class environment is mediated through the interaction between mother and child but will give more precise information about the effects of individual maternal environments on the cognitive growth of the young child.

References
Bernstein, B. Social class and linguistic development: a theory of social learning. In A. H. Halsey, Jean Floud, & C. A. Anderson (Eds.), *Education, economy, and society*. Glencoe, Ill.: Free Pr., 1961.

Bernstein, B. Family role systems, communication, and socialization. Paper presented at Conf. on Develpm. of Cross-National Res. on the Education of Children and Adolescents, Univer. of Chicago, February 1964.

Brophy, J., Hess, R. D., & Shipman, Virginia. Effects of social class and level of aspiration on performance in a structured mother-child interaction. Paper presented at Biennial Meeting of Soc. Res. Child Develpm., Minneapolis, Minn., March 1965.

Deutsch, M. The disadvantaged child and the learning process. In A. H. Passow (Ed.), *Education in depressed areas*. New York: Columbia Univer. T.C., 1963. Pp. 163-180.

Deutsch, M., & Brown, B. Social influences in Negro-white intelligence differences. *J. soc. Issues*, 1964, 20 (2), 24-35.

Eells, K., Davis, Allison, Havighurst, R. J., Herrick, V. E., & Tyler, R. W. *Intelligence and cultural differences.* Chicago: Univer. of Chicago Pr., 1951.

Hess, R. D. Educability and rehabilitation: the future of the welfare class. *Marr. fam. Lvg*, 1964, 26, 422-429.

Jackson, J. D., Hess, R. D., & Shipman, Virginia. Communication styles in teachers: an experiment. Paper presented at Amer. Educ. and Res. Ass., Chicago, February 1965.

John, Vera. The intellectual development of slum children: some preliminary findings. *Amer. J. Orthopsychiat.,* 1963, 33, 813-822.

Kagan, J., Moss, H. A., & Sigel, I. E. Psychological significance of styles of conceptualization. *Monogr. Soc. Res. Child Develpm.,* 1963, 28, No. 2.

Kagan, J. Information processing in the child: significance of analytic and reflective attitudes. *Psychol. Monogr.,* 1964, 78, No. 1 (Whole No. 578).

Kennedy, W. A., Van de Riet, V., & White, J. C., Jr. A normative sample of intelligence and achievement of Negro elementary school children in the southeastern United States. *Monogr. Soc. Res. Child Develpm.,* 1963, 28, No. 6.

Lesser, G. Mental abilities of children in different social and cultural groups. New York: Cooperative Research Project No. 1635, 1964.

Meyer, Roberta, Shipman, Virginia, & Hess, R. D. Family structure and social class in the socialization of curiosity in urban preschool children. Paper presented at APA meeting in Los Angeles, Calif., September 1964.

Olim, E. G., Hess, R. D., & Shipman, Virginia. Relationship between mothers' language styles and cognitive styles of urban preschool children. Paper presented at Biennial Meeting of Soc. Res. Child Develpm., Minneapolis, Minn., March 1965.

Shipman, Virginia, & Hess, R. D. Social class and sex differences in the utilization of language and the consequences for cognitive development. Paper presented at Midwest. Psychol. Ass., Chicago, April 1965.

Attribute-Treatment Interactions and Individualized Instruction: A Conceptual Framework and an Example from Project PLAN
John E. Rhetts

Skinner (1968) has suggested that: "We need to find practices . . . under which all students learn as efficiently as their talents permit." To do this, one obviously needs a variety of different materials available whenever a child's distinctive characteristics make one particular set ineffective or inefficient for him. But one of the limiting factors in achieving this goal is: how to match a given learner with materials appropriate to him? The answer to this question depends in large measure on our ability to differentiate successfully among learners and among the characteristics of materials to be learned. For the empirical scientist, this general question implies an interaction hypothesis.

One of the several unique features of Project PLAN (a joint venture of the American Institutes for Research and the Westinghouse Learning Corporation) is the specification of alternative learning activities designed to lead a student to master sets of explicitly stated instructional objectives. Discrete clusters of such objectives, coupled with learning activities, are called *modules.* The PLAN system identifies, from the entire inventory of available modules, those which are most appropriate for a given student via a complex set of decision rules. These rules are used by a computer to generate each year for each student a program of studies (POS) to guide his year's work. (Of course, the POS is flexible and can be revised at any time.) Each of the (more than 3000) alternative sets of learning activities leading to module mastery is referred to as a teaching-learning unit (TLU). Each student's program of studies, in addition to listing suggested modules, also indicates wherever possible which alternate TLU or set of learning activities within each module seems most appropriate for him. This procedure has been called *TLU matching.*

TLU matching assumes that a student will perform better when working on learning activities whose characteristics are matched to or are congruent with the learner's own (as compared with his performance on a TLU which is not well matched to his individual characteristics). In addition, this TLU matching procedure is predicated on the notion that there are measurable characteristics or variables which distinguish different learners and different learning activities or instructional treatments.

Several people have contributed to this paper. Drs. John C. Flanagan and Wells Hively II read drafts of a related paper, and Drs. David H. Feldman and Paul E. Johnson were the impetus for substantial improvements in this one.

Attribute-Treatment Interactions and Individualized Instruction

The reader may recognize this TLU matching procedure as a practical attempt at using individual differences to individualize instruction. Beginning with Cronbach (1957), the term *attribute-treatment interaction* (ATI) has been used to describe the same sort of phenomenon: the expectation that different learners will perform optimally under conditions differentially designed to accommodate each individual's habits, style of information processing, or acquisitive prerequisites. Thus, *individualized instruction* and *attribute-treatment interaction* are highly related terms. The former can be thought of as the practical application of principles derived from validated, empirical study under the latter's name. Indeed, without some at least vague notion about ATI's one cannot meaningfully individualize instruction.

A brief explanation might be in order about the meaning of the term *attribute-treatment interaction*. The first word is used to denote the learner characteristics of individual differences element in the problem. In the past many writers have used *aptitude* rather than attribute, but the former term has certain connotations in the measurement and testing tradition that would tend inappropriately to restrict the focus of ATI. *Attribute* implies that any individual difference variable is "fair-game," not just those constructs measured by conventional aptitude tests. This is not a trivial point, especially when one considers Carroll's (1963) definition that: ". . . Aptitude can be defined in terms of learning rate." Regardless of the utility of this definition (which Cronbach & Snow, 1969, have attacked), there are many variables other than rate of learning or aptitude, more broadly defined, of interest to the researcher looking for ATI's. Thus, the term *attribute* is broad enough to include any individual difference or learner-characteristic variable which proves to be empirically useful. Second, the term *treatment* in the phrase is the analogue to *instruction* in individualized instruction, and refers to the various organizations of material or procedures which the subject is asked to cope with and respond to. Finally, *interaction* is borrowed from analysis of variance terminology, meaning that there is an unequal, contrasting effect by the various treatments on the several subgroups of subjects.

A logical extension of this discussion might be to attempt to build a practical and meaningfully individualized program of instruction on the basis of the ATI research to date. However, it is quite likely that this would be a very frustrating undertaking. Present information could not support such a step, though there is no apparent reason why this could not be remedied by further careful work.

It should be kept in mind while reading the rest of this paper that the ATI model is only one way to respond to the problem of accommodating individual differences. Lesser (1971, and chapter 13 in this book) has reviewed a number of administrative, structural, and curricular accommodations which can be made to individual differences. In addition, there is a very large body of research and speculation which begin at the point of considering individual-difference variables—and may or (more often) may not explicitly deal with how to differentiate instruction for individual learners. However, the opinion is offered here that this last will not prove to be the most fruitful avenue for uncovering empirically validated procedures to optimize each individual's performance.

Certainly the situation is as Lesser (1971) describes, namely that ATI research involves

"... a fine-grained analysis of several of the major ingredients of complex classroom experiences: subject-matter differences, variations in instructional strategies and educational goals, and students with different learning styles. Forced to make numerous, moment-to-moment decisions, the teacher normally cannot aspire to such detailed analysis. However, any teacher can be alert to the following question in conducting classroom activities: Given the properties of a subject matter, several possible instructional approaches, different learning outcomes, and relevant observations of individual differences, what relationship among these classroom dimensions will provide optimal learning for an individual student? This complex question cannot be answered (or even asked) clearly by the classroom teacher under her normal daily pressures. It does, however, identify the major ingredients that the teacher must manage in her daily instruction ..." (p. 548).

Precisely because the classroom teacher does not have the time for such fine-grained analysis, there is need for careful work by the educational researcher. The position to be developed here is that the researcher should begin first with careful analysis of the tasks students are being asked to cope with, and then design treatments or "instructional approaches" only after the task analysis data have been used to conceptualize individual difference variables (or attributes) found to be related to performance differences. The opposite tactic, of beginning with either treatments or attributes, has not yielded powerful or clear-cut procedures or relationships. As Bracht (1970) has concluded in the research to date,

"... experimenters usually identified alternative treatments and then through trial-and-error tried to find personological variables to interact with treatments. The analysis of an interaction effect was often an afterthought rather than a carefully planned part of the experiment, i.e., the alternative treatments were not developed with the ATI concept in mind. This approach has not been successful for finding meaningful ... interactions" (p. 639).

The next section reviews the present state of ATI research, and subsequent sections deal with suggested modifications for improving the yield of meaningful procedures and relationships, ones which can be adapted for classroom use.

Status of ATI Research
One of the most extensive reviews of the state of ATI research is that by Cronbach and Snow (1969). Their review covered studies of learning rate, "tuning," specific abilities, and general abilities. In general, no sharp distinction is made (either by the authors or by the investigators whom they reviewed) between abilities and individual differences of other sorts. This fact probably represents either a lack of clarity in definition or individual investigator bias in labeling, or

both. Cronbach and Snow pinpointed two basic and pervasive handicaps of the research they reviewed: the first concerned basic methodology, and the second was related to overall conceptualization of the problem by individual investigators. The basic criticism of the methodologies employed centered on: questions poorly posed, contradictory findings among investigations, unduly brief experiments, lack of consideration of alternative or counterhypotheses, weak analysis, and failure to replicate experiments. (It would seem reasonable to conclude that these are faults of the particular investigations rather than necessary correlates of research in the general area.) Cronbach and Snow's criticism of the prevailing conceptualizations of the problem centered on the learner characteristics employed as variables by researchers; they concluded that the learner attributes studied to date are simplistic and therefore are

". . . unlikely to identify combinations of variables worth investigating. There is no instance where an ATI study defined in [simplistic] terms such as these, using familiar "content" constructs from the [Primary Mental Abilities], [Differential Aptitude Tests], Guilford or other such aptitude collections, has led to convincing evidence of interaction" (Cronbach & Snow, 1969, p. 184).

Indeed, Cronbach and Snow went so far as to predict that the attribute of general ability and its influence on an individual's performance could prove to be a useful construct in researching ATI's. This recommendation has been seconded by Bracht (1970), and by the procedures suggested later in this paper.

Overall, Cronbach and Snow's opinion of the state of knowledge about ATI's is somewhat pessimistic to say the least. However, they are not inclined to give up:

"Progress toward the goal of identifying and understanding ATI has been slight. . . . One reaction to this regrettable state of affairs would be to abandon ATI research on the grounds that such effects are nonexistent. We urge against this defeatist course. It is inconceivable to us that humans, differing in as many ways as they do, do not differ with respect to the educational treatment that fits each one best. To abandon the ATI model is to assume that there is only one path toward educational development, and that individual differences have no implications save the fatalistic one, telling the educator that some pupils will advance more rapidly than others, no matter what he does" (Cronbach & Snow, 1969, p. 193).

The general criticism is that relatively few investigators have managed to choose the most appropriate dimensions of learner characteristics and/or instructional methods, and that they have not always employed an optimal analytic methodology for revealing either of these dimensions of their research. The question then becomes: What—conceptually and methodologically—can be done to improve the validity and reliability of ATI research?

A Conceptual Framework for ATI Research

Tasks
The first area in need of improvement is the selection of tasks. In all of the experimental research to date, almost exclusive attention has been given to trait as
opposed to situational learner characteristics. Also, the hoped-for extrapolations
are clearly to classroom or training situations. But, experimenters have tended to
utilize short-term, artificially contrived, and relatively simple tasks, ones which
are noticeably (and possibly significantly) different from the contexts to which
they wish to relate their findings. Thus, several recommendations can be suggested:
   *Researchers should concern themselves with the ecological validity of the
experimental tasks they choose,* i.e., the question of the relatedness of the experimental task to other "natural" environment situations to which they would
like to generalize. (See Bracht & Glass, 1968, for a detailed discussion of problems with ecological validity.)
   *Investigators should utilize measures whose time span more nearly matches
the conceptualization of the individual-difference variables as being relatively
stable traits across some period of time.* For, it is quite possible, as Tobias
(1969) noted, that: "One-shot learning tasks demand more of the temporal
stability of measures used for classification than most of these tests are capable
of offering."
   *In designing an ATI study, an experimenter's first step should be to specify
the task* (as opposed to treatment or attribute variables, cf. Bracht, 1970, quoted
earlier) *and to conduct a detailed task analysis.* The preceding statement reflects
the belief that the task is the pivotal dimension of ATI, and that the development of treatments and salient attributes should be a function of the nature of
the task chosen. This thesis will be developed in subsequent sections.
   The dimensions of task characteristics are especially in need of refinement,
due to the pivotal nature in the process of generating potential treatments and
attributes for investigation. Many category systems for analyzing and categorizing tasks have been proposed, e.g., in terms of human functions (Miller,
1962, 1966; Gagné, 1962; Alluisi, 1967); internal processes and overt responses
(Folley, 1964a, 1964b; Berliner et al., 1964; Willis, 1961; Peterson et al., 1960);
and human abilities (Fleishman, 1962, 1967; Guilford, 1967). There are problems with each of these, and others as well. As Farina (1969) has pointed out:

"In general, the available schemes are hampered by one or more of several
factors: (a) imprecise terms; (b) little measurement capability; or (c) a lack of
development of the scheme to a point where it may readily be applied to real-
world tasks" (p. 68).
   "... What, for example, is the relationship between a function and an ability; Gagné (1962) defines his functions as transformations which convert an
input into an output. This implies a process-like nature. But what of abilities?
Fleishman suggests they are enduring "traits" or "capacities." Is a trait a pro-

cess? Or is it "something" an organism must possess in order to be capable of processing inputs into outputs? If a lack of ready correspondence exists between the two terms (functions and abilities) which are best defined, then even less success would be expected in interrelating the remaining types of descriptors (activities, behaviors, overt acts). . . . At our present stage of development, such a merger [of systems] might yield chaos as the disparate descriptors are not tied to any common framework, and hence, are unrelatable" (p. 66).

It would appear, then, that we simply do not know enough about describing and categorizing tasks with any existing taxonomies, and the basic impediment is almost surely both conceptual and semantic. The former requires considerable further work, clearly beyond the domain of this discussion. However, the terms *ability* and *aptitude* have figured in the semantic confusion, and the following definitions should at least help clarify this aspect of the problem:

Ability. A quantitative index of an individual's performance capability at any given point in time, for example, measured at the entry to some performance domain. The usefulness of this term would hinge on the predictive validity and reliability of the measure, as well as its test-retest reliability without the individual being exposed to any further training or practice. The assessment procedure theoretically should not put the individual under time constraint; the statement "He is able to do it" does not imply an arbitrary time limit within which the person is able to exhibit the ability. Ideally, the measurement of ability would yield a binary rather than qualitative assessment: The individual *is* or *is not* able to do X.

Aptitude. A qualitative index of an individual's (criterion) task performance at any given point in time, measured either as:

(a) the number of trials (amount of practice) or amount of time to criterion under a fixed task condition, or

(b) the number of errors under a fixed time condition.

With these distinctions in mind, the ATI problem can then be described as one where, based on the characteristics of the task, the investigator needs to devise differential treatments which remediate an individual's specific ability deficits, in order to optimize his aptitude scores on the criterion task measure.

The reader will surely notice that no answer has been offered as to how to describe tasks, and yet this is the prerequisite step to devising valid treatments and attribute measures. It would seem likely that use of the aforementioned schemes should continue to prove at least stimulating, and further (especially, integrative) work should be done. However, another tactic would be to approach the problem of task analysis from the performance measurement perspective of domain-referenced achievement testing (Hively, 1970; Rabehl, 1970; Sension, 1970.) A central element in this conceptual approach to measurement is to discover and articulate the rules by which test-item forms can be constructed, thereby giving one the ability to generate a very large number of test items covering the entire performance domain. A second element in this scheme is the analysis of item forms and the partitioning of the domain into interrelated item networks, each forming a stratum for ultimate item sampling. As the item-form and item-network rules are refined, these procedures should provide powerful conceptual tools for describing task components and prerequisite abilities, thereby assisting the ATI researcher not only in measuring task performance (a pervading problem) but also in generating important attribute and treatment variables.

Attributes
The conceptualization of attributes requires considerable further work. As Gagné and Gropper (1965) have strongly argued, ". . . measures need to be designed to assess capabilities that are task-specific . . . ." This same position is echoed by Bunderson (1970) in discussing procedures to guide his own future work:

"The measurement of cognitive [attributes in] ATI studies will increasingly be based on a careful analysis of information processing requirements generated by specific learning tasks, rather than on a selection of pre-existing tests."

This would suggest that, following the task analysis, the researcher needs to attend carefully to the cognitive skills abilities required to perform well on the task, as well as to motivational and other affective attributes needed to succeed on the task. The relevant individual difference measures should assess precisely those variables hypothesized to be required for or involved as mediators of performance. (The reader will notice later that the first phase of the recommended research design is focused on ascertaining the validity of this hypothesis.)

Treatments
The third area in need of remediation is the design of treatment conditions. It is obvious that the variations in treatment conditions should be related specifically to the task presented. From an examination of many of the treatments reported in the literature, there often seems to be only a tenuous relation between the contrasting treatments and the task itself. It would often appear that selection of the treatments was based more on their contrast or oppositeness than on their actual relation to the task. One remedy for this would be that:
    Experimenters should design treatment differences on the basis of characteristically different ways of coping with or solving the problem, e.g., on the basis of using different mediating cues or different cognitive information processes. This would mean that a researcher would use the task analysis data and his ideas about abilities individuals would need to perform well to generate contrasting treatments. The treatments to be designed should be procedures by which individuals lacking or failing to utilize specific abilities could acquire or make use of them. If, for example, task T involves some specific information processing or transforming ability (skill) A, then one treatment might provide more structured cues about the relevance of A to T. Or, the treatment might involve instruction designed to develop A in individuals lacking it. Experimentation with such procedures might help to clarify the usefulness of thinking of attributes as areas requiring prosthetic devices in the form of various specific

treatments which facilitate the performance of those who do not have certain specific processing skills in their operant repertoire. One of the reasons the previous work with specific abilities has not seemed to pay off may well be that the abilities under consideration in a given experiment had no known or strong inferential relation to the specific task the subject was asked to cope with. The task-analytic approach should increase the probability that treatment and attribute variables will show significant and replicable interactions.

Summary
The recommendations above suggest a sequential framework for designing ATI research: The experimenter's first task should be to select his task(s) and to conduct a careful analysis of the task characteristics. Second, this analysis should be used in conceptualizing measurable learner characteristics (defined in terms of cognitive and affective prerequisites for good taste performance). Third, and only then, work should be begun on devising contrasting treatments designed to remedy individuals' attribute deficits.

A Three-Dimensional Model
An implication of the need for careful analysis of taste characteristics in designing both treatments and in selecting attribute measures is that in order to be able to interrelate efforts at uncovering ATI's, it will be necessary to add another dimension to the ATI model, i.e., that of task characteristics. This would give rise to a schematic representation as in Figure 1.

Tobias (1969) has suggested renaming the ATI term: "Fruitful research in this area might well have to concentrate on the triple interaction [among] attributes, treatments, and tasks (ATTI) rather than only on the ATI double interaction." However, this would seem to be a premature move except in specific research designs where an investigator has generated specific three-way hypotheses (e.g., Tallmadge & Shearer, 1969). In the first place, the demonstration and validation of two variable interactions has not been solved, and the needed increase in precision is not likely to result from added design and measurement complexity. Educators and investigators are basically concerned at this point with establishing validated ways to enhance performance on individual tasks by predicting the probability and magnitude of subgroups' differential success under different treatments or moderating conditions. Second, the rationale for considering task characteristics as variables at this stage of research is that they be used explicitly in generating the treatments and attributes of concern for a given investigation. Only at a significantly more sophisticated stage of development will researchers generally be ready to attend to the degree to which patterns of ATI hold across tasks or the extent to which tasks should be treated as independent or related units for analysis and experimentation. One would certainly like to think, however, that ultimately science will have a fairly clear picture of multitask patterns of performance which are contingent upon the possession of some skill(s) and which could be significantly influenced by a known set of procedures or treatments.

Assuming that one could over time generate empirically important categories

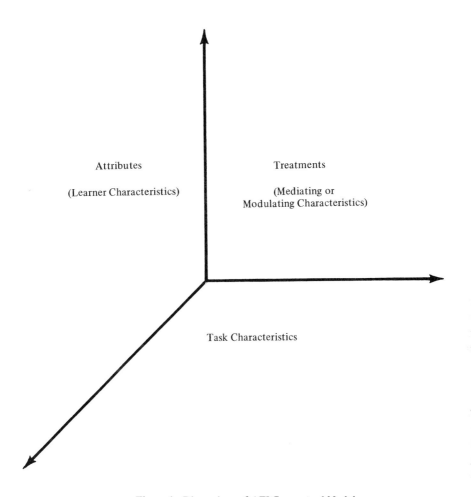

Figure 1 Dimensions of ATI Conceptual Model

for each of the three dimensions in Figure 1, then a major step would be accomplished toward a comprehensive classification system for cross-indexing and codifying ATI's. As has been suggested, the range of attributes is best thought of in general as large, but in a given experiment as task-specific and operationally defined (at least partially) by cognitive/information processing habits and/or prerequisites along with certain attitudinal and motivational variables pertaining to the specific task. The latter category certainly should be thought of as including personal preference, at least until empirical data make it possible to compare the magnitude of effect of this variable with others such as cognitive styles, etc. In addition to the previously outlined task-analysis sorts of treatment contrasts, other variables should be given serious attention, such as mode of task presentation, previous experience or exposure, and preparation (introduction, orientation).

As suggested above, a long-range outcome of validating categories of task, treatment, and learner characteristics could be the development of an ATI taxonomic structure for individualizing instruction. Such a structure could be pragmatically useful to an instructor in several ways. For example, given a task and students of varying abilities, what different treatments have proved to be effective in optimizing performance? Or, given a task, what attributes of learners should be attended to if the instructor plans to use some specific treatments? Unfortunately, though, these sorts of questions cannot be answered with much confidence or precision at the present time.

Methodology and Design in ATI Research

An implication of the conceptual framework outlined above is that the "one-shot" data collection procedure (typical of virtually all research to date) will not be adequate. A two-phase design will be needed. And, as Bracht (1970; Bracht & Glass, 1968) and Cronbach and Snow (1969) have pointed out quite clearly, the all-too-frequently used correlation and analysis of variance procedures are not the most powerful data-analytic tools.

One immediate solution to the data analysis *faux pas* would be for investigators to utilize regression analysis as the general tool. Cohen (1968) provides a very good discussion of multiple regression as a general data-analytic tool, as do Bottenberg and Ward (1963).

However, data analysis is only one aspect of research methodology. Upon close inspection, the one-shot data collection design typically used by ATI researchers could be expected to have contributed to the dearth of useful ATI's: Experimenters have sought to design treatments before having established that learners (differentially possessing some task-specific attribute) actually vary significantly in their performance on the given task. The implication is that a two-stage research design should be employed: the first stage collecting data regarding whether there is a task performance difference among learners varying on some specific attribute; the second, to test whether the performance differences can be eliminated by virtue of some carefully designed treatment. Both the better and poorer initial performers should be exposed to the treatment in such experimental work, to see not only if the poorer group improves but also if the treatment affects the initially superior group (especially in a negative direction, e.g., as a distractor).

The model then would permit either correlational or experimental procedures in the first stage, where one is seeking to establish performance differences. One might, for example, search for especially large general ability correlates with task performance. On the other hand, one might have more specific or narrowly defined and contrasting attributes to examine in an experimental design. However, stage-two work, studying the effect of selected treatments, would call for strictly experimental design, with (strongly suggested) multiple regression as the analytic procedure. Bracht's (1970; Bracht & Glass, 1968) criteria for a significant disordinal interaction seems eminently sensible. Figure 2 outlines the stages in such a model.

Feldman (1971) has pointed out that a design similar to this is one of the strengths in the research by Rohwer, and, indeed, one of Rohwer's studies can

1.0

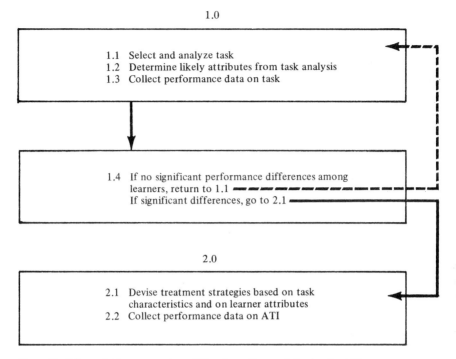

Figure 2   Schematic Representation of Two-Stage Research Design for ATIs

provide a concrete example. In a paired-associate paradigm, Jensen and Rohwer (1965) found a social class difference in learning performance. To test the effect of providing mediating concepts on this performance difference, they verbally suggested to the lower class subjects that they attempt to form *meaningful* connections among the stimuli and the response items. This instruction improved their performance to the extent of erasing the marked differences between the two social class groupings. This sort of work has also been investigated by Flavell and his associates under the heading of "tuning" (e.g., Flavell, Beach, & Chinsky, 1966; Corsini, Pick, & Flavell, 1968; Keeney, Canninzo, & Flavell, 1967; and Moely, Olson, Halwes, & Flavell, 1969). This general line of research shows that children may simply not make use of certain skills which they actually possess, and demonstrates that a simple instruction can markedly improve performance.

These are not true ATI studies, certainly not involving disordinal interactions as defined by Bracht (1970; Bracht & Glass, 1968). However, they are suggestive and perhaps point toward ways in which some of the language and conceptual structure from experimental verbal learning can be used in conceptualizing attributes for ATI research. For example, it would be tempting to hypothesize that providing help to the initially superior performers would tend to interfere with their performance; i.e., providing a cognitive strategy (make *meaningful* connections) at a conscious level might distract or interfere with the well-established (subconscious) habits, thus resulting in a performance decrement and a disordinal interaction.

Attributes and Treatments in the PLAN Program

The Variables
As indicated earlier, Project PLAN's TLU matching procedure is a practical attempt to capitalize on learner attributes to individualize instruction for each student in the program. The remainder of this paper will recount the procedures adopted to date and will indicate some of the further avenues for exploration. In terms of the research design proposed in the preceding section, the PLAN procedures are still at stage one, using a regression analysis to uncover performance differences.

After fairly extensive examination of both the finished curriculum units or modules and the design specifications issued to the module writers, seven variables were identified as describing salient aspects of the conditions (treatments) under which a module (task) was presented. These same seven variables also were phrased in terms of student attributes. Thus, as a treatment variable, each of the seven dimensions represented a TLU's characteristics; as a learner characteristic, each of the seven described an individual's attributes. The seven variables are listed in Figure 3, along with the number of scale intervals used in rating them for both learners and TLU's.

Each TLU for each of the 1071 PLAN modules was rated on the seven variables. The "teacher supervision" scale was dichotomous, indicating whether the teacher was or was not involved in the TLU, e.g., to be checked in with or asked to evaluate some intermediate performance. "Media richness" related to whether materials other than textbooks were used, including audio or visual hardware. The "social involvement" rating was an index of whether the TLU called for the student to work independently, with a partner, with others in a small group, or with the entire classroom. The "variety of activities" variable was designed to indicate the degree to which more activities than reading were called for in the TLU, i.e., whether the student was to engage in problem-solving and/or other activities. A composite variable of amount of reading was then constructed from the "media richness" and "variety" indices to be analogous to the students' "preference for reading" rating. The final rating was that of reading level; the reading materials for each TLU were examined and rated on their grade level equivalent difficulty.

In the spring of 1970, PLAN teachers in eight grades rated 3905 students on six variables (reading comprehension grade equivalents were derived from a group-administered objective test), each using a Likert scale varying from three to five response choices. By fall, about 15 percent of this number were not in PLAN classrooms, so the following teacher rating data pertains to 3338 (then) active PLAN students, slightly more than one third of the total number enrolled. (The other two thirds were new enrollees who had not been identified as potential PLAN students the previous spring.)

The Matching Paradigm
As stated earlier, the basic assumption underlying the matching idea was that a student would perform better on a task which required or drew upon abilities

Figure 3   TLU Matching Variables

Variable	No. Scale Points as TLU Variable	No. Scale Points as Attribute Variable
1. Reading level (difficulty[a] or comprehension[b]) in grade equivalents	12	12
2. Amount of[a] or preference for[b]: Reading	4	3
Degree[a] of or need for[b]:		
3. Teacher supervision	2	5
4. Practice or drill	1[c]	5
5. Single vs. multiple media	3	3
6. Variety of activities	4	3
7. Social involvement	5	4

[a]Treatment (TLU) descriptor
[b]Attribute (learner) descriptor
[c]Coded as "average" for all TLU's, due to insufficient time and data to develop empirically based scale.

or interests which the student himself also possessed. The actual matching paradigm called for a two-stage process, making reading comprehension the paramount variable. That is, reading comprehension was deemed the most crucial matching characteristic, with an explicit decision rule for assigning a TLU of equal or lower reading difficulty than the student's capability. The second stage of the algorithm involved the other six variables in a combinatorial way; a tabled value was ascertained for each of the possible combinations of a given student's ratings with those of each of the TLU's in a given module. The tabled values were constructed in such a way that a maximum value was obtained if the TLU and student characteristics were the same on any variable, and the tabled function provided less than a maximum value the more dissimilar the student's and TLU's ratings were. Thus, a composite score was obtained for each student-by-TLU combination within a module. The composite score itself was the sum of the six tabled values for each of the so-called style variables, giving each of the six equal weight in the sum. The TLU assigned a given student was the one for which in combination with student's rated characteristics the composite score was the highest. However, as stated earlier, the reading level of the material took precedence over the composite "style" index, so that the latter only entered into TLU assignment for those TLU's which were at or below the student's reading comprehension level.

Data on the Seven Matching Variables
An inspection of the frequency distributions (see Table 1) of the six teacher-rating variables reveals several interesting points. First, the restricted variance in usage of three scales suggests (a) that teachers are not very good raters (unable to discriminate or do not have the data to do so) of students' "needs" for multiple media, variety of activities, or preference for reading, and/or (b) that the trichotomized scales may have contributed to the attenuated variance. Considering

Table 1   Frequency Distributions of Scale Usage Expressed in Percentage of Total Number of Students Rated by Teachers

Stanine Value	Teacher Supervision			Practice or Drill			Social Involvement			Media Richness			Variety of Activities			Preference for Reading		
1	16[a]	12[b]	13[c]	14	11	17	18	18	24	13	16	24	8	11	16	30	19	22
2																		
3	18	16	14	16	20	26												
4							21	24	39									
5	28	25	24	38	37	33				65	63	52	78	76	64	53	63	54
6							49	49	30									
7	18	23	22	16	17	13												
8																		
9	19	22	25	15	12	8	10	7	5	20	20	22	12	12	18	16	16	23

[a] Data for students in grades 1-3, N = 1203
[b] Data for students in grades 5-7, N = 1716
[c] Data for students in grades 9-11, N = 419

the content of these three scales, it seems plausible that teachers might not be in the best position to make discriminations among students. However, rather than conclude these dimensions are worthless, it might well be appropriate to shift the source of such ratings to the student himself.

Table 2 shows the intercorrelations among the ratings of students' "need" for teacher supervision, drill or practice, and social involvement. The average correlation of .86 over the three age groups of subjects reveals a strong tendency on the part of teachers to rate students perceived as high in need for drill or practice as high also in need for teacher supervision. A revised matching paradigm should eliminate this redundancy.

The data on TLU coding is far too lengthy to present here, running to more than a dozen pages of computer output. However, these data can be summarized as follows: Of the 1071 modules in PLAN, 521 have more than one TLU available as alternative treatments. Of these 521, 349 have two nonidentical TLU's, 126 have three, and 7 modules have four nonidentical alternatives as rated on six of the seven variables in Figure 3 (number 4 had no variance).

Evaluation of the Matching Paradigm

With considerable variability among both TLU's and students (on some of the variables), an evaluation scheme was developed for the matching algorithm. The actual data are not in hand yet, but the design can be spelled out to indicate the direction of inquiry. The basic question was: Did students generally perform better after taking TLU's for which they were well matched or not? The null hypothesis was that the matching procedure, or more properly the extent to which a student worked on a well or poorly matched TLU, would not be correlated with module test performance. Because the matching procedure was a two-stage process, it was necessary to examine the relative contribution, if any, of each of the distinct sections. This required a tripartite evaluation, one for each of the three "matched-ness" indicators: first, for the combination of reading

Table 2 Intercorrelations of Teacher Rating Scales

	Practice or Drill	Social Involvement
Teacher Supervision	$.63^a$	.57
	$.98^b$	.43
	$.80^c$	.55
	$.86^d$	.44
Practice or Drill		.22
		.41
		.26
		.29

^{a}Data for students in grades 1-3, N = 97
^{b}Data for students in grades 5-7, N = 78
^{c}Data for students in grades 9-11, N = 106
^{d}Average correlation for all students, N = 281, using Z transformations.

comprehension plus the composite "style" value; second, for reading comprehension alone; and third, for the composite "style" value alone. A linear
regression format was decided upon, using module test results as the criterion,
independently for each of the three different "matched-ness" indicators. It
should be noted that simple zero-order r's would indicate to what degree the
"matched-ness" index was correlated with performance but would not reveal
how well matched the students had been. Thus, a covariate or control variable
was also included in the regression equation to index how well matched in
absolute magnitude a given student was. A low zero-order correlation would not
have discriminated between the situation where the low correlation was due to
low association between matching and performance and where the correlation
was suppressed because some portion of the students had worked on TLU's
which were a poor match.

The actual data on this question will have to be reported in another place,
as they become available. In the interim, PLAN continues to operate and to
collect data on large numbers of individual students' performance. In the future,
this PLAN data bank could prove to be one of the most significant resources for
research on individualized instruction.

Summary
This paper has argued that a potentially fruitful source of conceptual and empirical knowledge for meaningfully individualizing instruction will come from
further research on attribute-treatment interactions (ATI's). In order to maximize the payoff from this research, recommendations are made for the sequence
in which an ATI design should be developed: The experimenter's first task
should be to select his task(s) and to conduct a careful analysis of the task characteristics. Second, this analysis should be used in conceptualizing measurable
learner characteristics or attributes (defined in terms of cognitive and affective

prerequisites for successful task performance). Third, and only then, should work be begun on devising contrasting treatments designed to remedy individuals' attribute deficits. This step-wise process suggested that the ATI model should be expanded to include a task-characteristics dimension, and that future research might well use a two-stage design for data collection. Finally, preliminary work from Project PLAN was described, to indicate how a major individualized program at the national level is attempting to use and to build on ATI methodology.

References

Alluisi, E. A. Methodology in the use of synthetic tasks to assess complex performance. *Human Factors*, 1967, 9, 375-384.

Berliner, D. C., Angell, D., & Sheaver, J. Behaviors, measures, and instruments for performance evaluation in simulated environments. Paper delivered for symposium and workshop on the quantification of human performance, Albuquerque, New Mexico, 1964.

Bottenberg, R. A., & Ward, J. H. Applied multiple linear regression. (PRL-TDR-63-6). Lackland Air Force, Texas, 1963.

Bracht, G. H. Experimental factors related to aptitude-treatment interactions. *Review of Educational Research*, 1970, 40(5), 627-645.

Bracht, G. H., & Glass, G. V. The external validity of experiments. *American Educational Research Journal*, 1968, 5(4), 437-474.

Bunderson, C. V. Aptitude by treatment interactions: Of what use to the instructional designer? Research project report, University of Texas, Austin, 1970.

Carroll, J. B. Programmed instruction and student ability. *J. Programmed Instruction*, 1963, 2(4), 7-11.

Cohen, J. Multiple regression as a general data-analytic system. *Psychological Bulletin*, 1968, 70(6), 426-443.

Corsini, D. A., Pick, A. D., & Flavell, J. H. Production deficiency of nonverbal mediators in young children. *Child Development*, 1968, 39, 53-58.

Cronbach, L. J. The two disciplines of scientific psychology. *The American Psychologist*, 1957, 12, 671-684.

Cronbach, L. J., & Snow, R. E. Individual differences in learning ability as a function of instructional variables. *USOE Final Report*, 1969. OEC 4-6-061269-1217.

Farina, A. J. *Development of a taxonomy of human performance: A review of descriptive schemes for human task behavior*. Washington, D.C.: American Institutes for Research, 1969. AIR=726-1-TR-2.

Feldman, D. H. Personal Communication, 1971.

Flavell, J. H., Beach, D. R., & Chinsky, J. M. Spontaneous verbal rehearsal in a memory task as a function of age. *Child Development*, 1966, 37, 283-299.

Fleishman, E. A. The description and prediction of perceptual-motor skill learning. In R. Glaser (Ed.), *Training research and education*. Pittsburgh: University of Pittsburgh Press, 1962.

Fleishman, E. A. Performance assessment based on an empirically derived task taxonomy. *Human Factors*, 1967, 9, 349-366.

Folley, J. D. *Development of an improved method of task analysis and beginning of a theory of training.* Port Washington, N.Y.: USNTDC, 1964. NAVTRA-DEVCEN 1218-1. (a)

Folley, J. D. *Guidelines for task analysis.* Port Washington, N.Y.: USNTDC, 1964. NAVTRADEVCEN 1218-2. (b)

Gagné, R. M., & Gropper, G. L. *Individual differences in learning from visual and verbal presentations.* Pittsburgh, Pa.: American Institutes for Research, 1965.

Gagné, R. M. Human factors in systems. In R. M. Gagné (Ed.), *Psychological principles in system development.* New York: Holt, Rinehart & Winston, 1962.

Guilford, J. P. *The nature of human intelligence.* New York: McGraw-Hill, 1967.

Hively, W. Domain-referenced achievement testing. Paper presented to American Educational Research Association, February 1970.

Jensen, A., & Rohwer, W. D. Syntactical mediation of serial and paired associative learning as a function of age. *Child Development,* 1965, 36, 601-608.

Keeney, T. J., Canninzo, S. R., & Flavell, J. H. Spontaneous and induced verbal rehearsal in a recalled task. *Child Development,* 1967, 38, 953-966.

Lesser, G. S. Matching instruction to student characteristics. In G. S. Lesser (Ed.), *Psychology and educational practice.* Glenview, Ill.: Scott, Foresman and Company, 1971.

Miller, R. B. Task description and analysis. In R. M. Gagné (Ed.), *Psychological principles in system development.* New York: Holt, Rinehart & Winston, 1962.

Miller, R. B. *Task taxonomy: Science or technology?* Poughkeepsie, N.Y.: IBM, 1966.

Moely, B. E., Olson, F. A., Halwes, T. G., & Flavell, J. H. Prediction deficiency in young children's clustered recall. *Developmental Psychology,* 1969, 1, 26-34.

Peterson, R. O., Andrews, C. G., & Bryson, S. *Research on the training of outward operators, memorandum report number 1: Analysis of performance requirements.* Pittsburgh: American Institutes for Research, 1960. AIR-C30-60-IR-116.

Rabehl, G. J. The MINNEMAST experiment with domain-referenced achievement testing. Paper presented to American Educational Research Association, February 1970.

Sension, D. B. Future uses for domain-referenced achievement testing. Paper presented to American Educational Research Association, February 1970.

Skinner, B. F. Teaching science in high school—what is wrong? *Science,* 1968, 159, 704-710.

Tallmadge, G. K., & Shearer, J. W. Relationships among learning styles, instructional methods, and the nature of learning experiences. *J. Educational Psychology,* 1969, 60, 222-230.

Tobias, S. Research strategy in the effect of individual differences on achievement from programmed instruction. Paper presented at APA, Washington, D.C., 1969.

Willis, M. P. *Deriving training device implications from learning theory principles.* Port Washington, N.Y.: USNTDC, 1961. NAVTRADEVCEN 784-1.

Teaching Strategies
and Thought Processes
Hilda Taba and Freeman F. Elzey

The development of critical thinking has figured as an important objective of education for a long time. Yet, the implementation of this objective in curriculum construction and teaching has been sporadic and ineffective for a variety of reasons.

First, thinking has been treated as a global process. Consequently, the problem of defining thinking is still before us, as is the need to identify its specific elements, especially in terms which are helpful to planning effective teaching strategies. In a jungle of definitions, thinking has meant anything that goes on in the head, from daydreaming to creating a concept of relativity. Neither has knowledge of the development of thinking been too adequate. While Piaget has spent his lifetime in studying the development of thinking and has produced a quantity of reports, until recently his work received scant attention in the United States.

Implementation of thinking as an educational objective has also been handicapped by several questionable assumptions. One rather widely accepted assumption is that reflective thinking cannot take place until a sufficient body of factual information is accumulated. Teaching which follows this assumption stresses factual coverage and burdens the memory with unorganized and, therefore, rather perishable information.

An opposite, but equally unproductive, assumption is that thought is an automatic by-product of studying certain subjects and of assimilating the end-products of disciplined thought. Some subjects are assumed to have this power independently of how they are taught or learned. Inherently, memorizing mathematical formulae or the steps in mathematical processes is assumed to be better training than memorizing cake recipes, even though both may be learned in the same manner and call for the same mental process—rote memory.

The combination of these factors has prevented the focusing of attention on the development of teaching strategies designed to stimulate productive and creative thought. The curriculum is seldom organized to focus on active discovery and the use of abstract ideas. Classroom learning experiences are not usually designed to provide a cumulative sequence in the maturation of thought which is at once psychologically sound and logically valid.

All this has contributed to considerable underachievement in the mastery of autonomous and disciplined thought processes. Hence, a rather frequent criticism of current teaching-learning procedures is that they tend to cultivate passive mastery instead of an active discovery of ideas—a tendency to follow "recipes" in solving problems instead of analyzing them and searching for gen-

From *Teachers College Record*, 1964, 65, 524-534. Reprinted by permission of the authors and publisher.

eralizations with which to organize the needed facts and to plan an attack on them (Bartlett, 1958; Buswell & Hersch, 1956).

Cognition Revisited

Recently, there has been a renewed interest in the study of cognitive processes in general and thinking in particular. For example, Bartlett (1958) and Rokeach (1960) have been concerned with open and closed thought. Getzels and Jackson's study (1962) of creativity and Gallagher's study (1961) of productive thinking employed the classification of divergent and convergent styles of thought. Sigel (1961) has been interested in the relationship of the styles of organizing and labeling to personality dynamics.

The difficulty with such studies is that the findings about general cognitive styles fail to shed light on the processes by which these styles are acquired. Consequently, the data cannot be translated into guidelines for more effective teaching.

The study of thinking in elementary school children, on which this paper is based, set out to examine the processes of thought in the classroom in terms which are capable of shedding a light on the learning and teaching of certain cognitive skills in the school setting. The fundamental assumption was that thought consists of specific, describable processes which are subject to training, not in some category of powers which are inherent in the individual. Therefore, the study sought to create categories for analyzing thought which described learnable, and therefore also teachable, processes of thought. Specific processes in three cognitive tasks were identified: (1) concept formation, (2) the making of inferences and the induction of generalizations from interpretations of specific data, and (3) the application of generalizations to explain new phenomena and to predict the consequences of certain events and conditions. Critical thinking *per se* was excluded because the curriculum offered meager opportunities for its development.

The study was also conducted under conditions which presumably offered optimal conditions for the training of thought processes. First, the 20 elementary classrooms involved followed a social studies curriculum which centered on a series of basic ideas and was organized for an inductive discovery and development of these ideas. In addition, the curriculum outline also included a planned sequence of learning experiences designed to enhance the development of generalizations and their application to solving problems (*Contra Costa County Social Studies Units, Grades 1-6,* 1959).

Finally, the design for the study provided for special training of the teachers in the analysis of thought processes and in devising effective teaching strategies for their development. In other words, the study proposed to explore thinking under conditions which included the twin impact of the curriculum and of specified teaching methods.

The Theoretical Framework

The study, as well as the curriculum which provided the context for it, and the training of teachers were based on several concepts regarding the nature of thought and its development. First among these was the idea that the maturation of thought follows an evolutionary sequence in which the simpler mental operations form a basis for the creation of the increasingly more complex and abstract mental structures. For example, the learning experiences in the curriculum outlines were arranged so that each preceding step developed skills and cognitive operations which constituted a prerequisite for the next more complex or more abstract mental operations. The cycle of these operations usually began with the analysis of a concrete instance of the general idea on which the unit was centered and ended with the formulation of the idea and its application to new problems and situations (*Contra Costa County Social Studies Units, Grades 1-6,* 1959; Taba, 1962).

The exploration of the logical structure of the three cognitive tasks with which the study was concerned revealed another, more specific series of hierarchically ordered sequences of thought processes. For example, the sequence in concept formation begins with enumeration of concrete items, such as listing the differences one would expect to encounter when traveling in Latin America. The next step is that of grouping these items on some conscious basis, such as deciding the basis on which to group together "climate," "weather," and "altitude." The process ends with labeling or classifications, such as deciding to subsume a group of items under "standards of living." These steps constitute a necessary sequence in the sense that each preceding step is a prerequisite for mastering the next one. Underlying the steps are still other cognitive processes, such as differentiation of certain properties of phenomena or events with some degree of precision and an ability to abstract common elements and to determine the basis on which to group and label them.

In a similar manner, the logic of interpreting information and making inferences involves the assimilation of specific points of information, followed by relating several points to each other and making inferences or generalizations which go beyond that which is explicitly given.

The process involved in applying known facts and principles is a bit more complex, involving as it does divergent lines of prediction as well as the hierarchies of leaps in each according to the distance, ranging from the most immediate consequences to the most remote—such as predicting that water will bring grass, in comparison to predicting that the presence of water will cause nomads to cease to be nomads and turn to building cities.

The logic of the sequential steps in this process is not entirely clear. This unclarity is reflected in the rating scheme used. Obviously, the individual must draw upon his memory for the relevant information to form any predictions at all. But he must also relate this information to the requirements of the situation and construct the parameters of conditions necessary for the predicted consequences to occur. This process entails both the construction of chains of consequences, such as water → growing crops → settling down → building cities, and the perception of the logical relationships between the conditions and consequences.

The chief point about the sequences in the development of thinking is that a deficiency in mastering the first step, such as the analysis of concrete instances, leads to incapacity to function on the level of the final step, such as the formulation of generalizations. The chief task of teaching, then, is to determine the order of learning tasks and to pace each step appropriately. This is a crucial point in the formulation of teaching strategies, and one against which current teaching methods commit the greatest errors.

Cognitive Commerce

The concept that the cognitive operations are an active transaction between the individual and his environment or the material was another idea which influenced the design both of the curriculum and of the study. Children inevitably build mental schemes with which to organize the information they encounter. The quality of the learning experiences determines the degree of productivity of these schemes. All learning experiences teach what Harlow (1949) calls "sets to learn." Depending on the teaching strategies employed, children may learn to look for the structure of the problems set by the learning tasks or for arbitrary procedures. They may acquire a disposition to search for relationships and patterns among ideas and facts, or to look for single "right answers."

When the teaching strategies pay little attention to creating models for thinking, children tend to acquire faulty or unproductive conceptual schemes with which to organize information or to solve problems. For example, procedures such as asking students to name the important cities in the Balkans, without revealing the criterion for importance or without developing such a criterion with the class, leave students no alternative but to guess what the teacher wants or to recollect what the book said about the matter. Repeated experiences of this sort cause students to adopt irrational, unproductive, and arbitrary models of thinking and a dependence on memory rather than on judgment or inference.

Burton (1952) cites an extreme example of an irrational or mechanical model or schema. He describes an elementary school child who made good grades in arithmetic because she "came up" with the right answers. When asked how she decided when to use which process, she explained her method as follows: "I know what to do by looking at the examples. If there are only two numbers I subtract. If there are lots of numbers, I add. If there are just two numbers and one is smaller than the other, then it is a hard problem. I divide to see if it comes out even, but if it doesn't, I multiply." Evidently this child had built a scheme to fit the manner of presentation of problems in the arithmetic book. By applying the scheme, she was also learning an unproductive model of thinking or a "set" which excluded understanding the structure of the problems.

The idea of thought as an active organization of mental processes underscores the importance of addressing teaching strategies to the development of autonomy and productivity. Effective teaching is seen as consisting primarily of what we get out of the children instead of what we put into them (Sigel, 1961). In other words, helping students to develop a basis for and a method by which to judge the importance of cities may be of greater value than their simply knowing which cities are important.

Of special relevance is the idea that thought matures through a progressive and active organization and reorganization of conceptual structures. The individual fits the information he receives at any moment into the conceptual scheme he already possesses. When the requirements of the situation do not fit his current scheme, however, the individual is forced to alter it or to extend it to accommodate new information. Piaget (1947) calls this fitting process "assimilation" and the process of alteration "accommodation."

This process suggests a teaching strategy which includes a rotation of learning tasks, calling for the assimilation of new information into the existing conceptual scheme with information that requires an extension and reorganization of the scheme (Hunt, 1961). Prolonged assimilation of facts without a corresponding reshaping of the conceptual schemes with which to organize them is bound to retard the maturation of thought. On the other hand, a premature leap into a more complex or a higher level of thought is likely to immobilize mental activity and cause reversion to rote learning or, at any rate, to a lower level of thought. Students need a sufficient amount of assimilation to have the "stuff" to think with. But they need equally a challenge to stretch their modes of thinking and their conceptual schemes. An appropriate transition from one to the other demands a proper match between the current level and that which is required. Determining the proper match is perhaps one of the most difficult tasks in teaching and constitutes, in effect, a new concept of readiness and pacing. This task is complicated by the fact that the mastery of abstract communications, such as language and number, often masks the actual level of thinking. Verbalization may deceive the teacher and lead him to assume that thinking is more advanced than it is and, hence, to pushing the child's verbal habits of learning beyond his level of thinking (Peel, 1960).

Reasonable Hopes
It seems reasonable to assume that, given an adequate analysis of the learning processes involved in certain important cognitive tasks, and teaching strategies which effectively implemented the principles of sequence, of active mental organization, and of adequate rotation of assimilation and accommodation, it should be possible for all students to achieve higher levels of cognitive operation than seems possible under current teaching. Furthermore, it is not beyond possibility that by far the most important individual differences may be found in the amount of concrete thinking an individual needs before formal thought can emerge. This difference may distinguish the slow but capable learner from one who is incapable of abstract thought. It is not beyond possibility, therefore, that many slow learners can achieve a high level of abstract thought, provided that they have the opportunity to examine a greater number of concrete instances than the teaching process typically allows. The employment of teaching strategies which are scientifically designed for the development of cognitive skills may make it possible to develop cognitive processes at a much higher level and in a greater number of students.

This rationale set certain requirements for the methodology of studying the development of thought processes in the classroom. It required, first, securing records of classroom transactions. Second, it required a multidimensional analysis of these transactions in terms of what the teacher does, of what the responses of the students are, and of the product of the interaction.

Four discussions were taped in each of the 20 classrooms. Because the curriculum outline projected learning activities, it was possible to place each taping at a point in a sequence at which a specified cognitive task of concern to the study occurred. The first taping was made during the very first class session in which enumeration, grouping, and classification was the chief task. The next two tapings recorded discussions involving interpreting data and formulating inferences from them: one an interpretation of a film, and another at a point at which students reported information from preceding research, compared and contrasted their data, and attempted to express their findings in generalizations. These tapings were taken at the midyear. The final taping, at the end of the year, was of discussions involving application of previously learned knowledge to predicting consequences from described hypothetical conditions.

Units and Scores

One problem in analyzing classroom transactions for the purpose of describing thought processes is to decide on units of analysis which are at once capable of being scored accurately and which express sensible units of thought. In this study, the time sampling was discarded in favor of a "thought unit." "Thought unit" was defined as a remark or series of remarks expressing a more or less complete idea, serving a specified function, and classifiable according to a level of thought. It is, therefore, possible for one word or an entire paragraph to be designated as a "thought unit." For example, the word "cement," when it occurs in the process of enumerating materials for building houses, is considered a thought unit. So is a paragraph, such as "The people in the other country do not have electric saws and things that the men in this country use to build houses. The children help chop the wood and can do a lot of things to help build the houses. But the children over here cannot do very many things because of the danger."

In order to describe simultaneously the teaching acts and the levels of thinking of students, the verbal transactions were "scored" by three different "ratings." The first is that of *designation.* It describes the source of the thought unit —whether it emanated from the teacher or from the student and whether the person is giving or seeking information. The code symbols for designation are *child gives* (CG), *child seeks* (CS), *teacher gives* (TG), and *teacher seeks* (TS).

The rating of *function* describes how a thought unit functions in the context of discussion. When applied to remarks or questions by teachers, these ratings may be used to describe teaching strategies which affect the subsequent thought of children.

Two large groups of function ratings may be distinguished: (1) questions or statements made by the teacher or the students which are psychological or managerial in their function and unrelated to the logic of the content. Statements of this type include those that express agreement (A), approval (AP), disagreement (D), disapproval (Dp), management (M), and reiteration (R). (2) The second group includes teacher or student statements which function to give direction to discussions, but which at the same time can be rated according to the logic of content. Such ratings include focusing (F), refocusing (F_2), change of focus (FC), deviating from focus (Fd), controlling thought (C), extending thought on the same level (X), and lifting called to a higher level (L).

The third rating, called *levels of thought,* describes both the student's and the teacher's verbal behavior by specifying the logical quality and the level of thought expressed. A separate rating scheme was developed for each of the three cognitive tasks. For each of these tasks, categories were established which represent the hierarchical levels of thought, according to their level of abstraction and complexity. These categories refer to the specific thought processes which need to be mastered in a sequential order, because performing on the preceding level is a prerequisite to being able to perform on the next. Thus, the rating scheme represents the developmental sequence for each cognitive task. In addition, within each category, distinctions were made between the irrelevant, the disconnected, and the related information or content.

The rating scheme used for designating the levels of thought for each of the cognitive tasks is as follows:

Cognitive task: grouping and labeling[1] (giving or seeking)
  10 specific or general information outside of focus
  11 specific or general information within focus
  12 specific or general information with qualifications
  30 grouping information without basis
  31 grouping information with implicit basis
  32 grouping information with explicit basis
  40 categorizing information without basis
  41 categorizing information with implicit relationships between items
  42 categorizing information with explicit relationships between items

Cognitive task: interpreting information and making inferences (giving or seeking)
  10 specific or general information outside of focus
  11 specific or general information within focus
  12 specific or general information with qualifications and relationships
  50 specific reason or explanation that does not relate to the information
  51 specific reason or explanation that relates or organizes the information
  52 specific reason or explanation that states how it relates or organizes the information
  60 irrelevant or incorrect inference which is derived from information
  61 relevant inference which is derived from information
  62 relevant inference which is derived from information and expresses a cause and effect relationship, explanation, consequence, or contrast

---

[1]Categories in the 20 series were originally reserved for "general information" but were later combined with the 10 series.

70 relationship between information which implies an irrelevant or incorrect principle or generalization
71 relationship between information which implies a principle or generalization
72 principle or generalization which is derived from information

Cognitive task: predicting consequences (giving or seeking)
    90 correcting the cause or condition
Establishing parameter information
    100 relevant information
    101 relevant information for establishing the total parameter (if-then) or for a particular hypothesis or prediction
    102 relevant information for the total parameter or any particular prediction with appropriate explanation
Establishing parameters of conditions
    110 irrelevant or untenable condition for the total parameter or for the particular prediction or hypothesis
    111 relevant condition without connecting it with relevant information
    112 relevant condition and information and establishing logical connection between them
Prediction: Level one, immediate consequences
             Level two, remote consequences
120-220 incorrect or out of focus prediction
121-221 prediction with no elaboration
122-222 prediction accompanied by explanation, qualification, differentiation, comparison, or contrast
123-223 prediction accompanied by a stated or implied principle

In determining the level at which to rate a particular thought unit, it was necessary to consider the context in which the thought unit occurs. For example, the statement, "a hammer, because you can drive large nails with it," may be rated as "specific information with qualifying statement" if it is offered in response to the task of naming tools used in building a house; it merely gives additional information about the hammer and does not constitute a reason for naming "hammer." If the focus is on identification of tools most useful to primitive people, however, the same response would be rated as "relevant inference derived from information," because the phrase is an explicit reason for naming "hammer."

Function and Level
In describing the effect of teaching strategy on thought levels, four groups of function rating are especially important: focusing (F), extending the thought on the same level (X), lifting thought to a higher level (L), and controlling thought (C). Focusing establishes both the topic and the particular angle for its treatment. It sets the cognitive task. For example, the statement by the teacher,

"If the desert had all the water it needed, what would happen?" establishes the central focus for discussion and calls for prediction of consequences.

The coding system also specifies the shifts in subject matter (change of focus), the degree to which the teacher finds it necessary to bring the discussion back to the original topic (refocus), and the number of times that the discussion wanders from the subject (deviation from focus).

A statement of the teacher or a child is coded as extension of thought (X) when it gives or seeks additional information or provides elaboration and clarification on an already established level. The following example illustrates a series of extensions on the level of providing specific information:

(1)	C	Malobi took the money home with her.	CG 11
(2)	T	What did Malobi do with the money?	TS 11
(3)	C	She saved it.	CG 11X
(4)	C	She put it underground.	CG 11X
(5)	C	She put sticks and tin over it.	CG 11X
(6)	C	Before she did that, she put it in a little pot.	CG 11X

A thought unit is functioning to lift the level of thought whenever the teacher or child seeks or gives information that shifts thought to a higher level than had previously been established. In the following example, the teacher attempts to lift the level of thought from giving information to explanation:

(1)	C	They carried things in baskets on their heads.	CG 11
(2)	T	Explain why.	TS 61L
(3)	C	I suppose they can carry more things that way.	CG 61L

A question may function to extend the thought in one context and to lift it in another, as illustrated in the following example:

(1)	C	They were working fast on the house.	CG 11
(2)	T	Why?	TS 51L
(3)	C	They wanted to get the house done before the rain came.	CG 51L
(4)	T	Why?	TS 51X
(5)	C	Because unless it is finished, the rain will destroy it.	CG 52X

The inquiry on line two is rated as teacher seeking to lift the level of thought from the established level of giving specific information to the level of inference. The child's response provides the reason on the level sought by the teacher. The same inquiry on line four and the child's response on line five function to extend the thought because the level at which the question is asked has already been established.

Controlling of thought occurs when the teacher performs a cognitive task that students should be induced to do. This is the case when the teacher gives a category for classification, an inference in interpretation, or a prediction in the task of applying principles.

Strategic Patterns

As elements of teaching strategy, the frequencies of these functions may represent either effective or ineffective teaching strategies. For example, frequent shifts in focus may be needed at some points in the discussion to introduce sufficient information to form a basis for comparison and generalization. Other tasks may require that the discussion remain on one focus long enough to provide full treatment of the subject before proceeding to another, higher level of thought process. Frequent refocusing may indicate a faulty handling of the sequence in thought processes, which results in the necessity for constantly having to bring the children back to the focus.

This multiple coding scheme makes it possible to depict the flow of the classroom discussion by charting the sequences of transactions between the teacher and the children, the changes in the level of thought during the discussion, and the effect of these strategies upon the level and the direction of thought. The flow of thought can be reconstructed even though the specific content of the discussion is not given.[2] For example, an empirical sequence of thought may, when translated from the code, be read as *child gives specific information, teacher seeks an extension of that information, child provides the requested extension, teacher seeks to lift the level of thought from the "information" level to the "reason" level, child provides a reason as requested by the teacher,* and *teacher gives approval to the child.* In a similar manner, any sequence of ratings can be reconstructed from the observationally developed flow charts.

When the flow charts identify individual children, then one can describe the characteristic modes and levels of thought of particular pupils, such as a tendency to operate only on the level of concrete information or on the level of inference and generalization, the tendency to remain focused or to stray from the focus, to give relevant or irrelevant information, etc. It also permits the accounting of the frequencies of the various thought patterns which prevail in the classroom group and the discrepancies between what the teacher seeks and how the children respond.

Data of this sort depict the various strategies which teachers may employ and their consequences. For example, when the teacher attempts to raise the level of thought very early in the discussion, this typically results in the children's returning to a lower level and in their inability to sustain discussion at the higher levels of thought. On the other hand, a strategy representing an effective pacing of shifting the thought onto higher levels seems to follow a characteristic course. The level of seeking information is sustained for a considerable time during the first portion of the discussion. Grouping is requested only after a large amount of information has been accumulated. The result is that in a fairly brief period children transcend from grouping to labeling and then to providing reasons for labeling and to inferences.

---

[2] Charts based on empirical observation will be published later as a part of the report to the US Office of Education of a study of "Thinking in Elementary School Children" (Project No. 1574).

Other strategic patterns that have been empirically identified include the teacher's repeated attempts to steer discussion to the inferential level without permitting the development of a body of needed information; in such a case, the children repeatedly return to the information level. Or when there is a constant change of focus, the children's thought alternates between several levels, is not sustained at the higher level, and gradually stabilizes on the most primitive one.

Some Implications

This multidimensional analysis of classroom transactions has several advantages. First, by combining the description of the teacher's acts in terms of their explicit functions with the assessment of the logical quality of student responses, it is possible to evaluate the impact of the teacher's behavior in terms of its productivity. This addition of the dimension of the logical quality of the content of thought carries the analysis of classroom transactions a step beyond what has been available to date. Most current studies of classroom transactions concentrate more or less exclusively on the analysis of the psychological functions of teaching acts (Flanders, 1960; Hughes et al., 1959). This emphasis has evoked the criticism that teaching is explained and controlled exclusively in terms of psychological principles and that the logic of teaching and of its product in learning is overlooked (Smith, 1950).

A further advantage lies in the fact that, in addition to describing the impact of teaching exclusively in terms of the frequencies of specific acts, this scheme permits studying the cumulative impact of certain patterns or combinations of acts, including their pacing. It is at this point that a transfer is made from the study of teaching acts to the study of teaching strategies. Flanders (no date) has taken a step in this direction by describing the points of shift in the nature of teaching acts.

Finally, the scheme permits the examination of the effect of teaching strategies in terms of a measurable change in a specified outcome—levels of thinking in this case—and thus frees the study of teaching from the necessity of inferring the effect from the assumed consequences of the frequencies of certain types of teacher behavior.

A preliminary analysis of the typescripts of classroom discussion reveals an enormous influence of teacher behavior on the thinking of students. This impact is exercised in a variety of ways: by the nature of the questions asked, what the teacher gives to the students or seeks from them, the timing of these acts in the total sequence, which ideas are picked up for elaboration and which are passed over, points at which approval and disapproval are given, etc. For example, the focus which the teacher sets determines which points students can explore and establishes the models for thought they can practice. Of great importance is the sequence of mental operations called for and the appropriateness of this sequence to developing productive thought models.

It seems clear, further, that the level of thinking attained is influenced not only by the nature of the single act by a teacher just preceding a given response. The level of thought attained seems to be determined by the whole pattern of transactions: the particular combination of focusing, extending, and lifting; the timing of these acts; the length of time spent on a particular focus, such as exploring specific descriptive information before examining causes or attempting explanation; the distance between the mental operations of the students at the moment from the level required by the teacher, and the points at which the teacher seeks information from students and gives it. These combinations, not merely the frequencies alone, constitute a teaching strategy.

Only a casual identification of these strategies is available at the moment of writing this article. The variations in the patterns are too numerous to permit analysis by ordinary means. The staff, in cooperation with experts in computer programing, has developed a high-speed computer program designed to aid in accounting for these patterns. Such a computer program should permit the identification of the elements and the cumulative patterns of strategies associated with high and low performance.[3]

The findings so far suggest that if the acquisition of skills in autonomous thinking is to be a realistic objective, a much more thorough study of and experimentation with the appropriate teaching strategies and their impact of the development of thinking is called for. As Flanders (no date) suggests, any step in the direction of specifying productive teaching strategies should lead to a more adequate understanding of the connection between teachers' behavior and student response. A scientific mapping of such strategies should also add considerably to the developing theory of instruction, and especially to our understanding of the conditions which maximize the development of higher mental processes on the part of all students, not only the intellectual elite.

References

Bartlett, F. E. *Thinking: an experimental and social study.* New York: Basic Books, 1958.

Burton, W. N. *The guidance of learning activities.* New York: Appleton-Century, 1952.

Buswell, G. T., & Hersch, B. Y. *Patterns of solving problems.* Berkeley, California: Univer. California Press, 1956.

Contra Costa County Social Studies Units, Grades 1-6. Pleasant Hill, California: Contra Costa County Schools, 1959.

Flanders, N. A. *Teacher influence, pupil attitudes, and achievement.* Pre-publication manuscript of a proposed research monograph for the U.S. Office of Education, Cooperative Research Branch, Washington, D. C., 1960.

Flanders, N. A. Some relationships between teacher influence, pupil attitudes, and achievement. Ditto MS of a chapter submitted to the AASA, the NTBA, and the NEA Classroom Teachers Division. No date.

Gallagher, J. J., Aschner, M. J., Perry, J. M., & Afaar, S. S. A system for classifying thought processes in the content of classroom verbal interaction. Ditto MS. Urbana, Ill.: Institute for Research on Exceptional Children, Univer. Illinois, 1961.

Getzels, J. W., & Jackson, P. *Creativity and intelligence.* New York: Wiley, 1962.

---

[3] Such a computer program has been devised by P. J. Stone and M. S. Smith as a general sequence analyzer, planned to identify recurrent patterns in a list of events.

Guilford, J. P. Basic conceptual problems in the psychology of thinking. *Annals NY Acad. Sci.*, 1961, 91, 9-19.

Harlow, H. F. The formation of learning sets. *Psychol. Rev.*, 1949, 56, 51-60.

Hughes, Marie, et al. *Development of the means for the assessment of the quality of teaching in elementary school.* (Mimeo.) Salt Lake City: Univer. Utah, 1959.

Hunt, J. McV. *Experience and intelligence.* New York: Ronald Press, 1961.

Peel, E. A. *The pupil's thinking.* London: Oldbourne, 1960.

Piaget, J. *The psychology of intelligence.* London: Routledge, Kegan Paul, 1947.

Rokeach, M. *The open and closed mind.* New York: Basic Books, 1960.

Sigel, I. Cognitive style and personality dynamics. Interim report, Merrill-Palmer Institute, 1961.

Smith, B. O. Concept of teaching. *Teach. Coll. Rec.*, 1950, 61, 229-241.

Taba, Hilda. *Curriculum development: theory and practice.* New York: Harcourt, Brace & World, 1962.

Pedagogical Adaptations to Individual Differences: Some Research Findings
Gerald S. Lesser

The [aforementioned] adaptations to individual differences primarily deal with the organization of the school environment, operating within predetermined programs that generally are fixed and inflexible. Variations in school organization do provide certain benefits, but, according to Goodlad (1966):

"No scheme of school organization, however elaborately worked out, provides for the types and ranges of learner variability encompassed by the school. Thorough acceptance of this idea is some assurance that educators will not relinquish their educational responsibilities to limiting, classificatory contrivances and practices, such as ability groups, achievement levels, grade skipping, and nonpromotion. We've been around the clock several times before in our zeal to 'organize away' the stark realities of individual differences . . . In the matter of dealing educationally with individual differences, there are no educational panaceas" (p. 28).

We now shall describe adaptations to individual differences that stress *pedagogical* differentiation rather than *organizational* variations. Granting some

From "Matching Instruction to Student Characteristics." In *Psychology and Educational Practice* by Gerald S. Lesser. Copyright © 1971 by Scott, Foresman and Company. Reprinted by permission of the publisher.

limited value to organizational modifications, it is *differentiation for pedagogy* that affects educational practice in a fundamental manner.

From the teacher's point of view, the working model for pedagogical adaptations of instruction to individual differences often is informal. As she teaches a particular topic to her class, using the most powerful general form of instruction she can devise, she observes that a certain percentage of her students understand the topic clearly and thoroughly, others are on the verge of clear understanding but have not quite achieved it, others have only a vague sense of her meaning, and still others understand her not at all. What does she do? The answer depends on her diagnosis of why certain children fail to achieve a clear understanding. What obstacles exist for different children at their particular levels of incomplete or absent understanding, and how can her subsequent form of instruction be adjusted to meet these obstacles?

For those students who have narrowly missed complete understanding, perhaps she moved a bit too rapidly; minor adjustment of the pace of instruction perhaps is sufficient. For those who have achieved only a vague grasp, perhaps the idea was somewhat too abstract; a larger number of concrete examples may be necessary. For those who have understood nothing, perhaps some prior concepts were absent; the teacher must retreat to building the prior understandings the child must have before he can even attack the current concept.

Or, as an alternative, if the teacher judges that the topic being taught is not crucial to certain children who did not grasp it, or that some other topic is more crucial, she may adjust her educational goals accordingly.

Thus, the teacher constantly must use her informal diagnosis and analysis of individual differences to adjust both the forms and timing of instruction as well as her setting of educational objectives.

Cronbach (1967) also describes some informal classroom applications of the principle of matching instruction and individual differences:

"The teacher . . . barely acknowledges the comment one pupil makes in class discussion and stops to praise a lesser contribution from another who (he thinks) needs special encouragement. He turns away one pupil who asks for help—'you can find the answer for yourself if you keep at it'—and walks the length of the classroom to offer help to another, because he has decided to encourage independence of the former pupil and to minimize frustration of the latter. On the larger scale, he not only allows options for a term paper, but may custom-tailor a project for the student with special abilities or limitations" (p. 29).

The grounds for such teacher's adaptations of method to individual differences often are intuitive and implicit. These intuitive adaptations may be successful, but perhaps more explicit analyses of instruction and individual differences will be suggested by the following research examples.

Individual Differences and "Particular" Goals
for Different Children

In selecting "particular" goals of education for an individual child, the concept of individual differences demands that we find the particular, desired outcomes best fitted to the child's special aptitudes and motivations.

Defining "Particular" Goals Through Multiple Curriculum Options. It is an unfortunate commentary on American education that we are forced to turn to another educational system—in this instance, Sweden—to locate a case in which systematic attention is given to providing multiple curriculum options to match individual differences in aptitude and aspiration. There it was assumed that different mathematical ideas, at different levels of comprehension, were appropriate for students with different aptitudes and educational or occupational aspirations. In this framework, Husén (1967) describes the Swedish system's detailed specification of the different mathematical ideas essential in each of ten different vocational training and six different academic training programs, further identifying the exact level of each skill aimed for in each program. "Particular" goals in developing communication skills, understanding social studies, and other subjects have also been defined and made available to persons with different aptitudes and educational aspirations. Thus, the Swedish system attempts to provide an enormous cafeteria display of organized intellectual fare, presenting each individual with a wide range of options in selecting his "particular" goals of education.

Defining "Particular" Goals in Moral Education. Individual differences may influence the definition of "particular" educational goals in another way: when the particular objective is to modify or elevate the child's position on a dimension of individual differences in order to facilitate later learning. Kohlberg and Turiel's discussion of moral development in the present volume [Lesser, 1971, pp. 410-465] provides an example. Suppose that it is found that the rational discussion of a public-policy issue in a social studies class at the high school level (e.g., Oliver & Shaver, 1966) demands some ability to operate at Kohlberg's Stage 5, requiring the contractual-legalistic view which recognizes the rights of both individuals and groups. The purpose of rational discussion of such public-policy questions is to lead to a decision that will minimize the violation of important values, not to pretend that no conflict exists between individual and group rights. Yet, suppose further that many individual high school students have not progressed to this stage of moral development. If the teacher is to attack the curriculum issue at all, he must find ways to move his students from Stage 3 ("orientation to approval and to pleasing others") or Stage 4 ("showing respect for authority and maintaining the given social order for its own sake") to Stage 5 ("the contractual-legalistic view which recognizes the rights of both individuals and groups").

Thus, certain dimensions of individual differences (such as stages of moral development) form different hierarchies of steps of increasing developmental maturity. When the child's present position in that hierarchy of steps does not permit him to address a topic realistically, a "particular" educational goal becomes defined for him: elevating his position on that dimension sufficiently to enable him to deal with the issue.

We have reviewed some of the implications of the concept of individual differences for the selecting of particular goals for individual children, aims defined by their special aptitudes, interests, and the social forces in their particular environments. First, the teacher and the educational system must contrive a wide variety of options from which an individual student may select his particular direction. Second, it is necessary to recognize that the child often must be moved to a higher developmental level on a particular dimension of development before certain learnings can occur, this elevation of developmental level constituting a preliminary "particular" goal for the individual child, before a "universal" goal can be approached. We turn now to the interrelations among individual differences, instructional strategies, and some of these "universal" goals of education.

Individual Differences and "Universal" Goals of Education

We have identified certain "universal" goals of education—for example, literacy—as those we expect each child to achieve. In attempting to reach these universal goals more effectively, a teacher must find different instructional strategies to fit the individual child's strengths and weaknesses. Described below are some additional cases of research to illustrate this idea and to act as a guide to the teacher in fitting her instruction to individual differences.

Varying the Techniques of Instruction: "Socratic" and "Recitation" Methods with Students of Different Personalities. Oliver and Shaver (1966, 1968) aim at teaching junior high school students to think critically about issues of public controversy. They report that different teaching methods are of varying effectiveness with different subgroups of students.

Students were assigned to two different instructional groups for discussion of cases presenting public-policy decisions. In the *Socratic* discussions, the teacher encouraged individual students to take personal positions to handle the issue presented in the case and then defend the stand. In particular, the teacher was to force the student to face and deal with inconsistencies among his values and between his factual beliefs and his values in arriving at a defensible position. *Recitation* discussions were based on the same cases as the Socratic discussions, but the class as a whole explored the various factors that should be taken into account in making a decision. Rather than forcing students to take personal positions and defend them, the emphasis in the recitation discussions was on the nonpersonal aspects of the issue posed by the case. In general, no differences were found in student achievement under the two instructional techniques.

However, a number of personality measures had been administered to the students in order to investigate relations between student characteristics and learning, and interactions between personality and instructional techniques emerged. The Socratic style was more effective for students low in authoritarianism, low in the tendency to dichotomize, low in the need for structure, and high in the ability to tolerate hostile action. In contrast, the recitation technique was more effective for students high in authoritarianism and the tendency to dichotomize, and low in the ability to tolerate hostile action.

In the light of the adversarial nature of the Socratic technique, as compared to the low-affect, orderly nature of the recitation method, these findings make good educational sense. For example, the student low in authoritarianism would be expected to function better in the give-and-take of the Socratic discussion, while the student high in authoritarianism might find the Socratic teacher's aggressiveness so threatening as to interfere with learning, or he might reject the teacher as an authority figure because of the teacher's unorthodox behavior. By the same token, the person who tends to dichotomize is likely to find the open-ended Socratic discussions uncomfortable: either-or answers clearly are not acceptable to the teacher. The recitation technique does not pose this threat: clear-cut, definite conclusions are more accepted.

Closely related to Socratic and recitation methods are instruction through "discovery" and "exposition" techniques. These forms of instruction also show different effects upon different children.

"Discovery" and "Expository" Methods with Students of Different Reasoning Skills. The concepts of *mathematical sets* were taught to fifth- and sixth-grade students using discovery and expository methods (Kropp, Nelson, & King, 1967). In the discovery method, students were given numerous examples of sets and generated the definitional attributes of sets from these examples. In the expository method, the attributes of sets were defined by the teacher. Children strong in deductive reasoning profited more from exposition than discovery. Conversely, children strong in inductive reasoning learned more from discovery than exposition.

The interaction between techniques of instruction and individual differences has been proposed in the learning of other mathematics concepts.

"Spatial" and "Symbolic" Methods of Teaching Mathematics. Gagné (1960, 1962) suggests that the addition of signed numbers could be taught using either spatial, verbal, or symbolic concepts, and that students with different patterns of spatial conceptualization, verbal, and symbolic-reasoning aptitudes should show differential learning, depending upon the instruction-aptitude match. Bruner (1966) proposes a similar scheme:

"One can, for example, teach many of the same mathematical ideas in a spatialized iconic form (as with Venn diagrams) or in propositional form (as with the use of truth tables). That is to say, one can 'visualize' the statement 'if *a* then *b*' as a circle, *a,* within a larger circle, *b.* Or one can 'symbolize' it by the statement:

(*a* and *b*) is true
(*a* and no-*b*) is false
(not-*a* and *b*) is true
(not-*a* and not-*b*) is true.

Each mode has its virtues, viewed from a mathematical point of view. In the psychology of mathematics, the task is to delineate the virtues of the two modes (and their interaction) from the point of view of the learner or the user of mathematics" (pp. 155-156).

Several studies (e.g., Behr, 1967; Davis, 1967; Dougherty, 1967) now have tested these ideas, suggesting that in teaching mathematical ideas and operations there is merit in matching the model of instruction with the special aptitudes of students. On occasion, however, this research (e.g., Dougherty, 1967) is clearer about the destructive effects of mismatching than it is about the constructive benefits of matching. In teaching mathematical functions to children strong in space conceptualization but weak in number facility, Dougherty used graphic presentation; in teaching the same concepts to a child strong in number facility but weak in space conceptualization, he relied upon the manipulation of numbers in a tabular form. Such a matching of child and curriculum (e.g., a spatial child given a spatially oriented curriculum) resulted in some learning for most of the children, although there was wide variation in amounts of gain even within these correctly matched groups. Incorrect matching (e.g., a numerical child given a spatially oriented curriculum), on the other hand, resulted uniformly in insignificant gains. The inhibiting effects of mismatching seem well documented; the rational bases for arranging uniformly successful matches remain to be clarified.

"Manipulation" and "Verbalization" with Students of Different Reasoning Skills. The teacher often must use different techniques of instruction, depending upon the child's level of performance. In teaching classification skills to first-grade children, Tanaka (1968) used two instructional strategies: manipulation of objects and verbalization about pictures. For children with weak initial classification skills, Tanaka found that the object-manipulation method was more effective. For children at a higher initial level of classification skills, the picture-verbalization approach was superior. Thus, different initial levels of performance may indicate that different instructional techniques will be suitable.

"Phonics" and "Whole-Word" Methods with Students of Different Perceptual Preferences. Another instance of matching the techniques of instruction to known individual differences was suggested earlier in this volume [Lesser, 1971, pp. 152-155] by Bissell, White, and Zivin in their discussion of visual and auditory modality preferences. Referring to preliminary evidence provided by Robinson (1968) and deHirsch et al. (1966), it appears that the "visual" children acquired beginning reading skills more effectively in response to the "sight, whole-word" method of reading instruction, while children strong in the auditory modality learned best by starting with the phonics method. Again, fostering maximum reading skill apparently involves matching the technique of instruction to the child's strengths or weaknesses in the auditory or visual modalities.

Another instance of instruction-aptitude matching also involves the comparative effectiveness of phonics and whole-word methods with different children.

"Phonics" and "Whole-Word" Methods with Students of Different Language Ability. Snow (1968) studied alternative methods of beginning reading instruction in relation to the child's level of language ability. He reports that the

phonics method was more effective with children of low initial language ability while higher-ability children profited more from the whole-word method. Thus, higher reading achievement was obtained by the more able children when assigned to the whole-word group and by the less able children when assigned to the phonics group.

The same principles of matching instruction to individual characteristics apply in devising methods for the training of teachers.

"Self-Viewing" Methods in Teacher Training. One technique for teacher training involves seeing oneself in videotaped classroom lessons. Salomon and MacDonald (1968) report that teacher interns who were dissatisfied with their own teaching performance and had generally low self-esteem attended more to their physical appearance and after self-viewing had less favorable attitudes toward teaching. Those with higher self-esteem at the start tended to notice more cues relevant to their teaching performance and improved their self-evaluation. The investigators conclude that it is reasonable to expect that low self-esteem teachers will improve their self-esteem and their teaching behaviors not by self-viewing of videotaped classroom lessons, but by means of defense-reducing experiences—for example, satisfying first-hand experience in the classroom. The high self-esteem teachers, on the other hand, can be expected to benefit from the self-confrontation contained in the self-viewing of video-taped lessons.

Varying the Structure of Instruction. In addition to fitting the *techniques* of instruction to student aptitudes, the degree of *structure* within instructional methods has been modified to match the characteristics of children.

"Structured" and "Unstructured" Methods with Students of Different Personality Characteristics. The acquisition of basic reading skills also provides an illustration of the interaction between degree of structure in instruction and the individual characteristics of children. Grimes and Allensmith (1961) defined *structure* as the degree of clarity of procedures followed in a particular task, comparing primary reading achievement under a structured phonics program with achievement under a less structured whole-word approach. The structured treatment produced better results for highly compulsive children, while the unstructured, less organized method worked well with less anxious students. Apparently, compulsive students learned more when the teacher provided a structured environment by prescribing short-term goals, giving a maximum of explanation and guidance, and arranging feedback at short intervals to keep the student on the track. Less anxious students did not require such constant direction and reassurance, and instead may suffer from it.

The previous case matches the degree of structure of instruction with personality traits of children. Degree of instructional structure apparently interacts with cognitive functioning as well.

"Structured" and "Flexible" Methods with Students of Different Conceptual Levels. Hunt and Hardt (1967) studied the effects of both structured and flexible Upward-Bound education programs (precollege enrichment experiences for culturally disadvantaged high school students). Overall differences between structured ("clearly organized") and flexible ("allowing high student auton-

omy") programs were trivial. But the students had been classified according to *conceptual level;* those low in conceptual level being characterized as impulsive, poorly socialized, egocentric, and inattentive, those high being independent, questioning, and self-assertive. Clear interactions emerged between instructional treatments and conceptual level: Structured programs were more effective for students of low conceptual level, whereas flexible approaches produced greater gains for students high in conceptual level.

The complexity or simplicity of instructional materials also may be adjusted to individual differences among students.

"Complex" and "Simple" Methods with Students of Different Levels of Anxiety. Sarason (1960) found that high-anxiety subjects perform better than low-anxiety subjects on simple tasks, but the low-anxiety subjects increasingly perform better than high-anxiety subjects as task complexity increases. The teacher thus may find it useful to adjust the complexity of the instructional material to the child's level of anxiety.

Varying the Sequence of Instruction. We have illustrated the matching of both the *technique* and *structure* of instruction to individual differences. The *sequencing* of instruction also can be varied for different kinds of students.

"Visual" and "Oral" Methods with Students of Different Perceptual Preferences. We referred earlier to differences among individuals in the use of visual and auditory modes of perception and learning (Bissell, White, & Zivin, in this volume [Lesser, 1971]. Asher (1962), in teaching foreign-language vocabulary, found that subjects for whom the visual sense was dominant learned better if the presentation of visual stimuli preceded oral presentation, while for auditory subjects, the oral-visual sequences were more effective.

Difficulty Level of the Instructional Material and Personality Characteristics of Students. In another study on the sequence of instruction, Moore, Smith, and Teevan (1965) found that low-anxious, low-achieving subjects learned better when materials are sequenced in an easy-to-difficult order, while high-anxious, high-achieving subjects did better with materials presented in a difficult-to-easy sequence.

Varying the Setting of Instruction. Variations in the *technique, structure,* and *sequence* of instruction apparently have different effects on students with different aptitudes, personalities, and motivations. Interactions between student characteristics and the *setting* of instruction also exist.

Working Alone or in Pairs and Personality Characteristics of Students. Sutter (1967) attempted to teach problem-solving skills to students working alone or in pairs. She also measured the *affiliation needs* of the subjects, a variable defined as the desire to establish and maintain close, friendly interpersonal relations. Students high in affiliation need achieved better in the paired, interpersonal setting, while those low in affiliation achieved better alone. Also, high-anxious subjects learned more effectively alone, while less anxious subjects achieved better in the interpersonal setting. Apparently, the interpersonal conditions carried an "ego-threatening" quality for the highly anxious student.

Peer-Group Influence on Students with Different Levels of Academic Achievement. Since the peer group plays such a central role in determining the setting of instruction (see Schmuck's Chapter 17 in this volume [Lesser, 1971]), it is reasonable to expect interaction between peer-group influence and student characteristics, with students showing different responses to informal instruction from peers. For example, peer influence seemed to be most powerful in determining the educational aspirations of students with a history of poor academic achievement (Wallace, 1965), a finding which suggests that the student who is weak academically also is the one more likely to be susceptible to, and conform to, peer-group pressures.

Ability Grouping with Students of Different Personality Characteristics. Homogeneous and heterogeneous ability groups were discussed among the organizational adaptations to individual differences described earlier. Evidence exists (O'Connor, Atkinson, & Horner, 1966) that no overall differences are found under these two conditions of grouping in either learning or interest in school. Rather, the effect of homogeneous grouping seems to be advantageous for some students and disadvantageous for others. Students high in achievement motivation show greater scholastic growth and greater interest in school work given the challenge of a homogeneous ability-grouped class. Those low in achievement motivation show a decline of interest when placed in homogeneous ability groups, but no marked difference in scholastic achievement; they appear to perform as well but operating within a homogeneous ability group seems to be more stressful to the child with low achievement motivation. It would seem that achievement motivation is among the important factors to be considered in deciding which students should be assigned to homogeneous ability groups to maximize interest and learning.

Type of Reinforcement Accompanying Instruction. Teachers commonly adjust their reinforcements of classroom performance to their judgment of the student's needs and personality characteristics. Some research findings bear on this practice.

"Praise" and "Criticism" with Different Students. One of the older studies in the psychological literature (Thompson & Hunnicutt, 1944) reported that the effects of different types of teacher reactions depend upon the student's personality characteristics: "introverts" reacted with increased performance when praised by the teacher, while "extroverts" reacted more strongly when the teacher criticized them for doing poorly. Apparently, introverts were attracted by the carrot, extroverts were goaded by the stick.

Studies of the effects upon children of various types of verbal reinforcement generate other research instances of interactions between instructional treatments and student characteristics. For example, Van de Riet (1964) found that praise had stronger facilitating effects upon the learning of children achieving normally than those achieving below grade level, while criticism facilitated the learning of underachievers more strongly than the learning of normal achievers.

Other studies of verbal reinforcement not only report differential effects upon students with different characteristics, but emphasize the effects of one child observing the reinforcements directed toward other children in the class. In one such study (Sechrest, 1963), pairs of elementary school children were given jigsaw puzzles to complete. Each member of the pair worked on his own puzzle in the vicinity of the other member. After the first puzzles were completed, one of the two children was praised and the other criticized for his performance—and each child could overhear the reaction given to the other. Findings indicated that the greatest facilitation of performance came when a child heard his partner criticized, after which his own performance improved markedly. Hearing his partner praised had no effect on the child's performance.

"Personal" and "Impersonal" Reinforcement with Students of Different Personality Characteristics. The teacher can make reinforcements personal to the child by referring to the child's own individual characteristics or make reinforcements more impersonal by referring to the task the child is performing. Different children show distinctive responses to personal and impersonal feedback. For example, as Schmuck reports in Chapter 17 in this volume [Lesser, 1971], French (1958) found that teacher feedback had different effects on students with strong motivation to achieve and those with strong affiliation needs: Learners with high achievement motivation worked better when the teacher provided feedback relevant to the task performed; those with high affiliation motivation were more responsive to feedback of a more personal nature.

Magnitude of Reinforcement with Students of Different Levels of Persistence. The magnitude of reinforcements also seems to have a differential effect on students. For example, Nakamura and Ellis (1964) report that strong reinforcement facilitated performance for children low in persistence but did not facilitate the work of those high in persistence. Under conditions of weak reward, children high in persistence performed better than those low in persistence.

Students' Expectations Regarding the Outcomes of Instruction. The teacher also can adapt her instruction to the student's expectations regarding the likelihood of his success or failure in academic achievement.

Expectations of Success or Failure with Students of Different Personality Characteristics. Cronbach (1967) distinguished "constructively" motivated students (those showing high achievement motivation and low anxiety) from those "defensively" motivated (showing low achievement motivation and high anxiety). He summarizes the evidence that these students responded differently to the "perceived risk" involved in instruction, that is, the likelihood that they will be able to perform successfully: (1) The constructive students showed their best persistence when they thought that they were dealing with problems where there was a moderate risk, while the defensive students were most persistent when they believed that the chance of success was very low; (2) defensives were rigid when encountering difficulty, and unwilling to withdraw from a blind alley; (3) pressure in the form of stern supervision and pacing improved the work of defensives, constructives responded to such external, added pressures with lowered performance; (4) telling the defensive student that he had done well improved his work, while unfavorable comment improved the work of constructives.

Cronbach concludes that these findings support the hypothesis that defensive pupils learned most if the teacher defined short-term goals, gave a maximum of explanation and guidance, and provided feedback at short intervals—that is, if the teacher maximized opportunity for dependence. In contrast, the constructives should be given moderately difficult tasks where intermediate goals are not made too explicit; feedback should be provided at intervals for the purpose of teaching them to judge themselves rather than for motivational support. Cronbach (1967) summarizes as follows:

"If defensives learn faster under conditions of dependency, we probably want to arrange strongly supporting conditions for the schoolwork we take most seriously. But it would be short-sighted to restrict these pupils so that they remain defensive. Some part of the school program should be designed to increase their self-assurance . . . We have two coordinate problems: capitalizing on existing aptitude pattern and modifying that pattern. The school need not deal with both at the same moment, but neither should be neglected" (p. 36).

References

Asher, J. J. *Sensory interrelationships in the automated teaching of foreign languages.* San Jose, Calif.: San Jose State College, 1962.

Behr, M. J. A study of interactions between "structure-of-intellect" factors and two methods of presenting concepts of modulus seven arithmetic. Unpublished doctoral dissertation, Florida State University, 1967.

Bruner, J. S. *Toward a theory of instruction.* Cambridge, Mass.: Harvard University Press, 1966.

Cronbach, L. J. How can instruction be adapted to individual differences? In R. M. Gagné (Ed.), *Learning and individual differences.* Columbus, Ohio: Merrill, 1967. Pp. 47-90.

Davis, J. B. An investigation of the interaction of certain instructional strategies with the structure of basic mental abilities in the learning of some mathematical operations. Unpublished doctoral dissertation, Florida State University, 1967.

de Hirsch, K., Jansky, J., & Langford, W. S. *Predicting reading failure.* New York: Harper & Row, 1966.

Dougherty, K. Matching mathematics teaching to individual aptitudes in children. Unpublished study, Harvard University, 1967.

French, E. G. Effects of the interaction of motivation and feedback on task performance. In J. W. Atkinson (Ed.), *Motives in fantasy, action and society.* New York: Van Nostrand Reinhold, 1958. Pp. 400-408.

Gagné, R. M. Ability differences in the learning of concepts governing directed numbers. In *Research problems in mathematics education. Cooperative Research Monographs,* 1960, No. 3, 112-113.

Gagné, R. M. The acquisition of knowledge. *Psychological Review,* 1962, 69, 355-365.

Goodlad, J. I. *School, curriculum, and the individual.* Waltham, Mass.: Blaisdell, 1966.

Grimes, J. W., & Allensmith, W. Compulsivity, anxiety, and school achievement. *Merrill-Palmer Quarterly,* 1961, 7, 248-271.

Hunt, D. E., & Hardt, R. H. *Characterization of 1966 Summer Upward Bound Programs.* Syracuse, N.Y.: Youth Development Center, Syracuse University, 1967.

Husen, T., & Boalt, G. *Educational research and educational change.* New York: Wiley, 1967.

Kropp, R. P., Nelson, W. H., & King, F. J. *Identification and definition of subject-matter content variables related to human aptitudes.* Tallahassee, Fla.: Florida State University, 1967.

Moore, J. W., Smith, W. I., & Teevan, R. *Motivational variables in programmed learning.* Lewisburg, Penn.: Bucknell University Press, 1965.

Nakamura, C. R., & Ellis, F. F. Methodological study of the effects of relative reward magnitude on performance. *Child Development,* 1964, 35, 595-610.

O'Connor, P., Atkinson, J. W., & Horner, M. Motivational implications of ability grouping in schools. In J. W. Atkinson & N. T. Feather (Eds.), *A theory of achievement motivation.* New York: Wiley, 1966. Pp. 231-248.

Oliver, D. W., & Shaver, J. P. *Teaching public issues in the high school.* Boston: Houghton Mifflin, 1966.

Robinson, H. M. Visual and auditory modalities related to two methods for beginning reading. Paper presented at the meeting of the American Educational Research Association, Chicago, February 1968.

Salomon, G., & MacDonald, F. J. Pre- and posttest reactions to self-viewing one's teaching performance on videotape. Paper presented at the meeting of the American Psychological Association, San Francisco, 1968.

Sarason, I. G. Empirical findings and theoretical problems in the use of anxiety scales. *Psychological Bulletin,* 1960, 57, 403-415.

Sechrest, L. Implicit reinforcement of responses. *Journal of Educational Psychology,* 1963, 54, 197-201.

Shaver, J. P., & Oliver, D. W. The effect of student characteristics-teaching method interactions on learning to think critically. Paper presented at the meeting of the American Educational Research Association, Chicago, 1968.

Snow, R. E. Aptitude-instructional treatment interactions: Selected findings and hypotheses. Paper presented at the American Educational Research Association Convention, Los Angeles, 1968.

Sutter, E. M. Individual differences and social conditions as they affect learning by computer-assisted instruction. Unpublished doctoral dissertation, University of Texas, 1967.

Tanaka, M. N. Classification skills in first grade children: The effects of different instructional methods. Paper presented at the meeting of the American Educational Research Association, Los Angeles, 1968.

Thompson, G. G., & Hunnicutt, C. W. The effect of praise or blame on the work achievement of "introverts" and "extroverts." *Journal of Educational Psychology,* 1944, 35, 257-266.

Van de Riet, H. Effects of praise and reproof on paired-associate learning in educationally retarded children. *Journal of Educational Psychology,* 1964, 55, 139-143.

Wallace, W. L. *Peer groups and students' achievement.* Chicago: Aldine, 1965.

Part Five
Learning Performance
and Individual Differences

Chapter Fourteen
Learning Performance and Individual Differences: Prospective

The times are changing and the attitude of many educators and psychologists concerned with the instruction-learning process is likewise changing. This chapter summarizes the theoretical and practical implications of this changing view, and refocuses on the relationship of learning style, instructional style, and expectation to learning performance. Finally, it indicates some new directions for future research in this area and the application of those findings to classroom instruction.

Theoretical and Practical Significance of the New View

The centrality of classroom instruction and cognitive development is now seen by many as the primary focus of educational psychology. Consistent with this change in attitude has been a consequent change in thinking about the methodological aspects of research on instruction. Cronbach (1957, 1967) suggested that it is time to stop looking for the best instructional method and start looking for the particular method that has the most payoff in terms of achievement for a particular learner. Thus Cronbach's research and writing since his famed APA Presidential Address, "The Two Disciplines of Scientific Psychology" (1957), have considered the interaction of individual differences in learner aptitude with that particular class of environmental aptitide defined as instructional treatment or method. In a recent review of the literature, Mitchell (1969) concluded that,

"If educational psychology hopes to improve its predictive efficacy and utility, it must now make a strong effort to develop scientifically sound methodological approaches adequate to the task of making accurate predictions of individual behavior from the context of empirically assessed individual-environment interactions" (p. 699).

Throughout this book the reader has been exposed to two current areas of research involving person-environment interactions: Aptitude-Treatment Interactions (ATI), in the study of learning styles and expectations; and Verbal Interaction Analysis, in the study of instructional styles and expectations. This interest in person-environment interactions is quite consistent with Tyler's (1965) description of the impending second transition in the study of individual differences, where a rapprochement and synthesis between experimental psychol-
312

ogy and correlational psychology combine forces, and where the emerging theoretical framework of the study of individual differences is essentially idiographic and is a psychology of development rather than nomothetic and a psychology of measurement.

Theoretically, much interest has been generated concerning ramifications of this individualized approach to the learner for instructional theory and evaluation. A number of books, not to mention a plethora of magazine and journal articles, have appeared in the last few years. The N.S.S.E. (National Society for the Study of Education) Yearbook for 1969, Part II, *Education Evaluation: New Roles, New Means,* as well as symposium papers edited by Wittrock and Wiley (1970), discuss important methodological considerations relevant to individualized learning. Likewise, symposium papers edited by Gagné (1967b) and by Siegel (1967) illustrate the changing emphases in learning and instruction theories. And though there is much heated debate concerning aptitude-treatment interactions, there is guarded optimism that, at this stage in the development of educational psychology, the payoff may be great, especially for the disadvantaged learner. According to Jensen (1968):

"Perhaps our greatest hope of achieving equality of education opportunity lies in the possibility of finding significant *patterns* of individual differences in the development of abilities and in taking advantage of these differences to create the optimal instruction X pupil interaction. We have seen evidence that this can happen in the learning laboratory" (p. 23).

Practically speaking, the ramifications of really individualizing learning are even more encouraging than for the theoretician. Evaluation data from the following projects indicate that these programs are succeeding in increasing learning performance: Project TALENT (Flanagan, 1967); Project PLAN (Rhetts, 1970); and Individually Prescribed Instruction (IPI) (Cooley and Glaser, 1969).

Perhaps the most ambitious as well as exciting program to date is the Individually Guided Education (IGE) program developed by Klausmeier and his associates at the Wisconsin Research and Development Center for Cognitive Learning. Starting with seven schools in 1967-1968, IGE was being implemented by 2700 teachers in 170 schools during 1970-1971. IGE abandons all traditional arrangements that do not encourage provision for differences among learners in rate, style, and outcome of learning. Replacing the traditional schema for learning is a new organization for instruction which involves team teaching, differentiated staffing, and nongrading, with emphasis on flexibility in the use of space, materials, time, and better assessment of learner characteristics. Instruction is carried out for each learner in one-to-one relations with teachers, in small groups, in class-size groups, and in large groups (Klausmeier & Ripple, 1971).

Other notable projects include Wick's Individualized Continuous Assessment, or *corridors* approach (Wick & Beggs, 1971); The Stanford Tutorial System and other computer-assisted instruction (CAI) of Atkinson and associates at Stanford University (Atkinson, 1970); the Bucknell Continuous Progress Plan, a plan for individualized instruction at the college level (Moore, 1967); and continued development of Taba's school-based research on teaching thinking which is being refined and implemented by the Northwest Regional Educational Laboratory (Fredrick & Klausmeier, 1970).

The Relation of Learning Style, Instructional Style, and Expectation to Learning Performance

Earlier it was reported that Rosenthal interpreted Beez' study to mean that instructor expectations are not only translated into subtle verbal and visual messages to the learner, but actually alter instructional style which affects learning style and, ultimately, learning performance (see a discussion of this point in chapter 1). A number of other articles in this book have suggested the same or similar relationship among learning style, instructional style, expectations, and learning performance. At least four kinds of relationships were found: 1) among expectation, learning style, instructional style, and learning performance; 2) between expectations and instructional style with regard to learning performance; 3) how learning performance can be optimized by adjusting instructional style to existing learning style; and 4) how instructional style actually develops and can modify learning style, thus affecting learning performance.

In addition to the Beez study mentioned previously, Flanders' (1963) report seems to come to the same conclusion about the relationship of expectation, learning style, instructional style, and learning performance. Using the term *intention* much the same as expectation has been used in this book, Flanders concludes that when teacher intention changes, instructional style changes, thus affecting classroom social-emotional climate and, in turn, both learning style and learning performance.

The studies by Hills and Getzels indicated that expectations can and do influence instructional style and, consequently, learning performance. Hills' (1961) study pointed out that the level of social class of a community dictates that community's expectation for curricular orientation and instructional style as nomothetic, transactional, or idiographic. Getzels' model of behavior in social systems was the basis for Hills' research. In his article, Getzels (1963) delineated a number of relationships between various types of expectations and leader and institutional behavior, and how it affects social performance in that social system.

Paper and studies by Shumsky, Rhetts, and Bruner suggest that learning performance will be optimized when instructional style is modified to match existing learning style of the learner, which is, of course, the ATI hypothesis. Shumsky (1968) gave suggestions for the instructor regarding the assessment of certain dimensions of learning style, and how to modify instructional style in order to increase learning performance. Rhetts' (1970) description of the PLAN program of matching instructional style and method to learning style is by far the most ambitious undertaking which is testing the ATI hypothesis. Bruner, Goodnow, and Austin (1956) also imply that the instructor should adjust the selection strategy to the individual's particular learning style.

The papers by Hess and Shipman, Riessman, Kagan, and Taba and Elzey indicate how learning style is actually formed or can be modified by instructional style. Hess and Shipman (1965) showed how maternal expectations and instructional styles actually induce and shape learning styles in their children. Implied in Kagan (1966) and indicated in some of his later research is the idea that learners with styles characterized as impulsive could be deliberately changed to styles that were more reflective, simply by placing the learner with a reflective instructional style. Riessman's (1964) stated goal was to formulate the possible ways in which the strengths of the individual's learning style could be utilized and its weaknesses reduced or controlled as a function of instructional style. Taba and Elzey (1964) established a program which attempted to instruct all learners in certain styles of learning characterized by higher levels of thinking.

New Directions and Possibilities

It is too early to predict whether person-environment interactions, especially ATI and Verbal Interaction Analysis, will become the new shibboleths of the psychology of classroom learning; but in any case, new strategies and theories must be forthcoming if public education is to survive. Two rather new developments that offer promise are Fiedler's notion of organizational engineering and Fantini and Weinstein's comprehensive model of educational planning.

Organizational Engineering

It is almost axiomatic for students of organizational behavior to conclude that the effectiveness of a group is contingent upon the appropriateness of the leader's style to the specific situation in which he operates. According to Fiedler (1968), most people are effective leaders in some situations, and ineffective in certain others. This is no less true for education. An instructor may be most effective with one class in a given semester, and totally ineffective with another. Whereas Shumsky, Rhetts, and Bruner suggested that the instructor can and should adjust his instructional style to meet the particular needs of a particular group of learners, in practice this has not been easy. This attitude assumes that either by selection or training an instructor can be made to "fit" practically any learning group situation. Since it appears to be extremely difficult to change an individual's personality and leadership style, but relatively easy to change his work situation, Fiedler suggests that an organizational engineering approach be considered.

With this approach, the aim would be to fit the learning group to the instructor rather than forcing the instructor onto the learning group. Fiedler has offered a model and a set of principles which apparently can predict leadership effectiveness in interacting groups, and indicate factors affecting individual and group performance. This approach seems to be more sophisticated than the differentiated-staffing concept that educational administrators are currently discussing.

A Comprehensive Model for Instructional Engineering

Instructional development is usually a process involving four steps: 1) objectives or outcomes are stated; 2) content is delineated; 3) a method to convey the content is chosen; and 4) an evaluation schema to compare actual and desired outcomes is established. Instruction that is planned along these lines seldom takes into account individual differences, concerns, or needs. Fantini and Weinstein (1968) have proposed a more comprehensive model for planning instruction which seems very compatible with the main considerations of the present book. This ten-step planning model can only be briefly summarized here.

Each step of the model indicates a particular decision that must be made before moving on to the next step. The first four steps or decisions indicate about the same understanding as the concept of expectation used in this book. The first decision is to define the social class characteristics of the learners. The second step is to assess common concerns, which the authors suggest can be one or more of these three: self-rejection, disconnectedness, or powerlessness. Step three is to identify the learner's perspective or self-expectancy. The fourth decision is to clarify the desired learning outcomes in terms of the first three decisions. In the second phase, six decisions are required. In step five, the instructor selects an appropriate organizer, of which there are three types: generalizations, procedural organizers, and questions. Next a suitable content vehicle or subject-matter unit must be chosen. In step seven, instructional procedures and styles that are most appropriate to learner style, content vehicle, and desired learning outcomes are selected. The eighth and ninth decisions concern the learning processes (information processing) and skills that the learner needs in order to attain the desired outcomes. Finally, the tenth step is to assess the actual learning performance.

Classroom Applications

So far the discussion has focused primarily on experimental research and school-based research projects on expectations, learning style, and instructional style. This section will suggests ways in which the classroom teacher who wishes to teach in terms of individual differences can modify his instruction to optimize learning performance. The teacher will be shown how he can become cognizant of the learner's style, the need to match instructional objectives to the learner's expectations, and how to become aware of his instructional style.

Learning Styles

To be able to meet individual needs, the teacher first must be able to assess certain dimensions of the learner's style, i.e., dominant modality, tempo, and problem-solving strategy, etc.; and second, be able to accept these individual differences in the students, for if he does, he must modify his instruction to meet these differences. This acceptance is not easy, for its consequences demand much of the teacher. Perhaps this accounts for the fact that so little instruction is really individualized. In the absence of standardized tests that determine learning style, the teacher's own guided observation will suffice in assessing dominant modality, tempo, and problem-solving strategy.

Modality. According to Riessman (1964) and Bissell, White, and Zivin (1971), the primary modalities or reception channels for information processing are visual (reading), aural (hearing and speaking), and physical (doing). As previously mentioned, the learner's dominant modality appears to be formed early in life and is usually not subject to fundamental change. Therefore, it is imperative for the teacher to become aware of the dominant modality and plan instruction to take advantage of the strengths inherent in that modality to balance its weaknesses. The teacher should know:

What does the learner do when study time is announced?
How does he warm up for learning or starting an assignment?
How does he try to make himself concentrate?
What distracts him?
Does he tend to remember more of a story if he hears it, sees it, sees and hears it, or role plays it?

Tempo. Of all the experimental research on cognitive styles, the reflection-impulsivity dimension, or tempo, has the most direct application to classroom learning. It is important for the teacher to know:

Does the learner work slowly, cautiously, and accurately, or slowly and inaccurately?
Does he work quickly with good quality outcomes, or just to complete an assignment?
Does he work at a variable pace, depending on the nature of the task, or at one speed, all of the time?

Failure to recognize that learners differ in the amounts of time they need to complete a task not only ignores the fact that individuals move at different rates, but forces the learner into adopting undesirable ways of processing information. Whereas concern for dominant modality implies flexibility in grouping, teaching style, and materials, the teacher must also have flexibility in scheduling to enable each child to learn at the pace which will result in optimal performance. Yando and Kagan (1968) have found that impulsive children, especially boys, should be taught to read in groups led by an experienced reflective teacher. Yando and Kagan also found that while reflective teachers were able to foster reflectiveness in their students, impulsive teachers had little impact on their pupils' tempo of response, but it is hypothesized that impulsive teachers may be able to moderate the tempo of extremely reflective learners. Each teacher needs to know his own tempo, and how he perceives the learner's tempo. For instance, a teacher with a reflective tempo is likely to associate quickness with intelligence and will tend to reward impulsive learners who rapidly and accurately respond. The less able impulsive learner will then be at a disadvantage if speed of response is associated with inaccuracies in responding. This learner is being taught to value quickness, yet quickness may only enhance the learner's likelihood of failure. Finally, it should be noted that making errors and having difficulty in both short- and long-term memory are both highly related to a disposition toward impulsiveness, thus a teacher should hold judgment about "student laziness" or "lack of interest" until he can look at each incident with an eye toward the learner's tempo.

Thinking and Problem-Solving Strategies. Most persons have learned to think in abstractions (i.e., the concepts discrimination, democracy, etc.) without continually referring to specific concrete examples, indicating that they have learned to handle language at the symbolic level. Others, particularly the disadvantaged and low-income learner, find this more difficult. Taba and Elzey (1964) have noted that an individual employs certain modes of thought as a basis for grouping objects–labeling them, organizing them into personal experience, and making hypotheses about the solution to problems in terms of these modes. The teacher then should know:

Does the learner attack a learning task from beginning to end (part-to-whole), or does he first overview and then proceed (whole-to-part)?

Does his thinking process tend to proceed from the specific to the general, or from general to specific?

Does he tend to define things in terms of personal and concrete experiences and examples, or in terms of more nonpersonal and abstract categories?

Knowing this the teacher can better plan instructional strategies for that learner. And since the analytic thinker and problem-solver tends to have a reflective tempo, decisions about grouping and choices of curriculum orientation and instructional strategy can be based on fact rather than expediency and whim. For example, an inductive, discovery-oriented approach to science instruction is better geared to reflective and analytic learners, while a more expository, didactic approach is better geared toward the nonanalytic and impulsive learner.

Although these three dimensions of learning style are perhaps the most important for the teacher to be aware of, the reader may want to explore ways of observing the learner and consequently planning instruction in terms of these dimensions (e.g., attention, intolerance for ambiguity, independence, etc.)

Expectations
Knowing the student's learning style gives the teacher certain indications about how instruction can be modified in terms of grouping, scheduling, pacing, materials, and teaching style to optimize learning performance. In addition, instruction, particularly instructional objectives, can also be modified to optimize learning if teacher and learner expectations are examined.

According to Rosenthal (1971), as preservice teachers are taught that a teacher's expectations of a learner's performance may serve as a self-fulfilling prophecy, a new expectancy, that children can learn more than had been believed possible, will be created. This new expectancy will make it harder for teachers to say "Well after all, what can you expect from those kids?" Yet, teacher education does not have to change radically for a teacher to utilize his understanding of the expectancy function.

For DeCecco (1968) the expectancy function requires the teacher to maintain or modify the student's expectation of success or failure in reaching a particular instructional objective. This suggests two things. First, the teacher must have sufficient knowledge of the past school failures and successes of the learner to distinguish among realistic and unrealistic expectancies. This implies that the teacher know more than just learner ability and achievement as measured by standardized tests. It means that the teacher must know the reasons and circumstances in which failure took place: Is a learner's "failure" due to a personality clash with a teacher, a deficiency in language development, low self-esteem, impulsivity, a difficulty in concept-formation, problem-solving, or decision-making, etc.? A knowledge of the learner's style of processing information and his social interactions with peers and authority figures will usually suggest the cause for failure. Second, the teacher must describe concretely for the learner exactly what outcome the teacher expects and what the learner should be able to accomplish when the learning task is completed. Furthermore, DeCecco states that, since instructional objectives represent intermediate expectancies, the teacher must relate these intermediate expectancies to immediate and long-range goals of the learner to engage his full effort in learning, and thus increase his motivation and chances for success.

As Beez (1970) observed, when the teacher feels that a student can learn a task, he not only communicates that expectation, but he actually attempts to match instructional objectives and style to the uniqueness of the learner.

Instructional Style
Becoming aware of instructional style can also be an indicator of how instruction, specifically instructional strategy, can be modified to optimize learning performance.

According to Ober, Bentley, and Miller (1971), instructional strategy building begins when instructional objectives are formulated. Ober defines a strategy as a sequential linking of *functions* (a function being a specific teacher or learner behavior) as defined by a category of a systematic observational system. For example, the Reciprocal Categories System (RCS), an elaboration of Flanders' matrix system, presents nine functions that can be used in designing an instructional strategy. Similarly, the Equivalent Talk Categories (ETC), a cognitive behaviors system, presents five functions. Ober and his colleagues are suggesting that, once a teacher learns either or both of these systematic observation techniques, that teacher has the immediate resources and techniques for planning instruction in a systematic and scientific manner based on these basic functions or *pedagogical moves.*

In addition to its potential in developing instructional strategies, systematic observation can provide an objective analysis of a teacher's style of instruction, which can indicate a teacher's need for power and dominance and, in a sense, his expectations for his learners: Does he want and consequently teach them to learn how to learn and be convergent or divergent thinkers, or does he want and consequently teach them to be passive and compliant learners, capable of repetition but little else?

Training in observational techniques is becoming a requirement of many teacher training programs wherein teacher candidates learn a system and are able to evaluate their teaching performance on audio or video tape, in microteaching situations, and in student teaching. Furthermore, some observation systems can be learned individually with programmed materials that cost as little as $5.00.

The fact that a teacher has learned a system and can operate an audio tape recorder means that that teacher can now plan instructional strategies, teach the lesson, and provide himself with objective feedback. This feedback, in many cases, can be a more accurate indicator of learning performance than either teacher-made or standardized tests.

References

Amidon, E., and J. Hough, eds. *Interaction Analysis.* Reading, Mass.: Addison-Wesley Publishing Co., Inc., 1967.

Amidon, E., and E. Hunter. "Interaction Analysis: Recent Developments." In *Interaction Analysis,* edited by E. Amidon and J. Hough. Reading, Mass.: Addison-Wesley Publishing Co., Inc., 1967.

Anastasi, A., ed. *Individual Differences.* New York: John Wiley & Sons, Inc., 1965.

Anderson, H., and H. Brewer. "Studies of Teachers' Classroom Personalities: I. Dominative and Socially Integrative Behavior of Kindergarten Teachers." *Applied Psychology Monographs,* 1945, 6, 157.

Anderson, H., and J. Brewer. "Studies of Teachers' Classroom Personalities: II. Effects of Teachers' Dominative and Integrative Contacts on Children's Classroom Behavior." *Applied Psychology Monographs,* 1946, 8, 128.

Atkinson, R. "The Computer as Tutor." In *Readings in Developmental Psychology Today.* Del Mar, Calif.: CRM Books, 1970 Pp. 81-89.

Ausubel, D. "Viewpoints from Related Disciplines: Human Growth and Development." *Teachers College Record,* 1959, 60, 245-254.

Ausubel, D. *The Psychology of Meaningful Verbal Learning: An Introduction to School Learning.* New York: Grune & Stratton, Inc., 1963.

Ausubel, D. *Educational Psychology: A Cognitive View.* New York: Holt, Rinehart & Winston, Inc., 1968.

Barber, T., X. Calverley, A. Forgione, J. McPeake, J. Chaves, and B. Bowen. "Five Attempts to Replicate the Experimenter Bias Effect." *Journal of Consulting and Clinical Psychology,* 1969, 33, 1-6.

Bateman, B. "Learning Disorders." *Review of Educational Research,* 1966, 36, 93-119.

Beez, V. "Influence of Biased Psychological Reports on Teacher Behavior and Pupil Performance." In *Learning in Social Settings,* edited by M. Miles and W. Charters. Boston: Allyn & Bacon, Inc., 1970.

Bergin, A. "Personality and Social Behavior." In *Psychology of the Educational Process,* edited by J. Davitz and S. Ball. New York: McGraw-Hill Book Company, 1970.

Bissell, J., S. White, and G. Zivin. "Sensory Modalities in Children's Learning." In *Psychology and Educational Practice,* edited by G. Lesser. Glenview, Ill.: Scott, Foresman and Company, 1971. Pp. 130-155.

Bracht, G., and G. Glass. "The External Validity of Experiments." *American Educational Research Journal,* 1968, 5, 437-474.

Brown, B. "Experimentalism in Teaching Practice." *Journal of Research and Development in Education,* 1970, 4, 14-22.

Brown, B., R. Ober, R. Soar, and J. Webb. The Taxonomy of Cognitive Behavior. Unpublished manuscript, University of Florida, 1967.

Bruner, J., J. Goodnow, and G. Austin. *A Study of Thinking.* New York: John Wiley & Sons, Inc., 1956.

Campbell, J., and C. Barnes. "Interaction Analysis: A Breakthrough?" *Phi Delta Kappan,* 1969, 50, 587-590.

Chaplin, J., and T. Krawiec. *Systems and Theories of Psychology.* 2nd ed. New York: Holt, Rinehart & Winston, Inc., 1968.

Cooley, W., and R. Glaser. "The Computer and Individualized Instruction." *Science,* 1969, 166, 574-582.

Cronbach, L. "The Two Disciplines of Scientific Psychology." *American Psychologist,* 1957, 12, 671-684.

Cronbach, L. "How Can Instruction Be Adapted to Individual Differences?" In *Learning and Individual Differences,* edited by R. Gagné. Columbus, Ohio: Charles E. Merrill Publishing Co., 1967. Pp. 23-39.

Cuban, L. *To Make a Difference: Teaching in the Inner City.* New York: The Free Press, 1970.

Davis, J. *Technical Report #32: Concept Identification as a Function of Cognitive Style, Complexity, and Training Procedure.* Madison, Wis.: Center for Cognitive Learning, 1967.

DeCecco, J. *The Psychology of Learning and Instruction: Educational Psychology.* Englewood Cliffs, N.J.: Prentice-Hall, Inc., 1968.

Eckstrand, G. "Individuality in the Learning Process." *The Psychological Record,* 1962, 12, 405-416.

Fantini, M., and G. Weinstein. *The Disadvantaged: Challenge to Education.* New York: Harper & Row, Publishers, 1968.

Fiedler, F. "Personality and Situational Determinants of Leadership Effectiveness." In *Group Dynamics: Research and Theory,* edited by D. Cartwright and A. Zander. 3rd ed. New York: Harper & Row, Publishers, 1968. Pp. 362-380.

Flanagan, J. Project PLAN. Paper presented at the Aerospace Education Foundation, Washington, D.C., 1967.

Flanders, N. "Intent, Action, and Feedback: A Preparation for Teaching." *Journal of Teacher Education,* 1963, 14, 251-260.

Flanders, N. *Teacher Influence, Pupil Attitudes, and Achievement.* Cooperative Research Monograph #12. Washington, D.C.: U.S. Office of Education, 1965.

Flanders, N. "Teacher Effectiveness." In *Encyclopedia of Educational Research,* edited by R. Ebel. 4th ed. New York: The Macmillan Company, 1969. Pp. 1423-1437.

Fredrick, W., and H. Klausmeier. "Cognitive Styles: A Description." *Educational Leadership,* 1970, 27, 668-672.

Friedman, N. *The Social Nature of Psychological Research: The Psychological Experiment as a Social Interaction.* New York: Basic Books, Inc., Publishers, 1967.

Furst, N., and E. Amidon. "Teacher-Pupil Interaction Patterns in the Elementary School." In *Interaction Analysis,* edited by E. Amidon and J. Hough. Reading, Mass.: Addison-Wesley Publishing Co., Inc., 1967.

Gage, N. "Desirable Behaviors of Teachers." *Urban Review,* 1965, 1, 85-95.

Gagné, R. "Instruction and the Conditions of Learning." In *Instruction: Some Contemporary Viewpoints,* edited by L. Siegel. San Francisco: Chandler Publishing Co., 1967. (a)

Gagné, R., ed. *Learning and Individual Differences.* Columbus, Ohio: Charles E. Merrill Publishing Co., 1967. (b)

Gagné, R., and N. Paradise. "Abilities and Learning Sets in Knowledge Acquisition." *Psychological Monographs*, 1961, 75, Whole No. 518.

Gallagher, J., and M. Aschner. "A Preliminary Report on Analysis of Classroom Interaction." *Merrill-Palmer Quarterly*, 1963, 9, 183-194.

Galloway, C. "Nonverbal Communication." *Theory Into Practice*, 1968, 7, 172-175.

Gephart, W., and D. Antonoplos. "The Effects of Expectancy and Other Research-Biasing Factors." *Phi Delta Kappan*, 1969, 50, 579-583.

Getzels, J. "Conflict and Role Behavior in the Educational Setting." In *Readings in the Social Psychology of Education*, edited by W. Charters and N. Gage. Boston: Allyn & Bacon, Inc., 1963.

Getzels, J., J. Lipham, and R. Campbell. *Educational Administration as a Social Process*. New York: Harper & Row, Publishers, Inc., 1968.

Getzels, J., and H. Thelen. "The Classroom Group as a Unique Social System." In *The Dynamics of Instructional Groups, 59th NSSE Yearbook*. Chicago: University of Chicago Press, 1960. Pp. 53-82.

Goldberg, M. "Issues in the Education of the Disadvantaged." In *Psychology of the Educational Process*, edited by J. Davitz and S. Ball. New York: McGraw-Hill Book Company, 1970.

Gurin, G., and P. Gurin. "Expectancy Theory in the Study of Poverty." *Journal of Social Issues*, 1970, 26, 83-104.

Hess, R., and V. Shipman. "Early Experience and the Socialization of Cognitive Modes in Children." *Child Development*, 1965, 36, 869-886.

Hill, J., ed. *Minnesota Symposia on Child Psychology*. Minneapolis: University of Minnesota Press, 1967.

Hills, R. "Social Classes and Educational Views." *Administrator's Notebook*, 1961, 10, Whole No. 2.

Hoy, W. "The Influence of Experience on the Beginning Teacher." *School Review*, 1968, 76, 312-323.

Hughes, M. *The Assessment of Quality of Teaching: A Research Report*. Cooperative Research Project #353. Salt Lake City: U.S. Office of Education, 1959.

Jensen, A. "Programmed Instruction and Individual Differences." *Automated Teaching Bulletin*, 1960, 1, 12-17.

Jensen, A. "Varieties of Individual Differences in Learning." In *Learning and Individual Differences*, edited by R. Gagné. Columbus, Ohio: Charles E. Merrill Publishing Co., 1967. Pp. 117-135.

Jensen, A. "Social Class, Race and Genetics: Implications for Education." *American Educational Research Journal*, 1968, 5, 1-42.

Kagan, J. "Reflection-Impulsivity: The Generality and Dynamics of Conceptual Tempo." *Journal of Abnormal Psychology*, 1966, 71, 17-24.

Kagan, J., H. Moss, and I. Siegel. "Psychological Significance of Styles of Conceptualization." *Monographs of the Society for Research in Child Development*, 1963, 28, 73-112.

Katz, I., J. Robinson, E. Epps, and P. Waly. "Effects of Race of Experimenter and Test v. Neutral Instruction on Expression of Hostility in Negro Boys." *Journal of Social Issues*, in press.

Klausmeier, H., and R. Ripple. *Learning and Human Abilities*. 3rd ed. New York: Harper & Row, Publishers, Inc., 1971.

Kogan, N. "Educational Implications of Cognitive Styles." In *Psychology and*

Educational Practice, edited by G. Lesser. Glenview, Ill.: Scott, Foresman and Company, 1971. Pp. 242-292.

Kounin, J. *Discipline and Group Management in Classrooms.* New York: Holt, Rinehart & Winston, Inc., 1970.

Kuhn, T. *The Structure of Scientific Revolutions.* Chicago: University of Chicago Press, 1962.

Lail, S. "The Model in Use." *Theory Into Practice,* 1968, 7, 176-180.

Lazarus, R. *Personality and Adjustment.* Englewood Cliffs, N.J.: Prentice-Hall, Inc., 1963.

Lesser, G., ed. *Psychology and Educational Practice.* Glenview, Ill.: Scott, Foresman and Company, 1971.

Lewin, K., R. Lippett, and R. White. "The Social Climate of Children's Groups." In *Child Behavior and Development,* edited by R. Barker, J. Kounin, and H. Wright. New York: McGraw-Hill Book Company, 1943.

Medley, D., and H. Mitzel. "Measuring Classroom Behavior by Systematic Observation." In *Handbook of Research on Teaching,* edited by N. Gage. Chicago: Rand McNally & Co., 1963. Pp. 247-328.

Merton, R. *Social Theory and Social Structure.* New York: The Free Press, 1957.

Messick, S. "The Criterion Problem in the Evaluation of Instruction." Princeton, N.J.: Educational Testing Services, 1969. Also in *The Evaluation of Instruction: Issues and Problems,* edited by M. Wittrock and D. Wiley. New York: Holt, Rinehart & Winston, Inc., 1970.

Milton, O. "Two Year Follow Up: Objective Data after Learning Without Class Attendance." *Psychological Reports,* 1962, 11, 833-836.

Mitchell, J. "Education's Challenge to Psychology: The Prediction of Behavior from Person-Environment Interactions." *Review of Educational Research,* 1969, 39, 695-721.

Moore, J. The Application of the Continuous Progress Concept to the Natural Sciences in Higher Education. Paper presented at the Research for Better Schools Forum, December 8, 1967.

Morsch, J., and E. Wilder. *Identifying the Effective Instructor: A Review of Quantitative Studies, 1900-1952.* United States Air Force Research Bulletin # AFPTRC-TR-54-44, 1954.

Moskovitz, G. "The Attitudes and Teaching Patterns of Cooperating Teachers and Student Teachers Trained in Interaction Analysis." In *Interaction Analysis,* edited by E. Amidon and J. Hough. Reading, Mass.: Addison-Wesley Publishing Co., Inc., 1967.

Murphy, P., and M. Brown. "Conceptual Systems and Teaching Styles." *American Educational Research Journal,* 1970, 7, 529-540.

Murray, C. "The Systematic Observation Movement." *Journal of Research and Development in Education,* 1970, 4, 3-9.

Ober, R., E. Bentley, and E. Miller. *Systematic Observation of Teaching: An Interaction Analysis-Instructional Strategies Approach.* Englewood Cliffs, N.J.: Prentice-Hall, Inc., 1971.

Ober, R., R. Soar, and B. Brown. The Development of a Reciprocal Category System of Classroom Verbal Interaction. Paper presented to the American Educational Research Association, Chicago, Illinois, 1968.

Paul, I. "Retention Styles and Retention Ability." *Psychological Issues,* 1959, 1, Whole Issue.

Rhetts, J. "The Impact of Student Learning Style on Curriculum Assignment and Performance in the PLAN Program of Individualized Instruction." *Education*, 1970, 90, 248-251.

Riessman, F. "The Strategy of Style." *Teachers College Record*, 1964, 65, 484-495.

Rist, R. "Student Social Class and Teacher Expectations: The Self-fulfilling Prophecy in Ghetto Education." *Harvard Educational Review*, 1970, 40, 411-451.

Rokeach, M. *The Open and Closed Mind.* New York: Basic Books, Inc., Publishers, 1960.

Rokeach, M. *Beliefs, Attitudes and Values.* San Francisco: Jossey-Bass, Inc., Publishers, 1968.

Rosenthal, R. *Experimenter Effects in Behavioral Research.* New York: Appleton-Century-Crofts, 1966.

Rosenthal, R. "The Self-fulfilling Prophecy." *Psychology Today*, September 1968, 2, 44-51.

Rosenthal, R. "Teacher Expectations and Their Effects Upon Children." In *Psychology and Educational Practice*, edited by G. Lesser. Glenview, Ill.: Scott, Foresman and Company, 1971. Pp. 64-87.

Rosenthal, R., and L. Jacobson. *Pygmalion in the Classroom.* New York: Holt, Rinehart & Winston, Inc., 1968.

Rosenthal, R., and R. Rosnow, eds. *Artifact in Behavioral Research.* New York: Academic Press, Inc., 1969.

Sarbin, T. "Role: Psychological Aspects." In *The International Encyclopedia of the Social Sciences*, edited by D. Sills, vol. 13. New York: The Macmillan Company and The Free Press, 1968. Pp. 546-552.

Shulman, L. S., and E. R. Keislar, eds. *Learning By Discovery.* Chicago: Rand McNally & Co., 1966.

Shumsky, A. *In Search of Teaching Style.* New York: Appleton-Century-Crofts, 1968.

Sieber, S., and D. Wilder. "Teaching Styles: Parental Preferences and Professional Role Definitions." *Sociology of Education*, 1967, 40, 302-315.

Siegel, L., ed. *Instruction: Some Contemporary Views.* San Francisco: Chandler Publishing Co., 1967.

Smith, B., and M. Meux. *A Study of the Logic of Teaching.* Cooperative Research Project #258. Urbana, Ill.: U.S. Office of Education, 1963.

Snow, R., and G. Salomon. "Aptitudes and Instructional Media." *A V Communications Review*, 1968, 16, 341-357.

Soar, R. "Research Findings from Systematic Observation." *Journal of Research and Development in Education*, 1970, 4, 116-122.

Strodbeck, F. "The Hidden Curriculum in the Middle Class Home." In *Learning and the Educational Process*, edited by J. Krumboltz. Chicago: Rand McNally & Co., 1965.

Taba, H. "Teaching Strategies for Cognitive Growth." In *Behavioral Science Frontiers in Education*, edited by E. Bower and W. Hollister. New York: John Wiley & Sons, Inc., 1967.

Taba, H., and F. Elzey. "Teaching Strategies and Thought Processes." *Teachers College Record*, 1964, 65, 524-534.

Travers, J. *Fundamentals of Educational Psychology.* Scranton, Pa.: Intext Educational Publishers, 1970.

Tyler, L. *The Psychology of Human Differences.* 3rd ed. New York: Appleton-Century-Crofts, 1965.

Tyler, R. "Investing in Better Schools." In *Agenda for the Nation,* edited by K. Gordon. Garden City, N.Y.: Doubleday & Company, Inc., 1969. Pp. 207-236.

Uhlmann, F., and E. Saltz. "Retention of Anxiety Material as a Function of Cognitive Differentiation." *Journal of Personality and Social Psychology,* 1965, 1, 55-62.

Wallach, M. "Commentary: Active-Analytical v. Passive-Global Cognitive Functioning." In *Measurement in Personality and Cognition,* edited by S. Messick and J. Ross. New York: John Wiley & Sons, Inc., 1962.

Wick, J., and D. Beggs. *Evaluation for Decision-Making in the Schools.* New York: Houghton Mifflin Company, 1971.

Witkin, H., R. Dyk, D. Faterson, D. Goodenough, and S. Karp. *Psychological Differentiation.* New York: John Wiley & Sons, Inc., 1962.

Wittrock, M., and D. Wiley, eds. *The Evaluation of Instruction: Issues and Problems.* New York: Holt, Rinehart & Winston, Inc., 1970.

Wood, S. "A Multidimensional Model for the Observation, Analysis and Assessment of Classroom Behavior." *Journal of Research and Development in Education,* 1970, 4, 89-94.

Woodruff, A. "Cognitive Models of Learning and Instruction." In *Instruction: Some Contemporary Views,* edited by L. Siegel. San Francisco: Chandler Publishing Co., 1967.

Yando, R., and J. Kagan. "The Effect of Teacher Tempo on the Child." *Child Development,* 1968, 39, 27-34.

Zagona, S. and L. Zurcher. "The Relationship of Verbal Ability and Other Cognitive Variables to the Open-Closed Cognitive Dimension." *Journal of Psychology,* 1965, 60, 213-219.

Index

Index

A

Accountability, 2
Adapting instruction to individual
    differences, 251, 298-309
Aptitude- (Attribute-) Treatment
    Interaction (ATI), 8, 126
a conceptual framework, 273-276
definition, 270
empirical research on disordinal
    interactions, 136-138
and individualized instruction, 270
ordinal v. disordinal interactions,
    133
and person-environment inter-
    actions, 8, 312
status of current research, 271-272

B

Bucknell Continuous Progress
    Program, 313-314

C

Cognitive strategies. *See* Learning style
Cognitive style. *See* Learning style
Communication styles, 254-256
Computer Assisted Instruction (CAI),
    313
Control principles, 96. *See also*
    Learning style
Curriculum orientation and expecta-
    tion, 81

D

Demand characteristics, 56, 59, 61
Disadvantaged learner, 5
Disordinal interactions. *See* ATI

E

Expectancy. *See also* Teacher
    expectancy
conditions for changing, 12
definition of, 10, 104
ease of changing, 40
as an integrating concept, 38-40
interpersonal equation, 6
learning of, 43-45
a model of, 11, 26
and motivation, 10
personal equation, 6
psychological meaning, 10
sociological meaning, 11
teacher expectancy function, 5
theories of changing, 41
unintentional communication, 67
Expectancy bias, 15
Expectancy change
behavioral consequences, 46-48
stability and generalization, 42
Expectancy research
problems in, 48
research implications, 42
Experimenter bias effect, 6, 55-57, 61
magnitude of, 20
meaning, 5
studies of, 20

F

Field dependence-independence, 95.
    See also Learning style
stability of during development,
    151-155

H

Halo effect, 56, 59, 61
Hawthorne effect, 56, 58, 61

329

I

Idiographic dimension, 11, 25
Individual differences
  in response to educational
    treatment, 100-102
  trends in the study of, 6-7
Individual differences in learning. *See
  also* Learning style
  assessment of problems, 131
  attentiveness, 124-125
  grouping, 129
  independence, 123-124
  instruments for measuring, 130
  reaction to new situations, 125
  tempo, 122
Individualized Continuous Assessment,
  213
Individualized instruction. *See*
  Instructional style
Individualized learning, 313. *See also*
  Instructional style
Individually Guided Education (IGE),
  313
Individually Prescribed Instruction
  (IPI), 313
Instructional engineering, 315-316
Instructional style (teaching style)
  affected by social class, 83
  classroom applications, 319-320
  discovery v. didactic teaching, 232
  idiographic, 82
  instructional theory and, 191
  nomothetic, 82
  review of authoritarian v. democratic
    research studies, 219-231
  taxonomy of outcome variables,
    241-243
  transactional, 82
Interaction analysis, 193
  application to teacher education,
    204-206
  critique of research studies, 245-250
  interpretation of matrices, 200-202
  review of research studies, 208-211
  technique and procedure of
    observation, 197-200
Interaction quality hypothesis, 64

L

Learning disorders, 4
Learning performance, 2, 12
Learning style (cognitive style)
  and affective reactions, 100
  articulated v. global dimensions, 106
  a brief history, 95-96
  classroom applications, 316-318
  cognitive strategies, 112
  concept-formation and problem-
    solving, 140
  control principles, 96
  criterion tests of, 96
  as a criterion variable, 100
  definition, 94
  dimensions of, 104-105
  and discovery methods, 112
  and effects of early experiences, 254
  field independence v. field
    dependence, 95
  individual differences in learning,
    122-125
  and instruction, 111
  and learning performance, 97, 127
  and maternal child rearing patterns,
    107
  and memory (leveling v. sharpening),
    177-182
  a model of, 97, 140
  modification strategies, 119-121
  perception and, 106
  reception styles, 140
  reflection-impulsivity, 96, 165-176
  related psychological terms, 94-95
  retention styles, 140-141
  selection strategies, 157-164
  and sensory modalities, 116-121
  shaped by communication style,
    257-263
  status differences in concept
    utilization, 261
  of teachers, 111
  and types of defense mechanisms,
    110
  value judgments about, 102-104
Leveling v. sharpening. *See* Learning
  style

M

Matching instructional style and
  learning style, 7, 299-309
  different teaching methods, 302-308
  expectations, 307-308
  grouping, 306
  particular goals, 300-301
  peer group influence, 305-306
  sensory modalities, 303-304
  types of reinforcement, 306-307
  universal goals, 301-308
Motivation, 10

N

Nomothetic dimension, 11, 25

O

Organizational engineering, 315
Outcomes of instruction, 127

P

Performance contracting, 2
Person-environment interactions. *See
  also* ATI
  types of, 8, 312
Placebo effect, 56, 60, 61
Problem-solving, four phases of, 165
Project PLAN, 3, 251, 269, 280-284,
  313
Project TALENT, 313
Psychological differentiation, 95, 141

R

Reflection-impulsivity. *See also*
  Learning style
  measurement of, 166-168
  relation to memory and recall,
    172-174
Relation of learning style, expectations, instructional style, and
  learning performance, 191-192,
  314-315
Role, 11
Role conflicts, 23
  and expectations, 27-36
Role expectation, 11. *See also*
  Expectancy

S

Selection strategies. *See* Learning
  style
Self-fulfilling prophecy, 5, 11, 15.
  See also Expectancy
Sensory modalities. *See* Learning Style
Systematic observation of instruction
  cognitive climate, 189-190
  definition, 186-191
  implications of multidimensional
    approach, 215-217
  multidimensional assessment of
    climate, 190-191, 213-217
  nonverbal climate, 190
  social emotional climate, 187-188

T

Task of Public Education Studies, 81
Teacher expectancy. *See also*
  Expectancy
  and changes in student behavior,
    86-92
  classroom applications, 318-319
  and intellectual gains, 65
  shortcomings of the Rosenthal-
    Jacobson research, 68-75, 78-79
  and student learning performance,
    80
Teaching style. *See* Instructional style
Teaching thinking strategies, 286-298

V

Verbal Interaction Analysis. *See*
  Interaction analysis